Enactments

EDITED BY RICHARD SCHECHNER

To perform is to imagine, represent, live and enact present circumstances, past events and future possibilities. Performance takes place across a very broad range of venues from city streets to the countryside, in theatres and in offices, on battlefields and in hospital operating rooms. The genres of performance are many, from the arts to the myriad performances of everyday life, from courtrooms to legislative chambers, from theatres to wars to circuses.

ENACTMENTS encompasses performance in as many of its aspects and realities as there are authors able to write about them.

ENACTMENTS includes active scholarship, readable thought and engaged analysis across the broad spectrum of performance studies.

The Delight of Turkish Dizi

Memory, Genre and Politics of Television in Turkey

ARZU ÖZTÜRKMEN

WITH A FOREWORD BY

Richard Bauman

LONDON NEW YORK CALCUTTA

Seagull Books, 2022

© Arzu Öztürkmen, 2022

Foreword © Richard Bauman, 2022

Images © Individual photographers, agencies, networks, archives

ISBN 978 0 8574 2 898 1

British Library Cataloguing-in-Publication Data

A catalogue record for this book is available from the British Library

Typeset by Seagull Books, Calcutta, India

Printed and bound in the USA by Integrated Books International

To the treasured memory
of our dear
Latife Defne Mudun

Contents

Foreword

RICHARD BAUMAN

How does a folklorist and social historian, attuned primarily to traditional performance forms that are customarily enacted in situations of co-presence, come to undertake a study of a mass-media phenomenon that is in the process of extending its reach from a national to a global market? And once engaged, how does she pull it off? For Arzu Öztürkmen, a number of convergent factors drew her in almost before they coalesced into a full-scale research project: a fan's devotion to TV dramas of every-day life and their musical accompaniment, an abiding interest in performance and narrative, involvement in a research project on an Ottoman-era shoe factory repurposed as a film studio, a few serendip-itous personal connections to people in the industry, and almost before she knew it, she had embarked on a decade-long study of dizi. And now, we have before us the results of her ambitious, creative and illuminating study.

There are many problems that are inherent in the study of mass media for which Öztürkmen's transdisciplinary study suggests innovative and productive solutions. I will limit myself to only two, simply to hint at the kinds of insights the reader will find in the pages that follow.

First, there is the problem of scale: what units of analysis can give the analyst a purchase on the complex nature and broad reach of a mass-media form? For Öztürkmen, the question was one of how to manage the shift of focus from the co-present, immediate interaction order that is the province of the folklorist to the dispersed, distanced, technologically mediated domain of the mass-media television series. To negotiate that scalar gap, Öztürkmen draws upon a concept that is a familiar part of her folklorist's analytical repertoire, namely, genre.

In recent years, folklorists and linguistic anthropologists have left behind older philological approaches to genre essentially as a set of classificatory categories to a more practice-centered conception of genre as a conventionalized orienting framework for the production and reception of particular orders of texts. Conceived in these terms, genre is an inherently intertextual schema of cultural production. That is, when an act of entextualization is assimilated to a given genre, the process of its production and interpretation is mediated through its intertextual relationship with antecedent texts while, at the same time, anticipating future texts. Öztürkmen aligns herself with this approach and demonstrates it to be eminently scalable, temporally and spatially, as she upscales it to comprehend the genre of popular television drama: dizi. To this conception of genre, Öztürkmen adds a related an equally scalable understanding of the ways in which symbolic forms may be intermedially related to forms expressed in other media, as in her own earlier examination of pictorial representations of Ottoman festivals.

An important feature of Öztürkmen's investigation rests upon the recognition that the fit between intertextually and intermedially related forms is never exact. Elements of here-and-now contextualization enter into all acts of textual production and reception, opening the way to generic reconfiguration and change. Close attention to the historical evolution of the dizi as an emergent genre is one of the great strengths of Öztürkmen's study, from its beginnings in the 1990s, to the coalescence of the genre in the past decade, to the ongoing process of extending its reach from national to global audiences, all examined as the situated accomplishments of social actors.

In addition to the analytical problem of identifying a unit of analysis suited to the investigation of mass-media transformations, the other great problem attendant upon a shift from investigating folklore forms in co-present interaction to mass-mediated televisual forms is methodological: what empirical means will allow the investigator to get a purchase on the scalar complexity of, say, a television drama series? Here, too, Öztürkmen's well-honed toolkit as a folklorist and social historian of performance turns out to serve her very well.

For the folklorist, the production, circulation and consumption of cultural forms is a situated social accomplishment. That is, culture happens in places, in the situated practice of social actors. Therefore, to gain an understanding of how it works, the folklorist turns first and foremost to ethnographic fieldwork: onsite, firsthand, empirical observation of social agents engaged in the conduct of social life. Thus, in resorting to ethnographic fieldwork in her study of dizi, Öztürkmen is simply doing what comes naturally, seeking out the sites where the complex process of making dizi happens and engaging with participants. Gaining access to the relevant sites and participants may involve delicate processes of negotiation, and here, Öztürkmen's work really shines. She is a master of access, as witness the degree to which she becomes not only an onsite observer but a participant observer, drafted into an active role in the promotion and dissemination of dizi into global media markets. To her ethnographic work, Öztürkmen adds the skills of a social historian, equally adept at archival and oral-historical research, which enriches and gives historical depth to her study.

The fruits of Öztürkmen's richly synthetic and creative study, informed by her experience as a folklorist and social historian of performance, lie before you in the pages that follow. Her book, I believe, demonstrates clearly the energizing potential of disciplinary boundary crossing, specifically, the illuminating potential of what a folklorist and historian of performance can offer to the study of media forms in history and society.

IMAGE 1.1 The main alley at Beykoz Kundura film plateau. Image courtesy of the Beykoz Kundura Archive.

CHAPTER 1

Introduction

An ordinary day in Beykoz Kundura.[1] As I walk through the main alley, an Ottoman officer passes by me and run towards a Crusader. They hug and engage in a friendly conversation. I smile at their encounter, as one comes from the *Vatanım Sensin* set and the other from *Diriliş: Ertuğrul*. I walk to Demirane, a quiet place for refuge, where each table hosts another dizi team on different time slots. Some showrunners negotiate with the producer on the phone, a writer finalizes her script, a director gives a break from a long tiring day. In many cases, there is a communal table for an ensemble cast uniting for a late lunch or early dinner. As a folklorist, I cannot help myself but think how gossip is the main genre of the 'behind the scenes'. On my way back, when I cross to Yeniköy with a small ferry, I am pretty sure that I will cross path with a convoy of trailers along the Bosphorus, to shoot a scene on the pavements or in a *yalı*. As I write these lines, *Bir Zamanlar Çukurova* set runs in Adana, *Sefirin Kızı* in Bodrum, and *Hercai* in Mardin. In Istanbul, TIMS' Hadımköy set, first constructed for *Kösem*, and the set of *Diriliş* and *Kuruluş* in Riva are the new sites for dizis with historical content. It is in this fantastic realm that I began writing this book on a research I had started in the autumn of 2011.

* * *

---

1 Beykoz Kundura serves as a set for the television and film industry; numerous projects are shot amid the historical ambiance of a former factory.

These words would be my opening lines. Then Covid-19 hit the world and changed our sense of the 'ordinary' while I was writing the last chapters of the book. Like everywhere else, all action in the sets suddenly stopped in Turkey in mid-March 2020; stocks ran out in a few weeks, leaving their spots to reruns, while the audiences' attention was fixed on pandemic news. In mid-April, however, we heard that *Eşkıya Dünyaya Hükümdar Olmaz*, *Arka Sokaklar* and *Kuruluş* returned to sets, while *Kuşlarla Yolculuk*, a Ramadan series, had already began the shoots in a quarantine environment. *Çukur*, *Tutunamayanlar* and *Jet Sosyete* invented new strategies to produce new episodes, while producers began to search for new formulas to construct 'safe sets' to conclude the season finales, so that they would be available for sale in the global market. In the autumn of 2020, new sets opened for fresh content filmed 'under precautions'.

My friends in the industry and my students often teased me about the long time the completion of this book has taken. The historical frame of my research had pointed out too many turning points which changed the course of events. When the Covid-19 spread across the world, I first thought that this will hit Turkey's television industry hard. What emerged instead, however, was a rapid creative response. My friends in dizi distribution continued their business as usual, writers freshly appropriated Covid-19 in their scripts, producers hired large number of trailers to set up new safe conditions for work, and many joined the first MIPCOM online in October. In short, the dizi industry showed once again its capacity for adapting to a risky and precarious situation, which, I argue in this book, has built many of the structural characteristics of the dizi genre.

Dizi making is a marathon run by sprinters. The length of each episode is now more than two hours, and the pace of shootings requires the scripts to be written in haste and delivered to the set to be broadcast right after. This particular production process of the Turkish television industry has indeed directly affected the growth of the dizi genre that now circulates around the globe.

To many of us inside and outside of Turkey, the remarkable rise of interest in Turkish dizis and their amazing scale of global sales has come as a surprise. The entertainment industry was never seen as a promising 'revenue-producing sector' of the national economy. Historically speaking, the Turkish economy flourished through state support and subsidies until 1980s, through a national network of state-owned enterprises (KİTs), and accommodating the private sector along the way.[2] With the exception of the state-subsidized performances like theatre, opera and symphonic music, entertainment was a domain left mostly to private entrepreneurs.[3] If one leaves the national public network Turkish Radio Television (TRT) aside, the television industry has developed since the 1990s without any direct subsidy from the state. In a sense, this book is an account of the emergence of commercial television industry, in response to the changing economic, social and cultural conditions of the 1990s. In a context where different business opportunities emerged, a work culture and management style developed in Turkey with its own particularities, including weak unions, specific social codes of team-work and leadership models.[4] The vigour behind the rise of the dizi

---

2 For more on Turkish economy, see Korkut Boratav (2018). For KİTs, see Ch. 2, note 26.

3 See Sacit Akdede and Şansel Özpınar (2016); Himli Yazıcı (2016) and Kathryn Woodard (2007). Even tourism made its leap in the 1980s with state support; see Arzu Öztürkmen (2005). For the flourishing Istanbul night life in the 1990s onwards, see Mine Eder and Özlem Öz (2015).

4 From the 1990s onwards, Turkey entered, with the so-called handshake tradition, many markets in the Middle East and post-Soviet countries that Western business firms found too risky. With the rising global investments since the 1990s, 'business guides' gave tips to expats who came to work in Turkey. See Cameron Deggin (2017); John Howell (2018); *Expat.com* (2020). For academic research on Turkish work culture, see also Zeynep Aycan (2015); Peter Smith et al. (2006); Nevra Ersoy et al. (2011); and Adem Öğüt and Ayşe Kocabacak (2008).

genre is an outcome of this work culture, while its global sales owe greatly to Turkish ways of 'doing business'.

Remembering Turkish Television: The Subjective Entrance to the Research

My journey with television dates back to the late 1960s when TRT began its national broadcasting. As part of the first generation of television viewers, I grew up watching *Bizim Sokak* and *Casper*, TRT's pioneering children's programmes.[5] A television set in the household was a status symbol, and hosting relatives, friends and neighbours who did not own one, a social duty. Television evenings continued through my teenage years, with fascinating primetime British or American series like the *Avengers* or *Mission Impossible,* followed by *The Fugitive* and *Dallas.* These series introduced us to great actors like Barbara Bain, Diana Rigg, Martin Landau, Roger Moore or Tony Curtis, but also to addictive seriality through the 1970s and the 1980s. Ironically, we were more familiar, in those years, with the old stars of Hollywood like Tyrone Power, Rita Hayworth and many more, as TRT would rerun their movies every week. Like in many other households, television was central to the concept of entertainment in our family; it would keep playing until the day's broadcast ended.[6]

As a graduate student in the US during the late 1980s and early 1990s, I followed newer American formats, ranging from soap operas and sitcoms to various talk shows and news programmes. But I was in Turkey on 31 December 1990, to witness the phenomenal launch of

---

5 *Bizim Sokak* (Our Street) was an adaptation of *Sesame Street* using many local or traditional elements from Turkish culture. *Casper* was translated into Turkish as *Sevimli Hayalet*, the 'Pretty Ghost'.

6 Nostalgia narratives about the early years of television have been widely spread, often expressed in social media venues or memoirs. Among many others, see Halit Kıvanç (2002) and Vedii Yukaruç (2011).

Star TV, the first private channel, which celebrated New Year's Eve with eleven belly dancers, putting an end to the era of TRT's monopoly on entertainment television.[7] It was during 1990s that my mother and her peers were captivated by the serial broadcasting of soap and telenovelas. An urban legend holds that peasants of an Eastern village who were watching *The Young and the Restless* and *Marianna* dubbed in Turkish named their children Turkified versions of the characters' names: Viktır, Eşli and Maryana.[8] With the increase in private networks, imported telenovelas and soaps have helped the new channels to fill their programming hours, but also introduced a new habit of daily seriality among Turkish viewers. Private channels also boosted domestic productions, introducing from the 1990s onwards, the first samples of the dizi genre, the Turkish television drama. We often discussed *Süper Baba*, *Çocuklar Duymasın*, or *Sıla* with my friends at Boğaziçi (Nükhet Sirman and Selçuk Esenbel in particular) and our students. As a committed television viewer, I may say that I developed a good memory of television content over the years and their reception in different milieus.

'Studying television', however, became my agenda only in the early 2010s, when I was exposed to the phenomenal *Fatmagül'ün Suçu Ne?* (What is the Fault of Fatmagül?), which triggered my curiosity both as an academic and as an ordinary viewer. Produced by Ay Yapım and broadcast on Kanal D, *Fatmagül'ün Suçu Ne?* was first marked by its feminist content: the story of a young woman surviving rape, in the

---

7 The term 'private' channel or network refers to 'commercial television'. Following the Turkish terminology *özel televizyon* and *özel kanal*, I will use both the terms 'private' and 'commercial' network/television in order to position them in opposition to the long-dominating 'public' television, TRT.

8 The character's proper names were Victor, Ashley and Marianna. I collected this story from Ülkü Yılmaz, who heard it from the janitor of the school where she worked (see Yılmaz 2017). This trend turned the other direction when dizis became highly popular in Latin America (see *Hürriyet* 2018).

context of challenges in her own family and community.[9] As a folklorist, I was fascinated by the intermediality between the high quality of cinematography, acting, directing, the musical score, and the use of locations in and out of Istanbul. The serial also depicted everyday life in ethnographic detail. *Fatmagül'ün Suçu Ne?* represented a new cultural form, with a texture different from the serials that we had seen over the years. As such, the series had attracted a broad and enthusiastic audience and critical acclaim. I was not the only one taken by the wind of the dizis. The genre had become more consolidated through the 2000s, generating both social-popular and scholarly attention.

Exploring Dizi as a Media Text

Since the early days of television broadcasting in Turkey, television dramas, foreign and domestic alike, have been discussed among family and friends in the form of a 'meta-narrative gossip'. With the arrival of private channels in the 1990s, however, both the import and production of television programmes increased, triggering more and more popular and academic attention. During the 2000s, a magazine press emerged which offered a rich body of data on emerging stars and their dizis (Soygüder 2003; Dağtaş 2006; Satmış 2017). While many of these featured interviews focused primarily on personal issues, some also covered the experience of creative processes. The comprehensive dizi analysis platforms had yet to emerge, and the general attention of magazine articles was on the news and success stories of the leading figures—mostly actors, but also creative writers, directors and producers.[10]

---

9 It was the second adaptation of Vedat Türkali's short novel, following 1986 film adaptation. As a story, it has been closely examined from feminist perspectives. Among others, see Sevgi Yağcı (2011); Yasemin Yener (2012); Gökhan Gökulu (2013).

10 Ranini.TV, run by Rana Yıldız, regularly follows global markets and reports on international television news as much as domestic ones (see https://bit.ly/-3myzQ8b).

Dizis have attracted scholarly attention from the early 1990s. The initial studies explored more the Turkish audiences' sudden passion for the 'pink series', namely, American soaps and Latin American telenovelas (Budak 1993; Binark 1997; Gözlükaya-Tütüncü 1998a). Research focusing particularly on dizis appeared much later, in parallel with the rise of its production and global acclaim. Early dizi research included the works of Ayşe Öncü (1995, 2000), Asu Aksoy (2000), Hülya Uğur Tanrıöver (2004, 2005a, 2005b, 2005c), Nükhet Sirman (2007) and Feyza Akınerdem (2005), followed up by many others.[11] The scholarship on dizi has evolved in an exponential manner in the last decade.[12] There has also been a growing research on dizis from outside of Turkey.[13] These scholarly analyses came from different disciplines and approaches, mostly from sociology and media studies. They explored the dizis with an eye on their treatment of gender, class and ethnicity in Turkey. Be it on the pink series or on domestic dizis, the original source of interest was rooted in the viewers' passionate reception. The general approach to the pink series was that this was a phenomenon that needed to be examined and understood, often accompanied by a confessional

---

11 One should also cite the work of Asu Aksoy and Kevin Robins (1997), who published a critical and pioneering work on Turkey's landscape of culture industry, including the transition from TRT to commercial networks.

12 For more comprehensive reviews of the television industry, let me primarily cite the works of Evrim Özkan Töre (2010), Hülya Uğur Tanrıöver (2011) and Ayşegül Kesirli Unur (2016). Among many others, see also Melis Behlil (2010); Sevgi Yağcı (2011); Ayşe Öncü (2011); Enes Abanoz (2012); Cem Pekman and Selin Tüzün (2012); Yasemin Yener (2012); N. Yüksel (2013); Nuran Erol-Işık (2013); Gökhan Gökulu (2013); Serpil Karlıdağ and Selda Bulut (2014); Nuran Erol-Işık (2014); Berfin Emre-Çetin (2015, 2016); Firat Konuşlu (2016); Nükhet Sirman (2016); Feyza Akınerdem and Nükhet Sirman (2017); Deniz Özalpman (2017); Senem Çevik (2019).

13 See Alexandra Buccianti (2000); Penelope Papailias (2005); Christa Salamandra (2012); Mary O'Neil (2013); Mathieu Rousselin (2013); Marwan Kraidy and Omar Al-Ghazzi (2013); Miriam Berg (2017); Carolina Acosta-Alzuru (2018); Josh Carney (2019).

disclaimer that the author was not a fan of the genre.[14] My research took place during an era marked by simultaneous discourses of despise and pride about the dizi phenomenon. Like in the case of the Arabesk music genre in 1980s Turkey, there was a clear condescending attitude towards dizis, even by those who worked in the industry.[15] Compared with film-making processes, the dizi genre was framed as a 'shallow', 'non-artistic' or even harmful form, appealing to simple and unsophisticated minds.[16] Nevertheless, with their global success by the mid-2000s, dizis became the object of national pride, mobilizing different segments of the elite ranging from politicians to artists.

A preliminary review of scholarly analyses revealed that dizis were mostly explored through their content, that is, as a text embedding a story and its characters. Part of this approach may be related to the problem of access that many researchers in film studies have experienced (Ortner 2010). A large majority of scholarly work focuses primarily on broadcast episodes and published interviews, without giving much considerations to the contribution of actual social players and settings of the dizi industry. My method of textual analysis draws on my training in folklore and performance studies. It follows Richard Bauman's 'verbal art as performance' approach in which the rise of genres involves a historical process of and an ethnography of the social

---

14 These are quotes from two researchers who asked to remain anonymous. Distancing oneself from watching television has been an academic cliché, but I also observed that many other researchers' scholarly interest is rooted in their own passion for the television series and their actors.

15 Arabesk is a music genre in Turkey which became very popular mainly among working and lower middle classes during the 1960s through the 1990s. It was banned from public television for long years, and circulated mostly in live concerts and through audio cassettes. The attitude towards Arabesk music has greatly changed with time. See Betül Yarar (2008); Can Yalçınkaya (2008).

16 There is emerging research questioning the discourses on the impact of dizis. For an exemplary analysis, see Feyza Akınerdem and Nükhet Sirman (2019). On popular grounds, see *Ekşi Sözlük* (2008).

context of its performance (see Bauman and Joel Sherzer 1974; Bauman 1977, 1986, 2004). Dizis undoubtedly captivate their audiences with their stories and characters, but as a final product, they are also media texts that comprise many other visual and performative elements. They pass through a complex production process, which includes a collaboration between writing, shooting and post-production activities. A deeper understanding of the final media text therefore requires a thorough ethnography of these production processes, which generate each episode's broadcast tape and afterlife. As a media text, each episode of a dizi represents a collective creative effort on the part of writers, producers, directors, actors, editors, musicians and, in recent years, international distributors.[17]

My ethnographic research during the first two years revealed that dizis' production and broadcasting processes were tightly interwoven, offering a different mode of communication and consumption, and one that is extremely sensitive to the different conjunctures. When compared to many other national industries, the Turkish dizi industry operates with particular precarity, where many screenwriters begin to write without knowing whether the project in hand would remain on air until its finale. While the writing, producing and broadcasting processes are interactively linked, audiences and distributors have also a say in shaping the final outcome. Audiences give prompt responses to each episode; distributors give suggestions to producers on favourite topics and stars the market demands. In this regard, it is important to distinguish dizis from other television genres with which they are often associated—soap opera, telenovela, or *musalsal*.

---

17 Nowadays, dizi distributors are often consulted for their advice on 'working' content and actors. See Chapter 10.

Ethnography of the Dizi Industry: Methodological Challenges

My research began as a naive pursuit of my curiosity as a viewer, and I did not at first envision it evolving into a book project. It was 2011 and I was in the midst of editing two books on the history of performance in the Ottoman and Eastern Mediterranean world, carrying out a research project on the genres of borderlands, and co-organizing an international conference on the Alevi-Bektashi communities in the Ottoman geography. *Muhteşem Yüzyıl* (Magnificent Century), which depicted the life and times of Suleiman the Magnificent, dominated the domestic media at that time and became the centre of attention both in academia and in popular circles. Portraying everyday life of an imagined Ottoman harem, *Muhteşem Yüzyıl* captivated audiences through both its original content but also its production quality. But I found myself more taken by *Fatmagül'ün Suçu Ne?*, which brought its viewers to a series of different locations of Istanbul, gave realistic depictions of daily life, and layered its narrative with music and cinematography.[18] Shortly afterwards, during a dissertation defence committee meeting at Istanbul Technical University (ITU) Music Conservatory, I mentioned the powerful use of a folk song in *Fatmagül'ün Suçu Ne?* My colleagues told me that Toygar Işıklı, the music director for that dizi, was their graduate student, and put us in touch. So, I did my first interview with Toygar on 5 July 2011 at Boğaziçi University, praising him for the enhanced quality of his dizi music. We talked about music at first, but our conversation naturally shifted towards other aspects of a complex production process, such as the set shootings, film editing and the post-production line. What I learned from him paved the way for

---

18 The issue of location was central to the story of *Fatmagül'ün Suçu Ne?* which depicted the forced migration of a family, who travelled from one city to the other, while also discovering Istanbul from their own subjectivity. Some of these places, like Taksim Square or İnci Patisserie are now valuable archives of places that greatly changed in the last decade.

many other conversations and exchanges among friends and my former students of performing arts, who began to connect me with writers, producers, and actors from their own circles. To my surprise, Fahriye Evcen, one of the leading stars of the dizi world, happened to be a student in our History Department. My discussions with Fahriye, and later with her husband Burak Özçivit, also a star, warmly opened a privileged door to the subjectivities of the dizi world. In a snowball effect, the handful of people I met during the autumn of 2011 grew into 200 interviewees by 2015. Some of my interviewees became close friends, with whom I continued to consult and discuss many questions that arose during my writing process. The year 2015 was a breakthrough year in my research process, as I assisted in organizing a series of conferences at MIPCOM— the world's largest entertainment content market—when Turkey was the country of honour.

One important venue of my research was Beykoz Kundura film studios, which I have been visiting since 2013. There, I crossed paths with Serpil and Buse Yıldırım, who own and manage Kundura's multi-layered projects (see www.beykozkundura.com). Our initial common interest was the oral history of the landmark Sümerbank shoe factory that the Kundura complex once housed, a state-owned enterprise dating back to late Ottoman era. Since then, Kundura has been a field where I have been privileged to pursue ethnographic research while writing my book.

My research consisted of archival study, along with interviews with diverse social players of the industry, ranging from producers and network managers to actors, directors, and the technical crew. I also had the opportunity to closely observe a writers' study group, and to have ethnographic field observation of production spaces and global trade fairs.

My research showed the importance of a longitudinal media ethnography, a matter well discussed by Ece Algan and John Postil. Following the spatial metaphor of 'multi-sited ethnography' coined by anthropologist George Marcus, Postil underscores the notion of 'multi-timed ethnography' in the study of often slippery zone and rapidly changing contexts of media world. Postil suggests:

> [I]t is more helpful to think of actual social changes in the plural, as (a)countable, concrete, identifiable, unique and messy *processes*. But adopting a processual approach carries its own costs, for it requires that we rethink our ethnographic practice. For many years we have subscribed to the spatial metaphor of 'multi-sited ethnography' (Marcus 1995), but have yet to embrace its temporal counterpart: multi-*timed* ethnography. (2017: 28)

Without a decade-long ethnographic survey, it would have been very difficult to pursue the historical and contemporary dynamics I was able to raise in this study.[19]

Content of the Research

My interviews, ethnographic observations, and personal memory of television made pressing the need to understand the general context from which the dizi industry has emerged. This required intense ethnographic focus on film sets and television markets, along with archival research on published interviews. As my project developed, I grew more interest in the 'emergence' and consolidation of the dizi as a new genre that now circulates in global markets. To be able to appreciate the creative and collaborative structure of the dizi industry, one needed to look at the historical development of the genre and its professional and institutional memory. Additionally, as a folklorist and oral historian, my interest has been more in the historical-ethnographic context that shaped the dizi genre. With my training in the ethnography of artistic

---

19 For a discussion on longitudinal media ethnography, see Ece Algan (2017); John Postil (2017).

communication,[20] I targeted the collaboration in the creative processes, including the collective input of not just writers, directors, producers, but also location scouts, musicians, editors, art and photography directors, along with a pool of glamourous new stars.

The business aspect of the dizi industry has introduced me to a new epistemological realm of global television markets like MIPCOM, MIPTV, DISCOP and ATF. At these markets, one could observe firsthand how dizis are distributed, while also being able to contextualize them in relation to other genres and different industries. There, I drew on my undergraduate studies in business administration, dating back to the mid-1980s. This was an era where the academic focus was on the shift from a state-controlled economy towards neoliberal free-market policies. The study of the 'market' has also been central in my folklore research that looked at fairs and festivals as important cultural forms. Beginning in 2013, under the auspices of the Istanbul Chamber of Commerce (İTO), I began attending the MIPTV and MIPCOM television fairs, followed, in later years, by DISCOP, ITVF and ATF events. As much as sites for sales, these events served as venues for up-to-date conferences on the global television business. These conferences had a pace and structure of their own, where a particular, often abbreviated terminology prevailed. It took me two years to fully understand their dynamics and jargon, a know-how I greatly appreciated and used during the preparation for the 2015 country of honour year. The market conferences moved at a swift pace, with careful time management and moderation, and displayed a performative mode of their own, presenting CEOs or industry leaders as celebrities, complete with stage lighting and applause. Television industry figures followed these conferences closely, as did international television news outlets, including *Hollywood Reporter*, *World Screen*, *Variety*, *Prensario*, *Total* or *Todo TV*

---

20 Folklore has long been associated with artistic communication. See Richard Bauman (1992); Dan Ben-Amos (1972).

among others. Exchanging ideas with a wide range of international journalists and distributors greatly helped me to situate the dizi in a global perspective. I should admit, however, that the dual exposure to both academic and business-journalistic discourses has been one of the most challenging aspects of my writing process—in determining the content and the rhetoric of my own narrative.

Linguistic Realms and Their Discourses

Straddling two readerships, the academic world and the global markets, my aim has been to construct a historical ethnography that traces the rise of the dizi genre, and to do so in a language accessible to both. The jargon of the television market, I observed, was fascinatingly truncated. It took me a while to get adapted to its numerous acronyms, such as 'OTT' for 'over the top' viewing, or 'TVOD' referring to 'transactional video on demand'; I had heard of HD, but the markets also had experiment rooms for '8K' experiences. In one of the first conferences I attended, I heard a network CEO exclaimed: 'They showed me the project, and *it had content*'. It was obvious that all drama had content, but what the term meant here was what folklorists called the 'emergent', a remarkable creative leap that constituted a new genre. '*It had content*' meant that there was a novel creative element in it.

Moving between two worlds, I also quickly noticed a difference in the use of certain themes and concepts. The most important was perhaps how to approach to the term 'Turkish'. To the business world, the term 'Turkish' is simply a national attribute, similar to its use in the tourism industry. To the academic world, however, the term evokes a palimpsest of subtexts. The older nationalist paradigm would assign a more ethnic and national meaning to the term, while many recent studies adopt a more deconstructive approach, covering a larger framework. Since the 1980s, many of us in the social sciences in Turkey participated in this paradigm change, which explores the Ottoman Turkish legacy not just as an exclusive experience of Turkish-speaking Muslim

Ottomans, but acknowledging the multiple linguistic, cultural and religious communities of the Ottoman society. By 'Turkish', one now understands 'from Turkey', a society with diverse cultural communities bearing memories of cohabitation but also conflicts, war, migration and displacement. The term 'Turkish' may also refer to a social and cultural domain produced 'during the making of modern Turkey'.[21] What makes Turkish society intriguing today has been this palimpsest of historical-geographical traces and memories, transmitted through Republican generations and undergoing a continual change. The elaboration of the term 'Turkish' is therefore closely related to the issue of 'content', which lies behind the global success of the dizi genre. 'Turkey: Home of Content', the slogan launched during the 2015 MIPCOM, recalled at the end this historical-geographical cultural legacy of Turkey, with all its complexities and cultural affinities shared by various regions and communities around the world.

The Time Effect: Duration of the Research and Its Impact

My research covers a period of ten years, from 2011 to 2021. I conducted most of the interviews and collected the preliminary archival data between 2011 and 2016. With no grant commitment, I was able to freely follow my curiosities and delve into the many different directions in which the interviews led me. The core of the book has therefore been shaped through my research process during those years. When I finally began my writing on 24 January 2016, in Beykoz Kundura's Demirane, more set visits and interviews continued, along with conferences in academic and global market venues.

---

21 The concept of 'Turkish folk dances' is a case in point, where many regional folk dance traditions (also shared by other ethnic communities) grew during the Republican history into a different movement system to be identified by that term (Öztürkmen 2002, 2007). One can observe a similar trend in the making of 'Turkish folk music' as well (Öztürkmen 2015).

I began to conceptualize the preliminary data, while dealing with a series of academic and administrative commitments.[22] Not having a formally funded research freed me from a deadline, and I was able to extend the research over time.[23] This proved to be a methodological advantage as the 'temporality' of the academic world and that of show business differed greatly. Collecting data from different agents of the industry required surrendering to the irregularity and spontaneity of their schedules, while at the same time maintaining the routine of my own academic and daily life.[24] My research also coincided with a challenging period in Turkey, in which much of our energy was spent coping with the many intrusions that targeted our academic institutions and communities. Nevertheless, extending the writing process afforded me more time to observe the transformations within the dizi industry. Over the ten years, I witnessed the influx of Turkish content into global markets, significant changes in network administration and rating criteria, and the rising censorship, which altered the production trends, leading some towards digital platforms, and others to platforms aligned to government circles. One methodological challenge involved the career trajectories of industry professionals. By the time I started to write my first chapters, the assistant directors I had interviewed in 2012 had become directors, and some junior writers who had been part of writing teams in those years had become the lead writers of new hit

---

22 For the list of the academic meetings and lectures I attended or organized, see Appendix 6.

23 I did not receive any grant to start my research in 2011. However, in 2019 Boğaziçi University Research Fund (No. 14464) supported the final chapter of the project, which also generously funded the colour images used in this volume.

24 Appointments were quite often cancelled, set times and places changed, or given promises not held. The research coincided with a time at my career where I also had to pursue some administrative duties, as vice dean of the Faculty of Arts and Sciences, and director of both Confucius Institute and Asian Studies Centre at Boğaziçi University.

dizis. The scope of the interviews expanded more with published material, constituting a sizeable, somewhat unwieldy databank.

As my project evolved, my ethnographic explorations of the early years turned in time into a 'historical ethnography' of its own, and I am sure that other critical domains will emerge for further research by the time this book goes into press.[25] While I was researching and writing, many institutions in Turkey experienced a shifting political landscape. Networks changed hands, the Radio and Television Supreme Council (RTÜK)[26] established new ratings criteria, many of the decision makers of the dizi world left their establishments, and the digital domain became more visible with new global investments and domestic enterprises. To better understand this realm of precarity, this book begins by depicting first the foundational years of the dizis, and then focuses on the different aspects and dimensions of this now-globally-circulating genre. It tells also the story of an *ancien regime* of the dizi world, which first produced the genre but struggled to sustain it. Today's TRT cannot produce a cult dizi like *Leyla and Mecnun*, the absurd comedy, which developed a creative political critique with a language of its own.[27] Many talented writers now express their reservations about producing content for mainstream networks and would rather pursue digital platforms. Repetitive and 'safe' dramatic themes and narrative structures dominate the remaining space for mainstream broadcasting. These works unfortunately lack the power of the original Turkish content, which has captivated global audiences. Nevertheless, with the entry of global digital platforms such as Netflix, HBO and Disney, the industry has now

---

25 There remains a need for more ethnographies of particular set contexts and production processes, more analyses on the audience and affect, and a deeper content critique of narrative structures, genres and subgenres.

26 RTÜK stands for Radyo Televizyon Üst Kurulu, which was established in 1983, following the 1980 military coup, to control the content of TRT.

27 For more analysis on *Leyla and Mecnun*, see Berfin Emre-Çetin (2014); Demet Lüküslü (2018); Sarenur Özkan (2019); Mehmet Gerçek (2019).

launched a new form of dizi, licenced as 'New Generation Turkish Series', where the duration of the episodes is much shorter, targeting new markets in the Western world.[28]

On Theoretical Framework(s)

The production processes of the television world vary depending on the industries within which they operate. Given the hegemonies of big industries, genres emerged, for a long time, from well-established television industries and spread around the world.[29] This continued, even after different regional industries also began developing their own genres. The Latin American and Indian industries have emerged in parallel to American and British ones. Lately, one observes the rise of the Korean, Nordic, Israeli and Turkish content in global markets.

Research on television industries can be approached from different disciplinary venues. The most dominant has been to situate it in the general critique of the culture industry. There are ethnographical studies in the fields of media studies and anthropology.[30] Of late, business studies, more particularly organization and management studies, have also began to explore the creative industries from a different angle, in which they explore how cultural clusters are organized along with their stories of success or failure as economic enterprises.[31] Last but not

---

28 To cite a few, *Love 101* (2020), *Saygi* (2020), *Ethos* (2020), *Fatma* (2021), *The Club* (2021).

29 For a critical look at the one-way flow of TV programmes, see Daya Thussu (2007).

30 See Faye Ginsburg (1991); Ginsburg et al. (2002); Douglas Gomery and Luke Hockley (2006); Bonnie Rui Lui (2010); Tejaswini Ganti (2012); Christa Salamandra (2013b).

31 See Allen J. Scott (2005); Monika Mehta (2005); Bahar Durmaz, Stephen Platt and Tan Yigitcanlar (2010); Özlem Öz and Kaya Özkaracalar (2011); Ivan Turok (2003); Chris Lukinbeal (2004); and Neil Coe (2000).

the least, there is a rising number of journalistic research on the appeal of emerging television genres and their industries. These studies stand apart from television journalism, which regularly follow and report on industry news; instead, these are articles or books based on short-time ethnographic surveys and interviews with the fields' experts (Witt 2017; Bhutto 2019a, 2019b). However, even though they give a useful review, television industries are a more complex phenomenon than what they demonstrate.

Obviously all of these diverse approaches are complementary to one another for a better understanding of television industries; nevertheless, they are rarely brought together because of disciplinary canons and boundaries.[32] My research benefited from them all, while being strongly inspired by folklore and performance studies in exploring the historical growth of the dizi as a meta genre, through dimensions of interdiscursivity and intermediality (Bauman 2004; Bhatia 2017; Bartesaghi and Noy 2015). Oral-history methodology and approach helped me in searching for the foundations of the dizi industry. Ethnographic exposure to the sets, the offices of production and distribution companies, and the sites of global markets revealed how the subjectivities of various parties affected content. The timing of my research also coincided with a period in which audiences developed novel responses to the repertoire that they were offered in different streaming venues.

On the Critique of the 'Culture Industry' Approach

In the footsteps of the Frankfurt School, the study of culture industries approached modern popular cultural forms mainly from the point of

---

32 One important exception is John Thornton Caldwell's *Production Culture* (2008). The book explores 'the cultural practices and belief systems of film/video production workers in Los Angeles—not just those of the prestige producers and directors but also those of the many more anonymous workers, such as gaffers and grips, in Hollywood's lower castes and crafts' (2008: 1). He calls his approach 'an integrated cultural-industrial analysis' (2008: 4).

political and economic criticism, a matter which I believe still dominates academic discourses. Studies on culture industries have long criticized the role of modern capitalism in homogenizing and commodifying cultural forms. Georg Simmel (1997), Walter Benjamin (1969, 1999), Theodor W. Adorno and Max Horkheimer (2002) long ago formulated the notion of 'culture industry'. They brought a Marxist critique to capitalist industrialization, arguing that elites produced a standardized mass culture that facilitated social and political control. Calling attention to the 'class culture' embodied in specific social structures, Pierre Bourdieu (1983, 1984) demonstrated how culture works to legitimate the inequalities of modern societies.[33] Jürgen Habermas (1989), in turn, noted how a historically constituted public sphere became increasingly media-dominated under state-welfare capitalism.[34] One should also mention the early works of Vance Packard (1957) and Marshall McLuhan (1964), which brought a pioneering critique to commercial television's transformative effect of social life, while Raymond Williams (1974) pointed out to the role of technology, in shaping television's cultural forms. All of these works primarily focused on the power dimension of the cultural industries encountered in the mid-twentieth century, and expressed themselves through homogenized art and media forms, among which television played an essential role.

More recently, the analysis of culture industries has been reworked in the light of developments in communication technologies. For instance, the French philosopher Bernard Stiegler, questioned the relationship between autonomous individual consumers and the mass-

---

33 For a comparison of how Theodor W. Adorno and Pierre Bourdieu approach cultural industries, see David Gartman (2012).

34 The critics of Habermas contended his idealization of earlier bourgeois public sphere, which indeed excluded oppositional working class, plebeian, and women's public spheres. Nevertheless, his account underlined the increasingly efficient use of media in politics and everyday life, by means of powerful corporate interests (Calhoun 1992).

produced and broadcast programmes. The programme industry, Stiegler (2011) maintains, modifies the individual experience of time and thus consumption behaviour; on the other hand, audiences select their own 'time-tested content' through an intergenerational transmission—a matter which I explore in this study as television memory (Stiegler 2011). One important critique of the culture-industry approach comes from Tejaswini Ganti who explored the Bollywood industry. Ganti stressed how the producers' sentiments and subjectivities affected media productions and illustrated the importance of industry-based ethnographic research in better understanding of the practices, social relations and experience of media creation (Ganti 2012a, 2012b, 2014). Similarly, Christa Salamandra's comprehensive research on Arab tele-vision industry invites us to rethink the argument that popular dramas function as a means to control public opinion. Her work on Syrian television illustrates how realist dramas became an expressive form under an oppressive regime, depicting everyday life and class encounters, even if in melodramatic ways. In the changing Syrian public sphere, television drama as cultural commodities both accommodates and resists political currents, offering new models of artistic communication and consumption (Salamandra 2004, 2008, 2013a, 2013b, 2015). However modern and global they are, cultural products must be understood in their particular ethnographic contexts. Although they appear highly structured and regulated, television industries are also social settings where different performances produce different interpersonal and cultural encounters, which give rise to new cultural forms. The affective aspects of the dizi production processes confirms that the 'sentiments of disdain', in Ganti's words (2012b), touch upon the affect issues not only among producers but also among the other social players of the industry, particularly those in the set environment.

And finally, one can also mention the recent studies in 'digital lore', where emergent streaming logics or new conventions constitutively shape and reshape traditional broadcasting and production habits. With the advent of technology and distribution, streaming companies are now able to re-articulate viewing modes in building new strategies. Audiences' opting for 'quality' streams create new algorithmic responses, thus engendering new contents (Allen-Robertson 2013; Burroughs 2018). Digital lore now lies at the heart of the content debates in Turkey, where creative-industry figures endeavour to develop new strategies to circumvent censorship. This new approach also offers the possibility of examining 'big data' in television research. Through their face- or space-recognition abilities, new digital coding programs will soon enable researchers to make cross-cultural comparisons at a larger scale, where they will be able to explore the extent of how gender, violence, humour or romance is used in different industries.[35]

Although the assumption that culture industries politically control and manipulate the masses still prevails, changing technology and pace of the industry renders content more vulnerable to mass preferences. Traditional networks and their formulaic programmes survive, but with the arrival of the 'over-the-top' media service, we now speak of 'streaming contents' that empower audiences. Audiences of the twenty-first century are now more 'media-aware' and, compared with their predecessors, have more detailed and swift responses to the content they watch.

Folkloristic Approach to Genre and Fieldwork

Given the forces of capitalism, the growing power of mass media and the commodification of cultural forms, it is a challenging task to embark on a journey in which a postmodern genre is constructed in time. From a folkloristic and performance point of view, all artistic communication produces its own semantics in relation to its ethnographic context. Be it a product of 'programme industry' or a form of

---

35 For a recent example of digital research in Turkey see Aydın Çam and İlker Yüksel Şanlıer (2021).

'consumed art', the encounter between the cultural product and its viewer cannot be reduced to a simple, one-way power dynamic. It encompasses a complex matrix of relations during and after the so-called 'consumption processes'.

As folklorists, we have a strong awareness of how cultural forms have responded to modernity through time and place. Decades ago, folklorist Richard Bauman eloquently stated that

> the very idea of folklore itself was born of the epochal social transformation represented by the advent of modernity—the rise of mercantile and industrial capitalism, the growth of modern cities and the modern nation state, the emergence of a naturalistic and secular world view, and all the other political, economic, social, and intellectual elements of what we call the modern era. (1989: 175)

Folklore, Bauman added, can offer important tools to better 'comprehend in full scope the communicative constitution of social life in the modern world' (1989: 184). In the analysis of genre, folklore theory offers us fruitful concepts like 'interdiscursive' processes and their 'emergent' aspects, which I adopt to explore the historical construction of the dizi as a genre. It has also prompted me to explore the historical context of 'texts', and to situate the development of the dizi genre within its political economy and historical conjunctures, where leading institutions and figures contributed to its consolidation. Genre theory reminds us that cultural forms come into being not only by borrowing and transcending elements from an array of other genres, traditions and social institutions, but also through a historical-political process shaping their construction. For example, TRT, the initial home of 'Turkish content', has always reflected state policy in dizi content.

Folklore has also contributed to my fieldwork methodology. The collection of genres and a critical approach to ethnography have been at the centre of our training as folklorists, an approach which also sensitizes us to issues of ethics, subjectivity and reflexivity. Field research in entertainment industries poses particular challenges, where a folkloric approach to fieldwork helped me opening doors and raising my awareness as a researcher. As well pointed out by Sherry Ortner, ethnographic access to 'dream factories' has been strictly gated. Carrying out participant observations in 'inside' locations and interviewing industry insiders have been very difficult (Ortner 2009, 2010). With my folklorist instincts, I began my fieldwork focusing more on the crew than on the cast, which enabled me to collect a wide range of personal-experience narratives about the production processes. The magazine press highlighted actors, directors and writers, but there was not much coverage of the directors of photography, location scouts, editors, or other technical and post-production crew members. Ground knowledge of the industry that I gathered enabled me to develop a know-how and language to approach industry insiders and get their consent for participant observation on location. Additionally, performance theory helped to reveal the layered performativity of the film sets—the heart of the industry—where many aspects of 'Turkish work culture' were constructed and displayed.

Exploring the historical processes in which the dizi genre was shaped was not easy either. TRT has a rich sound archive, for which as we folklorists are deeply thankful, but its visual material on programmes' repertoire has not survived so well, given the recycling of tapes during the economic austerity of the 1970s and 80s. In the haste in which private networks were established, they too have not produced comprehensive archives. It was therefore rather difficult to trace the history of the content repertoire. Moreover, each dizi had a life and adventure of its own, through which its writers, directors or actors might change, offering another slippery zone for research. There was also a need to discover the social players who contributed to the production processes. In many cases, I had to find the first episode on YouTube in order to identify contributors from the credits. The producers, writers, directors and actors in decision-making positions changed over time—some early figures disappeared from the scene; others emerged as influential. I used oral history to connect the different phases of this historical process, which not only informed me on how a course of events unfolded, but also what kind of thought and emotions they evoked. The historical framework of the research relied therefore greatly on oral history, consisting of in-depth interviews with the leading figures of different institutions and creative industries, particularly from the TRT, cinema and advertising worlds.

Narrative Interpretation

I had previously researched two sector-ethnographies in my academic career, namely, the folk-dance industry of the 1980s and 90s and the tourism industry of the early 2000s (Öztürkmen 2002, 2005). In both cases, an oral-history approach proved to be extremely useful in gathering knowledge of past experiences and for retrieving the emotional meanings assigned to it. In this regard, published and broadcast interviews from various sources helped me to cross-reference the personal narratives I collected. Collecting the life stories of my interviewees enabled me to move from 'more history' to 'how history'.[36] As Alessandro Portelli argues, oral history 'tells us less about *events* than about their *meaning*', inviting the historian to encounter and explore the interviewee's subjectivity (Portelli 1991: 50, emphasis in the original).

Given the precarious terrain of the dizi industry, with its continuous movement of jobs and roles at all levels, interviews collected needed to be interpreted within the context in which they were given. Most of the interviews I collected were constructed 'front interviews', which needed to be contextualized as storytelling sessions narrated to a

---

36 Oral historian Michael Frisch called attention to the concept of 'more history' as an approach that oral historians adopt when they aim at revealing hitherto-undocumented or unrecorded aspects of the past. For the concepts of 'more history', 'anti-history' and 'how history', see Frisch (1990, 1993); Arzu Öztürkmen and Joanna Bornat (2009).

university professor, framed as an outsider to the industry. The interviews also needed to be cross-referenced with interviews taken from other counterparts, and with those published in the printed press. Whenever I mentioned to an interviewee an idea another industry figure had given me, I observed that they often disagreed, offering me an alternative account. This discursive realm of 'dizi experience narratives' undoubtedly deserves further attention. I also perceived that many of my interviewees worried about being misunderstood, misquoted or misrepresented, mostly because they feared the irresponsible reporting of entertainment news media. During my interviews, I often took notes instead of making recordings, and never asked to get a photograph. This methodology distinguished my researcher identity from the approach of journalists or fans. This encouraged interviewees to speak more openly about their experience, and many expressed their support for academic research on the dizi industry. Nevertheless, I could only quote a few by their names. From stars to set workers, many preferred to remain anonymous. Confidentiality is crucial, as many of my interlocutors continue to work in the industry. While supporting this research, they also wanted to protect their jobs.[37]

Researchers of the ethnography of speaking understand how contexts determine the expressivity of the texts, and how challenging it is to analyse the complex and often paradoxical nature of personal narratives. This is why I must state from the outset that my research, like all research, is destined to remain 'partial' and 'incomplete'. Drawing on the numerous set visits and interviews I conducted, along with academic and news media sources, this book tries to offer a historically inflected ethnography of production processes in Turkey's dizi industry. It focuses on the period from 2000 to 2018, when the last mainstream

---

[37] For the list of personal and public interviews, see Appendices 1 and 2; for the list of set visits, see Appendix 3; and for the list of global markets and events attended, see Appendix 5.

channel also changed hands, adopting a pro-government stance (Tunç 2018; Farmanfarmaian et al. 2018). The interviews I collected between 2011 and 2015 captured an 'age of rising energy', which has changed as the industry developed. The dizi genre that circulates now may be said to have consolidated in a particular moment of the industry, when ratings were set according to education, producers took risks, and networks had their own powerful position. There have also been important developments in the last decade, including the emergence of a pool of young talents, upgraded film sets, international investment in content and digital platforms. Many of the ideas I developed throughout the research consist of the ethnographic observations and the interviews I conducted over the years; the ideas benefited most from the decade-long time frame which enabled me to observe the evolution of different trends. The overall narrative in this book partly reflects the macro-political landscape of television history. The term 'politics' in the title refers, however, more to the power dynamics among the social players of the production processes. Many of the political issues, including censorship and propaganda in content or problems with unions and copyrights, certainly require further research than what is represented within the limits of this volume.[38]

---

38 Since 2015, I have elaborated some of these issues in the following academic venues: 'The Historical Rise of the Dizi Genre: Memory and Politics of Television in Turkey', ARTES Seminar, Amsterdam School for Regional, Transnational and European Studies, University of Amsterdam, 5 April 2019; 'Remembering Political Humor in Turkey: An Oral History of Television Genres', Oral History Association Annual Meeting, Montreal, 10–14 October 2018; 'On Politics of Political Expressivity in Turkish Television Series', Society for Cinema and Media Studies Conference, Chicago, 22–26 March 2017; 'Historical Drama in Turkish Television', Glimpses of the Past in the Cultural Expressions of Greece and Turkey, Lectures in Gennadius Library, Athens, 20 September 2016; 'Television Industry in Turkey: A Historical Ethnographic Approach', The 12th International SIEF Congress, Zagreb, 21–25 June 2015. I am grateful for the audience of these meetings, where I received constructive responses.

Chapter Overview

This book is an outcome of a research process that was sparked by curiosity about the dizi genre, which emerged in the 1990s, became consolidated in the 2000s and began to circulate globally in the 2010s. Although I originally focused on the dizi as a contemporary phenomenon, I found it necessary to begin with the historical process which produced the genre. The current television industry has greatly benefited from professional talent and broadcasting practices rooted in the early decades of TRT. This is why Chapter 2, 'Growing Up with TRT', begins by exploring the institutional memory of national broadcasting in Turkey, with a focus on TRT, the sole national channel until 1990. The chapter examines TRT's legacy and its emphasis on a newly developing concept of 'national content'. It illustrates how pioneering TRT directors developed their own distinct strategies for incorporating Turkish cultural elements in television drama. It also details TRT's efforts to reach beyond Turkey's borders by dispatching acquisition envoys to purchase American and European content from global markets. 'Growing Up with TRT' refers therefore to a state of learning about what distinguishes high-quality television drama, and of developing narrative devices to tell Turkish stories.

'Pillars of the Dizi Industry', the third chapter of the book, also adopts a historical framework in order to trace the shift from TRT's monopoly to an era of private networks. It maps out the sectorial and institutional roots of the industry, examining contributions from theatre, cinema, video, humour magazines and advertising, noting how each of these domains influenced particular aspects of the dizi genre. For instance, the advertising sector enhanced the technical quality of dizi production, and writers from cartoon media authored the early screen scripts. The quality of the dizis circulating today also owes much to experienced theatre and cinema actors, who helped to train new actors on the sets during filming. This chapter also touches upon how and why film distributors or managers became TV producers. It illustrates how, with the arrival of private networks and the rising demand from Euro-Turk audience, as well as the booming video market, distributors were led towards new entrepreneurships like production.

Following the same period of transition to private networks, Chapter 4, 'Emergence of Dizi as a Genre', recounts the formation of the dizi from the early years of TRT. Comparing it to a series of imported formats, the chapter examines local canonizations and terminologies. Approaching dizis as media texts, it also explores the processes of interdiscursivity and intermediality in the dizi genre.

The next three chapters look at the production processes from pitching to post-production and focus on the collective creativity, examining the participants' influence on one another in the formation of the final product. Chapter 5, 'The Turkish Styles of Pitching', explores the diversity of stories in the launching of the landmark dizis since the 1990s. It points to the work culture in Turkey and different mechanisms of pitching since the TRT times. This issue also refers to an important period, which introduced the first generation of producers, writers, directors and actors who contributed to dizis' initial global success. Chapter 6, 'Constructing Stories and Their Sets', delves deeper in the making of the genre as a convincing cultural form both as text (script) and as context (set) where it transforms into a moving image. It focuses on how writers and art directors engage in creating a sense of 'realness', using different tools and strategies, which contribute greatly to the construction of the dizi genre. Chapter 7, 'Coping with Fame', examines the world of actors and their diverse backgrounds and experiences. Actors are the visible faces of the dizis, and as such they are continuously in negotiation with writers, directors and producers, as well as with their domestic and foreign fans. Centring on the ethnography of the set, the next chapter, 'Behind the Scenes, Behind the Sets', explores the exhausting atmosphere of the dizi sets, with their bustle as well as emotional encounters. It also looks at the dual performativity of the cast and crew during the shootings. Chapter 9, 'The Wonderland of

Global Markets', moves to the international markets in which television content circulates, where the social players consist of producers, network directors, distributors and television journalists, who create a festive ground of their own. This chapter also discusses the disguised role of the distributors in creating the success of Turkish content.

Research for the book also brought to the surface certain 'dormant research'. Scholars have constructed what might be called an official history of TRT. Numerous memoirs written by former directors and employees needed to be incorporated into these chronological studies. The memoirs of directors İsmail Cem and Şaban Karataş, for example, form an illuminating dialogue. Additionally, the 1990s saw a boom in research on 'pink series'.[39]

These studies were mostly academic theses written under the aegis of the newly consolidating media studies departments. They were written in the wake of the enthusiastic audience reception of soap operas and telenovelas, before the rise of the dizi phenomenon. Nevertheless, their writers shifted away from television drama for their subsequent research. During my research, I also discovered that it was very difficult to access the recent history of certain fields, such as the growth of the advertising industry. There, I turned to oral-history research with former experts of the field, but further research would be beneficial to document the opening up of Turkish markets to global companies like P&G and Unilever in the 1980s. Advertising companies provided cutting-edge technological expertise to the Turkish film industry in general, and hence form an important chapter in the dizi story. One important development was the fact that the 2010s, when I conducted my research, witnessed the blossoming of academic interest and research on dizis. I could only partially reflect on this new scholarship

---

39 See *Beyazperde* (1989); Ferruh Binark (1992, 1997); Kadıoğlu (2010); Leyla Budak (1993); Asuman Taçyıldız (1995); Fatma Gözlükaya-Tütüncü (1998a, 1998b); Mehmet Mete (1999).

in this book, which will reveal many new perspectives of looking at dizi industry in the near future.[40]

The 2015 MIPCOM event, where Turkey was the country of honour, marked a pivotal point in my dizi research. As a member of the preparation committee, I found myself playing a role beyond that of an attendee. The experience of organizing Turkey's conferences at MIPCOM gave me a vantage point from which I could examine global television markets. It also affected my subjectivity as a researcher. Working closely with the insiders of the industry during the preparations of the panels, my position shifted from researcher to a social player, putting me in a multi-sited ethnography between the realms of academia and television industry. During 2014–15, as the voluntary coordinator of Turkey's conferences,[41] I closely collaborated with international television-industry journalists, along with other industry professionals.[42] This experience put me in later years to a position that anthropologist George Marcus calls 'circumstantial activist', [43] where I was often consulted as an 'opinion giver' or approached for a reference.[44]

---

40 See, for instance, Yeşim Kaptan and Ece Algan (2021); Özlem Arda, Pınar Aslan and Constanza Mujica (2021); Pierre Hecker, Ivo Furman and Kaya Akyıldız (2021); Eylem Yanardağoğlu (2022); Zeynep Sertbulut (2022).

41 I would like to stress here that my coordinator position was an unpaid voluntary work as a member of the Executive Board for MIPCOM 2015 Preparations.

42 Besides exchanging ideas with Xavier Aristimuno, Virginia Mouseler, Ted Baracos and Samira Haddi, conversations with the following international TV journalists were also very informative: Gün Akyüz (*C21*), Diego Alfagemez (*Revista Señal Internacional*), Mansha Daswani (*World Screen*), Fabricio Ferrara (*Prensario*), Andy Fry (*MIP Daily News*), Sebastian Novacovsky (*PRODU*), Rhonda Richford (*Hollywood Reporter*), Alejandro Sanchez (*Todo TV*) and Nick Vivarelli (*Variety*).

43 Marcus explains the position of the ethnographer as a 'circumstantial activist' as a negotiation between the multiple sites of fieldwork and academia: 'In practice, multi-sited fieldwork is thus always conducted with a keen awareness of being within the landscape, and as the landscape changes across sites, the identity of the ethnographer requires negotiation' (1995: 97).

My oral-history interviews have also been perplexing in the sense that they covered mostly the mainstream and powerful social players in the industry. Although I had the opportunity to interview many set workers, junior technicians and assistants during my set visits, I observed the constraints of labour ethnography in dizi industry. Interviews on the sets' working conditions offer complex 'narrative events', embedding paradoxical 'narrated events'.[45] Many cast and crew members complained and harshly criticized their work conditions, frankly sharing their stories while requesting anonymity. Producers and network directors, who also wanted to remain anonymous, repeatedly expressed that all parties are content to work, and would never want reduced salaries—which would be the case if they worked shorter hours.[46] I believe that more comprehensive oral-history research would

---

44 During my research, I carefully renounced professional industry offers to be a consultant or writer in various projects. Nevertheless, I voluntarily gave interviews to TV journalists. See https://bit.ly/3rxXTqP; https://bit.ly/3EllbW2; https://-yhoo.it/3k5teND; https://bit.ly/3EllfFg; https://bit.ly/3xwqxMQ; https://bit.ly/-3vJGMDV; https://bit.ly/3MbuieB (all links accessed on 11 April 2022). I also moderated or attended a range of international events. These are 'Turkish Content Arises', Prensario Virtual Screening Autumn Showcase, 7 September 2020; 'Mainstream Broadcasting and the Digital Turn in *Dizis*', 8th Bosphorus Film Lab, 25 October 2020; 'Institutionalization of the Dizi Industry in Turkey', Dizi Production and Export during The Pandemic, UNESCO Turkey National Committee, 11 May 2021; 'Consolidating the Dizi Industry: The Changing Content and Social Players', The Turks are Coming! The Popular Outreach of Turkish TV Series Conference, Leiden University, 6–10 December 2021; '*Three Cents*: Confronting the Racist inside Us', Brand Week, Istanbul, 10 November 2021; 'Domestic Priorities and Global Impacts: Turkish Television Explained', Roundtable Discussion on Turkish TV series at Ottoman and Turkish Studies at New York University, 28 January 2022.

45 Bauman commented on this doubly anchored character of narratives: 'Narratives are keyed both to the events in which they are told and to the events that they recount, toward narrative events and narrated events' (1986: 2).

46 There is growing scholarship on this issue that brings a critical look at the labour dynamics of dizi productions. See Evrim Özkan (2010); Fırat Konuşlu (2010, 2016); Ergin Bulut (2016); Duygu Saraç (2019); Aysel Kara (2019).

reveal a completely new idea about the more recent perceptions of the industry, where one could find many uncelebrated heroes, operating amid passive-aggressive decision-making processes.

I hope this book will become a useful reference for researchers who will expand the academic literature on Turkish drama, and for foreign readers who want to understand the strength and uniqueness of the dizi genre from the mid-2000s. The book also tries to reveal the distinguishing Turkish components of the television industry and show how this affected the evolution of the dizi genre. The dizi genre owes its rise to its own characteristics, including the pace of production, the use of real locations, and content touching upon cultural specificities, accompanied by distinctive original music—all of which carry strong emotional connotations.

CHAPTER 2

Growing Up with TRT

Remembering the Search for 'Turkish Content'

Television entered Turkish social life during the 1970s, through Turkish Radio Television (TRT) whose broadcasting began in 1968. As a member of the first generation of television viewers in Turkey, I vividly remember the different phases of this encounter. The early days of broadcasting was limited first to three, then five days a week, only during evening hours and in black and white until 1981. TRT was the only network and it remained as such for over two decades, until 1990, when the first private network began its broadcasting from a European satellite, breaking TRT's monopoly without breaking the law. The law that liberalized broadcasting towards a multi-network system was not officially enacted until 1993, by the time private networks had already started their de facto broadcasting.[1]

As the official national broadcaster in Turkey, TRT had a significant impact on the concept of 'Turkish content'. To understand the structure of today's dizi genre, the memory of the TRT period is important for two reasons. First, most of the first generation of dizi producers and directors of private television in Turkey were former TRT employees.

---

1 Private radio and television broadcasting were enabled by an amendment to the Turkish Constitution that amended Article 133 on 8 July 1993.

In this regard, TRT operated very much like a school to the television industry. Second, the way the dizi genre constructed itself over time has been deeply affected by the content imported from abroad in the early days of TRT. In other words, TRT trained not only the future players of the dizi industry but also its audiences, through a two-decade-long broadcasting of foreign content. Many network managers and acquisition directors who were in decision-making positions during those years shaped the viewers' taste and perception in television programming. Since its early years, TRT broadcast a variety of Italian, British and American shows, offering audiences a new genre of storytelling—that of the drama series—and helping build the very habit of television watching.

In terms of communication technologies, Turkey inherited from the Ottoman times the essential institutions that paved the way for television and its rapid reception. Turkish society has been known for its passion for both technological developments and social communication. Even today, Turkey ranks among the top countries in the world in the use of smart phones, internet and social media, a matter which closely affects television habits (*Habertürk* 2015; Özcan and Koçak 2003). Watching television fast became part of the domestic routine in the 1970s—also as an inheritance of the practice of listening to the radio, which was the most important source of news and entertainment for former generations.[2] Through the 1950s and 60s, it quickly made its way into urban households and homes of the elite in the provinces, and became a symbol of modernity in the domestic space.

Although news programmes always had a central place, music programmes and radio dramas were also favourable genres in broadcasting in general. During the early Republican years in particular, a regular

---

2 Turkey did not enter to the Second World War, but local audiences received the news through public radio broadcasts in People's Houses or neighbourhood coffeehouses. For People's Houses (1932–1951), see Arzu Öztürkmen (1994).

and continuous access to music was seen as a welcome change in women's daily life.[3] Radio was also the most important channel for the dissemination of new European and American popular music.[4] The impact of radio continued after the launch of television broadcasting as well. Given television's shorter broadcasting span and limited circulation, radio remained a dominant medium through the 1970s. While dependency on news and music continued, another genre, radio drama (*radyo tiyatrosu*), emerged as a powerful genre of serials in these years. *Arkası Yarın* (To Be Continued) was perhaps one of the most effective radio programmes of TRT in the 1970s, even after television broadcasting had begun. It captivated its listeners with adaptations of classic or bestselling novels, perhaps establishing the habit of following a time-bound 'serial'. Radio dramas also introduced a pioneering group of theatre actors from state theatres, whose voices remained etched in the ears of Turkish audiences. Many of these radio voices also dubbed for the stars of foreign dramas broadcast on TRT during the 1970s and 80s. Actors such as Zafer Ergin, Çetin Tekindor, Cihan Ünal, Tomris Oğuzalp, Can Gürzap, Arsen Gürzap or Işık Yenersu, whom audiences first got to know from their voices, later became familiar faces of many hit dizis to come.

Television broadcasting in Turkey began with a testing channel that opened in 1952 in Istanbul at Istanbul Technical University (ITU) (Kıvanç 2002: 23–29). ITU's broadcasting was limited to an hour every two weeks, and its content consisted of programmes on Turkish music and culture, health and children's entertainment. Studies show that even

---

3 For a thorough history of national radio broadcasting and its impact, see Meltem Ahıska (2010).

4 Special programmes like *Fransa'dan Müzik* (Music from France) or *Latin Dünyası* (The Latin World) were highlights for curious listeners who wanted to access to music from abroad. Some of these music programmes later made a transition from radio to television. One of them was Sezen Cumhur Önal's *Müzik Yelpazesi*, displaying Önal's repertoire of 'world music', when such a category did not exist in global music markets.

IMAGE 2.1 National Star Zeki Müren performing for Istanbul Techical University. Image courtesy of Istanbul Technical University Foundation Archive (İTÜ Vakfı Arşivi).

this limited broadcasting created an increasing demand for television sets.[5] The middle-income population rapidly embraced this new entertainment form despite its cost. Once the radio-link system was available, Turkey quickly entered the realm of foreign broadcasting, showcasing programmes from neighbouring countries. In the 1970s one could easily notice the rise in the number of rooftop antennas in big cities such as Istanbul, Izmir, Ankara, Adana and some Black Sea towns close to the border to receive foreign broadcasting. Demand for television sets soon created its own economy: there was a rise in imported or sneaked-in

---

5 Hale Kapsal (2012) reports that in 1966, the number of television sets had increased to 2,000. According to Ömer Serim, the total number of television sets both in Istanbul and Ankara was around 150,000 in 1971 (2007: 67). Given the fact that many television sets were located in public spaces such as coffeehouses, patisseries, hotels and schools, the number of viewers was surely much higher.

television receivers around the country. As journalist Semih Tuğrul reminds us, there was a high demand for television sets in the so-called 'American bazaars', regardless of their prices. The first generation of Turkish workers in Europe had also discovered that they could sell their television sets on the black market. Another reason for the increase in sales was the fact that neighbouring countries such as Greece, Bulgaria, Syria, Iraq, Cyprus, and the Soviet Union increased their investments in regional broadband broadcasting, establishing their transmitters near Turkish borders (Tuğrul 1975: 140–41).

The Complex World of TRT:
Launching National Television Broadcasting

Because TRT has been fundamental to the construction of what today one calls 'Turkish content', it is essential to understand the formative debates surrounding the choice of content since its early years. To begin with, TRT broadcasting was launched at a historic moment, marked by complex ideological challenges on the road to democratization (Ahmad 1977; Keyder 1987; Lovatt 2001; Uraz 1970). The transition to a multi-party system ended with a brutal military coup in 1960, followed by the 1961 liberal constitution. TRT was officially founded on 1 May 1964 (TRT 2017),[6] but national television broadcasting is usually dated to the evening of 31 January 1968, the day when the first monochrome broadcast on VHF band aired with a rather amateurish spirit. Political instability of the 1970s directly affected the TRT management. With governments changing hands almost every year or two, TRT directors also changed accordingly. In the midst of this political and administrative precariousness, TRT experienced different phases in structuring itself as the public broadcaster.

---

6 TRT Official website dates the founding date as 1 May 1964. Hülya Yengin (1994) dates it to 24 December 1963, when the TRT Law 359 was passed.

IMAGE 2.2 TRT's first news anchorman Zafer Celasun, broadcasting live from Ankara studio on 31 January 1968. Image courtesy of the TRT Archive Department.

One important challenge was related to the lack of material and technical resources. While the history of Turkey's radio broadcasting was similar to that of Western countries, television technology in the country lagged far behind.[7] TRT broadcasting had begun in a rather 'unplanned' manner. This important decision was not included in the five-year plan of the State Planning Organization (DPT) (Tuğrul 1975: 140). In the 1960s electricity had not yet reached Turkey's rural areas. In its early days, TRT did not have a professional studio, and used the ground floor of an apartment building in Ankara for this purpose. Many American and European companies competed to sell their technologies and approached Turkish authorities during these years. The government chose to collaborate with German technicians, who established the first

---

7 Both Hülya Yengin (1994) and Hale Kapsal (2012) agree that the cost factor had been the main reason in this delay.

studios of TRT. Both Semih Tuğrul and Mahmut Tali Öngören expressed in their memoirs their reservation regarding the Turkish-German Technical Cooperation Treaty. Öngören argued that the Germans wanted to transfer their out-of-trend black-and-white technical equipment to other countries. Tuğrul, on the other hand, criticized this move as a step towards dependency on German technology, resenting also the condescending attitude of the visiting German technicians. These ideas and observations may sound too detailed or even irrelevant for our analysis of todays' dizi industry. However, they constitute the deep emotional framework for Turkey's aspiration of keeping up with Western standards, often expressed as 'not falling behind' (Aksoy 2002: 15–16; Tuğrul 1975: 149–56).

While TRT relied on German technology in establishing its initial infrastructure, it had an eye on BBC in terms of content. In his analysis of TRT history, Özden Cankaya (2015) underlines the important impact of the BBC during the foundation years. Since 1959, TRT had established contact with BBC, taking it as a model for radio broadcasting. This continued in the field of television as well. Many TRT employees were sent to BBC in later years to be trained in the field of programming.[8] BBC was also seen as a model state institution just like TRT, having an 'autonomous' status and keeping a distance from governments. Since its early years, TRT struggled to keep such distance, as political turmoil always challenged its autonomous status. Following the 1971 military memorandum, for instance, Musa Öğün, a former military officer, was assigned as the new director of TRT. This brought more political pressure to move towards more nationalist content. The political milieu after the 1971 coup was quite different from the era which followed the 1960 coup. The 1961 Constitution granted many rights to civil

---

8 On taking BBC as a model of national but autonomous network, see Önen and İmik-Tanyıldızı (2010); Yusuf Devran (2011); Zeki Hafızoğulları and Ahmet Tarakçıoğlu (1998)

associations. TRT was launched as an 'autonomous' institution after this short-lived liberal era. The original management structure included only three members assigned by the government, but after the constitutional amendment of 1971, the power balance changed in favour of the government. In 1972, a new law was passed that declared TRT's status as an 'impartial' public corporate entity, putting an end to its autonomous status (İçel 1985: 263). There are different opinions about this transition from 'autonomy' to 'impartiality'.[9] For instance, in his memoir, Şaban Karataş (1928–2016), who acted as TRT's general director during 1976–77, criticized autonomy as a 'romantic idea', which he saw as the cause of management-related problems he faced within the TRT. 'Each added unit', stated Karataş, 'had become a dukedom of its own' (Karataş 1978: 25).

Historical accounts of the military's impact during this era underline two developments of that period: first, militaristic discipline and regulations; second, the focus on technical development. Both were related to the issue of autonomy in different ways. Following the 1971 coup, the TRT management, which had changed swiftly, replaced leftist employees with retired military officers. According to Tuğrul, there was a fear that television's power would 'awaken' and 'raise awareness' among the people (1975: 176). Nevertheless, writer and poet Özdemir İnce, who had worked in TRT during these years, drew attention to the defence mechanisms established within the institution. İnce was then the director of the Auditing and Editing Office, which was responsible for budgeting and programming. Many of the content proposals passed through this key office, caught between military wishes and TRT's own staff's progressive aspirations. 'This office', he said, 'became a shield to everything. It showed the front screen to martial law officers, but did not allow them to access the kitchen' (İnce 2010). In his survey of the

---

9 For a comprehensive analysis of the issue of TRT's autonomous status, see Kayhan İçel (1985: 263–66); Hıfzı Topuz (1990).

television world, Faruk Bayhan puts forth a more positive consequence of the military's impact. He says that, as a former military officer with technical training, TRT's new director Musa Öğün contributed greatly to TRT's technological improvement (2013). Karataş also confirmed that the military era brought material progress and improved the infrastructure of Turkish television (1978).

The Politics of National Content: TRT's Dilemma on Programming

TRT began its television broadcasting with a team of well-educated, young and motivated employees. The foundational law granted autonomy to this first generation of TRT employees with freedom of programming, production and selection of content. Television broadcasting prioritized technical know-how, which required hiring a staff who hailed from the 'learned' circles of Ankara. The 1960s and 70s also saw a rise in leftist movements.[10] In his analysis of TRT's history, Ömer Serim states that the young producers of these initial years had a particular passion for using television more for education rather than entertainment:

> It is hard to say that TRT was independent from what happened in the world and in Turkey during 1968–70. The ruling party of the time was angry at the producers, who were young and open to leftist ideas, and broadcasting about themes of oppression, exploitation and poverty; and at the directors of TRT, who were broadcasting the social movements of the time on television and radio. They were accusing TRT of provoking society while hiding behind their autonomy. (2007: 56)

As an institution that aspired to catch up with new technologies and modern cultural forms, while being under strict state control with rising nationalist concerns, TRT naturally experienced conflict in its

---

10 For a review of the leftist movements in Turkey, see Kemal Karpat (1966); Attilâ İlhan (1976); Mustafa Türkeş (2001); Murat Belge (2009); and Sabri Sayarı (2010).

work environment. The main conflict was ideological, which one can perhaps regard as 'Marxist-leftist' versus 'nationalist-right'. Seeing TRT as a castle to be conquered, each political party found in it a promising platform to promote their ideologies, making TRT 'an army of the dissatisfied' (Tuğrul 1975: 8).

The issue of 'national content' was in fact a central concern of TRT since its early years. There were different perspectives regarding what represents 'the national'. The repertoire of television programmes produced during these initial years was rather small. There was not much opportunity to finance domestic productions, but one can cite Şinasi's *Şair Evlenmesi* (Marriage of a Poet) as the first domestic production, which was performed and broadcast live from TRT's modest studio in Ankara.[11] The passion for 'education through television' revealed itself in children's programming, produced and performed by local talents.[12] Live broadcasts was also an important component of TRT's early years. One such event was the first steps of Neil Armstrong and Edwin Aldrin on the moon in 1969. Newspapers reported that many people travelled from neighbouring cities just to be able to see this scene on screen. The same year, TRT also broadcast live the Ankara concert of Zeki Müren, Turkey's phenomenally popular singer, an event watched by 150,000 people (Serim 2007: 58–59).

Nevertheless, the import of foreign content was a necessity for programming. To begin with, TRT was not well equipped for television production. Given the strong economic and political tensions of the

---

11 *Şair Evlenmesi* was written by İbrahim Şinasi and published in 1860 in *Tercümân-ı Ahvâl* as a series. It has often been called the first modern play in Turkish, although other such plays had been written and performed earlier by Armenians, such as Tovmas Berentz' *Aldatılan Eğinli* (Hermonn 2015). The play was directed by Tunca Yönder and performed by Ali Özoğuz and Mustafa Küçük. For more on this, see Ömer Serim (2007: 58).

12 Faruk Bayhan confirmed this, stating that the children's programming department was the highlight of TRT during the 1970s (2017).

times, its programmes were far below the technical level of television in the West. Foreign content helped to fill daily programming at a time where domestic production was costlier. There were disagreements, however, within the TRT management concerning dependency on foreign content. Some senior managers promoted the import of foreign feature films and documentaries along with American serials. Trained in the leftist circles of Columbia University, Mahmut Tali Öngören was critical of American content and opposed the idea of beginning Turkish broadcasting with dubbed foreign drama. Instead, he suggested producing local content, giving priority to other formats like news and debates (Aksoy 2002: 17).

In fact, TRT's autonomy allowed, in the beginning, many creative producers to come up with programmes with a focus on social and political issues. Given the intellectual aspirations and mostly leftist leaning of their producers, these programmes mainly consisted of political documentaries on issues such as historical memory, problems of economic development, or the difficulties of peasants.[13] There was also a general critique from left-wing circles that considered television a 'bourgeois tool', or some children's programmes as 'foreign indoctrination'.[14] Following the 1971 coup, however, a new era began in TRT in which the new administration and former employees had totally different approaches to programming. Ömer Serim reminds us that during this era, the military prioritized the expansion of TRT broadcasting to other towns and increased the broadcast time to five days a week, four hours a day (2007). The new administration also considered foreign acquisition a much safer strategy to control any controversial content produced from inside TRT. During these years, TRT began to broadcast

---

13 Among these programmes, Serim (2007: 57) mentions Gülseven Güven's *Türkiye'nin Kalıkınma Sorunları*, Adem Yavuz's *Buğday Çıkmazı* and *Tütün,* and a series of round-table discussions by Professor Mümtaz Soysal.

14 For a critical approach to *Bizim Sokak,* see Semih Tuğrul (1975: 193).

a certain amount of foreign content, including *Shirley Temple's Storybook, Mission Impossible, Star Trek* and *Fugitive* (*Anilarim.net* 2019). Another type of foreign content was the live broadcast of important events, as part of the Eurovision network (Serim 2007: 69–72). European Cup and the Eurovision Song Contest were among such programmes that connected Turkish audiences to European sports and entertainment.

In the post-coup period, domestic production was closely supervised. One important show of this era was the memorable children's programme, *Bizim Sokak* (Our Street). Inspired by *Sesame Street*, the programme turned out to be a successful adaptation—as an original production including dance, games, storytelling woven around playful and familiar characters from a Turkish neighbourhood. TRT used unscripted content as well. Besides language-teaching programmes in English and German, there were game shows, magazine programmes and a series of plays performed for television. The share of domestic television drama was rather small in the overall content. Plays meant for the theatre were performed live in TRT studios to be taped and later broadcast as television drama (Serim 2007: 72). Among them one should note *Hayattan Yapraklar,* which was perhaps the first Turkish drama produced and filmed for television. Written by Nezihe Araz and directed by Gürol Gökçe, it focused on one story in each episode and cast renowned theatre performers Yıldız Kenter and Şükran Güngör, whose students act today in many hit dizis (Serim 2007: 70–71).

A Short-Lived Leadership: The Impact of the İsmail Cem Era on Television Production

The period following the 1971 military memorandum is often referred as an 'interim regime', which was followed by the 1973 general elections. The leading party of the new era was the Republican People's Party (RPP), which had a social-democrat view. Their impact was perhaps most strongly felt in TRT when İsmail Cem (1940–2007), a charismatic research journalist, was appointed the new director of the organization. Cem was already a public intellectual, known for his critical approach to modernization and development, having published important books on these subjects (1970, 1973).

During his short service as the director of TRT in 1974–75, Cem made a notable impact on TRT's television division. His memoir *TRT'de 500 Gün* (2010) includes important observations on his first encounter with TRT as a state institution, and still stands as a comprehensive historical ethnography of its early years. Cem's first observation was about age; most of the TRT employees, he noted, were older than him, and as such, TRT looked like a giant organization, dispersed over different territories. Cem also observed that, amid changing governments and political clientelism, appointing new employees in TRT had been much easier compared with other state organizations, making TRT overcrowded. A figure from the world of print, İsmail Cem was new to the technical jargon of the television world, which had consolidated under different departments of the institution by the time he became director. But his greater reaction was to the cumbersome bureaucracy:

> *Telecine, Radio Link, Transposer, Ampex, Uher, First of the Fourth, Third of the Two.* As soon as I set foot in TRT, I found myself within a pool of foreign concepts. Most of it were related to technical issues. I grasped them in a short time, or even understood the general principles of television and radio technique, and of electronic communication, despite my lack of preliminary knowledge. But it took me months to get used to such meaningless—even unnecessary—legal references as the *first, second and third article of the Fourth rule.* It was like one had thought, 'What should we do to prevent TRT making progress; what kinds of irrational and illogical rules can we produce to abuse people's energy, consume it in inefficient areas?' and TRT as an institution was bound with these bigoted and incredible rules of personnel law (2010: 17).

Many key positions of the organization were filled by retired military officers. The head of the television division was a former colonel, as were the general secretary, and the heads of the human resources and planning divisions. Cem acknowledged the contribution of the personnel with military backgrounds in technical matters but had strong reservations regarding their decision-making position in content selection and management of television programming:

> To have the last word on radio and television programmes, to plan and take decisions about them requires a distinct education and upbringing; this is a matter of being specialized or at least having worked in areas like art, culture, sociology, journalism. The level of success of those who ruled TRT television and radio in February 1974 would be as much a success as I can achieve commanding an infantry regiment today. Or else, when they were assigned to these positions in the aftermath of March 12 [1971 military coup], what was expected from them were just to control these powerful media channels . . . . (2010: 21)

Cem's appointment as TRT's general director received broad coverage in media. His social-democrat background made him a controversial figure at the time. He was blamed for 'not even liking television', seeing it as the entertainment of a 'happy minority'. In his memoir, Cem tries to answer these claims:

> If a television is being used to the detriment of the masses, for opiating and freezing the order, this kind of usage is negative for the people, positive for the class who sees a benefit in keeping the order as it is. But if the same television is used in the direction of enhancing the development of the people, then it carries a positive function for the people, a negative one for those who have a benefit in people being calm and opiated. (2010: 47–48)

IMAGE 2.3 TRT director İsmail Cem (1940–2007). Image courtesy of the TRT Archive Department.

Cem emphasizes in his memoir how was indeed a careful viewer of European television, since the early years of his higher education in Switzerland and France. The 'European impact' was a significant factor in the projects he would develop during his directorship. Caught up amid political manoeuvres inside and outside TRT, Cem aspired for a high-quality broadcasting which also conformed to his own sociopolitical concerns. Many would agree that his short term at TRT had a remarkable influence in setting the frame for 'quality television' in the minds of generations to follow. Cem's projects were also the harbinger of what one may today call 'Turkish content', including not only dizis but also many unscripted formats such as political debate shows, animation and documentaries. Nevertheless, his idealism in building a constructive approach to creative television content triggered many debates on the definition of 'Turkish', 'national' and 'domestic' values, interpreted differently in the intellectual circles of the political right and left.

National Desires of 'Turkish Content':
The İsmail Cem Era and Beyond

When he was assigned to his post as the director of TRT, İsmail Cem expressed his plans in a press conference held on 11 March 1974, stating his ideas on the issue of 'content': 'One of my main criteria is what the public wants and what they like [. . .]. I will not treat the audience as virtual students, and TRT as a master mind which knows it all. TRT will pursue its informative and cultural mission, by evaluating public trends and by establishing a dialogue with people' (2010: 39). Building a new team, and collaborating with some former TRT employees,[15] Cem began to implement his vision fast, using a pragmatic approach to transcend TRT's clumsy bureaucracy. His approach was targeted and criticized by both the right-wing (2010: 145–49) and left-wing press (2010: 139–40). His priority was 'reaching out to the masses', a motto of the left in the 1970s:

> During our time at TRT, we had an action-reaction relationship with the left wing of Turkey. Especially during the last months, a part of 'the left' was highly critical of TRT [. . .]. According to them, news about the rightist parties, broadcasting shows on entertainment and sports was the epitome of betrayal. For example, a leftist folk singer on television would be enough to be praised by them. If I were to act as they wanted, TRT would get credit from some groups. But it would never have achieved strong dialogue and efficacy. (2010: 139)

Transmitting 'quality content' to the masses was crucial to Cem's policies. He was severely critical about the domestic production which preceded his era. In the domain of television drama, for instance, he

---

15 These were colleagues whom he could morally and intellectually trust to cope with technical deficiencies: Hıfzı Topuz, Mehmet Barlas, Haluk Şahin, Tarcan Günenç and Mustafa Gürsel, along with engineer Yılmaz Dağdeviren (see Şahin 2007).

only praised a few theatre plays as successful, even stopping the broadcast of a thriller series that he found 'unbearable' (2010: 55).[16]

Cem's era is also remembered with the rise of new local formats, including the legendary Sunday daytime entertainment programme *Telespor*, the forerunner of many similar shows. To 'reach out to people', Cem attached great importance to sports, approaching leading football clubs to broadcast their games live. In order to appeal to women and children, he invented a new format where live football was buttressed with programmes that included games, concerts and talk shows. *Telespor* was therefore not only a sports programme but one of entertainment, which promised long hours of fun to all family members. The broadcast of *Pink Panther* in *Telespor*, for instance, taught the public that animation could be enjoyed also by adults.[17] Audiences embraced this programme and it received genuine acclaim. In his memoir, Cem reports many phone calls TRT received during the first day that *Telespor* was broadcast. 'Are we watching TRT?' some asked. Friends apparently called him from Istanbul with news that the streets were all empty, and people were 'either at homes or at coffeehouses watching *Telespor*!' (2010: 63)

This feeling of success was closely related to the pride of producing a 'European-like' yet 'Turkish' programme. Novel news formats were also being launched, introducing the first news anchor of Turkish television: Can Akbel was introduced through the night-time news show *Güne Bakış*, and he took the liberty of presenting the news in his own friendly style (2010: 94). In fact, all television newsreaders were seen as stars during these days, and would be easily recognizable among the

---

16 I was unable to determine which series this was. One possibility could be from Araz's series *Hayattan Yapraklar* (see Kenter 2017, *Edebiyat ve Sanat Akademisi* 2015).

17 Şahin gives credit to Tarcan Günenç, who produced the show, along with Güneş Tecelli, who ran it. He sees them as the 'inventors' of this new all-round format which included music, entertainment, news and sports (see *Radikal* 2002).

public by their names. Nobel Prize-winning author Orhan Pamuk cites one of them, Aytaç Kardüz, in his novel *Museum of Innocence*: 'Unlike the relaxed women newscasters in the West, Aytaç Kardüz sat like a statue, never once smiling, and rushing through her reports as she read from her copy in her frozen hands' (2009: 489). Haluk Şahin also gives us humorous ethnographic accounts of the Cem's era regarding the myth of television appearance. He states that managers' rooms in the television division would fill up with people who fancied to appear on television, including 'mothers who wanted to watch their daughters on television; retired teachers who claimed to be good at reciting poems; young men who wanted to be a television announcer' (*Radikal* 2002).

The chaotic politics of the 1970s had a direct impact on TRT management, as directors changed each time there was a change in government. It is crucial to closely examine the directorships of these early years, because the foundation they built has been influential in the television industry for years to come. In the 1975 general election, RPP lost power and the right-wing coalition called the National Front came to power. One of the first operations of the new government was to dismiss İsmail Cem from his post, a matter which Cem took to court. Nevzat Yalçıntaş was appointed the new director, and began his term through this controversial transition. Through his short stay in TRT during 1975, Yalçıntaş hired new employees, but also continued to work with the managers Cem had appointed and pursued the prevailing policies and programming of the Cem era.[18] Following a series of legal controversies, Yalçıntaş resigned, leaving his post to Şaban Karataş, who ran TRT during 1976–77. Karataş was a self-made man: he came from a rural background and had become a professor in agricultural studies with close ties to nationalist circles. He began his directorship under strong expectations and pressure to pursue 'nationalist content'; but he

---

18 Both Yılmaz Dağdeviren and Özdemir İnce expressed their surprise at being allowed to continue in their positions after Yalçıntaş was appointed (Dağdeviren 2013; *Hürriyet* 2006).

found himself in a milieu of resistance from TRT's own bureaucracy. In a memoir he wrote right after he left TRT, Karataş commented on the challenges he faced there. Writing about what he wanted to achieve at TRT but could not, he complains about judgmentalism from the leftist opposition. He openly stated that he aspired to producing dramas with certain literary content embedding issues that would bolster 'national pride':

> What I wanted to insert in our television programming were the principal national works that made us proud. Some of these were vaguely introduced to our generation, but then they were left in oblivion so that they would be forgotten. I knew this would be a hard project. This was going to be a mission, a reaction to those that followed imported trends. (1978: 88)

Karataş resented the fact that some TRT employees made him a subject of contempt, portraying him as someone chasing only after national epics, heroes or myths (1978: 89–90). In fact, what Karataş wanted to launch was content that reflected the rising ideal of 'Turkish-Islamic synthesis'—proposing documentaries on the great figures or events from Turkish-Islamic history, or adapting for television the works of conservative writers, including Necip Fazıl Kısakürek's *Bir Adam Yaratmak* (Creating a Man), which was broadcast in 1977. Ironically, however, the Karataş era was also marked by the broadcast of many foreign dramas, which he justified as a way of remaining 'contemporaneous' with the Western world, selecting only content that 'conformed to Turkish values':

> As we all know, the most popular form in world television is the drama series. These dramas have almost become the common language of various national broadcasters. These are programmes that synthetized different tastes and worldviews, prepared by successful production companies. From the very beginning, Turkish television has been very careful in broadcasting them simultaneously with European and American

television, and in selecting those which inspired devotion, family bonding, loyalty, love, and civilized and good social conduct. (1978: 149–50)[19]

Nevertheless, his era is also remembered for censorship, such as cutting scenes kissing and drinking from foreign content. While religious content was first introduced in the İsmail Cem era, Karataş brought religious programming one step further by introducing religious talk shows as a new format to satisfy the National Front.

Karataş was followed by Cengiz Taşer, who was the first director appointed from within TRT. Hailing from a social-democratic background like Cem, Taşer prioritized quality domestic content as well, carrying on Cem's legacy, and producing miniseries like *Yorgun Savaşçı* (Tired Fighter), *Kiralık Konak* (A Mansion for Rent), *Paranın Kiri* (The Dirt of Money) or *İbiş'in Rüyası* (The Dream of İbiş), along with documentaries and children's programmes. He too needed to continue importing several American series, including hit series like *Love Boat, Baretta, Charlie's Angels* and the phenomenal docu-drama *Roots* (Serim 2007: 110). Taşer's successors, Doğan Kasaroğlu and Macit Akman, also continued the practice of importing programmes, though it was not very easy under the economic constraints that Turkey experienced in the 1970s. Confirming the significance of American content during these years, Faruk Bayhan, then the acquisition director of TRT, recounts how difficult it was to import television content because of strict Customs regulations:

> In the early years of TRT we had great difficulty because the prevailing regulation regarding film content did not include television programmes. Television series from abroad were

---

19 By the end of 1976, the imported drama included American series like *Bewitched, Little House on the Prairie, Bonanza, The Six Million Dollar Man, Police Woman, McMillan and Wife, Mission Impossible* and *Barnaby Jones,* among others (Karataş 1978:150).

treated as films meant for cinemas. They had to undergo a three-step inspection for censorship, and this meant a procedure lasting months and endangering regular broadcasting schedule [. . .]. We used to constantly go to and return from the Customs. There was some liberty regarding news programmes, so we used to get certain drama series out of the Customs by presenting them as 'news content'. In some cases, films would even be forgotten in Customs storage. (2013: 13)

In his historical analysis of TRT, Ömer Serim approaches the import issue from a different critical perspective. Despite all the debates on national content during its first decade, TRT had a dependency on foreign drama, whose content, Serim thought, was 'vain', and 'irrelevant' to Turkish society. He notes: 'Turkish television was dependent on airing shows that were based on foreign customs, traditions, culture and moral values. During that period, Turkish audience watched excitedly more than 50 imported productions; but those shows were no good to anyone' (2007: 94).

Turkish audiences, however, welcomed television entertainment, tolerating or not caring too much about the 'foreign elements', cherishing the feeling of being contemporaneous with the modern world. Serim states that one can distinguish Turkish social life 'before and after television', particularly in Ankara. Despite the early Republican performing arts institutions and many other cultural centres that Ankara had in those years, Serim argues that the city had maintained its quiet Anatolian town atmosphere: 'It was a big event when television broadcasting began in Ankara. People were initially distant from this uninvited guest in their homes. Because television sets were expensive and civil servants could hardly live and survive. But in three to five years, quite a number of houses could afford them. With television entering the house, visits had turned into "televisits"' (2007: 12).

The term 'televisit'—*telesafir* in Turkish—was a portmanteau formed from the words of *televizyon* (television) and *misafir* (guest), and it referred to the period of hosting friends, relatives and neighbours in households that had television sets. Watching foreign content during televisits now revived the old tradition of watching performances together, often while boisterously sharing a meal. The early Republican regime put great emphasis on establishing the modern practice of indoor theatrical performances, where audiences were expected to sit and watch quietly. In this context, television watching emerged as a liberating new form of entertainment.[20]

Imagining 'Turkish Content' while Watching American Drama

Besides the modernizing and socializing aspects of watching television, exposure to American television drama had yet another effect on Turkish audiences. Series like *Bewitched*, *Petrocelli*, *Dallas*, *McMillan and Wife*, *Bonanza*, *Little House on the Prairie* or *Roots* opened a window onto different aspects of American life, modern and historical alike. On the one hand, this exposure enabled Turkish audiences to access the representation of modernity and its enactment. One can better explain this experience through what the eminent scholar Şerif Mardin (2013) calls the 'gaze' in Turkish culture, inquisitiveness about other people's lives.[21] On the other hand, however, by watching foreign drama, Turkish audiences also went through a training process on up-to-date standards of television content, developing a certain taste for 'good-quality television products'. American series set an ultimate standard for the quality of content and technology for the early Turkish productions.

---

20 For the memory of the 1970s television culture, see Ayfer Tunç (2001); Halit Kıvanç (2002).

21 The gaze towards the West has been a rather well-documented aspect in the studies of Occidentalism, but Şerif Mardin carried the concept also to what he called the 'neighbourhood pressure' (*mahalle baskısı*) in which gaze operates as social control.

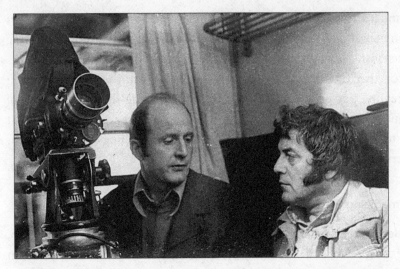

IMAGE 2.4 Director Metin Erksan (1929–2012) (right) during the shooting of his television films, adapted from stories of contemporary Turkish writers, 1975. Image courtesy of the TRT Archive Department.

In parallel to showing foreign content, however, TRT continued to produce Turkish television films and miniseries. In the early years, this meant adapting Turkish novels.[22] Under Cem's directorship, TRT had commissioned for the first time prominent film directors like Lütfi Akad and Metin Erksan to adapt a series of short stories for television. Of course, these otherwise well-known stories of modern Turkish literature had not been written for television. The great part of the Turkish audience, exposed to entertaining foreign content, found these pioneering television films rather short or, as one viewer expressed, 'depressing'. General audiences had a hard time interpreting the cinematic symbolism of film directors who adapted these stories.[23] In a way, watching Turkish

---

22 Some earlier examples were Halide Edip Adıvar's *Sinekli Bakkal*, Aziz Nesin's *Yaşar Ne Yaşar, Ne Yaşamaz* and Necati Cumalı's *Tütün Zamanı*.

23 For the difference between cinematic storytelling and the concept of cinematographic storytelling, see Jennifer Van Sijll (2005); Michael Bolus (2019).

television content became more a 'national duty' than a pursuit of pleasure; they gave a sense of underachievement in comparison with their Western counterparts. What was captivating as Turkish content in those days came from the sitcom *Kaynanalar* (The In-Laws, 1974) and the adaptation of the novel *Aşk-ı Memnu* (Forbidden Love, 1975) by director Halit Refiğ. In contrast to Erksan and Akad's story adaptations, *Aşk-ı Memnu* became a real success as a miniseries, receiving high public acclaim. Both *Kaynanalar* and *Aşk-ı Memnu* were therefore influential in giving the Turkish television the first sense of achieving a high-quality production—very much of 'Western calibre'.

Kaynanalar was written and directed by Tekin Akmansoy, a student of German director Carl Ebert (1887–1980), who had established the State Theatre in Ankara. Akmansoy proposed his story to TRT, building it up around two families, one traditional Anatolian and the other modern urban. The story stood upon the deeply rooted concepts of *allaturca* and *allafranga* (Turkish and European styles), which constituted the axis of the traditional Karagöz shadow theatre. The familiarity of the folk humour captured Turkish audiences, making *Kaynanalar* the hit programme and Akmansoy the first television star of Turkish dizis

IMAGE 2.5 A scene from *Kaynanalar* (1974), with Defne Yalnız, Leman Çıdamlı and Tekin Akmansoy. Image courtesy of the TRT Archive Department.

IMAGE 2.6 Director Halit Refiğ (1934–2009) on the set of *Aşk-ı Memnu* (1975) with actors Salih Güney, Müjde Ar and Itır Esen. Image courtesy of the TRT Archive Department.

(Akmansoy 2014). *Kaynanalar* was a low-budget project proposed to TRT director Cem, who approved of it because its content had a populist approach.

As a period drama, *Aşk-ı Memnu*'s production was a more expensive project. After Akad's and Erksan's television films, Cem had approached director Halit Refiğ, also known as an advocate of 'national cinema'. In his memoirs, Refiğ reported that they were all surprised to be 'selected' for these TRT projects: 'It was the first time one was producing a film with a mere national cultural goal, without any concern of ratings, and for the state television, which was totally an outcast from the commercial film market' (cited in Türk 2001: 302). Cem granted these film directors direct power, bypassing TRT bureaucracy with special regulations, drawing diverse reactions towards these productions. Refiğ reported the hardships and challenges he experienced at TRT: *Aşk-ı Memnu* received strong support from Cem and his top executives, but those in intermediary positions were largely against it (Türk 2001: 302). The filming took about nine months; by the time it was first broadcast in 1975, the government had already changed. Despite the grand success of the series, Refiğ did not receive any further call from TRT until 1978, when Cengiz Taşer invited him to adapt Kemal Tahir's *Yorgun Savaşçı* (The Tired Fighter), a historical novel on the Turkish Independence War.

The process of filming *Yorgun Savaşçı* went through different challenges, its shooting being interrupted several time during the political chaos of the late 1970s leading up to the 1980 military coup. The series remained in the memory of Turkish audiences as the first TRT production that was officially—and literally—burned after the military coup, on the premise of discontent over the representation of the army (*Radikal* 2009).

TRT's early attempts to adapt stories and novels from Turkish literature gave way to another idea in the 1980s: commissioning acclaimed poet and novelist Attilâ İlhan to write original scripts. İlhan wrote two dizis for TRT: *Kartallar Yüksek Uçar* (Eagles Fly High, 1983) and *Yarın*

IMAGE 2.7 Writer and poet Attilâ İlhan (1925–2005), who wrote the first original screenplays for TRT. Image courtesy of Biket İlhan.

Artık Bugündür (Tomorrow Now Means Today, 1986). The first was set in Izmir on the Aegean coast and focused on competing families, generational clashes and romance amid the sociopolitical landscape of Republican Turkish history. The second portrayed the rising awareness of a bourgeois girl when she is exposed to the problems of eastern Turkey, leading to her estrangement from her social circles. The content in these years thus focused more on the historiographic, with a desire to analyse Turkish society and history with a critical eye. With his leftist background and loyalty to traditional culture, Attilâ İlhan was the perfect choice as an intellectual writer with a foothold in Turkish cinema.[24] During this era, TRT also produced a drama touching upon an actual sociopolitical tension that Turkey was facing at the time with Bulgaria. *Yeniden Doğmak* (To Be Reborn, 1987), based upon a real story of families taking refuge in Turkey, escaping Todor Zhivkov's oppressive policies in Bulgaria, was temporarily banned for diplomatic concerns (Sevincokum.info 2018).

Historical novels and plays, focused on political figures and events, continued to be adapted for television. Adaptations of novels usually depicted the late nineteenth-century Ottoman social life and imperial political chaos. Following the footsteps of successful *Aşk-ı Memnu*, three other period dramas aired in the 1980s: *Üç Istanbul* (Three Istanbul, 1983), *Bugünün Saraylısı* (Today's Courtier, 1985) and *Çalıkuşu* (The Wren, 1986), all of which were shot as miniseries whose narratives revolved around class and romance, depicting the daily and political life of the late Ottoman period. Loyal to the original novels, they were effective domestic productions which appealed to Turkish audiences.

Produced by a state-run national network, historical dramas reflected the official approach to Ottoman history, depicting the 'foundational' period or the lives of powerful sultans. This genre had begun

---

24 İlhan's sister Çolpan İlhan and her husband Sadri Alışık were well-known performers of Turkish cinema.

with the phenomenal *4. Murat* (Murat IV, 1981), focusing on the lives of two powerful figures: the sultan, who ruled the Ottoman empire between 1623 and 1640, and his mother Kösem, one of the most influential women in Ottoman history. With performances by prominent theatre actors, the series adopted a strong theatrical frame. This trend continued with *Kuruluş* (Foundation, 1988), which was a grand, high-budget production depicting the foundational years of the Ottoman Empire. The series was filmed upon a plateau specially built for that production.

During the 1980s, TRT also made attempts to sell Turkish content abroad. Turkologist Apollinariya Avrutina reminds us the 'bombshell effect' of the 1986 adaptation of *Çalıkuşu* in Russia (*Haberler* 2014). Though Faruk Bayhan, who was then in charge of TRT's international sales, remembers the resistance they faced in foreign regional markets. Referring to the Egyptian market, he states:

> They had in their minds a notion of 'Turkish yoke' inherited from the Ottomans, and it seems that this is why they were reluctant to buy Turkish programmes. This was also the same for the Balkans; they would perhaps buy a few music programmes but would always keep away from our dizis, though we had great dizis in TRT. Their policies were to distance themselves from Turkish culture in order to establish their own identities. They did not buy any dizis for a long time as a state policy. In the Balkans, because they were broadcasting in Turkish, only Scopian television of Yugoslavia would buy— again not the dizis, but some other programmes. (2013: 12)

Bayhan's account points to a stance which is still common in 'post-Ottoman lands'. While Turkish content captivates these regions through cultural affinities and good production quality, national broadcasting institutions operate as the gate-keepers of the broadcasting processes. What is different today, however, is perhaps how new content transcends the boundaries put by national reflexes and circulate in global streaming platforms.

Breaking TRT's Monopoly: The Launching of Private Networks

The beginning of private broadcasting in Turkey has its intricacies. One may clearly state today that the launching of private networks happened under the auspices of the late Turgut Özal (1927–93), who served as the country's prime minister from 1983 to 1989 and then president from 1989 till his death, and who had a deep impact on the post-coup state policies of the 80s. Private broadcasting may be said to have started with 'stately support, despite the state' expressed in Turkish as '*devlete rağmen devlet destekli*'. As the official national broadcaster, TRT had the sole right of television and radio broadcasting—granted by Article 133 of the Constitution—and was in charge of controlling all transmitters in Turkey. This made any private television entrepreneurship legally impossible. In order to transcend this monopoly, Özal appointed Tunca Toskay, a former director of TRT (1984–88), as an advisor. Following a delicately pursued process on legal and technical issues, the law regarding transmission was revised, allowing the use of satellite broadband from a transmitter in Germany for broadcasting in Turkey. Even though the company looked German, the owners were actually Turkish and included Cem Uzan of Rumeli Holding and Ahmet Özal, the son of President Özal (*Alkışlarla Yaşıyorum* 2014). This partnership did not last long, but Magic Box Incorporated AG had been established in 1989 in Germany to start broadcasting in 1990 with Star TV as the first private channel in Turkey.[25]

---

25 Star TV was initially called Star 1, presuming that other Magic Box channels will follow. But with the break of partnership between Cem Uzan and Ahmet Özal, Star 1 simply survived as Star. For the sake of continuity, I shall refer to the Star 1 channel simply as 'Star'.

The 1990s were indeed an era in which many of the state-sponsored economic enterprises, known as KİTs, were privatized.[26] The opening of a private broadcaster can be evaluated within the framework of this transition, but there was more to this change. In the world of TRT, professionalism was taboo and discipline was stately. During its two-decade-long monopoly, TRT had established certain rules, which in time had become important symbols of what many of my interviewees called 'disiplinli yayın' (disciplined broadcasting). This included the display of the perfect use of Turkish, not just in terms of text but also as a performance of flawless pronunciation and intonation.[27] News anchors were seen as the lead performers of this 'professional seriousness'.[28] Moreover, as a pioneering new technology, television broadcasting was strongly associated with Western modernity, always aspiring for 'quality'. TRT also disapproved certain popular genres like Arabesk music or belly dancing. This solemnity and sterility of TRT broadcasting gave Star an opportunity to display the novelties that private channels could offer. Many viewers will remember the first New Year celebration broadcast on Star on 31 December 1991—a phenomenal night of never-before-seen entertainment. A variety of showmen and women talked to one another in an informal style, promising viewers a lottery of five cars, as ten belly-dancers performed on screen. The breaking of the monopoly also meant the breaking of a set of taboos imposed from above, allowing private

---

26 KİTs were state-owned enterprises created to build the national economy after the foundation of the Republic. They were active in fields like energy, textile, agriculture, transportation and communication, boosting production and industrialization until their profitability declined in time, particularly during the economic crisis of the 1970s (Celasun and Arslan 2001: 224).

27 For the use of language in Turkish television, see Ayşe Öncü (2000).

28 In its early years, broadcast news was watched not only as news but also as entertainment enacted by professional newsreaders—the lead actors. The fact that a camera caught Aytaç Kardüz fixing her blond hair would be news the day after. Likewise, a stutter or a mistake in any programme would be an 'odd moment' to be recalled in daily gossips.

television channels to promise more fun and entertainment than what public television had offered audiences so far.

It will be useful here to focus on the structure of Star as Turkey's first private network, with its controversial stance within the state apparatus. Star began with powerful support from President Özal. Although called 'private', the managerial profile of Star consisted, to a great extent, of former TRT managers. Following the end of his term as TRT director, Toskay had taken the lead at Star and gathered a team that comprised former TRT executives, including Mehmet Turan Akköprülü, Ekrem Çatay and Adem Gürses, all of whom would become influential figures of the television industry (Erdoğmuş and Koçer 2009). Competition with TRT grew stronger and fiercer as Star began to poach experienced news and entertainment presenters from the former. With these initiatives, Star managed to gather a large viewership within a short span of time—a development that rapidly attracted the attention of other entrepreneurs. Show TV was founded in France in 1991, which began its broadcasting in Turkey in 1992. HBB and Kanal 6 followed the same year; Flash TV, TGRT, Kanal D and ATV began in 1993. In the beginning, these networks broadcast from countries like Germany or France via satellite. Although TRT appealed to courts to ban private broadcasting, all legal and technical hurdles had been cleared by 1993. With Article 133, the right of broadcasting transmission was transferred from TRT to another monopoly: the Directorate of Posts, Telegraph and Telephone, or PTT. Since PTT could rent different wavebands that covered Turkish territory via satellites, it put an end to the precarious legal status of private broadcasters.[29]

It will be important here to assess the role and the place of TRT in the changing landscape of television broadcasting during the 1990s. Although TRT had lost its monopoly, its impact continued, as many of

---

[29] For more on this transition, see Haluk Şahin and A. Aksoy (1993); Ece Algan (2003); Betül Öngen (2017).

its former employees took the leading positions in the up-and-coming networks and their production processes. Programming, after all, was vital for the new networks, and it was a matter in which only former TRT directors had expertise. To give a few examples, when his partnership with Star collapsed, Ahmet Özal rapidly founded Kanal 6 but left its management fully to Mehmet Turan Akköprülü, former director of TRT's television department (Akköprülü 2015). Yılmaz Dağdeviren, also a former TRT director of television, had become the first director of Istanbul Greater Municipality Radio and Television (BRT), the first 'local' television network, with a 'public' characteristic. Dağdeviren brought in former TRT managers İskender Salgırlı and Altan Aşar. Former TRT director of acquisitions Faruk Bayhan also began a new career in private networks by 1991, first as the vice-director of programming in Show TV, and later as the general director of Kanal D and Star TV (Bayhan 2017).[30]

From the day it was established, TRT operated like a school, a fact that many former employees acknowledged after they became pioneers of successful dizis in the private sector. 'I learned dizi making at TRT,' states Tomris Giritlioğlu (2013), who designed and directed many ground-breaking projects in later decades.[31] Similarly, Ekrem Çatay, the founder of Ay Yapım, one of the leading production companies in Turkey, had long worked in TRT as the drama director in the 1980s. Bayhan himself acknowledged the important role TRT took in those years: 'TRT was such a school since the foundation of television that many important journalists, newscasters, directors were raised there— not only in the field of programming, but in the domain of technicians as well. These people have played a crucial role in the establishment of

---

30 One exception was Nuri Çolakoğlu, who had a background in journalism. He was instrumental in the establishment of Show TV, CINE5 and, later, NTV, the first news channel in Turkey.

31 Giritlioğlu has been the showrunner of such projects such as *Çemberimde Gül Oya*, *Hatırla Sevgili*, *Bu Kalp Seni Unutur mu* and *Kayıp Şehir.*

private networks' (2013: 13). In the 1990s TRT represented an 'established' state institution, and retained its status as the symbol of a well-disciplined and regulated broadcaster. 'Coming from TRT' was seen as a significant title, an assertion of a certain expertise in television with a well-trained and reliable background in the business.

Director Arzu Akmansoy remembers the momentum of change from public to private as an emerging nostalgia for TRT. As the newly launched private networks stumbled in their early years, this transition was 'painful and chaotic' at the same time. As the daughter of Tekin Akmansoy, who had starred and produced the legendary *Kaynanalar* series of the 1970s, she had witnessed, at first hand, her father's disappointment when a private network remade *Kaynanalar*: 'There was such a difference in the quality of management and the way in which payments were made. In TRT, you would deliver the tape and receive your money the following week.' From her own perspective shaped by deeply rooted TRT experience, Akmansoy noted the failure of the private sector in regulating the financing of production: 'People who had no idea about the television business were employed, and many of them had no clue about the financial circulation, which was key to running a production process' (Akmansoy 2014). She also called attention to how the new attitudes in broadcasting policies differed from TRT's: 'Today, because of the lack of unions, networks can cancel the broadcast of a dizi in a one-sided decision' (2003: 13).

Producer Mustafa Karahan, on the other hand, drew attention to another impact of the transfers from TRT—managers of new channels who came from TRT continued the tradition of 'harsh contracts' between the producers and networks:

There is an important reason for the weakness in the relationship between networks and producers today. When the private networks were founded, they were run by the former managers of TRT, who continued to act as if they still had the stately power in signing contracts with independent producers. They put copies of contracts similar to those prepared for TRT and told the producers to sign them. Producers, on the other hand, never had the opportunity to examine, oppose or give their opinion on these contracts. (2018)

Ekrem Çatay recalls the TRT years' 'luxury of the monopoly' in a different way:

We produced a lot of adaptations in those days—literary adaptations. This was a different pleasure back then and people also enjoyed it [. . .]. Since TRT was the only network, and because there was no such concept as ratings, and we felt as if everybody liked all the productions that we ourselves liked. (*MagazinMax* 2018)

The transfer of TRT programmers and producers to private networks also had a significant impact on programming, which helped create the initial infrastructure of the blossoming dizi world in the 2000s.

Challenges of Programming for the New Networks: The Competitive Ground of the 1990s

Exploring the programming of the new networks has its own methodological difficulties. The principal challenge is to set an accurate chronology of the production processes and broadcasting policies of the 1990s. Many of the early production companies and private networks did not keep a proper archive, and if they did, it is very difficult to access them. As many have changed hands, information has also been scattered in private archives. The record of many dizis, filmed and broadcast during that time, are available on the internet, which as a source of information is never fully reliable. Access to correct dates and names often requires a thorough cross-examination with oral and published interviews, and at times checking the closing credits of the first episodes of the dizis from the Internet.

One can start perhaps by describing the landscape of the television world in the 1990s, a time when a more liberal television programming had become possible. TRT stood at the centre as a reference point for both 'good' and 'bad'. The new networks had transferred many executives from the TRT circle, but what they needed the most was a large repertoire of shows and commercials to survive, and programming had become a key issue of this process. In the beginning, sports offered a good opportunity to fill the programming. Particularly, football broadcasting that was long monopolized by TRT had become a profitable ground to conquer. This was followed up by a series of imported foreign drama—mostly daily telenovelas and soap operas—and variety shows usually adapted and displayed as Turkish formats. To fill the empty slots, new programming also welcomed the rerunning of old Yeşilçam movies, along with some domestic dizi production, which was also taking a new turn. It is important to lay out each of these developments as they all prepared general audiences to a new mode of watching television, where the new networks were offering a more liberal programming for different segments of the society.

A Port in Storm: The Re-running of Yeşilçam Movies

Let us begin with the impact of the Yeşilçam cinema as a source for programming and production purposes in private networks. Beginning by the 1992 and thenceforth, networks like Star TV, Kanal 6, Flash TV, Tele On, Show TV, ATV, Kanal D and TGRT began to broadcast their own drama projects.[32]

During these initial years, the film industry provided all of these new networks with many directors and cinematographers to produce

---

32 Director Ayhan Özen assigned a particular importance to TGRT, which produced its own dizis, talk and music shows, while many other networks imported mostly packet programmes. TGRT also hired many people from the financially strained movie sector, employing not just many technicians but also directors for new television productions (Özen 2014).

their domestic content (Sekmeç 2011). But more important, in the need to fill up their daily programming, many private networks turned also to the repertoire of former Yeşilçam content, which heavily consisted of melodrama and humour. These movies which were vastly consumed during the 1960s and created the leading stars of Turkish cinema, establishing a powerful memory for Turkish audiences. However, just like the cases of Arabesk music and belly dancing, TRT ignored Yeşilçam popular movies for a long time. With the exception of the works of some important directors, like Metin Erksan or Halit Refiğ, TRT had kept a certain distance with Yeşilçam, broadcasting instead dated Hollywood movies—of the 1950s and 60s—as a prime-time show. The re-running of old Yeşilçam movies offered private networks a genre to which Turkish audiences were affectively attached. In a strange way, these old Yeşilçam movies also brought together a trans-generational audience, who enjoyed the melodramatic storytelling in their own different ways. Adult audiences who had watched many of these movies in the past in theatre halls across Turkey, were reunited with the stars and romance stories of their youth. The quintessential Turkish beauty of Türkan Şoray—the Sultan of Turkish Cinema whose image was established on her disguise— was now available on screen on a daily basis (Büker 1993). On the other hand, however, for the youth of the 1990s, Yeşilçam's melodramatic storytelling was perceived primarily as 'absurd' or 'humorous'. Both generations shared a similar interest in seeing old Istanbul or old Turkey as 'historical ethnographic sceneries', either in a nostalgic way or in a curiosity mode. The new private networks benefited greatly from these re-runs to connect to wider audiences, offering them a familiar and affectively remembered melodrama tradition.

Director Engin Ayça, a figure who is familiar with both Yeşilçam and TRT traditions, explored this transitional process in two directions (see Savaş Arslan 2011: 247). He first called attention to television as a new venue for the display of Turkish movies and saw this as a positive development in the 'experiencing of a film culture' in Turkey. For the first time, he thought, the elite who barely followed Yeşilçam melo-drama movies was exposed to them via the new private networks. Meanwhile, Yeşilçam's former viewers were introduced to not only different genres of contemporary foreign films, now available on television as dubbed in Turkish, but also different forms of narrative films, especially documentaries: 'Their culture and the language of seeing cinema got diversified. [. . .] Today's Yeşilçam spectators have not given up their tendencies, but they have become more tolerant, with more perspectives and openness to a diversity of products' (Ayça 1994: 43–52). This was indeed a very important training for both the elite and the masses. Cinema scholar Savaş Arslan confirms that these developments encouraged 'the spectators of two different strands of cinema, to learn each other's language, thus increasing their tolerance of each other's tastes' (2011: 20). This encounter was very significant in the construction of a television viewer's profile as well, transcending social class when it comes to dizi watching.

Football and More Football

Besides showing old movies, private channels began exploring new forms of domestic content. One lucrative domain consisted of unscripted formats like games, sketches, variety, talent or reality shows. Many of these were adapted from the foreign format, but their novelty captivated Turkish audiences, as they were presented with a certain domestic flavour, and creating in time their own stars.[33] In the landscape of this new establishment, one other challenge came from the field of football (i.e. soccer). Leading football teams accepted the new and profitable deals that private networks offered. Establishing the first broadcast-encryption system (*şifreli yayın*), Show TV took the copyright of certain games at the Turkish Super League. Other networks initiated other

---

33 One of the earliest match-making formats began in Show TV, for instance, with Nurseli İdiz. İdiz was a State Theatre actress, but she earned fame with this show (*Saklanbaç*) which also offered her a new career in the dizi world.

football-related programmes such as roundtable debates or magazine shows, focusing on the private lives of the players. This changed the way football was watched in Turkey. New public spheres emerged for those who could not afford to subscribe to the paid-view system. A great majority of the male audiences gathered in coffeehouses, restaurants, local clubs or a friend's house to watch the games. The new genres of football-related programmes provided private networks with more opportunities to fill their air time. These new roundtable debates and football magazine shows differed a lot from the serious sports-news style of TRT. Engaging football fans on screen for long hours of passionate conversations, these programmes opened the way to another television genre, in the form of paparazzi magazine programmes. Seeing the popular interest in screening football talks, there emerged more interest in players' personal lives. Following the programmes like *Sporvizyon* and *Televole* in the 1990s, reporting about their love lives or consumptions, but also making football stars 'talk', this genre combined football and magazine, evolving in time to tabloid television programmes, reporting more on the lives of the rich and the famous. This new form developed in parallel to the growth of the dizi industry, which had a direct impact on actors' social lives and their perception by the general public.[34]

Welcoming Seriality on Television: Turkish Perceptions of Soap Operas and Telenovela

The successive opening of private television networks brought forward a need for seriality in programming. Turkish audiences were exposed to seriality through 'radio drama' since the 1940s.[35] The search for seriality in programming led private networks to open their doors to melodrama

---

34 The interplay between actors and tabloid television in Turkey deserves a closer analysis. See Erdal Dağtaş (2006); Oray Eğin (1999); Erol İlhan and Adalet Görgülü Aydoğdu (2017).

35 Radio dramas had a more didactic form in the early decades, which evolved in time to a more entertaining form in the 1970s. See Meltem Ahıska (2010).

content from around the world, but mostly to telenovelas and soap operas. Turkish television audiences began to be exposed to both telenovela and soap opera simultaneously, naming them 'pembe dizi', or the 'pink series'. In fact, TRT had broadcast such genres during the 1980s, which included series like *Escrava Isadaura*, *Generations*, *Santa Barbara* or *Alcanzar*. But watching of the pink series on a daily basis and in abundance introduced an addictive aspect of day-time television watching that had not been experienced before.

The intense and rapid spread of pink series received severe criticism about the qualitative aspects of their content. The audiences embraced them, but their content was 'foreign', a matter which brought forward once again the issue of 'domestic content' in programming. In her study on this transitional period, Filiz Erdemir compared the different views regarding the broadcasting of pink series on TRT and the private networks. She found out that it was mostly TRT which was criticized for broadcasting these series, particularly by some state officials who expressed their concerns regarding some moral issues. In their views, many of these series did not conform to the Turkish customs and rituals both in terms of their stories and value system, and some were directly opposed to Turkish traditions. By broadcasting them as such, they thought, TRT had a negative effect on the Turkish youth and family structure (Erdemir 2009: 207).[36]

The new challenge from the private networks and the emergence of a critique towards its programming led TRT to revise its content in favour of domestic programmes. In the aftermath of a series of surveys, the daily *Cumhuriyet* published a report which showed how foreign productions exceeded domestic ones. The headline announced that there would be more focus on domestic production and stated: 'Starting from 1987, the duration of the "Latinbesk" series among the total

---

36 See 'Çiçek'ten TV'ye Eleştiri', *Cumhuriyet*, 5 August 1990; 'Diyanet'ten Eleştiri', *Cumhuriyet*, 10 September 1990. Quoted in Filiz Erdemir (2009: 207).

broadcasting duration had been increased up to 24 hours because they were cheap and in demand. But the local dramas were only limited to 10 hours. With a new regulation [. . .] it will give more priority to local dramas.'[37]

Latinbesk was of course a pejorative term, combining two 'disdained' genres, telenovela and Arabesk. The latter was a musical genre which had emerged during the 1970s, as the music of the first wave of rural migrants to big cities (Özbek 1991; Stokes 1992). Be it the telenovela or Arabesk, the critique has usually been directed to the melodramatic expressivity of these genres. Despite the criticism for broadcasting pink series, Erdemir reports that TRT was also praised for the successful documentaries it produced. A report in Cumhuriyet in 1990, stated that at the international television market in Cannes, TRT's most favoured products had been the genre of documentary.[38] A few years later, compared with the programming of private networks, TRT was distinguished as producing more domestic content in the fields of arts and culture as well as documentaries.[39] Duygu Asena, an important figure of the feminist press during the 1990s, drew attention to the 'ratings' issue, then a newly developing concept for Turkey (1999). Asena, who had taken part in well-received TRT cultural programmes, had developed a reflexive critique.[40] Reminding how TRT lost its privilege of broadcasting with no rivalry, she stated that this could be turned into an opportunity. Private networks, she thought, had banal, low-quality and unregulated broadcasting while TRT still pursued its quality content, exactly because it could survive broadcasting without commercials.

---

37 See Cumhuriyet, 20 December 1990. Quoted in Erdemir (2009: 208).

38 See 'Belgeseller İlgi Gördü', Cumhuriyet, 9 May 1990; 'TRT'nin İçinden', Cumhuriyet, 7 August 1990. Quoted in Erdemir (2009: 210).

39 See 'Sanat Dünyasının Sesi: 25. Kare', Cumhuriyet, 22 March 1993. Quoted in Erdemir (2009: 210).

40 One was Ondan Sonra, a cultural programme where Duygu Asena had a weekly conversation with prominent writer Selim İleri.

In any case, the success of pink series led both TRT and private networks to produce daily dramas as well (Taçyıldız 1995).[41] The simultaneous broadcasting of multiple soaps and telenovela had produced a new state of 'watching serial'. The term *dizim var* meant 'I cannot miss watching it'—it referred to the passionate and addictive mode of watching the series on its real broadcasting time. The term emerged during this era to be later used for domestic dramas as well. The surprise of the success of pink series soon created a genuine interest in exploring Turkish audience behaviour. A considerable amount of research was undertaken during the early 1990s to understand this addictive phenomenon.[42] Today they are valuable documents of a long-forgotten memory, but they lay out a very important pool of data to understand today's dizi-watching modalities.[43] The intense reception of the pink series brought forward a debate on the triviality of the content and the social status of those who watched it.[44] The research of Asuman

---

41 During the 1990s, TRT produced *Kalbin Sesi* (1991), an adaptation from renowned Turkish writer Muazzez Tahsin Berkant's novel *Küçük Hanımefendi*; ATV's *Son Söz Sevginin* (1993) was also broadcast on a daily basis for 56 episodes. See Asuman Taçyıldız (1995).

42 See *Beyazperde* (1989); Ferruh Binark (1992, 1997); Sebnem Kadıoğlu (2010); Leyla Budak (1993); Asuman Taçyıldız (1993, 1995); Fatma Gözlükaya-Tütüncü (1998a, 1998b); Mehmet Mete (1999).

43 Many of these studies tried to analyse audience responses to these new genres. Most of them consisted of fieldworks in sample neighbourhoods in Ankara and Istanbul in the form of polls and face-to-face interviews. In searching to deconstruct these genres, they searched for whether the audiences' bonding originated from the power of the melodramatic genre or from their personal sociocultural needs. They also examined how the soaps and telenovela have been evaluated by Turkish audiences, and revealed that in many cases viewers underlined such common aspects like escape from daily routine, serial curiosity, emotional expressivity, luxurious fashion and home decoration. See Leyla Budak (1993); Ferruh Binark (1997); Fatma Gözlükaya-Tütüncü (1998a, 1998b); and Asuman Taçyıldız (1995).

44 There was a clear elite critique that condescendingly categorized both the soap and telenovela as 'simple', 'cheap' or 'easy'. Fatma Gözlükaya-Tütüncü's research,

Taçyıldız reminds us, however, that these genres have in fact prepared Turkish audiences to decode complex and parallel narratives. Opposing the idea that the pink series are 'simple' or 'easy' genres, Taçyıldız argues that their cinematic narrative is in fact complex, requiring a grasp of the multiplicity of characters and of different shots into sequences of a meaningful narrative (1995).[45] For the heavy viewers of these genres, this was indeed a training in cinematic decoding. One other impact of the pink series was on the idolization of characters, a phenomenon which would be later observed for dizi consumption of the 2000s. For the first time, audience behaviour took a new turn through a much closer association with the characters of the series. Audiences who bonded with the characters on the basis of their names (like Rosalinda, Marianna, Nikki, Victor or Ashley) developed a new fandom model, which was later applied to the emerging dizi world.[46]

---

for instance, revealed how academic women particularly covered their association with pink series, as a 'hidden or forbidden pleasure' which they often tried to legitimize (1998b: 93).

45 Asuman Taçyıldız's ethnography consists of a poll and face-to-face interviews conducted over three months with 245 viewers in Dikilitaş neighbourhood of Istanbul, among the middle- and lower-class residents living in apartment buildings as well as shantytowns (1995).

46 I remember my own shock when my mother recognized Eric Braeden—who played Victor in *The Young and the Restless*—in the crowd of New York's Fifth Avenue in 1993.

Chapter 3

Pillars of the Dizi Industry
The Performance, Media and Advertising Sectors

One question often asked about the dizi industry concerns whether its success is conjunctural, or if it would be sustainable. Understanding the contemporary structure of the dizi industry requires a closer look at the institutions and individuals who played an active role in establishing it. The development of the dizi genre as we speak of it today happened mainly during a period which began in the 1990s, taking different turns in time, in terms of its content, format, distribution and material investment. This chapter aims at looking closer at the foundation pillars of this industry, which came together at a particular historical conjuncture to constitute the dizi genre. The background of the dizi world consists of the interaction of different cultural sectors, which responded to the demands of Turkey's liberalizing market from the 1990s onwards. The growing dizi world profited greatly from the expertise accrued under TRT, but it also benefited from the cinema, theatre and caricature traditions, rooted in early Republican reforms, which may even said to have begun with the Ottoman modernization. Dizi industry also owes to the changing economic demands of the post-1980s, an era of neoliberal policies, where the sectors of video, fashion and advertisement blossomed. Each of these cultural sectors contributed in different ways to the construction of the dizi industry, which now reaches out to global markets.

Reborn from its Ashes: Yeşilçam Cinema and the Video Market

It is important to assess the role of cinema in the establishment of the television industry in Turkey. As in many other parts of the world, cinema entered the Ottoman Empire in the late nineteenth century, and local productions date back to 1910s.[1] Fascination with cinema spread rapidly during the early Republican era. The boom, however, came after the Second World War, when cinema's appeal transcended the demand coming from big cities like Istanbul, Izmir or Ankara, and extended to provincial towns as well. Depending of the accessibility of electricity, old church buildings or wedding halls were transformed into indoor cinemas, while open-air summer cinemas were also widespread as new entertainment platforms. Alongside such cinema halls, many KİTs, the state-owned-enterprises, also offered indoor film screenings to their workers and employees.[2] With the rise of a star system in the 1960s, going to the movies had already become an entertainment habit, boosting local demands for more film production. During the 1960s and the 70s, family-oriented melodrama became the dominant film genre. At a more elite level, the 1960s also witnessed the launching of cinematheques in both Ankara and Istanbul. *Türk Sinematek Derneği,* established in Istanbul in 1965, operated more like a cinephile club, organizing screenings and panels, and publishing magazines. Beginning in the 1980s, urban audiences had more access to Hollywood and European movies, a fact, which in time developed a genuine artistic curiosity for world cinema as well. A passion for filmmaking also flourished, creating more need for expert technicians for the industry.

---

1 For different historical reviews of Turkish cinema, see Özde Çeliktemel-Thomen (2019); U. Daniel et al. (2019); Gönül Dönmez-Colin (2013); Nezih Erdoğan (2011); Saadet Özen (2010); Nijat Özön (1968); Özde Çeliktemel-Thomen (2018); Asuman Suner (2010); Rekin Teksoy (2008).

2 Sümerbank shoe factory in Beykoz was one of them, where there were regular film displays. See www.kundurahafiza.com (last accessed on 28 September 2021).

In his book *Cinema in Turkey: A New Critical History*, Savaş Arslan makes the distinction between the 'Yeşilçam' tradition with the 'new cinema' in Turkey. 'Yeşilçam' refers to the Yeşilçam Street in Beyoğlu area in Istanbul, where many film companies were founded during the 1950s. Arslan's historical analysis takes the Yeşilçam period (1950s–80s) at its centre, as a key period to understand its preceding era and its aftermath. He calls attention to the emotive aspects of this history where aspirations for Westernization produced 'desired images' often expressed in a certain 'melodramatic modality'. Melodrama became the dominant genre of the Yeşilçam period, offering cinemagoers a filmic experience to satisfy their desire of Westernization through cinema (Arslan 2011).

Yeşilçam lived its heydays from the 1950s up to the 70s, a period where around 300 films were being produced annually. This was a fundamental era for Turkish cinema, a period which gave us influential directors such as Ömer Lütfi Akad, Metin Erksan, Osman Seden, Memduh Ün, Atıf Yılmaz and many others. The number of cinemagoers also increased tremendously during those years, while 'cinema courses' made their way into different university curriculums. This was an epoch where the Union of Turkish Film Producers was established along with the Cinema-Television Institute, where well-known directors of the 1960s and 70s began teaching. Yet, once access to television spread rapidly and a severe economic crisis struck during the 1970s, Yeşilçam lost its former production power, and began looking for other sources of revenue: one was to invest in erotic films;[3] another, to use the stars as live icons displayed in the so-called *gazino*s, theatre halls combining food, music and entertainment. Many film stars like Filiz Akın, Hülya Koçyiğit and Göksel Arsoy began 'singing' in these *gazino*s during the 1980s (Mater 2002). One final source of revenue was in fact the rise of

---

3 For a critical review of erotic cinema in Turkey, see Giovanni Scognamillo and Metin Demirhan (2002).

the video market both in Turkey and abroad, as an outcome of the spread of television sets, offering a cheap and comfortable platform for film watching. In their study on television audiences' programme preferences, Hülya Tufan-Tanrıöver and Ayşe Eyüboğlu underlined how television dramas followed the news in Turkish audiences' watching habits. The reason for this heightened interest, they argued, developed in time, when Turkish popular cinema faded with the entry of television in the households. With their former habit of watching Turkish movies in the cinema, and given the precarious economy of the film industry, audiences welcomed first the re-running of former Turkish movies on television, and then the newly produced domestic dizi genre (Tufan-Tanrıöver and Eyüboğlu 2000).

In his critical review of cinema in Turkey, Arslan underlines that while the quality of films improved in the 1980s, the number of productions was far from approaching the glorious days of the 1960s.[4] Arslan also draws attention to the tensions between TRT and Yeşilçam during those years. As a state television, TRT gave very limited broadcast time to domestic films, and preferred foreign movies and television drama dubbed in Turkish (Arslan 2011: 20–21). The 1970s and 80s were also the years where a massive migration of workers from Turkey to Europe took place. Building their own communities in Germany, France, the Netherlands, Belgium and Switzerland, the so-called Euro-Turks were inventing their own local economies, which produced a domain for different entertainment genres.[5] The video market boomed

---

4 Savaş Arslan evaluates the post-Yeşilçam era as a transition towards a 'new cinema in Turkey', a period marked by art house films and independent cinema, exploring alternative venues (2011: 1–21).

5 As Köken Ergun's work shows us, among Turkish communities in Germany, 'wedding', for example, has been a main genre of entertainment, overarching the family who organizes it. See Köken Ergun's video art at https://weddingkokenergun.wordpress.com (last accessed on 28 September 2021). See also Ergun (2020, 2016).

during this period as a lucrative business opportunity for many Turkish entrepreneurs, who opened small-scale companies both in Turkey and in Europe, to sell—or even produce—Turkish films for Euro-Turks.

Producer Cengiz Ergun narrates the vibrant atmosphere of these days, when film business moved from distribution to production and vice versa. Ergun was originally in the world of print publishing. His interest in production began when he assisted director Tunç Okan (also his brother-in-law) for the production of his prominent film *Otobüs* in 1974.[6] With the success of the film, they soon made a circle of respectable friends in Yeşilçam community, including Ömer Kavur and Atıf Yılmaz, the leading film directors of the 1980s. In 1982 Ergun established ESTET, a company which was to dominate the video market in the upcoming years. He also opened Odak, a production company with Atıf Yılmaz in 1985:

> The video phenomenon had just started, because Yeşilçam was right in the middle of a crisis. Yeşilçam was over. Then video entered our lives through Türker İnanoğlu. We followed him afterwards. I began first with the distribution, I had access to 11 movies by Atıf Yılmaz and Ömer Kavur in the same system. They were very good-quality movies [. . .]. I bought their movies as well as the rights to these videos. (Ergun 2017)

Ergun recalls that he also rented films from other producers, who in time came to him asking whether he could sponsor their next project:

> We financed all films that Neşe Film Company had produced. Let's say, this is a Kemal Sunal movie and Kemal Sunal receives an amount of 40 million, while the overall movie costs 80 million. So, let's say the producer is Uğur Film and they want 80

---

6 *Otobüs* (1974) depicted the harrowing story of smuggling illegal migrant workers in Sweden. The film was banned for several years in Turkey but won many awards at international film festivals in 1975.

million from us. I bring 80 million to Uğur Film, and I only buy the video rights for the next five years. The producer shows his film in movie theatres, and he owns the negatives and everything. We were selling in Turkey to 3,500 video clubs at the time. (2017)

Arslan also confirms this transaction between distributors and producers. He states that Yeşilçam ceased to produce films for theatre exhibition after the 1980s and instead focused on producing and distributing for the video market. Arslan also highlights how the 1980 coup marked a 'cultural break', bringing a change in viewers' attitudes. 'Spectators,' he states, 'who in the late 1970s had already started to watch films on television and video instead of going to theatres, almost stopped going to theatres altogether during and after the military intervention' (2011: 203–04). Critics differed in their view whether to see the video market as a 'dead end', or as 'beneficial' to cinema (2011: 205–06). Producer Türker İnanoğlu published an interview in *Video/Sinema* with a headline 'Video and Cinema Are Not Enemies', calling attention to how the copyright issue can be useful to film industry at large: 'As the video market enforces copyrights, public screenings at coffeehouses and restaurants, or the circulation of pirated tapes could be better controlled and would be a new source of continual income' (1984: 68).

The direction of this transaction operated in the other sense as well, as the world of film distribution generated new producers, showrunners and directors in the film industry, many of whom later became influential figures of the dizi world: including Türker İnanoğlu, Abdullah Oğuz, Erol Avcı and Mustafa Karahan, among others. Yet, while the production budgets were funded by video sales, Arslan reminds us that production companies also began to distribute videotapes. The rising involvement of Hollywood in the distribution and exhibition of films in Turkey brought a further challenge to Turkish producers and distributors. One more development was that although the launching of television had shaken the film industry by the 1980s, the proliferation of television sets in households had opened a new platform for old and new Turkish films distributed via the video film market. The audiences of the 1980s video boom consisted of the middle classes and workers in Europe who could afford to buy VCRs and regularly rent videotapes from the rental stores popping up throughout the country. This trend slowed down, however, in the late 80s, especially when new private networks emerged, further hampering Yeşilçam's film production (Arslan 2011: 203–06).

The video market also brought a challenge to TRT monopoly on content. With the increased number of television sets in the 80s, there emerged a demand for popular Hollywood and European movies, along with world cinema and trendy television series not shown on TRT. The limitations of TRT programmes were now transcended through video stores, mushrooming not only in the big cities but in small towns as well. Murat Çolakoğlu, now partner of PwC Turkey, recalls the aura of these days in an interview, sharing his impressions when he first discovered a video store in his neighbourhood:

> When I entered the shop, I felt as if I was in an amusement park; I could not believe it: the shelves on the walls are full of film tapes. Does this mean that I can take any cassette and watch it at home? Hooray! I approached the man behind the counter who was trying to rescue a tape stuck in the VCR as if he was a rocket engineer, and asked him with my heart pounding: 'I want to rent a *cassette*' (That was the term to ask for it). (Çolakoğlu 2013)

Çolakoğlu remembers the video storeowner asking him back: 'Beta or VHS?' The transaction also needed to be insured by a request of an official 'residential document' or a reference from the neighbourhood. Cengiz Ergun reports on the inflated number of people who wanted to enter this profitable business:

> It was so pitiful—we would see a boy coming with his father, whom he convinced to sell his house to open a video club.

[. . .] We would advise the father not to do so, that this is a temporary phenomenon. The video phenomenon was indeed temporary, lasting only five years, because of private networks which had just started. (2017)

Ergun shares his own experience as an actual social player of this era and comments on the changing dynamics of the movie industry of the 1980s:

As you know, when you produce a movie in Turkey, you first collect an advance payment from the provinces, and the producer profits mainly from the Istanbul screenings. The advance payments come from cinema managers in İzmir, Adana, the Black Sea, Ankara and other regions. You tell to them what kind of a movie you will make, who will star in it and who will direct. Director is also important for the manager, who thinks whether his movies will do well at the box office. Atıf Yılmaz and Ömer Kavur were on-demand directors of these days; but once the video market spread also in the provinces, movie theatres really collapsed. At that point, private networks offered a new advantage. Right at the moment the movie industry was about to give up, networks started to buy movies. And there began a new upsurge. (2017)

While Yeşilçam started to lose its production powers in the domestic context, movie distributors were able to sell previously screened Yeşilçam movies—first to the European video market, and later, in the 1990s, to the newly opening private networks in Turkey, which urgently needed to fill their programme time. While the nostalgic demand for Turkish films was developing in Europe, the profits coming from the Turkish video market become a source of income for new productions with contemporary stars. Entrepreneur Sabri Demirdöğen had established Türk-Kan Film and Video (1980), a film and video production company in Germany, to produce many movies with stars including Bülent

Ersoy, Ferdi Tayfur, Orhan Gencebay, Hülya Avşar and Kemal Sunal (Demirdöğen 2007). Similarly, Tahir Minareci's Minareci Videola TV Studios (1982) also produced many music clips and video films, growing into a legendary producer-distributor of Turkish content. These companies also organized live concerts in diverse European cities for Turkish migrants.

IMAGE 3.1 Singer and actor Ferdi Tayfur with the legendary Tahir Minareci (1923–2014), posing in front of Minareci's music and video shop in Munich, c.1980. Image courtesy of Ferdi Tayfur (https://twitter.com/-ferdiitayfur/, posted on 17 March 2014).

Turkish Desire for Cinema and Its Academic Consequences

The flow of films in the video market, both in Turkey and abroad, had another important impact which is related to the later developments in the dizi world. The roots of Turkish content and the production quality of the film industry in general owe a great deal to a historical conjuncture in the 1980s, where both the television industry and its audiences received formal and informal training. Arslan reminds us the change in the profile of filmmakers and filmgoers during this era, which grew to be 'younger and well educated' compared with earlier periods. Arslan links this change to an increasing 'awareness of global developments in cinema'. With this change in demand, he states, 'spectators increasingly compared the films made in Turkey with those made abroad' (2011: 20–21).

One should acknowledge the contribution of the video market in the development of this new audience. Besides its popular culture consumerism, the booming video industry of the 1980s had also backed up the 'knowledge of cinematheques', circulating the classical repertoire of world cinema. With no regulations of copyrights, many households cherished this era as a home-entertainment epoch. While mothers rented some American primetime drama not shown in Turkey like the then famous *Dynasty* series or feature films, younger generations and curious cinephiles found an opportunity to watch for the first time the works of renowned directors like Andrei Tarkovsky, Federico Fellini, Michelangelo Antonioni or Pier Paolo Passolini. The launching of the cinematheques and the film festivals also led to a visible rise of interest in what had been called 'art movies'. With the initiations of cinephiles in the 1980s, there also emerged cinema magazines that offered critical articles on the history of cinema, along with reviews of contemporary films. And last but not the least, beginning in 1983, Sinema Günleri (Cinema Days)—which later transformed into International Istanbul Film Festival in 1989—had a big impact that lasts to this day. Sinema Günleri not only gave a certain access to the archives and memory of

IMAGE 3.2 Sinematek's modest entrance from Taksim Sıraselviler Road, Istanbul. Founded as an NGO in 1965, this space was opened in 1970, and has been one of the film venues most widely attended by cinephiles. Image courtesy of *1+1 Express* (https://bit.ly/3O7THqH, last accessed on 12 June 2022).

world cinema but also put cinephiles in touch with contemporary global trends and cinematic visions (Uçansu 2012). As one of the early attendees of this event, I vividly remember the 'craze' of going to three or four movies per day in the 1980s. These were the years where self-training in cinema was an important part of the youth culture among university students. Cinema clubs and film centres were being established in different universities.[7] Arslan distinguishes this post-Yeşilçam era, as a period marked by 'serious filmmaking'—of films that won awards, and auteur or art films—where educated urban audiences learned to demand more and more 'quality films' and film publications.

---

7 Boğaziçi University was such a venue. Many notable directors began their first self-training process at Boğaziçi University Cinema Club, among whom are Nuri Bilge Ceylan, Derviş Zaim, Emin Alper and Ezel Akay. Cinephile Mithat Alam donated his personal film archive to the university, making Mithat Alam Film Center a unique venue for media students, scholars and artists.

I agree with him that the contemporaneous opening of many vocational and academic schools beginning by the mid-1970s owed greatly to fulfil the aspirations of this cinephile community in Turkey. The desire to make and sell cinema created a film industry which demanded now a new profile of people educated in film studies.

In her study on higher-education institutions for communication, cinema and television, Deniz Bayrakdar informs us that these institutions initially gave a more theoretically oriented training than a technical one. Technical training improved in the late 1990s, when the first generation of communication scholars returned to Turkey after their graduate studies abroad and began teaching in these departments. The first institute for cinema and television (Sinema Televizyon Enstitüsü) was established in Istanbul in 1974. It was followed by a Department of Cinema and Television founded under the Eskisehir Academy of Economy and Commerce (Eskisehir İktisadi Ticari İlimler Akademisi) in 1977. Both institutions were established as vocational schools, and in the beginning, the team of professors consisted of leading producers, directors, editors and sound and lighting experts. In the 1980s, there opened other departments of film studies, with a more theoretical focus, in Ankara, Istanbul and Izmir, training the first generation of *okullu* (schooled) directors and technicians of the film industry, including the dizi world (Bayrakdar 2016).

The concept of *alaylı* versus *okullu* is worth explaining at this point. Even today the film industry employs a large number of technicians and workers who did not get a formal training in film studies but were trained in the field. *Alaylı* refers to this category where you learn 'by doing' and by being part of a group, be it a cameraman, a boom operator, an editor or a lighting technician.[8] An oral-history project conducted by

---

8 The category also applies to actors who did not get a formal training. Many actors raised in a conservatory call themselves as *konservatuarlı* (from the Conservatory), a status which distinguishes them from models or self-made actors.

the Mithat Alam Film Centre at Boğaziçi University reveals that the *alaylı* category in fact goes back to the Yeşilçam period.[9] With a few exceptions, many cinema directors and cinematographers were self-trained artists at a time when the love for cinema was at its peak.

The Technological Leap from the Advertising Sector

The development of academic departments during the 1980s coincided with the growth of another area related to film industry: the advertising sector. Television commercials date back to the 1970s, which were received in the beginning with genuine interest and watched almost like a new television format. I remember the first broadcast of advertisements on TRT, because it was discussed among our friends as a 'funny thing to watch'. Viewers were not yet annoyed by the genre, and given the limited broadcasting time of TRT, advertising of the 1970s was rather a well-received aspect of programming. The real change came with the 1980s, when the advertising sector began to flourish and took on a more multinational structure when Turkey shifted towards a free-market economy under the leadership of Turgut Özal after the 1980 military coup (Nas and Odekon 1988; Turan 1994; Erdemir Göze 2011).

In his historical survey of Turkish advertising industry, Hamza Çakır reminds us how consumption was encouraged and pumped after the so-called 24 January 1980 Decisions launched by Özal. He cites businessman Fuat Süren who described the Özal years as a shift in Turkish society from a 'contended' (*kanaatkar*) stance to a 'consumerist' one. Neoliberal policies created a competitive domestic market, opening its doors to multinational partnerships, which is precisely when multinational advertising companies arrived in the Turkish markets (Çakır 1996: 255). These companies raised the standards of the Turkish

---

9 See the archive of Turkish Cinema Visual Memory Project (Mithat Alam Film Merkezi, Türkiye Sineması Görsel Hafıza Projesi). Available at: http://www.gorsel-hafiza.org.tr (last accessed on 7 April 2022).

advertising industry to an international level, while also benefiting from a large amount of profit.[10] Similarly, R. Ayhan Yılmaz gives a thorough survey of the companies during this period, showing the dynamic blossoming, separations or mergers between them (2001).

The advertising sector nourished the dizi industry in two ways. First, it trained a considerable number of scriptwriters who had been carefully observing the sociological and emotional elements of Turkish society in order to write creative and effective commercials. They knew how to appeal to targeted audiences. Some of these writers were in fact literary figures including poets and novelists. Ayfer Tunç, one of the pioneering screenwriters of today's dizi industry, gives us a sincere account of these days:

> The advertising industry was just blossoming but there was no institution to train copywriters. They knocked on the doors of the poets. Many poets worked in advertising [. . .]. As the industry professionalized, it was realized that it would be hard to proceed with these semi-professional copywriters; professional copywriters had to be trained. They expected poets to become copywriters. Some adapted to this and quit poetry; some gave up advertising. (İnci 2014)

Second, the advertising sector operated with much more generous budgets than the film industry. Beginning in the 1980s, filmmakers had the opportunity to reach out to higher technologies, including technical equipment like high-resolution cameras, quality boom operators or jimmy jibs. They also had access to better labs for post-production in editing or colouring. Director of photography Aydın Sarıoğlu, who has worked in both cinema and the dizi world, remembers this transition period:

---

10 As a result, advertising expenditures reached 20 billion lira in 1981 and 150 billion lira in 1986 (Çakır 1996: 251–60).

The advertising sector was an advantage for us. It trained us in its technical quality. At school, they would mostly give us a theoretical training [. . .]. We learned from advertisement shootings how to get prepared with a well-done preliminary research. This had no mercy. With the advertising industry, the number of boom operators, editors also increased, and they developed a certain technical expertise, which surpassed at the time many cinema directors. Advertising was a sector we approached for a better revenue, but also to test our creativities. With the rise of the advertising industry, creative contribution also made a leap. (2012)

Literature on the contemporary history of advertising in Turkey focuses more on the economic aspects of the industry, and the memory of technological progress experienced in this era is often neglected.[11] There are a few memoirs (Baransel 2003; Davutoğlu 2002), but one needs oral-history research to learn more about this important transitional period. My interview with Moris Sarfati, a pioneer and doyen of the advertising industry in Turkey, revealed, for instance, the entrepreneurial efforts of these early years:

When the big manufacturing companies entered the Turkish market, I was at Grafika and we were mostly working with Unilever. Incoming new big companies like P&G and others demanded new film formats that we did not have back then. So, to respond to the new demands, I decided to quickly establish our own studio and laboratory under our own roof. We searched for and found a director from Yeşilçam. We hired a scriptwriter through a newspaper ad, and we found actors from opera and theatre circles. As demand increased, other advertisement

---

11 See Mustafa Dilber et al. (2012); Recep Yılmaz et al. (2019); Yakup Baruh (1968).

production companies followed us. Neşet Kırcalıoğlu's Telesine was one of them. (2017)

R. Ayhan Yılmaz reminds how with the rise of neoliberal economic policies during the 1980s, advertisers who wanted to use television as a commercial marketing platform began to put more pressure to break TRT broadcasting monopoly. The increasing number of television networks and printed media brought in the 1980s a search for new advertisement and marketing techniques, like the use of billboard or advertising in movie halls. Yılmaz reminds us that this rapid change also necessitated new market research. Global companies like Unilever and P&G, who were sensitive to their advertisement investments, had already began such research during 1980s (Yılmaz 2001: 362–63).

Moris Sarfati gives us a closer look to the technological developments in the advertising industry during the 1980s and 90s. Advertisement production companies had significantly increased by now. As the sector became more competitive, it was possible to be more selective in hiring cameramen or buying high-quality technical equipment. Sarfati remembers how shootings were still being done with negative films, although analogue videos were available in the film industry. One other important change that had happened was in the domain of graphic design. As stripping was the only way for data visualization, many agencies had to establish their own colour labs, and hired new personnel. 'We had a scarcity of graphic designers,' states Sarfati, 'We even organized exams to hire people': 'This continued as such until 1992, when our company bought a Mac for the first time. But then finding a Mac operator became a problem. So we invited a university professor, and opened a training course under our agency. We selected those who could learn and adapt to our hard-working conditions' (2017).

When the Turkish market began to offer lucrative business opportunities, foreign advertising companies also entered the Turkish market, some of which established partnerships with existing Turkish firms. These mergers offered a profitable exchange for both sides, as foreign companies brought their own portfolio of products, which secured revenues for local agencies. It is important to remember at this point that this era has also marked the beginning of the establishment of a rating system in Turkey (Bir and Ünüvar 2000). With the rise of many research companies, awareness of public-opinion polls also increased, a matter which gradually affected political life, particularly during election campaigns.[12] Television Audience Measurement began in 1989 with AGB-Anadolu. In 1992, interested parties of the media industry, including networks, advertisement agencies and companies involved in commercial campaigns, came together to establish TİAK, the Research Committee of Television Viewing, while global manufacturing companies also began to establish their own media departments with Turkish partners (Sönmez 2010; Yılmaz 2001: 362–63). That the rise of private broadcasting and the development of advertising industry happened simultaneously affected significantly the finance mechanisms of the dizi industry. As former Kanal D CEO İrfan Şahin states, financing has been one of the determinants of how the 'genre' of dizi was constructed and became consolidated (2015). The advertisement industry has therefore influenced the dizi industry in two respects: first, by improving equipment and helping a new generation of filmmakers to develop their technical, directing and storytelling skills; second, by imposing rising numbers of commercial breaks, and thereby shaping the length and the storytelling technique and style of the dizi production.

The Performative Background of the Dizi Sector: The Domains of Theatre, Acting and Modelling

The 1960s and 70s are often referred at as the 'golden age of theatre' in Turkey. A generation of devoted actors who were also entrepreneurs of

---

12 One should remind here the pioneering entrepreneurship of Nezih Neyzi, who established the first market-research platform PEVA in 1961 and then TÜAD (Turkish Researchers' Association) in 1988.

their own newly built theatres were the first performers of Turkish television productions.[13] In the very beginning TRT broadcast some of the plays, putting them on screen as they were. From the 1970s onwards, these leading actors played an entrepreneurial role in proposing certain television productions, which today can be considered the prototypes of what we call dizi.

The increasing demand for dizi production in the 1990s boosted the demand for actors from the fields of cinema, theatre and modelling. In the field of theatre many young actors trained in state conservatories and other theatre departments graduated and joined the blossoming television industry, acting not only in dizis but also in talk and game shows. From that generation, one can cite such well-known names like Derya Alabora, Mustafa Avkıran, Hasibe Eren, Halit Ergenç, Mehmet Ali Erbil, Demet Evgar, Barış Falay, Mahir Günşiray, Nurseli İdiz, Binnur Kaya, Fikret Kuşkan, Erkan Petekkaya and Bennu Yıldırımlar, among others. Many of these young actors were already cast in the feature films heralding the New Turkish Cinema. With the rising demand for new stars, modelling agencies also played an important role in organizing beauty pageants for men and women, producing a follow-up generation of stars like Kenan İmirzalıoğlu, Cansu Dere, Burak Özçivit, Serenay Sarıkaya, Hatice Şendil, Çağla Şıkel, Kıvanç Tatlıtuğ and Çağatay Ulusoy, among others.

Many of these actors and actresses trained themselves through private drama schools, acting studios and special coaching. When dizi

---

13 Among others, one should cite Haldun Dormen's Dormen Tiyatrosu (1955), Yıldız and Müşfik Kenter's Kent Oyuncuları (1959), Naşit Tiyatrosu (1961), Gülriz Sururi-Engin Cezzar Topluluğu (1962), Ayfer Feray Tiyatrosu (1968), Devekuşu Kabare Tiyatrosu (1967), the Nisa Serezli–Tolga Aşkıner Tiyatrosu (1968) and Poyrazoğlu Tiyatrosu (1971). Turkish theatre also witnessed in these years a search for new form and content. Haldun Taner's Devekuşu Kabare Tiyatrosu (1967), for instance, introduced the cabaret format for the first time, with a dose of political humour in the 1970s. AST–Ankara Sanat Tiyatrosu (1963) and Dostlar Tiyatrosu (1969) became important models for political theatre from the 1970s onwards.

production accelerated in the 2000s, theatre became a central pool for casting, particularly for the 'character roles'. There also emerged well-trained actors who chose in time to be behind the camera, pursuing new careers in casting, coaching and managing. Mine Güler, who now holds a key position in dizi casting, began her career as an actress in Seyhan State Theatre in Adana. Discovering her power in training actors for auditioning, she soon shifted her work towards casting teams, finally establishing her own company (Güler 2012). İpek Bilgin, a key figure in many leading dizis, has been coaching dizi actors of different backgrounds, alongside her own acting career (Bilgin 2014). Ahmet Koraltürk, who got a degree in acting became the agent of leading actors like Emre Kınay, Caner Cindoruk, Barış Arduç and Necip Memilli. He states that he took this path when he realized that he enjoyed it better than acting in the dizis (Koraltürk 2016).

Initiating the Dizi Sector: Individuals and Institutions

With the contributions of both cinema and advertisement worlds, and using TRT's experience in programming and production, the dizi industry as we know it today began to develop in small steps from the 1990s . The main pillars were the first generation of television network owners, channel directors and producers. They were the ones who set the ground for a second generation of producers in the 2000s, who eventually established the contemporary dizi market. As mentioned earlier, the transition from the supremacy of TRT to the establishment of private networks happened through a number of entrepreneurs who took the initiative to step into the media world.[14]

---

14 Among the first generation of television network owners, one can cite Cem Uzan (Star 1991); Erol Aksoy (Show 1992); Kadir Has (HBB 1992); Ömer Ziya Göktuğ (Flash 1993); Enver Ören (TGRT 1993); Dinç Bilgin (ATV 1993); Aydın Doğan (Kanal D 1993); and Cavit Çağlar (NTV 1996).

The first generation of television network owners came from diverse backgrounds. Most of them belonged to middle-class families who had established their businesses since the 1950s in different sectors other than the media. Although some had a former connection to printed press in their youth, a quick overview of their profile shows that their primary interest was soft power in enhancing their holdings' investments in other fields like textile, construction, automobiles, banking or tourism. Media gave them a visibility and prestige which helped their desire to rise through the ranks in the neoliberal establishment of the 1980s and 90s. As businessmen, they had close ties with the state, developing in time familiarity with political leaders or high-ranked bureaucrats. Cem Uzan and Besim Tibuk had at some point founded their own political parties. Cavit Çağlar, who owned the first news channel in Turkey, was a minister of state in the early 1990s. Many also established their own banks, which caused some to fall from grace in time.

Figures like Dinç Bilgin and Cem Uzan came from families who had former ties with the publishing, and Enver Ören expressed in an interview that he worked as a proofreader at a newspaper (*Türkiye Gazetesi* 2014). Yet, most of these investors lacked particular experience in and the know-how of the television business. This is why they quickly turned to a pool of programmers and directors who mostly came from TRT, Yeşilçam cinema and the printed press, which in time started an immense traffic of transfers among the general directors of the new television channels and programme managers.

Among the first network managers, Nuri Çolakoğlu, Serpil Akıllıoğlu, Mehmet Turan Akköprülü, Adem Gürses, Ekrem Çatay, Faruk Bayhan had all former TRT experience. There were also new figures, coming from other fields. İrfan Şahin, who began with Show TV in 1992 and later led Kanal D for long years, had worked in the fields of police and banking. TGRT's owner Enver Ören entrusted the drama section to Professor Beşir Tatlı of Istanbul University. Tatlı had begun by writing a chemistry entry for an encyclopaedia published by the İhlas

Holding, which also owned TGRT. He later served as a general advisor to the encyclopaedia, and Ören invited him to the newly established drama section of TGRT. Tatlı's initiation story reveals in fact the founding anxieties and amateurish spirit of the early days of the industry:

> What do I know about television? I did not have much technical knowledge. They told me 'we have a section on production where you can read scripts'. I thought, at least it is about reading, not something technical. I began reading the scripts, but then I realized scripts also had a particular style of writing; *mis en scène* on the left side, dialogue on the right. And the first script I read and criticized was one by late Osman Seden, the great writer-director-producer, who in fact appreciated my feedback. (Tatlı 2017)

With his skills in research, Tatlı gathered valuable knowledge in a short time and took a decision-making position in the early years of TGRT. Similarly, İrfan Şahin's earlier exposure to public service and financing placed him among the trend-setting drama managers. The landscape of producers also offered a rather diverse profile. Given that they leapt into the television world from different fields, one could call them 'producer-entrepreneurs'. One of the most effective figures of this era was Türker İnanoğlu, a doyen producer of Yeşilçam, who had an important impact on the programming of the newly launched private networks.

Having founded Erler Film in 1960, İnanoğlu was known as a multitasker. Besides producing many Yeşilçam movies, he operated several cinema halls, was a pioneer of video industry and chaired many public film-industry associations. Founding Ulusal Video in 1979, he established the first network of video clubs in Turkey, and his pool of copyrighted Yeşilçam movies filled the programming of many private networks during the 1990s. In 1985, İnanoğlu established a film studio, where he produced diverse entertainment programmes for these networks. He also launched a brand-new political programme in 1987,

IMAGE 3.3 TÜRVAK (Türker İnanoğlu Foundation, Museum of Cinema-Theatre) was founded in 2001, exhibiting a valuable collection of TRT technical equipments. Image courtesy of the author.

İcraatın İçinden (From Inside [Political] Performance), where prime ministers delivered televised public speeches. In 1997 he established his own foundation TÜRVAK; and in 2001 the Museum for Cinema and Theatre in Istanbul, which today holds an important collection of original documents, photographs, technical equipment and accessories from the Turkish film industry (Scognamillo 2001; *Sözcü* 2018). İnanoğlu brought his expertise in film industry to the dizi world, producing not only hit dizis but long-lasting subgenres as well, which focused on taxi stations, police offices or ethnic humour, all contextualized within a framework of Turkish family life.[15]

Putting Türker İnanoğlu aside, it is rather difficult to make a general classification of the pioneering television producers of the 1990s and

---

15 Among many others, one can cite *Yabancı Damat, İkinci Bahar, Tatlı Kaçıklar, Çiçek Taksi, Cennet Mahallesi* and *Arka Sokaklar.*

2000s. They came from different paths of life and many were also writers, directors, distributors, cinema operators and even actors and singers. Their common characteristic may be presumed to be their 'entrepreneurial skills'. One key figure was Osman Yağmurdereli, a popular singer, who always had close ties with politicians.[16] Founding his own production company Yağmur Ajans in 1988, Yağmurdereli began to produce dizis first for TRT and later for the private networks during the 1990s and 2000s.[17] His narrative on the memory of this period reveals the precarious social context of dizi making in its initial years:

> Yücel Yener, who later became the director of TRT, was the vice-director of Ankara Television in 1988. I visited him to take some advice, because I wanted to do something different. Asım [Turgut Özal's son-in-law] had tried textile and construction businesses, but they did not go well . . . 'TRT will call for new project applications,' he [Yener] told me, 'Be a producer.' Tunca Toskay was then the director. I was shooting a dizi called *Kıbrıs'ta Vuruşanlar*. Our producer was Enver Özer, the owner of Özer Film. He was a very honest, affectionate man; I proposed to him that we be partners. *Samanyolu* was our first job together. But the administration changed in TRT; Cem Duna became the new director, and Serpil Akıllıoğlu the director of the television department. *Our* dizi passed the supervision process. The director was Kartal Tibet. He did not have any job back then. I did not only propose that we work together, but offered him partnership as well. This is how Yağmur Ajans was born. The first task was to adapt Kerime Nadir's *Samanyolu* for

---

16 Osman Yağmurdereli was elected to the National Parliament in 2007 as a deputy from AKP, before he died in 2008.

17 Yağmurdereli also acted in many dizis, beginning 1988, including *Sev Kardeşim, Yeni Bir Yıldız, Evdekiler, Bizim Mahalle, İz Peşinde, Kıbrıs'ta Vuruşanlar* (*diziler.com* 2020).

TRT as a dizi. I did not betray TRT, but I produced *Evdekiler* for Star, which was my first project that became very popular. (Karakuş n.d.)[18]

Another important producer of these early years was Faruk Turgut, who had joined the film industry as a director in the 1980s, shifting to television after he established Gold Film in 1994, and produced many dizis the 1990s onwards. Both Turgut and Yağmurdereli produced popular series in the genre of melodrama or singers' drama (*şarkıcı* or *türkücü dizisi*), which were widely watched but not highly esteemed for their content. Singers' dramas had started as a melodramatic movie genre during the late 1970s and the 80s, to lure audiences with the stars of the rising Arabesk music that had been banned from public radio and television. One main star was certainly Orhan Gencebay, who was seen as the king of the Arabesk, and who had filmed many movies in the 1970s and 80s and was the first to be put on screen in four different miniseries in 1993.[19] Two other leading singers, İbrahim Tatlıses and Osman Yağmurdereli, produced and directed several dizis for newly opened private networks, featuring popular women singers like Gülben Ergen or Seda Sayan.[20] One should also mention Küçük Emrah and

---

18 Kartal Tibet was a famous Yeşilçam film star who had begun a new career in directing. He directed many of the dizis of the 1990s and 2000s, launching many of the first generation of dizi actors. Burak Özçivit, now a leading dizi star, has a warm memory of Tibet's charisma: 'Coming from acting to directorship, he had a powerful style of training us—both on and off the set. He would tease our naivety and insist that we develop a more assertive style' (2018).

19 These were *Bayan Perşembe, Kızımı Arıyorum, Gerçek Bir Masal* and *Hamuş*.

20 İbrahim Tatlıses had made a phenomenal entry in the music markets in the mid-1970s with his interpretation of a folk song called 'Ayağında Kundura', after which he made his film debut 1978. He acted in more than 30 movies—some of which he wrote and directed himself. He also produced television series in the 1990s, among which one can cite *Tetikçi Kemal* (1993) and *Fırat* (1997), featuring the star Gülben Ergen. When Tatlıses began producing musical melodrama for private channels, Yağmurdereli was also a popular actor and singer. For *Geceler*

IMAGE 3.4 A scene from *Fırat* (1997), featuring stars Gülben Ergen and İbrahim Tatlıses. Image courtesy of *Medya Radar* (https://bit.ly/3OeoxOv, last accessed on 12 June 2022).

Ceylan, who were both child singers discovered and cast in more than ten movies in the 1980s.[21] Many of these melodramas were written in a very short time by Sefa Ünal or Sergin Akyaz, even sometimes by singers themselves, like İbrahim Tatlıses. The leap in content came in the 1990s, when writers became producers of their own projects. Güner Namlı and Umur Bugay are among the pioneers of this group. As copy-writers in advertising world, Namlı and Bugay had established their own firm Ar Ajans and collaborated to write and produce dizis like *Perihan Abla* and *Bizimkiler* for TRT (*Gazetemag* 2019). Based on a range of realistic characters in a neighbourhood, these dizis captivated audiences with the familiarity of their content.

Dizi production also greatly benefited in its early years from the well-established humour and caricature magazines (Georgeon and Fenoglio

---

(1993), one of his earliest dizis, he had approached Seda Sayan, who was introduced as the Turkish music diva of the 1980s.

21 Emrah was the lead actor in *Gündüzün Karanlığı* (1993) and *Unutabilsem* (1998). Similarly, Ceylan, also a child singer, had performed in 1998 in *Aynalı Tahir*.

IMAGE 3.5 A scene from *Perihan Abla* (1986), featuring Şevket Altuğ, Tuluğ Çizgen, Ercan Yazgan and Perran Kutman as 'Perihan'. Image courtesy of *aHBR* (https://bit.ly/-3twexZ4, last accessed on 12 June 2022).

1996; Davulcu 2015). Humour has been a rooted genre of Turkish television since the TRT era, as many scriptwriters like Kandemir Konduk began their careers by writing comedy sketches for television shows. One important figure is comedian Levent Kırca, who produced *Olacak O Kadar*, a social and political comedy show which began airing in 1988 and continued for two decades (Arık 2006). The circle of *Olacak O Kadar* introduced many talented writers and actors to the dizi world, among them Yılmaz Erdoğan. With his entrepreneurial skills, Erdoğan established his own production company BKM in 1994, which produced many dizis in the genre of comedy and dramedy (Uysal 2015, 2016; Yüksel 2009).

The caricaturists' circles were organized around *Gırgır*, Turkey's best-known humour magazine that offered sharp political satire and enjoyed a wide circulation in the 1970s and 80s (Tunç 2001; Kürüz 2007; Arı 2008). *Gırgır*'s founding editor Oğuz Aral was influential in the launching of new humour talents, each of whom established new

IMAGE 3.6 The cast of *Çocuklar Duymasın*. Image courtesy of *Sputnik News* (https://-bit.ly/-3ts8RiD, last accessed on 12 June 2022).

cartoon characters from Turkish daily life.[22] Trained by Aral, cartoonist Gani Müjde made an important leap in the early 1990s, establishing Tükenmez Kalem, a writing team for the blossoming television world.[23] Müjde closely collaborated with another humour writer Birol Güven. Both had entrepreneurial skills and they provided a platform for many cartoonists to write dizi scripts in the genre of comedy or dramedy. Güven founded MinT (Made in Turkey) Production in 1996, and produced successful comedies like *Ayrılsak da Beraberiz, En Son Babalar Duyar, Çocuklar Duymasın* and *Kadın İsterse*. Müjde also acted as the project designer and produced several dizis. Türker İnanoğlu, who noticed the potential of the caricaturists' world, also produced long-lasting dizis like *Tatlı Kaçıklar, Cennet Mahallesi* and *Gurbetçiler,* including cartoonists in the writing teams.

---

22 A few examples of these characters are Bezgin Bekir by Tuncay Akgün, Timsah by Mehmet Çağçağ, Kötü Kız by Ramize Erer, Sıdıka by Atilla Atalay or Eşşek Herif by Hasan Kaçan.

23 Scriptwriters who also happened to be caricaturists incliude Kemal Kenan Ergen, Fatih Solmaz, Selçuk Erdem, Mehmet Çağçağ, Caner Güler, Metin Açıkgöz, Resul Ertaş and Yılmaz Okumuş, among others.

Among influential figures of the early decades of dizi production, one should mention Fatih Aksoy, who developed a genuine interest in filmmaking, through his association with eminent writer Onat Kutlar. Aksoy founded MED Production in 1993 and began producing talk shows and entertainment formats. He has been the first to launch direct adaptations from foreign content, including that of *The Nanny* (*Dadı*, 2001) and *Grey's Anatomy* (*Doktorlar*, 2006). His adaptation of *Desperate Housewives* in 2011 was sold for higher prices than its original version in the Middle East and North Africa region. Aksoy continued with many more hit dizis in the 2010s, founding MF Production with partner Faruk Bayhan.

Beginning in the 2000s, producers Şükrü Avşar, Erol Avcı and Mustafa Karahan also came forward from different paths of life, but with grassroots knowledge of what Turkish audiences like to watch. Avşar was a cinema operator from a very young age, who had founded Avşar Film in 1984 for cinema operation, film import and distribution. He moved to the production side, producing many hit dizis like *Çemberimde Gül Oya*, *Ihlamurlar Altında*, *Yer Gök Aşk*, *Lale Devri* and *Fazilet Hanım ve Kızları*. Avcı hailed from the film import and distribution business. With his partner Karahan, he had established TMC in 1993, trading videos in the European market, mainly in Germany. Remembering these early days of the video market, Karahan gave me a thorough narrative on how they decided to shift to dizi production:

> In those days, we were buying Turkish movies to sell in Germany. Most Yeşilçam producers were keeping old movies in ratty storages. We used to collect them, and sign contracts for those we could buy. We claimed a five-year copyright for screening on TRT and future private networks. Türker İnanoğlu had his own pool of old Yeşilçam movies that he produced himself. We collected around 400 such films. After us, Erol Aksoy, the owner of Show TV, also began collecting. The competition was very fierce. We approached networks but

some were not interested in our offer at first. But after strolling through the market, they would realize the size of our movie repertoire and would come back. We would then sell it for a higher price of course. TMC continued for two years like that. Our business settled, we now had free time. We decided to import foreign movies. We went to an international film market. But the competition was so fierce that even Turkish import companies, which were around 20 in number back then, cut us out. Then we decided to invest in learning English and do some research in LA. Erol went and learned English and established direct contacts with many global firms. We started to buy the rights of their future films, before they were even produced. So we had the rights for foreign content before they went to the market. In time, we collected a very strong list of content that we could sell at a more reasonable price than the major companies in global fairs. (2018)

Among other prominent entrepreneurs of the 1990s and 2000s, one should mention Abdullah Oğuz, Tomris Giritlioğlu and Sinan Çetin, who have been influential figures as leading projects designers. Oğuz had begun his first business in the US, founding ANS-International in 1983, a company marketing video and online video sales. He came back to Turkey with valuable know-how of advertisement production. In 1992, he founded ANS-Turkey, which operated as a production company in cooperation with Kanal D. Oğuz worked as project designer and director of many dizis, movies, game shows, music videos, gathering teams of new writers, young directors and executive producers, including Meral Okay, Çağan Irmak, Timur Savcı and Pelin Diştaş, who became influential figures in the coming years. The mere credits of his *Asmalı Konak* may be seen today as a future list of powerful decision makers of the dizi industry to come in the 2010s. The late Okay and Savcı were the writer-producer team of the phenomenal *Magnificent Century*; and Savcı continues to be one of the leading producers of the industry. Çağan Irmak directed many influential movies and dizis in the 2010s, while Pelin Diştaş rose in the administrative realms of the dizi industry first as the drama director of Kanal D, then as producer in Ay Yapım and nowadays as the manager of original Turkish content for Netflix.

Another figure who had a long-lasting impact in the formation of the dizi-making initiatives was Tomris Giritlioğlu, who was a TRT producer with expertise in documentary filmmaking. After her retirement, Giritlioğlu worked as the project designer of a series of period dramas, closely cooperating with Şükrü Avşar. With her background on documentaries, Giritlioğlu touched upon delicate historical and social issues like the memory of military coups (*Çemberimde Gül Oya, Hatırla Sevgili, Bu Kalp Seni Unutur mu?*), Independence war (*Kara Yılan*) or the urban poor (*Kayıp Şehir*). She also produced or directed romance stories (*Asi, Ihlamurlar Altında* and *Gönülçelen*) which circulated well both in domestic and global markets. Many actors she cast in these dizis became the first generation of stars, who now have millions of international followers.

Director Sinan Çetin has produced more movies than dizis, but he had an impact on filmmaking circles particularly after he founded his production company Plato in 1986, and a film school in 2004. Besides his cinema career, Çetin produced some formats and dizis for television, but mostly advertisements. The path of many assistant directors, executive producers and technicians have crossed with Plato. Among others, Nermin Eroğlu, the eminent executive producer of hit projects like *Magnificent Century* and *Vatanım Sensin*, began her career as an assistant director of Çetin (Eroğlu 2012; *tsa.org.tr* 2017).

All these figures belonged, of course, to a much wider pool of producers, drama managers, directors or talent agents who contributed to the construction of the dizi industry in the years to follow. Director Kartal Tibet, for instance, was among the prominent social players of these early years, having an important role in the success of many early dizi projects. Today's prominent directors Zeynep Günay-Tan and Hilal Saral began their careers in such projects, and later directed many of the hit dizis of the 2010s. Fatih Edipoğlu and Ömer Özgüner, as network directors of ATV and Star, and Lale Eren, as the manager of Kanal D's in-house productions, have also been closely involved in the decision-making processes of the dizi world in 2010s. One should also mention Ayşe Özer, Nermin Eroğlu, and Nevin Ayaz as executive directors or coordinators who developed their own styles of organizing sets and coordinating production processes.

CHAPTER 4

The Emergence of Dizi as a Genre

From Script to Media Text

Analysing film genres is a complex undertaking. While the term 'dizi' has been used since the 1970s, the growth of the dizi as a metagenre has evolved over time. From the 1990s, the dizi genre matured into its latest version, which now circulates in the domestic and global television markets. In global markets, where television drama is simply referred at as 'scripted format' (see Chalaby 2016), the dizi has usually been called 'Turkish soap', 'Turkish novella', or more generally 'Turkish drama'. Until recently, producers, distributors and even academic researchers from Turkey had also adopted this nomenclature to situate the dizi within the categorization of its global counterparts.[1] The momentum driving Turkey's emergence as a leading exporter in global markets caught the attention of international journalism and academic research; this development will certainly lead the dizi to be compared

---

1 For the use of 'Turkish soap' term, see Paulina Abramovich (2014); Michael Kaplan (2016); Jenna Krajeski (2012); Amy Spiro (2019); Nathan Williams (2013). For the term 'Turkish Telenovela', see Adam Jacobson (2018); Manuel Betancourt (2018); Sam Ford (2017); Carolyn Miller (2014). On the term 'Turkish Drama', see Giulia Achilli (2016); Ryan Watson (2018). Turkish scholars and reporters often used the term 'Turkish soap' or 'Turkish TV series'. For the usage of 'Turkish soap', see Selda Bulut and Serpil Karlıdağ (2014); Ziyad Varol (2012, 2016a, 2018). For the usage of 'Turkish TV series', see Aslı Öymen (2012); Ziyad Varol (2016b).

even further with its counterparts. Nevertheless, many leading producers and distributors revealed a sense of resentment to me when dizis were nominated for global awards under the category of 'telenovela' instead of 'drama;' they claimed that dizis were 'different'.

Scholarly research distinguishes dizi from similar genres in terms of its structural elements. The genre differs from American or British primetime series and daytime soap operas, the Latin American telenovela, or the Arab *musalsal*. Although many dizis have predominantly melodramatic or dramedy content, their formal features are quite distinct from their counterparts. Carolina Acosta-Alzuru notes, for instance, how telenovelas and soaps differ from dizis in terms of their duration, narrative style and episodic structure (2017). There also exists a Turkish vernacular classification of subgenres based on content, actors or regional setting, including '*türkücü dizileri*' (folk singers' series), '*mahalle dizileri*' (neighbourhood series), '*ağa/töre/Doğu dizileri*' (landlord, tradition, Eastern series), '*komplocu/askeri dizileri*' (conspiracy, military series) or '*tarihi/dönem dizileri*' (historical or period drama).[2]

The insiders of the dizi world underscore different components, which define what makes up the genre. Eminent director Hilal Saral highlights how the visual narrative of dizis merge the 'emotive' and 'realistic' aspects in a unique manner:

> We use a visual narrative based on feelings and expressions, and we do this rather slowly. On top of this, we tell the stories more realistically. In the Western world, sets are in fixed studios, and frankly, they have better working conditions; but there, they tell their stories through a more technical method. Here we catch the real feeling with shooting on real location. Our most important distinction is the use of real locations. Our

2 See Feyza Akınerdem (2005). For the analysis of neighbourhood drama, see Zeynep Gültekin-Akçay (2011). For the Eastern serials, see Ayşe Öncü (2011).

other difference is our ability to visualize the emotions. Now we also have all the technical equipment we wanted for so long. We also do tell our stories with great motivation and an amateurish spirit. We are really passionate to produce (2015).

Beşir Tatlı, former general manager of Calinos, details dizis' power in terms of their content: 'Turkish dramas narrate love, family, human relations, through well-written scripts and masterful shoots. [. . .] Turkish dizis have the capacity to embed at the same time completely dissimilar narrative forms like tales and real-life stories into a same frame' (*Milliyet* 2016). Similarly, Adam Theiler, the former general manager of Fox Networks Turkey (2014–16) says: 'Turks are very good at telling stories of jealousy and revenge, and stories that are based on families' (Vivarelli 2016).

Fredrik af Malmborg, managing director of Eccho Rights, which has long distributed Turkish drama around the world, draws attention to two key aspects of the dizis: that they often interweave elements that appeal to both females and males, such as romance and crime, and that their production values are fantastic (Carney 2016). Today's dizi can therefore be described succinctly as a weekly serial, with a duration of around two hours; it is usually shot on real locations and adopts a visual narrative style, where stories mingling romance, action and family life are delivered with an emotive and natural slowness.[3]

This chapter approaches the dizi genre as a 'media text' with its own intermedialities between its script, film, music and post-production. I also consider dizi a 'metagenre', which grew from the creative fields of theatre, literature, cinema, video, advertising, fashion, humour and

---

3 'Natural slowness' refers to a temporality close to 'real-time' action, but also to an acting absorbed in this slow pace in a natural way, rather than being artificially stretched. Editors have an important role in accommodating this real-time acting in slow motion, which is often accompanied by music to convey better the 'emotion' of the scene.

music, and was shaped during a specific period of Turkish television industry, the years between 1990 and 2018. Since the 1990s, dizis have benefitted from many related fields and institutions to become what one may now call a new genre of media text, 'performed' in its particular context of 'accelerated production' and broadcast within a very condensed time frame, where writers hand over their script to the sets to be shot right away, with episodes broadcast the following week. Dizi industry directors and cinematographers have developed a new style of storytelling in response to Turkey's unique production and market conditions. The tightly paced and almost interactive structure of the dizi industry helped them to follow closely the desires and responses of their audiences. I take 2018 as an end date that marks the sale of Kanal D to pro-government owners, following similar takeovers of other mainstream networks.[4] My primary focus is on understanding the dynamics of the historical process that paved the way for this metagenre. My other aim is to emphasize that dizis are media texts, exploring dimensions beyond textual content heretofore neglected in scholarly research. Cinematic storytelling, or what Henry Jenkins calls 'transmedia storytelling' (2006), is a complex process, and its discussion will offer a better understanding of television genres that attend to their interdiscursivity and intermediality (see Bolus 2019; Van Sijll 2005).

---

4 The sale of Kanal D marks a shift in outlet, pushing 'bold' content towards digital platforms. Romantic comedies increased, replacing dramedies touching upon social issues or political memory. There appeared also a new subgenre, merging a more culturally conservative language and aesthetics with a production using mainstream, secular actors and directors, who had not performed in such dizis before. For examples, see *Vuslat* (2019), *Hercai* (2019) and *Halka* (2019). For the change in Turkish media, see Birol Akgül and Ebrar Feyza Kılıç (2019); and Aslı Tunç (2018).

Situating Dizi Research within Genre and Creative Industries Studies

I offer two lines of inquiries in researching the dizi genre. First, I show how the creative circles in Turkey came together to construct and consolidate the dizi genre that now globally circulates. This involves an interdiscursive process that needs to be delineated. Second, I want to emphasize that the dizi, as a cultural form, is more than just its story and its characters—the textual content with which it is often analysed. For sure, dizis' scripts resonate through intertextuality and by placing everyday life and discourse in stories that draw on cultural, social, political and historical memory. However, the dizi genre owes much of its power to the intermediality it establishes successfully between words, sounds and images; the dizi is a media text that needs to be analysed with the richness of all the creative aspects it uses.

It has been challenging to find a literature to inform this analysis and to compose a theoretical and methodological framework to comprehend the above-mentioned characteristics. Studies on creative industries are usually written from perspectives of media, anthropology and management studies.[5] Some studies were particularly inspiring for the historical process I wanted to explain. The work of Özlem Öz and Kaya Özkaracalar focused, for instance, on the dynamics between different clusters in Istanbul's film industry (2011). Christa Salamandra's approach to Arab television drama showed the importance of combining both macro and micro analyses (2013a). Ivan Turok faced similar challenges in showing the complex set of relations during the historical development of film and television production in Scotland (2003).

Discussions of intertextuality, or even interdiscursivity, mostly focus on verbal genres, and television studies often overlook intermedialities involved in genre analyses. To move beyond this focus, I drew from a diverse range of disciplinary approaches, including folklore,

---

5 For two different approaches to Bollywood, for instance, see Tejaswini Ganti (2012) and Monica Mehta (2005).

management and genre studies. They all helped me to both delineate the historical process and interdiscursivity through which dizis were constructed as a metagenre, and explain the intermedial nature of the dizi as a media text.

Genre Studies

Genre studies often underscore the dynamic processes of genre formation and transformation over time. Many genres develop by challenging established generic conventions and moving towards new ones. Mikhail Bakhtin indicated decades ago that a genre's unity is defined by its chronotope: 'Chronotopes are mutually inclusive, they co-exist, they may be interwoven with, replace or oppose one another, contradict one another or find themselves in ever more complex interrelationships [. . .] The general characteristic of these interactions is that they are dialogical (in the broadest sense of the word)' (1981: 84–85).[6] In his critical essay 'The Law of Genre', Jacques Derrida reminds us that 'at the very moment that a genre or a literature is broached, at that very moment, degenerescence has begun, the end begins' (1980: 66). Literary historian Ralph Cohen also notes how genre concepts arise, change and decline for historical reasons: 'Since each genre is composed of texts that accrue, the grouping is a process, not a determinate category. Genres are open categories. Each member alters the genre by adding, contradicting, or changing constituents, especially those of members most closely related to it' (1986: 204). Scholars of genre evolution, and particularly rhetorical genre studies, largely agree that genres are dynamic and constantly changing entities.[7] Genres also embody communal knowledge and

---

6 Chronotype can be described as the bodily and behavioural response one gives to circadian rhythms, such as the sleeping habits or energetic cycles during the day. The term chronotope refers at the way 'time-space' configurations are represented in language and discourse. See Timo Müller (2010).

7 Some adopt more situational approach, treating genres as the outcomes of recurrent social situations and actions. See Carolyn Miller (1984). Amy Devitt (1993,

become a way of navigating social activity (Berkenkotter and Huckin 1994: 4). They take shape in dialogue with the world of prior cultural forms, and as such, they are destined to change over time and in relation to the social, political and cultural dynamics. Often there is a historical momentum: a genre arises within a certain political and economic context.

Literature on the emergence and development of other television serials, like the American soap opera or primetime TV drama, the Latin American telenovela or the Middle Eastern *musalsal*, points either to a particular historical-political context which made these genres appear, or to a traditional artistic domain which precedes them (like popular theatrical forms or radio shows). The American soap opera, for instance, has been politically situated within the escapist mood of the developing economies that followed the Great Depression and the Second World War in the 1950s. It later evolved into a more didactic genre on social behaviour in the 1970s (Allem 1995; Levine 2009: 173). The telenovela soared during the authoritarian military coups in Latin America during the 1970s and 80s (Ribke 2011). Both genres had initially started on radio. The soap narrative had literally been formulated by advertising executives working on behalf of soap and other retail industries, while the telenovela genre has been linked to traditional circus combined with the populism of the Brazilian theatre. In the footsteps of the *hakawati* storytelling performances, radio serials opened a way for the *musalsal* genre in the Arab world, to be later adopted as a genre of Ramadan entertainment (Salamandra 1998, 2004, 2013a, 2013b). The emergence of Turkish dizi also happened amid a particular sociopolitical context, borrowing elements from different professional sectors and institutions. To explain the historical factors that generated these creative sectors is a difficult task, as the historical

---

2000), for instance, approaches genre as both the product and the process that creates it.

course of events, establishments and networks is neither linear nor evolutionary. Hence, the approach developed in the organization and management studies that explored creative industries can be helpful in understanding how an uneven but combined course of developments prepared a ground for the blossoming of dizi production.

Creative Industries Studies[8]

As part of the creative industries, television has long been analysed in media studies, history and anthropology. Industry ethnographies have been scarce; the primary focus has been on television content, exploring different formats like news, drama series, games and other entertainment shows. However, in recent years, interest in the study of creative industries has also burgeoned in the fields of political science, management and organization studies, which recognized the value of television products in the areas of soft power, economic growth and potential for exportation (Erol-Işık 2013; Alankuş and Yanardağoğlu 2016). These fields offer valuable frameworks which can be helpful in explaining the 'unintended' industrial developments, like the rather surprising emergence of a dizi industry, with all the different cultural circles contributing to its growth. The approach of 'historical institutionalism', or concepts like 'clusters', 'path dependence', 'spillovers' or 'critical juncture' may provide us with tools to describe the process in which a variety of old and newly structuring, formal or informal cultural institutions and networks contributed to the development of a television industry in Turkey, within which the dizi genre became consolidated.[9] For the sake

---

8 I would like to thank my friend Professor Özlem Öz from the Department of Management at Boğaziçi University for her generous and valuable guidance.

9 In the fields of political science, management and organization studies, these ideas and concepts have originally been developed for political-economic analyses. Studies on creative industries can benefit from their conceptualizations in order to explain the historical cultural processes that shaped them.

of analysis, I will focus here on the concept of 'cluster', which can be defined in several different ways.

To economist Michael Porter, the cluster is 'a geographically proximate group of interconnected companies and associated institutions in a particular field, linked by commonalities and complementarities' (Porter 1998: 199). Other scholars underline clusters' regional proximities (Enright 1996) or their incoherent and chaotic nature (Malmberg and Maskell 2002; Martin and Sunley 2006). What makes the concept of cluster useful for dizi analysis is the flexibility in which one can explain different ways business and artistic groups associate with one another. Clusters also refer to geographical proximities, which in the case of creative industries tend to be the big cities. The emergence of today's dizi is closely related to the public and private institutions of the cultural industry established during the Republican era, including the fields of television, cinema, theatre and video, along with the worlds of fashion, modelling, literature and caricature.

Each of these fields comprised different creative clusters, in touch with each other but having their own group or institutional cultures. Theatre, for instance, was multi-sited in different ways in Ankara and Istanbul. Located in Ankara, the capital city, TRT was part of the state bureaucracy, and despite all of its internal debates and disputes, it had produced its own institutional culture. In its historical development, the dizi industry benefited from creative clusters in Ankara, Istanbul, İzmir and Eskisehir, while having close contact with European cities, mainly in Germany. Television, theatre and literature circles were predominantly multi-sited in Istanbul and Ankara, while various clusters of cinema, music, caricature and fashion were mainly based in Istanbul. Many film technicians on dizi sets were graduates of film schools in Istanbul, İzmir and Eskisehir, and continue their collaboration and solidarity during their job search or working on the sets. Video and music domains operating in-between European cities and Istanbul offered important clusters and networks of people and companies. Many distributors of music or video content later became producers in the dizi industry.

The Sociopolitical Context of the Rise of the Dizi as a Metagenre

To understand the dynamics within which dizis have matured, it is important to examine how the main structural features of the dizi genre were shaped over time. To reach today's production quality and entry into global markets, dizis benefited from the merger of creative powers that blossomed in different cultural and economic clusters and institutions at a historical juncture that began in the sociopolitical context of 1990s Turkey. In this sense, it may be approached as a metagenre, embedding elements from different genres in the fields of theatre, literature, cinema, video, advertising, fashion, humour and music. It would be useful to remember here that the term metagenre has various usages, particularly in film studies, where the term refers to a genre that transcends some other specific genres like in the case of 'melodrama' or 'docudrama' (see Dancyger 2001). I use the term metagenre here as a way to apprehend the dynamics of interrelations between different creative forms.

What was the general sociopolitical climate of the 1990s that gave birth to the dizi as a significant cultural form in Turkey? During this decade, Turkey aimed to 'catch up' with the material forms of Western modernity. Since the Tanzimat era, Turkey's modernization has been inspired by Western modes of development in the fields of education, gender and secularism, as Republican intellectuals and writers have thoroughly analysed.[10] The 'traditional-modern' paradigm found its highest expression in literature, where generational clashes and their

---

10 The Tanzimat programme, declared in 1839, aimed to reform the traditional political and legal institutions of the Ottoman Empire to resemble Western norms. For different approaches to Westernization, see Attilâ İlhan (1972); Şerif Mardin (1991); Tarık Zafer Tunaya (1960); Mümtaz Turhan (1959).

implications for class and gender relations were treated in novels, plays and movies.[11] Among the series of important changes of the 1990s, one should highlight the material transformation that came with the rise of the neoliberal policies that began in the 1980s. Often called the 'Özal years', this period saw the launch of cell phones, credit cards, and many global brands sold in the shopping malls that mushroomed in the country. Tourism flourished, with new 'holiday villages' constructed along Turkey's Mediterranean shores. Istanbul was promoted as a lifestyle brand, with burgeoning nightlife and clubs, chain cafes, restaurants and hotels.[12]

One important change in the Turkish economy was the customs union agreement with the European Union in 1995 (see Yılmaz 2005). Many industries benefited from this, notably textile and fashion, along with other manufacturing sectors like electronics and household appliances. The construction industry boomed as well. New neighbourhoods rose up in big cities, introducing luxurious residences with swimming pools, but also subsidized high-rise compounds for the provincial middle classes who began to migrate to urban centres in their own pursuit of modernity. The 1990s saw waves of forced migration from the rural southeast to surrounding towns and cities as well, in a pattern never before experienced during the Republican times.[13] This changed the demography in both the countryside and the cities, as former villagers emerged as the new 'urban poor'.[14] These years witnessed the

---

11 For discussions on modernization in literature, see Ulaş Bingöl (2017); Olgun Gündüz (2002); Nüket Esen (1990); Yadigar Şanlı (2013). For theatre, see Yavuz Pekman (2002); Tamer Temel (2016). For cinema, see Filiz Çelik (2011); Aydan Özsoy (2004); Mehmet Öztürk (2004).

12 For discussion on the history of tourism in Turkey, see Arzu Öztürkmen (2005).

13 See B. Akşit (1998); D. Çakmak (2012); Gülçin Erdeniz (2011); Anna Grabolle-Çeliker (2013); Ö. Sevim (2000); TESEV (2008); TMMOB (1998).

14 See Rojin Akın and Funda Danışman (2011); E. Özgür and M. Yüceşahin (2006); Sevilay Kaygalak (2009); Yeşim Mutlu (2009).

expansion of printed media into private television networks as well. Through satellite technology, access to international channels became available. The rise of the internet produced a visible leap in scholarly and popular publication, with important foreign publications rapidly translated and circulated.

The 1980s and 90s have also become known as the heyday of *dergicilik*, popular news magazines which could focus on issues that had long been taboo.[15] Through these magazines and a series of new dailies, debates on sexual orientations and experiences, ethnic identities, and nostalgia and memory for displaced non-Muslim communities found a new discursive platform. These emergent topics found expression in academic scholarship, literature, cinema and, of course, on television. One important development was experienced in the field of arts consumption. International Istanbul Film, Music and Theatre Festivals, the newly opened Warner Bros movie halls, and mega-concerts of world stars[16] became new venues for urban entertainment, creating a feeling of connectedness to the global art world. With greater access to the global cinema, Turkish entrepreneurs and audiences developed a desire for the Turkish versions of what they observed. 'We too have big families like the Italians,' said an anonymous producer, 'we have our own natural beauty, historical textures. So we thought, why not write our own stories, with our own people and places?'

Dizi production of the 1990s was modest compared with today's industry, but both the producers and network directors sought to 'make a difference' and to benefit from the financial opportunities of commercial television. Landmark dizis emerged at a historical juncture where their content reflected the concerns and issues of a certain sociopolitical climate, while their production quality benefited from the new technology and increased material resources of neoliberal economy.

---

15 See Nurdan Gürbilek (2011); Arzu Öztürkmen (1998).

16 These included Madonna (1993), Michael Jackson (1993), Ricky Martin (1998) and Tina Turner (1998).

On the Interdiscursive Processes and the Concept of the 'Emergent'

Since the early years of the television broadcasting in Turkey, the dizi genre has responded to other international formats (American prime-time series, BBC dramas, soap operas and telenovelas) and borrowed cinematic and technical elements from different domains of the Turkish media industry, including cinema, advertising and video. Two concepts drawn from folklore and genre studies will be useful in our discussion of the dizi as a metagenre. One is the process of 'interdiscursivity'; the other is the 'emergent' aspect of genres.[17] Generally speaking, genre studies have developed within linguistic studies. Ancient and modern literary genres have been thoroughly analysed, and contemporary genre debates have emphasized the dynamic, processual and subjective features of genre-making, calling attention to the issues of taxonomy and coding. My approach to genre is more performative than literary-textual. Inspired by the works of Richard Bauman (2004) and Vijay K. Bhatia (2017) on the ethnography of communication and genre, I approach the dizi as an outcome of an interdiscursive process that has emerged through borrowings from various forms of media making, which were recontextualized within an emerging television industry, at a particular moment of Turkey's recent history.

Explaining the interdiscursive processes of dizi as a media text becomes a complex issue, as the cultural forms from which dizis appropriate structural elements may not be media texts per se but, rather, certain elements drawn from various creative clusters or institutions. Communication scholars Mariaelena Bartesaghi and Chaim Noy

---

17 I am grateful to Richard Bauman for his guidance in approaching the complex problems I faced while examining dizi as a genre. His genre theory offers us many valuable concepts on the dialogic interactions between genres. The concept of entextualization, for instance, relates to the processes of decontextualization and recontextualization to producing specific texts, and this approach will be very beneficial for specific dizis' content analysis and intertextuality. With my focus on the historical emergence of dizi as a genre, the concept of interdiscursivity has been a better tool to explain the interaction between dizis and other existing forms.

approach the analysis of interdiscursivity as the dialectical relations between texts, discourses and the realm of the social, and emphasize how 'discourse types are bound to particular institutional settings or spheres of social life' (2015: 2):

[I]nterdiscursivity refers to the heterogeneity of texts, how they fold within them other texts, other utterances, and draw upon multiple discoursal contexts. By taking up the productive inter-action between text and discourses, the concept of interdiscur-sivity proposes an examination of how, on the one hand, discourse is typified and ordered into more or less permeable or hybrid genres, and, on the other, how genres are prescriptively bound to accountable social action across multiple sites. (Bartesaghi and Noy 2015: 1)

Folklorist and anthropologist Richard Bauman explores the relationship of texts to other texts and generic blending in his seminal book *A World of Others' Words: Cross-Cultural Perspectives on Intertextuality*. Laying out the relationship between genre, performance and the production of intertextuality, he details his approach to interdiscursivity:

The perspective that I am suggesting here is founded upon a conception of social life as discursively constituted, produced and reproduced in situated acts of speaking and other signifying practices that are simultaneously anchored in their situational contexts of use and transcendent of them, linked by interdis-cursive ties to other situations, other acts, other utterances. The sociohistorical continuity and coherence manifested in these interdiscursive relationships rests upon cultural repertoires of concepts and practices that serve as conventionalized orienting frameworks for the production, reception, and circulation of discourse (2008: 2).

These scholars draw attention on the discursive realms constituted in social life, where artistic and economic domains converge to produce their own conventions as genres. The rise of dizi as a metagenre is an outcome of such discursively constituted spheres of social life that included public and private institutions, artistic and business clusters, which emerged through a particular historical process. As explained in the previous chapters, the dizi's latest form owes greatly to the production skills developed in TRT, Yeşilçam and theatre tradition, the business experience in advertising, fashion, video and music industries, along with the storytelling power of the fields of literature and caricature.

As a scholar of applied linguistics, Vijay K. Bhatia brings a critique that the study of genre analysis focused extensively on the linguistic and rhetorical analysis of discourses, and argues that it neglected how and why such discourses are used to achieve their communicative purposes. Bhatia explores the dynamics of interdiscursivity, in the context of professional communication, focusing on genres like advertising, promotion campaigns or fundraising practices. His approach to interdiscursivity brings us a valuable framework to study what he calls the 'text-external factors' such as generic norms and conventions, discursive space and participation mechanisms in dizi analysis (2017: 12). He states:

> Interdiscursivity [. . .] is always across discursive events (may be genres and disciplines, professional activities and/or identities, or even more generally professional cultures, and/or discursive space). It is often based on shared generic or contextual characteristics across two or more discursive constructs, and some understanding of these shared features is a necessary condition to an adequate understanding of the new construct. (2017: 35)

In the light of above framework, our question becomes: What were the dynamics of the interdiscursive processes through which dizi rose as a novel genre? There are different layers paving the way for the gradual development of the dizi, including viewing habits, technological infrastructure, and acting styles from cinema, theatre and modelling.

Let us begin with the audience reception of seriality since the early days of television broadcasting. Turkish audiences developed their television viewing habits through TRT which, during the 1970s and 80s, featured hit series imported from the international markets. Two such imported series—*The Fugitive* (1967–67) and *Dallas* (1978)—tied up viewers to screens, 'emptying the streets'.[18] *Kaynanalar* and *Aşk-ı Memnu* were the first dizis creating a serial habit in the 70s, followed by *Perihan Abla* in the 1980s. Nothing compares, however, with the passionate reception of Turkish viewers for the soap and telenovela series that aired on private networks in the 90s, establishing a new mode of daily serial watching.[19] The producers of proto-dizis in the 90s searched for ways to create content that would appeal to both domestic audiences in newly launched commercial channels, and Euro-Turks, who had begun to demand more Turkish content in video format. This era coincided with a boom in the advertising industry, which introduced updated technological knowledge and equipment to television. The 90s were also a decade of debates over identity politics, historical nostalgia and the women's movement in Turkey, stimulating new desires for content on social and historical issues. This was also a period in which new platforms in the fields of theatre and modelling generated a new pool of actors and media schools supplied new directors and technicians to the film industry.

Dizis as media texts took elements from each one of these fields, including viewing habits, technological infrastructure, and acting styles from cinema, theatre and modelling, and recontextualized them in the

---

18 *The Fugitive*'s lead actor David Janssen was invited to Istanbul in 1974 (see *Hürriyet* 1974). For remembrances of 'empty streets', see Facebook (2014, 2017). I remember how the question 'Who shot J.R.?' dominated the agenda of the printed press as much as the small talks on *Dallas (*see CNNTURK 2012).

19 For a review on the reception of the 'pink series', see *Beyazperde* (1989); Ferruh Binark (1992, 1997); Leyla Budak (1993); Fatma Gözlükaya-Tütüncü (1998a, 1998b); Şebnem Kadıoğlu (2010); Mehmet Mete (1999); Asuman Taçyıldız (1995).

sociopolitical climate of the 1980s, marked by the effects of the military coup, and neoliberal economic policies. The process of interdiscursivity in the dizi genre may be said to have drawn 'seriality' from soap opera and telenovela, production quality from commercials, and professional acting from theatre. *Bir Çocuk Sevdim* (2011–12) is a case in point. The series was produced by TMC, a company which ventured into production from Turkish video-content distribution in Germany. Executive producer Ayşe Özer and director Cevdet Mercan have formerly worked as assistants to Yeşilçam cinema directors before joining television. Similarly, director of photography Aydın Sağıroğlu had experience both in cinema and advertising industries. Writer Gaye Boralıoğlu was a renowned literary figure, who began writing for television in the early 2000s. The ensemble cast included senior State Theatres actor Çetin Tekindor, along with Gülcan Arslan and Ilayda Alişan as young actresses with no former experience.

Another important concept here is that of the 'emergent genres'. As dynamic sites of tension between stability and change, genres are sites of inventive potential, a matter which folklore studies long ago examined in borderland folklore. Americo Paredes' analysis of the *corrido* is the best case in point, demonstrating how this ballad genre emerged at the Mexican–American border, a site which is itself 'a historical emergent', as 'the product of a complex and turbulent development' (Bauman 1993: *xii*; Paredes 1958). Contemporary folklore scholarship also emphasizes the relations between artistic communication in everyday life and the individual creativities emerging from it.[20] In their article on genre

---

20 The recent website of the New Directions in Folklore section of the American Folklore Society approaches the concept of 'emergent folklore' in the modern world as follows: 'Emergent folklore arises out of the need for new kinds of community or new strategies for maintaining and dealing with communities faced with change. Emergent folklore may make use of traditional genres—jokes, song, narrative, material culture or may create new genres. The materials, sources, or means of transmission such as electronic media are influenced by the issues and problem

systems, Jo Ann Yates and Wanda Orlikowski (2002) approach this issue through the concept of 'kairotic moment', expressing that genres change exactly when a 'kairotic moment' presents itself and necessitates the performer to adapt to the new demands or preferences of the audience. Media studies benefit from this concept in the analysis of how new social media forms like blogs, tweets, YouTube or Amazon sites emerged (Kelly and Miller 2017).

The development of the contemporary dizis happened at such a kairotic moment of Turkish history. The emergence of a series of groundbreaking dizis marks this era, uplifting the genre to another form distinct from its predecessors. Examples with an enduring legacy include *Perihan Abla* (1986), *Bizimkiler* (1989), *Bir Demet Tiyatro* (1993), *Süper Baba* (1993), *İkinci Bahar* (1998), *Asmalı Konak* (2002), *Çocuklar Duymasın* (2002), *Kurtlar Vadisi* (2003), *Yabancı Damat* (2004), *Aliye* (2004), *Çemberimde Gül Oya* (2004), *Gümüş* (2005), *Yaprak Dökümü* (2005), *Hatırla Sevgili* (2006), *Elveda Rumeli* (2007), *Elif* (2008), *Aşk-ı Memnu* (2008), *Ezel* (2009), *Behzat Ç.* (2010), *Fatmagül'ün Suçu Ne?* (2010), *Muhteşem Yüzyıl* (2011), *Leyla ile Mecnun* (2011), *Kayıp Şehir* (2012), *Karadayı* (2012), *Suskunlar* (2012), *Uçurum* (2012), *Öyle Bir Geçer Zaman ki* (2013) and *Kiralık Aşk* (2015) as the prototypes of many more to come. The importance of these dizis has been confirmed by the number of scholarly studies written about them over the years. One can cite the articles written on *Çocuklar Duymasın, Asmalı Konak, Hatırla Sevgili, Magnificent Century, Kurtlar Vadisi* and *Ezel*.[21]

---

of "modernization", which both includes and transcends popular culture. New Directions in Folklore questions the concept and role of tradition as a cultural and intellectual construction working with, as well as against, forces of modernity' (American Folklore Society 2019).

21 For *Çocuklar Duymasın*, see Armoni Bayar (2019); Nergiz Gündel (2003); Mustafa Tekin (2003). For *Asmalı Konak*, see Filiz Aydoğan (2005); Ebru Gülbuğ Erol (2009); Seçkin Özmen and Y. Yıldızhan (2004); Evrim Yörük (2010). For *Hatırla Sevgili*, see Pelin Başçı (2017); Ali Eyüboğlu (2008); Remziye Özelçi (2010);

The significance of these dizis lies in the fact that they responded to the desires of new audiences by offering original content, a new mode of visual storytelling and a new way of portraying social issues, creating characters and producing stars who earned international acclaim. Some of the emerging content was rooted in the upsurge of interest in Turkey's political and social taboos during the neoliberalization policies in the aftermath of the 1980 military coup. Sociologist Nurdan Gürbilek saw this as a break from the hegemony of political ideologies: in the post-1980s ideological vacuum, ideas and concepts which had long been suppressed by extreme Left or Right found an opportunity to surface (2011). Sexuality, women's issues, ethnic or religious identities, all of which featured in popular news magazines during the 1980s, made their way into political talk shows on the private networks, but also constituted the thematic framework of many dizis to appear in the 1990s and the 2000s. One may say that the themes of these emergent dizis often belonged to the issues discussed in the media. For instance, taking its theme from the Turkish-Greek rapprochement in the late 1990s, *Yabancı Damat* and *Elveda Rumeli* depicted the issue of ethnic memory, addressing both its conflict and humorous dimensions.[22] *Yabancı Damat* emerged as an object of mutual nostalgia, studied by both Greek

Güliz Uluç and Mehmet Yilmaz (2008); Emre Ünsallı (2008). For *Magnificent Century*, see Serpil Aydos (2013); Aygün Sen and Selin Tüzün (2014); Mustafa Şeker and Fadime Şimşek (2011); Hasan Günal and Ramazan Kaya (2015). For *Kurtlar Vadisi*, see Erol Aksoy (2014); Zeynep Gültekin (2006); Lerna Yanık (2009). For *Ezel*, see Ş. E. N Can (2018).

22 Two pioneering academic meetings are worth mentioning here: 'Exploration of a Cultural Heritage: History of Turkish-Greek Communities in the Ottoman World', Boğaziçi University, Istanbul, 16–18 April 1997; 'Sociopolitical Sciences and Historiography in Turkey Today: Major Currents', Symposium under the Auspices of UNESCO and Panteion University, Athens, Greece, 28–30 May 1998. The Turkish-Greek rapprochement happened also with efforts in the diplomatic, literary and media circles. For a review of the Turkish-Greek rapprochement, see Ali Çarkoğlu and Kemal Kirişçi (2004); James Ker-Lindsay (2000 and 2007); Ziya Öniş and Şuhnaz Yılmaz (2008).

and Turkish scholars and journalists.[23] Two other dizis, *Çemberimde Gül Oya* (2004) and *Hatırla Sevgili* (2006), provoked strong responses in the public media and academic circles by triggering traumatic memories of military coups. Both series were the first dramatic reimaginations of the recent past that was experienced by every household in one way or another. These 'emergent' dizis of political memory were followed by others such as *Bu Kalp Seni Unutur mu?* (2009), *Öyle Bir Geçer Zaman ki* (2010), and *Ben Onu Çok Sevdim* (2013).

Dizis that explored issues of sexuality drew inspiration from discourses of the growing feminist movement of the 1980s.[24] A series of emergent dizis picked up on taboos and desires, captivating large audiences. *Bir Demet Tiyatro* and *Asmalı Konak* touched upon the suppressed sexual desire of lower income provincial women. *Fatmagül'ün Suçu Ne?* directly took on rape and forced marriage. *Aliye* depicted a fraught divorce case, an issue which continues to be a big concern regarding crimes against women.[25] Two dizis tackled other long-silenced sexual issues. *Uçurum* explored women's trafficking in Turkey. Forced prostitution, which had increased as a regional problem after the collapse of the Soviet Union in the 1990s, had not received the press coverage it deserved.[26] Although it was adapted from Barry Levinson's *Sleepers*, *Suskunlar* bravely brought forward the issue of child sexual abuse, a widespread but rarely discussed issue.[27]

---

23 See Robbie Moore (2013); Penelope Papailias (2005); Mehmet Yılmaz and Güliz Uluç (2009).

24 For a review of women's movements in Turkey, see Arzu Öztürkmen (2013); Nükhet Sirman (1989); Şirin Tekeli (1986).

25 Demand for divorce may be a brutal process leading to women's murder or honour crime at times. See Murat Balcı (2019); İhsan Çetin (2015); Pınar İlkkaracan (1998); Dicle Koğacıoğlu (2004); Yonca Altındal and Songül Sallan-Gül (2015).

26 For a review of this issue, see Emel Coşkun (2014).

27 For child abuse in Turkey, see Alanur Çavlin-Bozbeyoğlu (2010); Mazlum Çöpür (2012); Ayten Erdoğan (2011).

Some ground-breaking dizis portrayed class issues emerging from the cultural memory of folk theatre genres like Karagöz or Ortaoyunu. These traditional genres are usually set in a neighbourhood context and include a set of characters representing different segments of society (Mizrahi 1991). The protagonists play the two poles of the modernization process: one represents the traditional value system (*alaturka*) and the other a modernist personality (*alafranga*). The success of *Bizimkiler*, which lasted 13 seasons, and of *Çocuklar Duymasın,* which aired sporadically during 2002–14, owed much to the humorous tensions between such traditional and modern characters.

Some dizis' emergent quality derived from the new appropriation of old places, using the imagery of authentic locations. The dramedies *Perihan Abla, İkinci Bahar* and *Süper Baba* situated new urban classes into the old neighbourhoods of Istanbul, like Kuzguncuk, Samatya and Çengelköy. In this way they reinvented these old places as new sites of gentrification, and as *lieux de mémoir* for fan tourism.[28] Melodramas like *Gümüş* or *Aşk-ı Memnu* tackled the class issue through tense encounters between the rich and the poor, set in fancy houses and with characters dressed in stylish clothes. Shot in big *konak*s or *yalı*s (old mansions), these dizis provided visual access to contemporaneous upper-class lifestyles for the first time. These were taken from the circulating imagery of the rising fashion industry: the magazine press depicting the prosperous upper-class society at glamorous parties, yachts or luxurious cars. This process coincided with the branding of Istanbul's historically rich but also glamorous texture, and its trendy nightlife (Eder and Öz 2015). Dizis continued to use touristic imagery of other sites as well. *Yabancı Damat* featured Gaziantep, *Asmalı Konak* was set

---

28 The street where the shootings of *Perihan Abla* took place has now been officially renamed Perihan Abla Street. The shop which was used as the site of the kebab restaurant of the main character Ali Haydar in *İkinci Bahar* is turned into a real restaurant called 'İkinci Bahar–Ali Haydar'. And finally, the historical tea garden continues to be visited both as a traditional but also *Süper Baba*'s filming site.

in Cappadocia and *Sıla* in Mardin, each adding their shootings sites to these towns' rising tourist industries.[29]

The depiction of everyday life has also been an important factor in why certain dizis became the emergent of their type. Dizis like *Perihan Abla, Bizimkiler, Bir Demet Tiyatro* or *İkinci Bahar* captivated the audiences by mirroring the living rooms and kitchens of the urban middle-class. Set in the intimacy of a small neighbourhood and displaying unending gender and class conflicts, these dizis immediately won the hearts of audiences by celebrating the dignity and solidarity of ordinary—and mostly lower-income—people. *Çocuklar Duymasın* became a phenomenon in the depiction of the middle-class quotidian, treating gender wars as a source of conflict and humour. Terms and expressions from some of these dizis became part of everyday lexicon.

Some emergent dizis captivated audiences with innovative art directing. The reception of period and historical drama owes greatly to art directors who created an emotive effect, stimulating the visual memory of bygone eras. *Muhteşem Yüzyıl* reimagined the political, social and cultural domains of the sixteenth-century Ottoman court, convincing audiences as historical ethnography but also sparking controversy in its depiction of fratricide. *Çemberimde Gül Oya, Hatırla Sevgili, Elveda Rumeli, Karadayı* and *Öyle Bir Geçer Zaman ki* were pioneers of period drama, with a range of thematic focuses, decontextualizing glimpses of a commonly shared visual memory of places, artefacts or costumes along with body language and speaking styles. Drawing elements from cultural memory and recontextualizing them in dizis produced powerful emotive effects on viewers.[30] These projects captivated audiences

---

29 See Arzu Kılıçlar and R. Şahbaz (2009); Işıl Arıkan-Saltık, Yeşim Coşar and Metin Kozak (2010); G. Y. Yaraşlı (2007); Hakan Yılmaz and Medet Yolal (2008); Emel Gönenç-Güler and Cemal Yükselen (2009); Evren Güçer, Asli Taşçı and Mithat Üner (2006).

30 A similar encounter happened in the Balkans and the Middle East, which still nurture memories of the Ottoman-Turkish cultural domination (see Mihalakopoulos 2013; Paschalidou 2014; Tunç 2012).

through successful art direction along with powerful cinematography. Last but not least, the decontextualization of the themes from all these different sociopolitical venues was accompanied by that of technical know-how from the advertisement industry, both adding appealing quality to these emergent dizis.

Approaching Dizi as a Media Text

Generally speaking, scholarly research on dizis has focused primarily on particular shows, with an eye on treatments of gender, historical, class, ethnic or national conflicts.[31] Dizi research has also highlighted their negative impacts on Turkish culture, arguing that commercials affect young people and trigger extreme consumption habits.[32] Dizis were often analysed in terms of their content—story and characters— sometimes with an eye to audience reception.[33] The general approach has therefore been 'textual', analysing the narrative in terms of both its plot and its characters, usually situated within the general cultural critique of Turkey's sociopolitical context. The dizi genre, however, is a 'media text' which lies at an intersection of production processes, broadcasting marketplaces and audiences. Its material existence consists of a recorded tape or a digital file to be broadcast at a regular time. Its true existence, however, is realized only when it reaches its audiences, who assign to it multiple meanings. As media texts, dizis include many signs and symbols. In this regard, they operate within a polysemic

---

31 For treatment of gender, see Pınar Aslan and Derya Ünlü (2016); Tanıl Bora and Aksu Bora (2010); Feride Çiçekoğlu (2010); Ece Ünür (2013); N. Aysun Yüksel (1999). For national and other conflicts, see Sinem Arslan (2015); Ali Bilis (2013); Sevilay Çelenk (2010); Berfin Emre-Çetin (2015); Tuvana Gülcan (2010); Zeynep Gültekin (2006); Harun Er, Cengiz Özmen and Fatma Ünal (2014); Pınar Sayan (2010); Günseli Pişkin (2007); Evrim Yörük (2012).

32 See Mustafa Çağlayandereli and Yaşar Erjem (2006); Levent Cantek (2010); Zeynep Özen (2010); Ayfer Tunç (2010); Mihriye Yurderi (2014).

33 See Feyza Akınerdem (2012); Mete Kazaz and Yasemin Özkent (2016); Binnaz Saktanber (2010).

media language that conveys a multiplicity of features. These include non-verbal elements which complement the dizi text, like the site of the set (a real location or decor), actors' gestures, expressions, along with costumes and props.

Because the study of genre developed primarily in the fields of literature, linguistics and folklore, the primary focus has been on verbal texts. Therefore, the analysis of any television genre as a 'media text' requires an adaptation of the prevailing genre theories. As part of a 'media language', media texts are inherently layered. They involve the enactment of a text, but also an intermediality between cinematography, music and post-production, among others. In his work on moving image texts, Steve Campsall describes 'film language' as follows:

'Film language' describes the way film 'speaks' to its audiences and spectators. Directors, producers and editors work to create meaning from the moving images of film, video and television. We 'decode' these meanings in a not dissimilar way to interpreting spoken and written language. As with words, but more so, we don't merely 'read what we see'—we bring to our interpretation of moving images a range of pre-existing expectations, knowledge and shared experiences that shape the meaning we take from what we see. An important aspect of film language is its compelling nature and its appearance of reality (what is called 'verisimilitude'); it is not only as if we are watching an authentic 'window on the world', it's a window we want to keep on watching—like peeking nosily through the window at an argument in the street, enjoying guessing where it will lead! Through these means, moving images work to entertain, inform and educate but also persuade us to see the world in a particular way. (2002)[34]

---

34 Campsall (2002) also calls attention to the multiplicity of the constituents of the film genre, ranging from the mise-en-scène, editing and shot types to camera

The strong reception of dizis from the 2000s onwards coincided also with the change in material life brought by shopping malls, the internet and cell phones. To begin with, the rise of information circulation boosted the Turkish public's desire for modernity. Mall visits boomed for all segments of the society, making showcases of fashionable brands available to everybody.[35] The ease of media language rapidly replaced reading habits, inviting audiences to a different mode of visual and oral communication. To watch a trendy dizi became a must in order to discuss later its characters but also their life styles among friends and family. Or television magazine programmes produced elaborate talk shows about dizis' content and the styles of their stars. This also became an affective venue for inter-class communication, an important concern for Turkish society. Comparing stars' lifestyles or discourses with one another led audiences to make a selection of whom to identify with.

Distinguishing Narrative Text from Media Text

The camera's framing of a scene through various shot sizes and camera angles, and the actors' interpretation of characters drawn in the script, are crucial elements in the media text's communication to its audiences. While the scripted content—the story and its narrative— constitute the main axis of the dizi, the polysemic character of the media text invites the viewer to read many other elements of its media language. Be it *alaylı* or *okullu,* dizi directors are trained in this media language and are skilled at delivering their intended meaning through moving images. Using camera moves and juxtaposing different shots, they add to the scene's other emotional or informative signs.[36] There are, for

---

angles and movement, lighting, sound, visual effects, along with the story. Media language conveys how the camera sees the scene through shot size and camera angles, but also how the actors interpret the script.

35 See Ufuk Doğu and Feyzan Erkip (2000); Feyzan Erkip (2003).

36 An establishing shot, for instance, is often a long shot to contextualize the action for the viewers. Close-ups communicate the characters' thoughts or feelings,

instance, specific conventions that mark the genres of romance, horror, action and humour films. These may be particular locations, props, types of characters, the speed of the editing and the beat of the music. In many cases, they pair with one another as well. Therefore, the media text embeds, both a literal, denotational meaning of what a particular scene depicts, and also its connotation, with its different potential interpretations linked to a particular cultural sphere.

To distinguish the 'communicative' aspects of the media text from the narrative of the script, it would be useful to refer to Russian director Andrei Tarkovsky's concept of 'poetics of cinema', where he underlines the unique impact of the moving image on the viewer. Often criticized for his intellectual approach to narrativity in film composition (the matter of 'what his movies mean'), Tarkovsky defines the essence of the director's work as a process of 'sculpting in time':[37] 'No other art can compare with cinema in the force, precision and starkness with which it conveys awareness of facts and aesthetic structures existing and changing within time' (1986: 68–69). To Tarkovsky, experiencing the poetics of the cinema image is a unique mode of communication between the author-director and their audience. In other words, cinematic communication cannot be reduced to a verbal story; like in all other forms of performance, watching a moving image is a unique communicative experience. Tarkovsky illustrates his thoughts, commenting on what happens when a literary text is adapted for a play script or a scenario:

> When you read a play, you can see what it means, even though
> it may be interpreted differently in different productions; it
> has its identity from the outset, whereas the identity of a film

---

whereas a high-angle shot makes them look more vulnerable, while a shot taken from below usually assign more strength to them.

37 For a further analysis of Tarkovsky's poetics of cinema, see Thomas Redwood (2010).

cannot be discerned from the scenario. The scenario dies in the film. Cinema may take dialogue from literature, but that is all— it bears no essential relation to literature whatsoever. A play becomes part of literature, because the ideas and characters expressed in dialogue constitute its essence: and dialogue is always literary. But in cinema dialogue is merely one of the components of the material fabric of the film. Anything in the scenario that has aspirations to literature, to prose, must as a matter of principle be consistently assimilated and adapted in the course of making the film. The literary element in a film is smelted; it ceases to be literature once the film has been made. Once the work is done, all that is left is the written transcript, the shooting script, which could not be called literature by any definition. It is more like an account of something seen related to a blind man. (1986: 134)

Dizis as scripted moving images must be approached from a per-spective beyond their 'textual content', the predominant methodology adopted for dizi analysis. In addition to the analysis of their narrative composition, the process through which dizis take shape as media texts is of particular importance. Given the rhythm of dizi making in Turkey, the text is subject to change through different phases of the production process. Through collaboration, directing, acting, editing and scoring are mutually constitutive, and dizis transcend their scripts today as media texts. It would be useful to remember at this point the historical dimension of the dizis' pitching and production processes as well. As dizis are written, produced and broadcast simultaneously, the writing of a script is closely affected by the producers and network directors' continual comments and by the responses coming from the social and printed media after the broadcast of each episode. Dizis are unique in this sense, as their writing and broadcasting are interconnected and operates in an interactive–performative way, within a unique tem-porality, a production style which emerged and is still prevailing in

Turkey. In this sense, the dizi genre encapsulates a multifaceted semiotic text, which goes beyond the scripted narrative composition and its characters.[38]

Crossroads of Intermediality in the Dizi World

The concept of intermediality is particularly useful for examining the interdependence among various creative aspects of the dizi media text, as a palimpsest of text, cinematography, music and drama, among others. Current conceptions of intermediality covers however, wider range of phenomena, which I would like to address here, to distinguish and clarify my own usage of the term. Communication scholar Klaus Bruhn Jensen sums up the three main approaches to the concept of intermediality as follows:

> First, the term denotes communication through several discourses at once, including through combinations of different sensory modalities of interaction, for instance music and moving images. Second, intermediality represents the combination of separate material vehicles of representation, as exemplified by the use of print, electronic, and digital platforms in a communication campaign. Third, intermediality addresses the interrelations among the media as institutions in society—interrelations that are captured in technological and economic terms such as convergence and concentration. (2016: 1)

---

38 A similar speedy filming process exists in the Indonesian film industry for the *sinetron* genre, where writers have very little time for plot development, actors barely have time to develop characters, and crews are pushed to get things done before the next episode airs the following day. Nevertheless, *sinetron* is one of the genres of the Indonesian film industry, and although there are formal similarities in the production processes, the dizi genre is very different in terms of its production size and quality, and domestic and foreign reception. See Edira Putri (2018).

In a comprehensive article, literary scholar Irina O. Rajewsky also elaborates the different approaches to the concept of intermediality, referring to its historical roots in Fluxus artist Dick Higgins' concept of 'intermedia',[39] and the long tradition of *interarts studies* (Fischer-Lichte 2016; Vos 1997). Rajewsky asserts: 'intermediality [. . .] designates those configurations which have to do with a crossing of borders between media, and which thereby can be differentiated from *intra*medial phenomena as well as from *trans*medial phenomena (i.e. the appearance of a certain motif, aesthetic, or discourse across a variety of different media)' (2005: 46). Given the vastness of the concept, I approach the concept of 'intermediality' in a narrower sense of media combination, which Jensen describes as the 'communication through several discourses at once, including through combinations of different sensory modalities of interaction' (Jensen 2016). There is, however, a rich diversity of approaches even within these boundaries. Gabriele Rippl illustrates this diversity in a volume she edited on the intermediality between literature, image, sound and music, combining a series of studies on the relations between texts and images along with musicalization of poetic texts.[40]

In my exploration of the historical process in which dizi emerged as a distinctive television genre, I observe how the dynamics of intermediality had an important role in this process. The interaction between dizi's script, score, setting, cinematography and post-production editing that includes cutting, colour grading and sound adjustment make up the final product: the tape to be broadcast. The combination of these

---

39 Fluxus was an avant-garde art movement which developed in Western Europe during the 1960s and 70s. Dick Higgins first coined the term 'intermedia' in the 1960s in reference to interdisciplinary art activities between different genres (2001[1966]).

40 Eckart Voigts' (2015) article explores in this volume the intermediality between literature and television series, examining the dynamics of a literary adaptation in a situation of transmedia engagement.

features and their interaction is certainly not unique to dizis. Intermediality is intrinsic to all television series; however, they are often distinguished as separate subgenres. What makes the case of dizis different is how the interaction between these features is interwoven within the particular context in which they are produced, and how dizi takes its power from this interaction. This section elaborates the roles of directors, directors of photography, editors and musicians in this collective and creative process, which takes place under tight time and budget constraints. As writer Eylem Canpolat puts it, 'every episode is a miracle' (2015).

The diversity of professional backgrounds among creative teams is an important factor facilitating intermedial relations. Screenwriter Nilgün Öneş, for instance, was a graphic designer, and many comedy writers like Resul Ertaş and Gani Müjde were cartoonists who moved between texts and images. Popular music stars like Osman Yağmurdereli, İbrahim Tatlıses, Mahsun Kırmızıgül and Özcan Deniz produced and sometimes directed their own projects. Their experience of close encounters with live audiences guided them in predicting viewers' demands. Öneş believes that different art fields inspire one another, 'like imagining a text through visual material, or reflecting a feeling that an object triggers in you while writing' (2017b). Actor Timuçin Esen believes that his education at the California Institute of the Arts prepared him for the intermedial dimensions of the film industry: 'We were trained in dramatic storytelling, enhanced with a photography education.' He also underlined how important it was to receive technical training—not only to learn every aspect of this collective art to best tell its story, but also to be able to direct all these different units (Esen 2019).

Director Mehmet Ada Öztekin refers to the process of combining text with images as 'visualizing the story' (2012), while Ayhan Özen calls it 'constructing the atmosphere' (2014). Each dizi project usually has a showrunner, a position which operates differently in the dizi world. In the American context, a showrunner is the head writer who

IMAGE 4.1 Writer Nilgün Öneş during her Famelog Academy Sunday Talks at Beykoz Kundura, Istanbul, 24 March 2019. Image courtesy of the author.

is also an executive producer, and the concept is associated with writers who are closely involved in the creative processes (Archer 2017). The 'showrunners' of dizis are not writers themselves but operate more as executive producers, with diverse styles. Director-producer Tomris Giritlioğlu is known for 'designing' her own dizi projects, remaining closely involved from art department to casting and writing. In *Hatırla Sevgilim,* she entrusted the script to Öneş, but maintained an eye on the story's evolution. Giritlioğlu launched a new generation of actors who later came to be the stars of today's globally circulating hit dizis. Writers Pınar Bulut and Kerem Deren both operated as the showrunners of their projects. For instance, Bulut remembers that on *Ezel,* 'there was a team spirit, covering all departments ranging from art, costume, actors, lighting, and this is how this became a groundbreaking work'. Bulut also closely monitored the choice of locations and costumes while writing for *Suskunlar.* Her involvement had changed by the time, however, the second season began: 'Dynamics changed when networks and producers interfered more' (Bulut 2014).

Many writers agree that producers try to reduce expenses during a dizi's second season. 'Once the audience accepts us,' one writer said, 'they want to minimize the costs, and if the production cost of a scene is high, they prefer omitting that scene or propose one which is cheaper to produce.' Producer Timur Savcı remembers the lack of expertise and personnel in the early days of the dizi industry: 'They were like kitsch weddings, there was no soul in them. You need to blow spirit into the project, as its writer, musician, actor, producer—all collectively' (2014). He recalls that as the showrunner of *Asmalı Konak,* he experienced a multi-sited life, split between the writer in Istanbul and the film location in Cappadocia.

The Intermedial Role of the Director in Constructing the Dizi

The art of directing demands competence in cinematic storytelling (see Van Sijll 2005). According to acclaimed director David Mamet, a film director must, above all, think visually; the burden of cinematic story-telling lies less in the individual shot than in the collective meaning that shots convey when they are edited together (Mamet 1992). Filmmaking comprises a language with specific vocabularies and technical sub-languages. To director of photography Aydın Sarıoğlu, 'a good director is one who can do a "*decoupage*" over the script' (2012). Editor Gökçe Bilgin-Kılıç underlines the importance of mutual understanding, a 'common language' between the director and the editor in the course of long-lasting dizi production (2012). She explains her job through the metaphor of jewellery design. Referring to close-ups and long or medium shots, she describes how editors collaborate with their directors:

> In bead design, there are big stones and small stones. If they are too symmetrical or too similar, then the piece becomes boring. You have to be creative in your design. Sometimes the *mise-en-scène* is too long, and you have to open up between the scenes, to stretch it or to intensify it. To give another example, sometimes there are only three lines like 'The girl walks towards the

shore, the guy wants to approach her, but he hesitates'. The director may ask us to stretch the scene to 1.5 minutes. Or sometimes, when there is a break between the scenes and I connect
them well in the montage, she can say 'better than what I
expected'. The reverse also happens, she may say 'It does not
work the way you edited, I do not want so much silence.' (Bilgin-Kılıç 2012)

Like the editor, the director of photography plays a crucial role in
the making of the final media text. Aydın Sarıoğlu, a doyen among
directors of photography, has worked in all domains of filmmaking—
from commercials to cinema and to dizi. He recalls how their collaboration evolved through time, particularly through the rise of
advertising industry in Turkey. Some of the film directors of early dizi
days came from the advertising world, and they faced specific challenges in adapting to dizi making. 'Many advertisement directors used
ready-made plans for commercials,' says Sarıoğlu, 'they would not know
how to read long scripts or understand dramatic structures. Some
found this transition very difficult' (2012). In the early days, dizi directors had to work with directors of photography who were raised in the
old-school Yeşilçam industry. Over time, the art, lighting and photography units who came from advertisement backgrounds became more
influential in dizi production. Sarıoğlu also recalls that the skill level
and creative input further increased during the 2000s, when a new generation of film-school graduates joined the industry.[41] Dizi directors
and directors of photography affected greatly one another in imple-
menting their knowledge on cinematic storytelling. Their collaboration
is essential for the timely delivery of daily shots into the editing labs. In
all my set visits, I observed this rush and focus to complete a certain

---

41 The Institute for Cinema and Television was founded in 1976 in Istanbul. The
'new graduates' referred mostly to those coming from Dokuz Eylül in İzmir and
Anadolu University in Eskişehir, who formed their own creative and collaborative
clusters in later years.

number of scenes, with rapidly shot 'close-ups' and 'long shots'. Nevertheless, using different lights or angles, both the directors and directors of photography express that they aim 'to pass the feeling' or convey 'the sense of realness' that the story requires.

Prominent dizi directors describe their process of constructing these media texts in detail. Director Mehmet Ada Öztekin notes that in the pace of dizi making, 'every day is a new construction site for the cast and crew' (2012). Öztekin reminds us how directors 'open up' the scripts: 'Sometimes, an important scene is expressed in a few words in the script. In such situations, we do open up, by breaking the scenes. In the end, you move forward to transform the story into a visual narrative' (2012). Similarly, director Hilal Saral notes that she starts by 'studying the script', and then imagines it: 'As the master of the overall domain, I think of every detail, make decisions for selecting, editing, placing— doing this all from a perfectionist mindset' (2012). Director Zeynep Günay-Tan

IMAGE 4.2 Director Zeynep Günay-Tan on the set of *Istanbullu Gelin* at Beykoz Kundura, 6 March 2019. Image courtesy of the author.

also makes sure to always assist in the editing and scoring processes, even during her *repos,* her off days during shootings (2019).-

Despite the division of labour among departments, directors are the ones who have final approval of designs and styling. I have seen several instances of sets, waiting for final check-ups or revisions. Directors are also crucial in the act of casting. Casting manager Renda Güner describes the process:

> The description comes like this: 'A girl from the Eastern Anatolia, oppressed by her family, with a timid personality.' You provide three candidates to the director. The director should also give you the right feedback. When you do this successfully and make the match happen, you really enjoy the process. Sometimes directors don't know exactly what they want and cannot explain it well. Some directors are not that talkative, or sometimes they are very polite. Sometimes an idea is not mature enough. They may say, 'You thought of this option, but it does not work for such and such reasons.' This is how the final matches mature. (2012)

As soon as screenwriters submit their scripts, directors engage in what they call '*senaryo çalışması*', the study of the script. This is almost like a process of translation, reading the script every week, interpreting it, and delivering it to cast and crew. Doğan Karaca describes his own working style as follows:

> I read the script in a mode of 'imaging'. In the beginning, I read it very slowly. The atmosphere, the sentiment, the dialogues. There are a lot of subtexts. For example, the heroine is facing a tough situation—how can I help the actress deliver this hardship through the camera or lighting? Finding the correct expressivity, situating it in the right context—and the balance of all of this is so important. (2013)

Karaca also offers an account of the negotiation process between directors and screenwriters:

> We work most with the screenwriters on the places and the period. The place should be appropriate for a stable filming environment. For example, in *Çalıkuşu*, the rooms are on the same floor, but according to the script, the dining room should be downstairs, bedrooms should be upstairs. Feride finishes her dinner and goes to her room. I insisted that the dining room cannot be upstairs, and we discussed this a lot. In fact, this is wrong, but if it is a detail that the audience will not notice, we let it go. (2013)

Dizi directors do these preparations on a weekly basis, for months. Karaca reminds us that what distinguishes directing dizi from directing cinema is the race against time, which structures the modes of preparation and actors' motivations (2013).[42] He also calls attention to the challenges a director faces, working with hastily written scripts that may be incoherent or inconsistent. In many cases, Karaca states, directors are expected to adjust accordingly or interfere in the script. They must deal with input from a variety of sources. Shooting in a remote location offers another challenge. Karaca directed *Elveda Rumeli* in 2007–09, in Bitola (Manastır) and Ohrid in Macedonia. He recalls how local people hosted the team as soon as they stopped the daily shoot: 'Once the shoots finished, we all used to go back home. We socialized with people. Back then, we had made the headlines in Belgrade "Bali Bey, thanks to you, we forgive the 500 years of Ottoman yoke"' (2013).

Director of photography Hüseyin Tunç draws attention to another aspect of intermediality. He expressed how working closely with a director on different projects affects both sides: 'They influence our imaging, and we influence their directorship. During the shootings, in the

---

42 When I had this interview, the team was shooting 85 pages of script in 6 days.

presence of others, I ask *par politesse* what they want, although I know very well what they want' (2012).

Dosing the Visual: The Role of the Director of Photography

Cinematography is an important component of the dizi's visual narrative. The terms cinematographer and director of photography are often used interchangeably in film industries.[43] The Turkish dizi world uses the term *görüntü yönetmeni*, director of photography, which I will use as such in this volume. On the sets, directors of photography are the right hand of the directors in crafting the dizi's visual style. They also serve as the leader of the entire technical department. Producer Stephen Follows articulates their tasks:

> They report directly to the director and have a large number of people answering to them. They run the camera department and also manage the gaffer (who runs the lighting department) and the grips (who are responsible for moving the camera on dollies, cranes, rigs, gibs, etc). Whilst their work may be most apparent during the shoot, it actually starts in pre-production, when they will be working with the director to plan the look, hiring their team and managing decisions over what equipment to use. And after the shoot is over they will often be included in the grade (the post-production process which tweaks the look and colour of the final film). (2018)

---

43 Film data researcher Stephen Follows explains that the historical reason why both terms prevailed is that 'many national film industries evolved independently from each other and so different terms developed for similar roles' (2018). It is therefore mostly a matter of fashion and convention that some want to be credited as cinematographers while others may prefer to be called directors of photography. After studying 4,000 films released during 1997 and 2016 and analysing the credits, Follows finds out that 'director of photography' is more commonly used: 'The fashion for one term over another does seem to be cyclical with cinematographer overtaking director of photography in the late 1990s and again in the early 2010s' (2018).

In its early decades, the developing dizi industry benefited greatly from the Yeşilçam's directors of photography, who over the years were replaced by new film-school graduates. Since the 1990s, both directors and the directors of photography have gone through a mutual process of learning, adjusting and surviving in the pace of dizi making by developing their own style of cinematic storytelling. This requires a 'field solidarity', which usually creates bonds but sometimes ends in disappointments. The daily shoots greatly depend on the gaze and talent of the director of photography, who decides on visual textures and techniques to deliver them.

Senior actors and directors of photography distinguish themselves by their old-school knowledge of filmmaking. Actor Rutkay Aziz notes that the early days of the dizi shoots, when 35 mm format was used, 'were difficult times for filmmaking'. He remembers, 'We were not yet in the digital world, and pellicle films would be imported on a dollar basis. We would say "play as if we only have two metres of film"' (Aziz 2016). Director of photography Aydın Sarıoğlu calls attention to the importance of being surrounded by visual art: 'The art director or director of photography matures with visual exposure.' This includes not only light and colour but also sculpture and painting. He remembers his early days of cinema-making and its technical challenges:

> We were forcing the technical conditions to be better, assembling, for example, film lenses onto the video cameras. You have to know how to deal with lights. I learned this profession by using film cameras, not video cameras. If you know well how to work with negatives, you film well. Film camera has a different aesthetics from the digital one. In digital video, you may place the lights and make visible every corner, whereas film negatives are organic chemical material. You have to start working by predicting the result. By using exposure meter, I usually say 'We need more light here' or 'Let's cut here, there is too much light'. You have to film by knowing this infrastructure. Once you

know this, digital shooting is very easy. You may turn daylight into night by changing the shadow's sharpness. The digital brings a certain visual ease which contributes to the cinematic storytelling, and it is also true that it is more beneficial for the budget. (Sarıoğlu 2012)

The pace of today's dizi shooting often does not allow time for the directors of photography to go beyond simple recording, but many aspire to a more refined cinematic storytelling. As a doyen director of photography of the dizi world, Sarıoğlu underlines the importance of preliminary study in developing the project. 'If you start thinking on the set,' he says, 'you sign your own collapse' (2012). In the rush of shooting, directors may often urge him to work faster and to refrain from scrutinizing shots. 'I have respect for my job,' Sarıoğlu notes, 'I take my time until I am convinced' (2012).

Directors of photography express how their own styles of lighting and colour distinguishes them from others. Hüseyin Tunç, who was the director of photography on many top dizis, believes in the virtue of 'natural light', which he thinks greatly contributes to the final media text: 'I don't like much light. Filming in darkness sometimes delivers better the feeling of a scene' (2012). Sarıoğlu also believes in the essential role of lighting's calibration in capturing a sense of realness: 'I do not light up a night scene, for instance. They tell me "It's not visible" and I reply "Yes indeed!" Making it visible does not make it real' (2012). Both Tunç and Sarıoğlu also underscore the delicacy of colouring: 'You need shabby imagery in certain scenes', Tunç says, 'We often need to control very closely the colouring process' (2012). Similarly, Sağıroğlu approaches dizis in terms of their colour tones: 'Houses and characters, they all have a different tone. This is why I always carefully assist colouring in post-production process' (2012). Colour operators are usually young technicians who cannot say no to the producers who sometimes pressure for more colouring: 'Imagine a colour operator may work for four different dizis at a time. Obviously they all end up looking alike.

What they do is not colour correction but colour grading. The producer may ask for more "red" to have a sparkling general view, but then the skin colour looks metallic' (Sarıoğlu 2012). Drawing on his cinema experience, Sarıoğlu does colour grading while he is shooting: 'I arrange the mid-tones, for instance', he says, 'to suit to general broadcasting standards' (2012). Tolga Kutluay points to different styles of 'performing' the director of photography's job from a different angle: 'There are some who just stay open or close the camera's diaphragm. I cannot contain myself, and I always want to see behind the camera. We come from the old school of negative films, and we were on our own. Now, working constantly with three cameras, I need at least two other camera operators' (2019).

Tunç stresses the distinction between movies and dizis: 'In television, priority is given to the actor, not the angle. I usually ask the actors first. In scenes with strong dramatic structure, or those with powerful dialogues, I give priority to actors, and if not very necessary, I do not interrupt them much' (2012). Tunç also underlines the challenge of shooting in crowded urban areas: 'For the Taksim scenes in *Fatmagül'ün Suçu Ne?*, we surrounded the actors from the front, back and sides, using all other crew members as extras; this is how we provided actors with some space to perform' (2012).

The directors of photography have a symbiotic relationship with their technical teams on the set, particularly the lighting team. Kutluay, who has worked as director of photography in the hit dizis *Karadayı*, *Son* and *Çukur*, underlines his position vis-à-vis his team members:

> Director of photography is the person in charge of constructing the entire picture composition, responding to what the director demands. My gaffer is my right arm. We sit and decide where we will set the lighting. I've worked with the same technicians since 2011. This is not an official team, but one bonded in heart (*gönül bağı*). We have to endure the set conditions altogether. Last year's average was eleven hours of shooting per day, five

days a week, and two days of break. In time, the camera assistant becomes a focus puller, the focus puller becomes a cameraman, and the cameraman director of photography. In this way, I train and 'graduate' them and send to other jobs. (2019)

While directors frame and control cinematic storytelling, directors of photography assist them as the engineers of the cinematographic quality. Once they get the cue from the directors, they use their technical competence to produce effective images on screen. Along with dizi directors, they work to ensure that the 'spirit of the scenes' reaches out to the audiences. Training junior technicians on site, they are like professors in live laboratories. During my set visits, I observed them 'performing their expertise', finding the right angle, or solving a lighting problem. In many cases, they also advise directors on how to construct the frame of particular scenes, establishing the link between cinematography and storytelling. *Bir Zamanlar Çukurova*'s executive producer Emrah Karacakaya describes the collaboration between the director, director of photography and location scouts. His narrative illustrates the intermediality between the text, visual imagery and the technical craftsmanship of cinematography:

> *Bir Zamanlar Çukurova* is filmed in Adana. Once the script arrives, our director reads it and comes to us with an imagery in mind. Let's say he says, 'I want a site by the river, and lots of trees around.' Location scouts search and find a few possible sites. Then we go to the site with the director and director of photography. The director says, 'I want the camera move from here to there.' The director of photography may say he cannot work from that angle because of sunlight or the trees' shadow. He may say, 'We can put the camera here. If we shoot with a crane, we can do it.' Then everybody turns to me and asks, 'Can you get us a crane over here tomorrow?' (Karacakaya 2020)

Directors of photography are masters of the camera, and it is up to them whether, for instance, they will use a camera on shoulder, a jimmy jip or a chariot. Directors are usually very busy managing both cast and crew; they often delegate the execution of what they imagined to the hands of their directors of photography who indeed put the last touch on the shoots.

'Blowing the Spirit' into the Project: The Role of the Dizi Musicians

Music is one of the strong pillars of dizis' intermediality and cinematic storytelling benefits greatly from the musical narrativeit. Like visual input, sound is also a determinant of the genre. Musical scoring enhances the mood of the scenes, depending on the situations or dialogues from the scripts, or at times accompanying general landscape or other outdoor views. Songs from cultural memory (folk or popular) are also used, displaying an intermediality for the audiences. Burcu Yıldız, a pioneering scholar of dizi music studies, confirms that producers and directors in Turkey use the narrative quality of music as a driving force in the dizi. *Magnificent Century*, for instance, used music in approximately 85 per cent of episodes each week (Yıldız 2016). In fact, dizi music making grew along with the genre's development. In the early years, for example, a simple theme song accompanying the opening credits sufficed. Derya Köroğlu, who composed the opening score of the hit dizi *Süper Baba,* remembers the excitement of publishing a soundtrack for a dizi for the first time—'Tell Me a Tale, Father', which became a hit that year (Köroğlu 2019).

In time, as competition among dizi creators increased and the duration of episodes lengthened, dizi composers invented a musical form of their own in response to the changing needs of a dizi industry-in-progress. Paralleling the visual track, they gradually began to support more of the audiovisual narrative, constructing dizi music as a new genre with its particular production conditions, dynamics and practices (Yıldız 2016).[44] Along the way, musicians also discovered new ways of

---

44 Research on dizi music is a relatively new field for dizi studies. See Süleyman Fidan (2018) and Nural İmik (2006).

coping with the challenges of this new industry, excelling in composing new tunes under time constraints, developing editing skills and training their technical crew to assist them. Köroğlu remembers the early days of composing original instrumental score: 'Western classical music consisted of instrumental music. We thought Turkish music is also based upon a tradition of modal instrumental music, like the *fasıl*s or *saz semai*s. We produced film music from this side of our tradition.'

Composer Aytekin Ataş, named among 'Turkey's most talented TV composers' at MIPCOM 2015, also points to the merger of the Western and Turkish sounds in dizi music making: 'For *Magnificent Century*, we created a hybrid sound by using Alaturka melodies and Western instruments like the electric guitar and a symphony orchestra, in order to create a glamorous imperial sound' (2019). Toygar Işıklı, the music director of many hit dizis, maintains that he pioneered 'symphonic orchestration' in dizis (2013). Işıklı's sound had indeed made a memorable impact on different dizis that aired simultaneously since the mid 2000s, such as *Yaprak Dökümü, Aşk-ı Memnu, Ezel* and *Fatmagül'ün Suçu Ne?* Burcu Yıldız also confirms that 'dizi music has overwhelmingly moved towards large orchestrations'. In the case of *Kaderimin Yazıldığı Gün*, for instance, producers even hired the Prague Symphony Orchestra, 'to have a special, authentic sound never before used in the dizi industry' (Yıldız 2016).

Intermediality of the musical domain has been studied in its relation with both the text and the image. Some scholars explored musicality of a literary text or the lyrics of a musical piece in historical or contemporary contexts.[45] A wider literature examines the relationship of film to music.[46] To explore the dynamics of intermediality in dizi music, I will focus here on a conventional distinction that film music

---

45 See Erik Redling (2015); Steven Scher (1992); Philipp Schweighauser (2015); Werner Wolf (2015).

46 See Walter Bernhart and David Urrows (2019); Mervyn Cooke (2008); Richard Davis (2010); Roger Hickman (2017); Andy Hill (2017).

theorists make between source music (*diegetic* music) and dramatic scoring, also called underscore (*non-diegetic* music).[47] Conventionally speaking, diegetic music has been seen as a part of the fictional setting, and is heard by the characters. Non-diegetic music refers to what is played over the scenes for the viewers to hear, not the characters. Some criticize this distinction, arguing that film music always operates in a liminal space between the two categories, an important issue in the discussion of intermediality. For instance, Ben Winters proposes the term *intra-diegetic,* foregrounding the cinematic (rather than narratological) idea of diegesis (Winters 2010). Dizis offer both diegetic and non-diegetic music in different venues. Diegetic music was a strong part of the 'singers' dizis' genre (*türkücü dizileri*) in the early 1990s, where characters (often played by famous popular singers) themselves sang in almost every episode. In recent years, folk songs have also been used as an affective communication between the characters.[48] Dizis' power, however, comes from their non-diegetic dramatic scoring, which is a defining characteristic of the genre.

The involvement of musicians to dizi projects begins during or right after the pitching process. In many cases, producers consult the musicians at an early stage of the project, when they gather the creative team of directors, screenwriters and art directors. Dizi musician Cem Öğet

---

47 Among many others, see Giorgio Biancorosso (2016); Kevin Donnelly (2005); Claudia Gorbman (1987). Greek philosophers' approach to the terms *diegesis* (narration) and *mimesis* (imitation) suggested that *mimesis* shows by enactment, while *diegesis* tells by narrating. In filmmaking, the term refers to the story as depicted on screen, as opposed to its real-time happening. See Stephen Halliwell (2014).

48 To give an example, in *Fatmagül'ün suçu Ne?*, the character of Kerim singing 'Evlerinin Önü Mersin', where the lyrics say 'That God gives you to me', became a turning point of the story, marking an emotional consensus between the couple, where the woman character had been forced into a marriage. Burcu Yıldız reminds us that in some cases where ratings are low, making a lead actor sing becomes a strategy to improve the ratings. See also Süleyman Fidan (2018).

states: 'When the creative team is on the same page, success is reflected on the overall project. There are cases where the popularity of a project boosts its music, or others where the music boosts the overall content of the project' (2019).

Drawing on her personal journey as a performer and researcher in dizi music industry,[49] Burcu Yıldız offers a comprehensive review of how musicians combine the arts and crafts of dizi music making during production. She begins with a comparison with the Western standards of scoring for television, where production companies work with a music crew that includes a composer, a music supervisor in charge of the overall musical landscape, and a music editor to synchronize music with images. In the case of dizi production, many of these separate jobs merge in the figure of 'music supervisor', who acts as composer, sound engineer (recording, mixing and mastering) and editor, and who delivers the upcoming episode's score on time. Stressing on the time factor, Yıldız explains:

> The entire production process should be completed as quickly as possible. Dizi musicians must respond at the speed imposed by the TV industry; they must compose, arrange and orchestrate, record, and complete the mixing, mastering and editing at superhuman speed. Music is one of the last stages in the post-production process. Dizi musicians take each episode and edit the music two or three days before screening day. Music editing must be completed in approximately 24 hours. Once the music editing is complete, the entire soundtrack is unified at the final mixing stage, comprising the dialog, music and sound effects. The issue of speed is, in reality, one of the most basic challenges

---

49 These include *Fırtına* (Storm), *Bir Bulut Olsam* (I Wish I Were a Cloud), *Baba Ocağı* (Family Home), *Muhteşem Yüzyıl* (Magnificent Century), *Suskunlar* (Game of Silence), *Yer Gök Aşk* (Love in the Sky), *Çalıkuşu* (Lovebird), *Kardeş Payı* (Equal Shares) and *Kaderimin Yazıldığı Gün* (The Day My Fate Was Sealed).

faced by dizi musicians. This is embodied most clearly in the struggle with sleep deprivation; most dizi musicians must have a strong enough constitution to remain awake for 48 hours. (2016: 213)

Finding an original score is the most challenging aspect of dizi music making. Many dizis begin with an original opening score and musicians are expected to create new melodies along the way. Aytekin Ataş describes this aspect of his job as an intermedial experience between the story and his tunes:

I see composing as a process where one extracts the story of the script and translates it to a musical language. The most important and difficult part of this process for me is to explore what kind of soundscape a dizi content demands and come up with a sound which suits it. What I mean by 'suit' here refers to an aesthetically relative concept. And in order for it to be solidly based, it must always embed artistic, commercial and technical meanings. (2019)

Cem Öğet expresses similar ideas, focusing on the soundscape of the dizis: 'I try to understand the spirit and the feeling of the project in hand. I believe the better I grasp the world and the characters to be created, the better the music that I compose will serve its purpose' (2019).

Yıldız asserts, however, that music editing is as critical as finding the tunes. Besides composing original melodies, a dizi musician must have the necessary editing skills to maintain the integrity between the music and images. He also needs to have the versatility to adapt the main tune to different emotive versions, which may range from romance to fear or humour. Many decisions are taken during the editing process. Yıldız notes: 'This is where the art of music editing comes into play, to select and put the right music on the right scene, and to achieve harmonious, flowing transitions between scenes' (2016: 212). Musicians must also find the proper diegetic music, researching and deciding on the music content and its related instruments, and at times rehearsing with the performers. For period or historical dizis, there is usually a need for preliminary research about the music of the era. Dizi musicians must also have a multifaceted musical background and the competence to adapt the tunes they find to scenes of romance, action or humour (Yıldız 2016: 213). They are also expected to control the precise coordination of film and music, an equation they each create by experience. Developing these professional skills in a wildly competitive television industry led many dizi musicians to devise strategies for effective editing for each episode:

> They compose and arrange themes in a layered structure to provide transitions between the actions, moods and/or speed of scenes. Dizi musicians also assemble a musical theme pool consisting of music tracks derived chiefly from thematic transformations. They record the same theme in different moods, happy or sad, and use them in different scenes. If the script of an episode does not require new musical material for a special scene, they usually use already existing versions of the same material from this theme pool. Music editing, rather than composing, is thus one of the most time-consuming areas for dizi musicians. (Yıldız 2016: 212–13).

To find the right leitmotif, a catchy tune is of great importance, as it sets the dizi's emotive atmosphere. Yıldız states: 'The producer, director, and TV channel manager demand an authentic, original and identifiable musical sound for each TV series they produce. They expect that the audience will be able to identify the series by its musical sound' (2016: 212). In Aytekin Ataş' words, 'Nobody will remember the music of a dizi that aired only three episodes. What one needs for success is a long companionship between a good drama and compositions' (2019). Ataş also calls attention to the creative challenge that dizi musicians face under time pressure:

The process of dizi production has a rapidly rolling calendar; it is on the air in the blink of an eye. Composing so many pieces in such a short time makes you get lost in-between different sounds. [. . .] These pieces need to be short tunes, easily caught by the viewers, artistically satisfy the composer and have an individual style and an original language of its own. And all of this need to be done sometimes within a few days in order to air on time. (2019)

Yıldız notes how network directors and producers believe that dizi musicians must have a 'magic touch' that draws women out of the kitchen and in front of the television. Music is also expected to cover up shortcomings in the production process. As one musician told to me, 'When acting is low energy, music comes in!' Dizis' dramatic scoring usually employs symphonic orchestration, which can construct a musical narrative parallel to the story:

I believe that instrumental compositions have a storytelling function, whose theme is borrowed from the content of the drama. This means that when we close our eyes and only listen, we can visualize the world depicted by that particular drama content. I think this is when one can say that a good chemistry is forged between the sound and the image. (Ataş 2019)

Other musicians also underline the intermediality between dizi content and music. Ümit Önder says that finding the tune that identifies with the project's theme is the basis of the music-production process: 'Music must integrate with the essence of the dizi, its story, its imagery and give a closure to it; no one can forget such music' (2019). Nail Yurtsever calls attention to the important role of the *jenerik*, the opening score of the dizi: 'To find the theme which suits the script and the spirit of the dizi is so important. If you think, we construct a building, it is like the entrance door to it. Once you have a consensus on the opening score, you can build the rest on it' (2019). Ercüment Orkut stresses how the content of the script and its interpretation by the director shapes the project: 'We construct a music language, on the basis of the time period and location of the dizi, and from the information we receive from the script and the director' (2019). Toygar Işıklı has a different method where he attributes great importance to preliminary research: 'I read the script and begin imagining three to four months ahead of the time the dizi production starts. I take this very seriously, and I compose all the music without seeing any image' (2013b).

Musicians also take inspiration from the characters of the story. Orkut, for instance, points out: 'We first work on the characters in the script, and then start composing by thinking about the similarities and contrasts between these characters' (2019). To Cem Tuncer, 'exchanging ideas with the directors is what affects the creative process the most'; he also adds, 'our instincts, based on experience, also lead us' (2019). Focusing on characters puts musicians in contact with the actors, mostly indirectly but sometimes for face-to-face collaboration. How well the characters are enacted may sometimes affect how the story evolves. As I analyse further in Chapter 7, the stories are often paved on the road and actors' characterization inspires musicians as much as the writers. Vice versa is also true. I have observed over the years that many actors respect or become close friends with the musicians, whom they see as a significant component of the overall creative process. Actual rehearsals become a necessity when musicians need to work face to face with actors who are asked to perform songs for a certain episode.

Işıklı turns our attention to the intermediality between the sound and image: 'To use the right music in the right scene is what makes successful dizi music' (2013b). The balance between the image and the music is a delicate issue: 'Normally, music does not need to be stronger than the scene. However, I did the reverse consciously in the first three or four years of my career. I wanted to show the power and importance of music, simply because back then people were not noticing music in the dizis' (Işıklı 2013b). Maintaining the importance of the balance of intermediality between music and images in the construction of a scene, Barış Aryay summarizes the rules of a 'successful dizi':

> In fact, music also helps the director to unify the scene he has in mind. This is why your music should never get ahead of the image. It needs to carry the scene and pass the emotion delivered by the script to the audience. [. . .] Dizi music can be successful if it is original, composed according to the scene and played with the right instruments. That the composer understands well the world that the director wants to construct and reflects its spirit in the music is very important. (2019)

Musicians are also in close contact with actors, writers and directors. They occasionally visit the sets and are well-respected. They also take part in promotion galas.

Constructing the 'Local' between Music and the Landscape

The soundscape of the dizis also aims to match the landscape and the material world in which dizis are situated. Dizi musicians deploy their knowledge of different regional musical forms in dizis set in various locations. Yıldız explains: 'Balkan sounds for the narratives which takes place in Thrace or the Balkans, or Kurdish laments or *duduk* in sad peasant stories from Eastern Turkey. They may choose a special instruments' timbre to create a hook effect. They may use vocal themes, mostly the cries and exclamations of women' (2016: 212). Ataş, on the other hand, underlines that regional or historical tunes can give the composer certain cues while composing. Nevertheless, he adds, composition mostly consists of the composer's imagination, inspiration and his own musical repertoire (2019). Reputed Armenian singer-composer Ara Dinkjian's concept of 'music finder' explains very well how the act of composing relates to a recontextualization of tones from the learned repertoire of the musician (Ara Dinkjian Quartet 2013).

In some cases, actual sounds collected from the place in which the dizi is set are inserted in the music. Aytuğ Yargıç who worked with director Osman Sınav for *Sakarya Fırat*, a dizi with a military theme, gives an account on how the psychological atmosphere and the sense of place affected the dizi music: 'Sınav wanted sounds from the real location to be inserted into dizi music in order to pass the proper feelings to the viewers. Two such examples are *Sakarya Fırat* and *Pusat*. We collected sample sounds from real locations and adapted them in a successful way to the music' (2019). Since many projects now begin with the meetings of creative teams, musicians find the opportunity to build friendships and exchange ideas. Cem Öğet says: 'From the very first moment, we become part of a very big team and we exchange ideas. If the director, screenwriter, editor, art director, composer-musician understand one another while chasing the same dream and develop a common language, that project becomes successful' (2019).

Almost all musicians are gratified that their compositions circulate globally. Ataş received the El Premio Latin Awards in 2019 for his music for *Kösem*. 'In fact, it is joyful, but also surprising,' he says, 'because they gave the award to the top 50 songs; and *Kösem*'s original opening score has been one of these that was broadcast and heard in Latin American media' (2019).

The Behind-the-Scenes Storyteller:
The Transtextual Role of the Film Editor

As much as the text and the music, film editing is also an important component of intermediality in dizi production. This is where the textual narrative is transformed into cinematic storytelling. In this continuously changing industry, editing technology has also changed, shifting from analog to digital. Nevertheless, editing is an experience involving emotions as well, and as such, it needs to be interpreted as more than just a technical process of cutting. Graphic narratives can perhaps be used as a metaphor, where each image is loaded with particular information. In his work on comics, Scott McCloud emphasizes how sequences of images have a certain primacy, where the nonlinear narrative is afforded a closure by the reader's choices and interactions (1994). Film editing also has its own narrative tools, where scenes are lined up in a certain manner, inviting viewers to articulate the story, and to imagine and foresee the scenes to come. A suggestive look, for instance, may communicate an emotive message 'in the blink of an eye'. Renowned Hollywood editor Walter Murch follows this metaphor in his book exploring the aesthetic concerns of film editing. Film cutting, Murch suggests, is a complex artistic process which involves a craftsmanship in the pursuit of a 'good cut', that is to make the decision of 'why' and 'where' to cut (2001). Steve Hullfish's book *Art of the Cut* illustrates how film editors develop their own individual methods and styles of cutting. Interviewing top film editors from around the world, Hullfish reminds us how editors approach different scenes in regard to their structure, rhythm, storytelling, along with their sound and music design (2017).

The principle of editing for television series, therefore, concerns the construction of a cinematic storytelling in each particular episode. This is why directors and editors need to work very closely on a weekly basis. Most directors keep working with the same editors over years, as 'to be on the same page' is seen as key to their common success. Many editors note that they develop a sense of what their directors like, want or prefer in different situations.

Long-time dizi editor Gökçe Bilgin-Kılıç, who for many years worked closely with director Hilal Saral, shares her early experience of dizi editing in the Şafak Studio, while she was editing *Fatmagül'ün Suçu Ne?*:

My biggest experience was in *Aşk-ı Memnu*. Because the content was related to forbidden love, a big hidden lie, the story was communicated through suggestive or allusive glances. Our writers Ece and Melek[50] had this particular style of explaining

---

50 Melek Gençoğlu and Ece Yörenç worked together for long years to write hit dizis.

IMAGE 4.3 Editor Gökçe Bilgin-Kılıç with director Hilal Saral, working at Şafak Studios in Istanbul. Image courtesy of Gökçe Bilgin Kılıç.

every detail on the side. 'Angry, but why angry?' they would explain this like in a novel. Now in *Fatmagül'ün Suçu Ne?* I often think: Should I keep the scene with Fatmagül longer—to make the audience feel better and understand that scene? I would also know what Hilal Saral, our director, would approve of. Sometimes, it would be better to use Fatmagül's face while Kerim is talking. If there is a running glance, then it becomes important not to have eye contact on that scene. Or if there is high tension, silent scenes work much better. (2012)

To Haluk Arus, who also edited many hit dizis, instinctive talent is the key to successful editing. 'You need to line up the plans first in your head,' he says. 'Which plan can be associated with what—this should all be lined up' (2014).

IMAGE 4.4 Writer Meriç Acemi with editor Aykut Yıldırım during their collaboration for *Kiralık Aşk* (2015–17). Image courtesy of Meriç Acemi.

While editors know their directors well, the reverse is also true. Above all, knowledge of editing enables the director to make better decisions in the shooting of different plans. By understanding all the different ways a scene can play out, directors may provide editors with more choices for different cuts. All the directors I talked with emphasized how they assist in the final editing of each episode. Nevertheless, with the lengthy set hours and the haste of the production, editors now take more initiative than they did before. 'Once we learn what the director wants, we take the initiative and do the cuts,' says an editor who worked for hit dizis. 'In most cases it is the aesthetic decision of the editor that shapes a dizi's cinematic narrative; directors often come in to approve the final cut.'

In the absurd comedy *İşler Güçler*, writer-director Selçuk Demirel and editor Aykut Yıldırım created a visual language by using editing to give a particular rhythm to the narrative. Aydemir began his career shooting and editing short films. He stated, 'I had edited 10 short films just by myself; this is when I learned the power of visual effects' (2014). In *İşler Güçler*, Demirel and Yıldırım collaborated on innovations that squeezed walks in a fast-forward style, or narrowed the screen view to a smaller rectangular frame in each scene which included the character Şenol Baytar. Inventing their own style of dynamic cutting, Aydemir and Yıldırım created an editing language that became a strong component of *İşler Güçler*'s cinematic storytelling. 'It was like a game for us,' Yıldırım stated, 'Selçuk was coming up with an idea, and I was coming up with another. It was like a dialogue, and very exciting.' As a result, *İşler Güçler*'s addictive rhythm challenged other comedic dizis. One viewer commented: 'After I got used to *İşler Güçler*'s tempo, I did not find the newly airing *Yalan Dünya* so funny' (*Ekşi Sözlük* 2012).[51]

Like musicians, dizi editors work 'in-between four walls', enclosed for long hours in an edit suite, trying to wrap up scenes which are delivered to them while the shoots continue. Bilgin-Kılıç has a humorous memory while editing *Fatmagül'ün Suçu Ne?*: 'Imagine me as I was passing all my time cutting and editing these characters, I knew them all—all the actors' mimics, gestures, body language. One day I saw one of them in the subway, and instinctively, I waved my hand to him, only to remember that he had no idea who I was' (2012).

In many cases, editors may also point to a need for an extra shooting or dubbing on the very same day they receive the tapes. Given the detailed craftsmanship involved in the cutting and colliding of shots, editors are as picky and perfectionist as Turkish women lace makers. When I visited them in their editing studio London Post, Aykut Yıldırım, the editor of *Kiralık Aşk*, called the set manager in my presence

---

51 *Yalan Dünya* was another hit comedy which aired during 2012–14.

to ask that a dialogue be retaped and sent to him right away. The dubbing was completed before I left their office. When I visited Haluk Arus in Post Dükkanı studio, he described the delicacy of his art:

> Imagine, one film frame is the ½₅th of a second. And with the frame counter, I can clean some of the palpitations, but this takes so long. The more you put time in it, the better it gets. Because I do have a cinema background, I have a very meticulous approach. My editing can sometimes take longer than the shooting. (2014)

The continuity of light (day or night), props and costumes is maintained by special assistants. But in the pace of shoots, mistakes happen; editors ask for many scenes to be reshot. In the days of analog filmmaking, when editing literally required the cutting of the pellicle films, actors were more careful to memorize their lines. Director Mehmet Ada Öztekin distinguishes the television industry from analog cinema:

> Old cinema directors had to finish their films using limited amounts of negatives. They had to calculate very well the mathematics of each plan to be shot, and wonderful films were made with an auto-control mechanism. Now, because the digital gives you the liberty of shooting endlessly, people have become lazy. They say we can decide while shooting. And this produces an excessive number of images. The dizi world demands too many plans, and this brings an extra load to the editing process. My editor uses 90 per cent of what I shoot; we have now a settled common language. He knows what I want and do not want. I have many rehearsals with my actors, decide how to shoot beforehand, then shoot and finish. (2012)

In the current state of digital editing, many actors benefit from the comfort of reshooting a certain line or even a scene. It is the editor who covers up for actors. An anonymous editor described the process candidly:

Here, everybody covers one another's weak points. I chose the scenes where acting is better. In cases where actors have low energy, we need to enliven the scene through cutting or music editing. Sometimes we have faulty editing, which colour grading covers. There are also certain scenes you cannot shoot again—then we place some formerly shot plans in-between the scenes. Let's say the manual lighting trembled—then colour editing corrects it.

Film sets and music and editing studios are settings where one can observe how intermedialities are constructed, even performed. Screen-writers write their stories as texts, which the directors visually imagine and directors of photography technically deliver, a process where visual narratives are completed by editors and musicians. Throughout my research, it has often struck me how all these different units work in a self-contained manner, interconnected only through messengers, where everybody has a particular mission to assist or complete the other. In the dizi's 'accelerated production', most of the social players call this a 'duty', but when witnessing a creative performance, each of them takes pride in it.

CHAPTER 5

The Turkish Style of Pitching

Different Forms of Project Design

Television production processes vary depending on the national industries within which they occur. In the case of the dizi, it is the production process that defines the genre. All drama genres are the outcome of a collective work and creative interaction, but the complexities of human and technological resources of the dizi industry create a work culture particular to Turkey which determines the structural elements of the genre. Pitching processes constitute an important aspect which displays the Turkish particularities in launching creative projects. Pitching processes have changed over the last four decades of television broadcasting in Turkey, displaying a diversity of strategies implemented by the network managers, producers, directors and writers.

Compared with the structured pitching processes of Hollywood, one may perhaps call Turkish pitching more a process of 'project design' than a performance for selling an idea. In his analysis of Hollywood, John Thornton Caldwell approaches pitching as a kind of performance art, closely related to the idea of 'high concept' in marketing (2008: 81). He notes 'the use of the full-length screenplay as the point of origination for the show/deal now long obsolete', and adds how pitching concerns now 'the interpersonal ways that both are enacted and performed among individual creators within the production/development chain'

(2008: 81). The available guidebooks for newcomers are informative on the key steps in approaching major network or to casting directors,[1] referring to a system much different than the one in Turkey, where how a dizi's idea is developed and processed offers diverse cases. Therefore, the use of the term 'pitching' in the Turkish context refers to the different forms of project design. These pitching activities required networking and relationship building like elsewhere, but content development happened sporadically, depending on how different parties including networks, producers, directors and writers took the initiative. Because the establishment of the television industry and the rise of the dizi as a genre are simultaneous, one can easily say that dizi projects developed in a 'Turkish style', where networks, producers and writers each had a different say. While pitching partly related to the institutionalization of the Turkish television industry, another significant impact came from the political framework, where content has always been subject to control.

A historical overview of project developments in Turkish television reveals its vulnerability to political and historical conjunctures: Turkish content, so to speak, has always mirrored the boundaries of political freedom in a given historical moment. In this respect, dizis as media texts directly reflect the possibilities and limits of filmmaking of their time as well.[2] Until the 1990s, under TRT, it was either the top managers

---

1 See Ken Aguado and Douglas Eboch (2018); Charles Harris (2016); Michael Hauge (2006); Jacquie Jordan (2006); Squeaky Moore (2017).

2 *Yorgun Savaşçı* is a case in point. TRT ordered director Halit Refiğ to film *Yorgun Savaşçı* before the 1980 military coup. The shoots were interrupted several times for political reasons, and the film was finally completed only to be—literally—burned by the military. Although one copy is said to have survived, the story of *Yorgun Savaşçı* remains unresolved. Similarly, *Leyla and Mecnun* could continue with a jargon they invented to transcend regulations of post-1980 Radio and Television Supreme Council (RTÜK). The dizi was discontinued because of the actors' social media comments on the Gezi Park protests that took place in May–August 2013.

who approached creative directors or writers to launch new projects, or vice versa. Many private theatre companies sought opportunities to appear on screen during these years, to enhance their reputation, but also to earn money from the more reliable state venues. From the 2000s, however, the power dynamics between producers and network directors began to change, creating new key figures as industry decision-makers. As private networks became more and more the influential players, a successful project passing necessitated a certain diplomacy between them during the pitching processes.

Pitching under TRT: Negotiating Content with Bureaucrats

In the early days of TRT, domestic production was limited and dizi projects were planned in-house. Directors of TRT directly approached prominent film directors, such as Ömer Lütfi Akad, Metin Erksan, Halit Refiğ and Yücel Çakmaklı, calling for proposals from them.[3] Years later, Refiğ would comment on his surprise at this invitation:

> Lütfi Akad and Metin Erksan were names which the cinema circles in Turkey would value and approve of [. . .]. It was not a surprise to approach them, if one needed to select a director from Yeşilçam. [. . .] As for me, I was a front-line advocate of 'national cinema' those days. [. . .] TRT was mainly based in Ankara, and had a rather small contact office in Istanbul back then. . . . The Ankara bureaucracy had strong reactions to the fact that TRT asked directors of from outside, and particularly from Yeşilçam they long despised, and granted them special permission to transcend TRT's rules. [. . .] Aşk-ı Memnu had

---

3 These included Aşk-ı Memnu (1975) and Yorgun Savaşçı (1982), directed by Halit Refiğ; Ömer Seyfettin Hikayeleri (1975) and Bir Ceza Avukatının Anıları (1979) by Lütfi Ö. Akad; Beş Hikâye (1976) by Metin Erksan; IV. Murat (1981) and Kuruluş (1987) by Yücel Çakmaklı; and İttihat ve Terakki by Ziya Öztan (1982). See Ali Sekmec (2012).

a strong support of Director İsmail Cem and his team, but the bureaucracy behind them had a great resistance and a negative attitude. (Türk 2001: 300–02)

The way the project of *Aşk-ı Memnu* was designed illustrates the difference from the pitching concept where the creative team tries to convince the networks or the producers. As a Yeşilçam director, Refiğ was used to working with very modest budgets. That TRT were meeting the expenses was an indulgence he had not experienced before. As already mentioned, these TRT projects were part of a search for establishing a national content with a popular appeal in the 1970s. In that regard, Akad, Erksan and Refiğ chose their stories from Turkish literature. Refiğ described his reasoning behind *Aşk-ı Memnu*: 'This is the story of a family, and families constitute television viewers. This is why when TRT asked me to adapt a classic Turkish novel, I thought of a valued novel which would appeal to Turkish viewers not only culturally but also with its dramatic content' (*Milliyet* 2020). Similarly, Akad chose four stories by Ömer Seyfettin, a writer associated with Turkish nationalism (see Dikici 2008). In the political context of the 1970s, leftists fiercely criticized Akad for having idealizing the authoritarian state. Akad defended himself, stating that his aim was not to interpret Seyfettin's worldview but to reflect the ideal of Turkism as it was adopted in the time he was writing these stories (*Milliyet* 2020). Although TRT left to the directors to choose the content of the films, it was interesting how Akad, who had made so many films on various social issues, chose a nationalist writer's stories. Erksan, an award-winning film director, used this opportunity to try his surrealist approach to filmmaking, which was very unfamiliar to the general Turkish audience.[4] He was

---

4 These stories were Sait Faik Abasıyanık's *Müthiş Bir Tren*, Kenan Hulusi's *Sazlık*, Samet Ağaoğlu's *Bir İntihar*, Ahmet Hamdi Tanpınar's *Geçmiş Zaman Elbiseleri* and Sabahattin Ali's *Hanende Melek*. For an analysis of their critique, see Murat Kirişçi (2015) and Melek Yeşilyurt (2016).

also severely criticized, and two of his films made for TRT were not broadcast.

The encounter between TRT and cinema directors proved to be a precarious experience for both sides, and cannot be considered as pitching. There is not much information regarding the negotiations between TRT and the directors, but in light of a few published interviews and memoirs, one can see that all had a personal approach to their first encounter with television. Occasionally, TRT commissioned screenplays from prominent writers. Two such projects which covered social issues were *Kartallar Yüksek Uçar* by Attilâ İlhan (1984) or *Sızı* by Mehmet Eroğlu (1987). The pitching processes of these projects were negotiated by TRT bureaucrats of different ideological backgrounds and independent freelance writers and directors.

Television programming benefitted more from theatre circles to reach larger audiences. Since the 1970s theatre plays were known to have been performed in TRT studios, to be broadcast as drama.[5] But many television projects were also undertaken by entrepreneurial theatre actors themselves. *Kaynanalar* (1974), for instance, was launched by actor-director Tekin Akmansoy, who wrote the script himself, casting his own actor friends (Akmansoy 2014). Leading theatre actors also approached TRT for the adaptation of some of their plays to screen. In that regard, the performative aspect of pitching that John Thornton Caldwell stressed was enacted by these entrepreneurial theatre actor-directors. These projects were mainly musicals adapted from stage to screen, including *Yedi Kocalı Hürmüz* (1983), directed by Cüneyt Gökçer, the long-time director of Ankara State Theatre; Gülriz Sururi and Engin Cezzar's project *Keşanlı Ali Destanı* (1988); and *Hisseli Harikalar Kumpanyası* (1989), directed by actor-director Haldun Dormen. These shows succeeded for a number of reasons, but mostly because of

---

5 Ömer Serim cites *Vişne Bahçesi, Cengiz Han'ın Bisikleti, Kaktüs Çiçeği* and *Yağmur Sıkıntısı* (2007: 72).

the fame of the renowned theatre actors that the audiences knew but could not watch live. Gülriz Sururi gave an ironical account on how *Keşanlı Ali Destanı* developed. Her memoir details a general picture of this era, where TRT bureaucrats had a performance of their own:

> We go to Ankara, with Engin [Cezzar], we have an appointment with Director Mehmet Akköprülü. As you know, we are highly esteemed at the level of directors or ministers. They receive us at the doors, praising us, mentioning details and every good thing even we have forgotten about our theatre. 'We don't do enough for you,' they say, 'this would not be like that; actors in Europe, in America, they have mansions, yachts, etc.' I forgot the number of rooms I entered with such reception and then left hoping for good results. We left our proposal, they sent us off saying, 'Such a timely project, you will be so successful.' After a while, we received this answer: 'As it does not conform to the principles of TRT, we cannot accept your *Keşanlı Ali* project.' I was going mad. [. . .] So many prime ministers, presidents had strongly applauded *Keşanlı Ali* in this country. [. . .] The good thing was, however, that the top management changed very quickly in TRT, and it was within that a year that a new management came. (2003: 158)

Keşanlı Ali was finally shot in Eskişehir at Anadolu University's newly opened film studios, while bureaucratic challenges concerning censorship and payments continued along the way.

In the 1980s, it was customary to initiate a dizi by finding the stars first, then building the project around them. The story of the phenomenal *Perihan Abla*, for instance, began when TRT television director Atalay Akçalı approached movie star Zeynep Aksu, offering to make a dizi 'for her'. Aksu declined the offer because it would take her away from her child, and proposed that her comedian friend Perran Kutman take her place (see Köşger 2018). Kutman, in turn, took the project to

IMAGE 5.1 Screenwriter Kandemir Konduk with legendary humorist Aziz Nesin and actors Müjdat Gezen and Perran Kutman, at a ceremony during the 1980s. Image courtesy of Tekin Deniz (https://twitter.com/-TekinDeniz_, last accessed on 8 June 2022).

her sketch-writer friend Kandemir Konduk, and they worked a whole summer on it, conjuring diverse characters ranging from shopkeepers to bank employees and housewives. Konduk remembers this process as 'mere fun'. This collaboration between sketch-writer and a comedian produced a script rich in puns, teasing, and laughter. They based the main character on the humorous personality of Perran Kutman herself, as an enthusiastic, energetic middle-class woman, and built a neighbourhood comedy around her. They proposed four episodes to TRT, and were asked for eight. The series ended up expanding to 74 episodes broadcast over a period of two years (Konduk 2014).

New Networks, New Projects

With the opening of private networks, pitching processes naturally moved in a commercial direction. Holding broadcasting monopoly, TRT had no competitors during the 1970s and 80s. The general pressure concerning dizi production was due to content and its political implications. TRT was also subject to a rising demand for wider broadcasting coverage and technical quality, giving priority to content that promoted 'national values' and 'reached out to the masses'. It was therefore during the1990s that TRT faced competition for the first time. The initial goal of the new private networks was to broadcast popular cultural forms, like belly dancing or Arabesk music, which TRT refused to 'deliver' because of its political proclivities. With private networks in play, priority for 'national content' in the pitching processes changed direction towards 'popular content' that could captivate the audiences. This is how the dizis starring singers, known as *şarkıcı* or *türkücü dizileri*, emerged when entrepreneurs like Osman Yağmurdereli, Güner Namlı, Faruk Turgut and Kaya Ererez founded their own companies and produced a round of profitable dizis. Yağmurdereli founded Yağmur Ajans; Güner Namlı, Ar Ajans; Faruk Turgut, Gold Film; and Kaya Ererez, Rüzgar Filmcilik. As a doyen of the Turkish film industry, Türker İnanoğlu's Erler Film played an important role in launching new television drama as well. With an eye towards international television hits, İnanoğlu offered, from the 1990s onwards, a series of dizis, which lasted many seasons; these included *Çiçek Taksi*, *Haşlama Taşlama* and *Yaseminname*, among others. Coming in İnanoğlu's footsteps, cinema directors like Yusuf Kurçenli and Atıf Yılmaz also proposed dizi projects that were produced by new networks; Kurçenli directed *Taşların Sırrı* for Star in 1992, while Atıf Yılmaz, *Tatlı Betüş* for Show TV in 1993.

In this era, screenwriters sometimes led the pitching of new projects. The longstanding neighbourhood dramedy *Mahallenin Muhtarları* began with Kandemir Konduk playing a leading role. As a pioneering screenwriter of the 1980s onwards, Konduk introduced many other

IMAGE 5.2 Writer Umur Bugay, who wrote the scripts of many dizis, including *Bizimkiler*. Image courtesy of *Gazetemag* (https://bit.ly/3xqyLUV, last accessed on 8 June 2022).

writers, such as Melek Gençoğlu and Ece Yörenç, who became important pens in the following decades. Playwrights also approached new networks with their own projects, mostly comedies. Playwright Umur Bugay opened his own firm, Bugay Yapım, in 1990, producing the long-lasting hit *Bizimkiler* (1987–2002). Leading theatrical actors also spearheaded occasional projects. In 1993, the production company Devekuşu, run by comedians Zeki Alasya and Metin Akpınar, pitched *Hastane* to the newly founded ATV, which broadcast the series for three years. Another comedian, Şevket Altuğ, pitched the ground-breaking *Süper Baba* from his company, Kare Film, which was also broadcast in 1993.

Networks also undertook in-house production. Responding to its new competition, TRT sponsored a number of series, but was overshadowed by Kanal 6, ATV and TGRT's dizi productions. Kanal 6 produced *Tetikçi Kemal*, starring the pop star İbrahim Tatlıses. ATV produced *Gurbetçiler,* a humorous family drama centring upon a German bride, written by cartoonist Murat Kürüz. TGRT began producing its own projects by the end of the 1990s, with *Komşular, Mutlugiller* and *Deli Balta,* among others.

The pitching process became more complicated in the 2000s, as mainstream networks consolidated their brands and became more established. During the 2000s, some directors with former TRT backgrounds began offering new projects to private networks. For instance, after she left TRT in 2001, director Tomris Giritlioğlu founded her own production company, SİS, where she developed landmark dizis like *Asi* (2007) and *Bu Kalp Seni Unutur mu?* (2009). Giritlioğlu acted as the showrunner of different projects as well, establishing her own creative team, that included writer Nilgün Öneş, and collaborating closely with producer Şükrü Avşar and network directors like İrfan Şahin and Kenan Tekdağ. The pitching process of *Hatırla Sevgili,* which was perhaps the most influential of Giritoğlu's projects, revealed this alliance:

> *Hatırla Sevgili* was born out of my inspiration for a Turkish movie. I told Nilgün [Öneş] to make a story on the coup period, based on three fathers. I just said, let one father be a judge in Yassıada Court, and the other an imprisoned member of the Democratic Party. [. . .] Nilgün is a writer whom I really appreciate and like. We both have a political past in our youth and that's why we were so excited about this project from the beginning. But the real hero of *Hatırla Sevgili* is Kenan Tekdağ. Back then he was the media group director of ATV and gave us tremendous support. If he did not help, one would not talk about *Hatırla Sevgili* today. (Giritlioğlu 2014)

My interviews with the leading producers and network directors of the dizi world quickly revealed difficulties in collecting the complete stories behind pitching processes.[6] Although on paper, the rights for

---

6 Interviews with Kerem Çatay, 8 March 2012; Türker İnanoğlu, 19 November 2012; Timur Savcı, 6 February 2014 / 21 April 2014 / 28 May 2014; İrfan Şahin, 11 February 2015; Lale Eren, 31 March 2014; Pelin Diştaş, 31 March 2014; Beşir Tatlı,

each dizi belong to its producer, the pitching process involves many more stakeholders, including network managers, directors and writers, who all play significant roles in creative processes.[7] In the final analysis, however, network directors wield the greatest power in deciding which projects will pass to the next stage.

The negotiation table may include writers, directors and producers, but the networks make the final decisions. Many of those network managers who constituted the first generation of these pitching mechanisms had come from TRT, which had always enjoyed the upper hand in negotiations over projects coming 'from outside'. Producer Mustafa Karahan expressed that this practice has greatly affected the ways contracts were written and proposed to producers, as networks run by former TRT managers continued to keep their 'stately attitude'. This granted a higher status to networks during negotiation processes as well as decisions in continuing a dizi on screen (Karahan 2018).

An anonymous writer explained to me how the mercenary aspects of this process worked during the 2000s: 'If you have an acquaintance from among the members of the board of a certain network, you make a deal with them. If they convince the decision makers, they get their commission.' Certainly, this old model does not represent today's pitching mechanisms. Producers and writers I consulted often described a model closer to the Western style of pitching. They underlined the importance of social network and a memory of former collaboration for launching new projects. Nevertheless, the first encounter with network managers is always an anxious process involving lengthy negotiations. Hollywood producer Jonathan Treisman reminds us how a

7 July 2017; Faruk Bayhan,14 February 2017; Elif Dağdeviren, 23 February 2013; Yılmaz Dağdeviren, 22 March 2013 / 3 April 2013; Armağan Cağlayan, 25 March 2013; Erdal Tuşunel, 28 March 2013; Nevin Ayaz, 11 June 2013; Cengiz Özdemir, 19 July 2013; Birol Güven, 13 February 2014.

7 Until the recent global rise of the dizi, writers and directors did not greatly benefit from copyrights.

screenwriter's 'acting skills' are as important as their 'writing skills': 'We all know that Hollywood is not a meritocracy where only the best scripts, books or ideas get made into films. You have to learn how to pitch effectively to get your projects purchased in this very competitive marketplace' (Treisman 2003, in Caldwell 2008: 81). To describe the Turkish ways, a screenwriter anonymously detailed the 'performance of power' in pitching:

> There are 'kings' and 'queens' among the network decision makers. They see many projects come and go, and of course develop a certain knowledge about what would garner high ratings. But over time they build an authoritarian attitude. They forget that if we don't write, or if producers do not produce, they would not have anything in their hands. They feel over-confident as the ultimate decision makers in pitching. There are many cases where they also make mistakes, and miss projects which later become very successful in other networks. This is a power play.

Accounts of pitching vary from project to project, and each of them reflects the historical momentum of a developing industry. A producer like Türker İnanoğlu, a doyen of the film industry, need not put great effort into pitching. As a close follower of the international film industries, he develops his projects based on research (İnanoğlu 2012). Among his most successful dizis one can cite *Yabancı Damat* (2004) and *Cennet Mahallesi* (2007), which treat time-tested themes of sympathy and nostalgia for ethnic communities. He is also known for his research of 'globally successful' themes which he adapted into series on taxi drivers (*Çiçek Taksi*, 1995; *Akasya Durağı*, 2008) and an episodic thriller using middle-class Turkish cultural codes (*Arka Sokaklar*, 2006) that still airs. İnanoğlu is a truly successful entrepreneur whose formulas always win, making his dizis run for several seasons.

Some projects happened at a certain 'conjuncture', without a real pitching process. *Çocuklar Duymasın* (2002), the phenomenally popular dizi which attained the highest ratings during the 2000s, is a case in point. Birol Güven, its writer and producer, recounted that the project began with the TGRT networks' instant need for domestic content within which to air commercials. 'They literally told us, give us space for commercials', Güven stated, 'without even asking about the content; their main concern was to air it on December 16, a certain deadline they had' (2014). In the case of *Kiralık Aşk*, the big hit of 2016, the project began as a tentative, modest production following the success of *Bir Kadın-Bir Erkek,* where Meriç Acemi and Müge Turalı had collaborated as writer and producer: 'Müge told me, "Let's do a romantic comedy." *Bir Kadın-Bir Erkek* had just finished, and she was ready for a new job. I received many offers to adapt Korean content, but I was not inspired to go in that direction. I thought I can do better.' Acemi prepared a few episodes, basing her story on a set of characters she had long nurtured in her mind. The network happened to need a summer project, so the dizi rapidly took shape, becoming a big success that summer and continued for a new season (Acemi 2016).

The story of Sema Ergenekon and Eylem Canpolat also reveals much about the pitching processes of the 2000s. Before they became the chief writers of hit dizis like *Gümüş* (2005), *Karadayı* (2012) and *Kara Para Aşk* (2014), both Ergenekon and Canpolat studied at Ankara University's Dramatic Writing Department. They were critical of the dizis that they watched and Ergenekon's husband, actor Uğur Arslan, encouraged and funded them to begin writing their own projects. They bravely came up with six different stories. With no former connection in the industry, they emailed their unsolicited projects at random to directors and producers. Their first response came from director and producer Ezel Akay, who warned them against naïvely sharing their stories on the internet. They also approached Mahinur Ergun, a pioneering dizi screenwriter, with these words: 'We are two house-based writers, and if unnoticed, we

IMAGE 5.3 Sema Ergenekon and Eylem Canpolat, in their office, working on *Siyah Beyaz Aşk*, 8 February 2017. Image courtesy of the author.

will stay as such forever. Show us a way out, so that we will be your greatest rival.' Ergun invited them to Istanbul and helped them send their scripts to diverse production companies. They were first approached by İrfan Şahin, then the director of Kanal D (Soydemir 2008).

Following the success of *Gümüş*, producer Kerem Çatay commissioned them to write a project for Kenan İmirzalıoğlu, a leading male star of the dizi world. *Karadayı* was produced through long deliberations over its theme and narrative structure. Their initial conception differed vastly from the final product, 'We wrote 10 different versions. Even if the production company said it was okay, we didn't feel like it. "This isn't good." we would say. We still don't like our first episode. Also the one which was broadcast. [. . .] We could have written better. But *Karadayı* has been the dizi in which the written version matched the filmed version the most closely' (Ergenekon and Canpolat 2015).[8]

Director Zeynep Günay-Tan recalls that in the early days, directors were rather kept out of the preliminary pitching process. She is grateful

8 Ergenekon and Eylem Canpolat began writing separately in 2020.

to Kanal D production for changing her perception of production. Before it was sold in 2018, the network instituted a new collaborative pitching formula:

> When I first entered this industry, the director had no relations with the network. They used to have a direct relationship with the producer. But later on, my perception of the network and production changed as I started working in D Production for *Öyle Bir Geçer Zaman ki* and *Kayıp*. Because it was an in-house production company, D Production had a wonderful working system. There was a great atmosphere in which Pelin [Diştaş], İrfan [Şahin], Lale [Eren] and I sat on the same table and had a brainstorming sessions including with the scriptwriter. Before I started working for D Production, my perception of any network was this: 'Oh! Here comes the inspector!' But when I sat down on the same table with them—and this was the brightest period of Kanal D—I entered an environment in which we could express and discuss our ideas equally with the CEO of the holding, head of dramas, and the network director. From then on, I started not to accept anything the other way around. I still don't. Because these names form the head of the creative process. The production company that respects me and the network director who sits with me like that is very worthy and this is how it should be. (2019)

The critically acclaimed *Fatmagül'ün Suçu Ne?* also emerged from a collaboration with the producer Kerem Çatay and Kanal D managers (Çatay 2014). The project was first proposed to Çatay by Barış Pirhasan, son of prominent author Vedat Türkali, who had written it as a film script. The details of the pitching negotiations even included the faith of the characters. The adaptation of the film script for the small screen needed extending and brought important decisions in order to make the story last longer (Diştaş 2014). 'This business has no mathematics,' Pelin Diştaş, long-time director of Kanal D stated, and underlined the centrality of the script in pitching processes: 'The preliminary preparations of dizis [. . .] can generally take a year or a year and a half. The most intense preparations are done while working on the script. Last year, when we started *Öyle Bir Geçer Zaman Ki*, the scripts for 17 episodes were ready. The longer you prepare, the stronger you proceed' (Vural 2011).

The pitching process often begins with a collaboration between writer and producer, as was the case for the globally successful *Muhteşem Yüzyıl*. This project reunited writer Meral Okay with producer Timur Savcı, the team that made the successful *Bir Bulut Olsam*, which introduced many young actors and musicians to the dizi world. Okay approached Savcı saying, 'Why don't we do the *Tudors* of the Ottoman Empire?' and thus launched this ground-breaking project (Savcı 2014). In the case of *Bir Çocuk Sevdim* (2011), it was the producer who came forward with the initial idea, proposing 'Let a 17-year-old girl get pregnant!' First, he approached writer Gaye Boralıoğlu, with whom he had collaborated in *Kapalıçarşı* (2009). After a series of meetings with the director and casting agent, they agreed that the story should centre on two families, one rich and the other middle class.

IMAGE 5.4 Writer Meral Okay (1959–2012) with producer Timur Savcı at a panel on *Muhteşem Yüzyıl* (2011–14). Image courtesy of Banu Savcı.

Director Cevdet Mercan proposed that the middle-class family come from Ankara. Then casting agent Renda Güner brought photographs and auditions began (Özer 2012).

The pitching of foreign format adaptations also requires delicate deliberations between networks and the producers. Diştaş related how, after a period of hesitation, the network finally agreed to a remake of *Umutsuz Ev Kadınları*, the Turkish version of *Desperate Housewives*: 'We don't like much adaptations. They never fit and they never seem Turkish. When Fatih Aksoy came with this idea a year ago, I asked him about the script. It was a very hard task. But the result has been so well. [. . .] The women, the events and the dialogues, they were all are from us' (Vural 2011).

Produced by Med Yapım in 2011, *Umutsuz Ev Kadınları* became a hit that completed 100 episodes, the only adaptation reaching such a number. The series was also sold in the Middle East at a much higher price than the original. How foreign content is adapted also has a unique Turkish style. The story and the script are approached as separate 'adaptation units'. In the beginning, a number of episodes are produced that closely follow the script. But in most cases, contracts are made in such a way that the story can take a new direction after a few episodes. This is why it becomes difficult to identify whose story it is; the inspiration may come from the original content, while the follow-up story can develop completely new threads. This was so with *Kuzey Güney* (2011).[9] The case of *Suskunlar* (2012), on the other hand, is more complex. Writer Pınar Bulut, asserts that their starting point had been the Turkish press, and states that it has more 'thematic' commonalities

---

9 The initial character set followed Irwin Shaw's novel *Rich Man, Poor Man*, originally written in 1969 and fully adapted to television as an American mini-series in 1976. The Turkish adaptation took off in very different directions after a series of episodes. But it was also criticized, giving no credit to the story, which at the end turned out to be a very different story. See Burhan Ayeri (2011) and *Gecce* (2011).

with Barry Levinson's 1996 movie *Sleepers* than with its own 'story'. Here as well, the follow-up narrative deviated from its original axe (see Deren 2016). Questions occasionally arise regarding a script's originality, as was the case in *Sıla,* where the story, which appeared under the producer's name, was said to have been plagiarized from Turkish author Dürsaliye Şahan. The issue was brought to court, which ruled in favour of Şahan (*Hürriyet* 2001). Nevertheless, the controversy paled next to *Sıla*'s pioneering success in the traditional Eastern drama genre. At times, a producer will extend a movie project into a dizi. Writer Berkun Oya first proposed *Son* as a feature film that later became an internationally acclaimed dizi. Producer Kerem Çatay believed that the story should be expanded for television, with a fixed number of episodes, and produced it as such (2014). *Son* was remade in various national industries.

As the number of projects and interested networks steadily increased from the 2000s, competition also intensified, generating anxiety among project designers over 'losing momentum'. For instance, during the launch of *Asmalı Konak*, Timur Savcı, who was then the production coordinator, remembers how he continued to work on the project even during his obligatory military service, handling his business during break times. 'This was a rather *alaturka* method,' he stated, 'but it was the only way I could manage' (2014). Both Savcı and producer Abdullah Oğuz also recall the urgency to assemble the team for *Asmalı Konak* within a very short time (Savcı 2014; Oğuz 2016).

There were not many male stars. I found Özcan Deniz [. . .]. I invited Mahinur Ergun, the only director I knew back then [. . .] Meral Okay provided the original story. Mahinur got back to us the next day. She did not like the script, and volunteered to write it herself, and proposed that her assistant Çağan Irmak direct the project. This would be the first-time Irmak had full credit as a director' (Savcı 2014).

Nilgün Öneş joined the *Asi* project team first as a script advisor while she was still writing *Hatırla Sevgili*: 'It was such a wonderful project, I accepted despite all my other load. I found myself first joining their writing meetings, then their story discussions, and finally revising the script' (Efendioğlu 2016; Öneş 2017a).

In the 2000s, dizi directors began to establish their own production companies, like Tomris Giritlioğlu's Sis, Gül Oğuz's Most or Serdar Akar's Adam. In such cases, their social networks would be the source of projects to come. The ground-breaking *Behzat Ç.* is a case in point. Producer Serdar Akar called writer Emrah Serbes to Macedonia, where Akar was working on another dizi, *Elveda Rumeli.* He asked him to adapt his novel *Behzat Ç.* into a film script. After more than a year of meetings, travel, and other projects, Akar turned *Behzat Ç.* into a hit television series (Serbes 2012).

In some cases, projects take a new turn from the way they had been imagined. The pitching of *Elveda Rumeli* has such a story. Writer Ali Can Yaraş and his producer friends approached ATV network for a rather high-budget project. The network approved it in principle, but to earn the funding they needed for the first project, they proposed meanwhile a lower-budget summer sitcom situated in an Ottoman context. The team of writers and producers then came up with the idea of adapting *Fiddler on the Roof*, situating the story in an Ottoman Macedonian village. The dizi used the family humour of the original story, but situated it in the context of ethnic conflict and local solidarity in the nineteenth-century Balkans. The sitcom evolving into period drama transcended the idea of a summer dizi, which continued to air for three seasons (Yaraş 2008). In some cases, persistent writers revise their turned-down proposals. The pitching of 'marginal' content, for instance, is often seen risky and producers or networks see such projects as time-consuming. Ethem Özışık, the writer of the hit dizi *Poyraz Karayel*, recalls how the first time he approached a producer, he was advised to 'go and find another job': 'He was right, but I did not give up, worked hard, and prepared *Poyraz Karayel* (2017). His project attracted attention, but most networks deemed it 'marginal' or 'experimental', content that 'aunties who shell the beans won't watch it' (2017). The dizi finally aired on Kanal D for three years to great acclaim with its 'emergent' content.

Networks have been the key to the decision makers in the pitching process. Many projects may initially be launched by the writers or producers who designed them, but the fate of a dizi—whether it will start and if it will continue—is determined by the will of the network. TRT has always held a special position among networks, not only with its budget and technical resources but also with its solid and widespread broadcasting capacity. Since its early years, 'to access TRT' had been an important goal for many project designers for all sorts of content, including dizis. Writer-director Burak Aksak, for instance, expressed his anxiety about approaching TRT, stating 'Everybody was telling us, "You need to have your own man within TRT."' When his company applied, they were first asked to produce a very low-budget sitcom for the month of Ramadan (Aksak 2015). TRT called them back for another similar dizi, which in time turned out to produce a cult of its own: *Leyla ile Mecnun* aired for three seasons on TRT, as an absurd comedy with political commentary, becoming one of the strongest social phenomena of the dizi industry.[10] In fact, one can also state that launching comedy projects always has its own dynamics, where the chemistry between the comedians and writers produce a 'play', with a creative producer taking the lead or the writer-directors pitching their own projects to networks. *Avrupa Yakası* (2004), *Leyla ile Mecnun* (2011) and *İşler Güçler* (2012) each emerged as creative projects which produced their own special fans. And finally, it is important to remember that as in other realms, producers always hunt for good

---

10 The cast of *Leyla ile Mecnun* toured universities around the country, bringing fans face to face with the cast at events that became performances of their own. I attended one of these events during the 3rd Antalya Television Awards on 21 April 2012 at Akdeniz University.

writers, assistant writers in successful productions are often noticed, and producers assign them new projects. The idea for the *Kara Sevda* project, for instance, had come from producer Kerem Çatay, and was offered to Özlem Yılmaz and Burcu Görgün-Toptaş, in their first chief writing position, after they had worked as assistant writers on many other projects (Görgün-Toptaş and Yılmaz 2016).

In the pace of dizi production of the 2010s, during which many networks changed hands, the direction of how dizi projects were designed also varied. Interpersonal courting and social networking undoubtedly continue to be important components of the pitching process. However, the mechanisms in which new projects are launched operate in a much more established industry, where players speak of experience and decision-making processes are more prudent.

CHAPTER 6

Constructing Stories and Their Sets

The World of Writers and Art Directors

How does the production process take place once the pitching is completed? Here, we delve into the creative and administrative components of this process. The process begins with the story, which is presented either in the form of a script treatment[1] or the scripts of the first few episodes. Then the art-related departments such as location, décor and costume come up as the more visible and tangible creative aspects of the production process. In tangent runs an organizational work for casting, but also for rapid assembling of directors, with their technical crew and assistants.

Dizi-production processes determine the essential features that characterize the genre. The length of the episodes shapes very much the interaction among the writing, shooting and viewing elements. Filming venues are constructed in newly emerging film plateaus or on real locations. Both the story and the artistic construction of the set aim to captivate a certain sense of 'realness' (*gerçekçilik*) displaying 'the natural' (*doğal*) in the use of language and lifestyle conveyed in the story. This chapter explores the two significant domains of the production process

---

1 A film treatment is the prose synopsis of the story that happens in a screenplay, which tells about the actions and dialogues, as a roadmap for producers and writers.

that render dizi projects more 'convincing' to their audiences. It focuses first on how the writers deal with the production process, looking at their different ways of imagining their stories and coping mainly with demands of producers, directors and actors. It then examines how art departments create from scratch the entire worlds in which dizi stories are situated.

The World of the Writers

The Loop of the 'Length Issue'

When I interviewed İrfan Şahin in 2015 about the state of the industry and the historical development of the dizi, he stressed that it is the free market which has shaped the structure of the genre. The transition to commercial television, Şahin argued, necessitated longer duration for the dizis, and the prevailing form had affected the style of storytelling (2015). Actress Hasibe Eren puts this in a humorous way, saying 'We practically produce dizis to be placed in-between the commercials' (2016). The length of dizi episodes affected the genre in different ways. First, the dizi industry developed a pace of its own, as the duration of each episode stretched from 60 to approximately 180 minutes. This structure allowed writers and directors to stretch their storytelling to almost match the rhythm of everyday life. Captivating the emotions expressed in real-time slowness, dizis were able to 'pass the feelings' (*duyguyu geçirmek*) to the viewers in a 'natural' way. The fact that most dizis used real locations enhanced this sense of natural slowness, and distinguished them from genres such as the soap. Second, the writing, production and viewing processes of the dizi industry merged into one another, with each component informing the others. Dizis begin their journey with a harsh test of the ratings. If they pass this hurdle, their scripts are written in parallel to shootings. A script delivered to the production team may be shot the week after, and be broadcast immediately, allowing the writers to gauge audience responses and work them into scripts. Dizis are also tied to the dynamics of the set milieu, where incidents or crises arise and may affect the writing process. For instance, actors may get decide to quit, daily politics sometimes provokes censorship, production costs may limit the shooting of certain scenes, and viewer demands on social media may worry the broadcasters. The dizi genre, perhaps more than its counterparts, is therefore produced and consumed in a more a tight-paced cyclical mode of production, which squeezes the creative writing, shooting and viewing practices into just a few weeks. This becomes an almost interactive process, which is also subject to rapid change. Writer Melih Özyılmaz describes his daily routine during production: 'Writing a dizi in Turkey isn't complete until the filming is over. If you have a dizi that is broadcasted on Wednesdays, you don't give it an ending until Saturday. You have to be ready for revisions at any moment. Putting an ending to a work is a matter of time and patience in the local dizi industry' (2018).

If a dizi survives, its writer faces another challenge. As director Onur Ünlü puts it, 'After the end of the second season, you fall into a cycle of repetition. The number of side stories needs to be increased. One begins consuming stories in hand' (2012). One can also add another factor to the interactive mode of production. Very often, behind-the-scenes stories accompany the broadcast episodes, a matter which heightens the viewers' experience and puts extra pressure on the writers.

Episodes' length differently impacts actors and writers. Writer Nihan Küçükural calls attention to what she calls 'dolgu diyalog', or filler dialogues, which help the writer to stretch out the duration of the episode and allow room for commercials. 'In American dramas,' she states, 'time perception is totally different; there is no room for unnecessary chit-chat. For us, this is the only way we can reach the demanded duration' (2011). A lead actor notes, 'Chit-chat dialogues are really boring for us as actors, but they also give us time to rest in-between more demanding scenes.' One viewer who complained about the extended length of dizi episodes notes that her friends insisted that she switch to foreign drama. 'There,' she said, 'you have to really watch; I don't have so much time to focus, so I remain in my dizi world.'

Commercial television's reliance on advertisements produces vulnerability for dizis. If the ratings for the first few episodes are low, the networks can easily break their contract, sometimes forcing writers to wrap up the story with a contrived end. Ironically, as the duration of the episodes increases, the industry and its social players find themselves in an absurd rush for a slowed-down storytelling to create more time for commercials. In other words, the fast-forward dizi industry owes its success to its slowly told stories. Özlem Yılmaz, one of the writers of *Karasevda* and *Kuzgun,* calls her process a marathon: 'You try to keep the audience's attention high throughout a marathon of four hours, which also includes the ads . . . When it comes to inspiration, it is never enough by itself" (Uras 2016). Writer Pınar Bulut looks at the length issue from a different angle. For writers, she argues, the key is knowing how long the dizi will last: 'We turn an idea for a story to a universe. This is a technical issue. Setting up the drama in a dizi is a technical thing. It is like a relationship arc. How one season is going to go? When it is a long journey, you need to keep it longer' (Bulut 2014).

Meriç Acemi points out that writers need to follow how the dizi is broadcast. She notes, 'We stay close to broadcasting, trying to "smell". I usually watch like a regular viewer, trying to understand what is likeable, which story works well' (Acemi 2016). Similarly, Ali Can Yaraş paid attention to the ups and downs of the broadcasting process while writing *Elveda Rumeli*:

> I knew it could be popular, but it didn't start well. The first five episodes went badly. Then they switched it to Mondays. Once they start changing dizis' day and hour, its end is obvious, it is straight away labelled to be discontinued. When the results of the fifth episode were bad, we went to ATV. We said, 'We do not insist on continuing for 13 episodes; we can close the set after

IMAGE 6.1 Writer Meriç Acemi at the Beykoz Kundura with the surviving set of typewriters from Sümerbank Shoe Factory, 16 October 2016. Image courtesy of the author.

the 19th episode and return.' The rating slightly improved while in Prime Time 2 on Monday. This time, they changed it to Prime Time 1 on the eighth episodes. But there, we got very good results. It came second in the first week, then it came first. Later on, things got settled. Its success increased and continued. It is important for a project to find the right day and time. (2008)

Writers' Backgrounds

Writers of the dizi world come from various professional and personal backgrounds. The early dizi content of the 1990s was mostly the work of comedy writers, some of whom also wrote and/or drew for cartoon magazines.[2] In the early 2000s, journalists and literary writers also

---

2 Among humour writers of the 1990s not discussed here, one can cite Resul Ertaş, Ömer Pınar and Yılmaz Erdoğan.

developed an interest in writing dizis as a new source of income.[3] These writers were pioneers in establishing their own circle of assistants. One of the earliest screenwriters, Kandemir Konduk, describes how he picked his team of mostly women writers:

> Our job was predominantly related to women, children, home, food and clothing. We used to have fun working as a team. Actually, most of them didn't know each other. It is totally a coincidence that they came together and started working. There were others who worked only for a short time and quit. Some had a different sense of humour, or couldn't stand the workload, or would not perform well enough . . . There were insurance agents, or those who brought their friends. I used to ask: 'Would this character talk like this?' If their style was not satisfying, we would ask them to bring a new friend, even though they would feel sorry. (2014)

Structured writing groups became more frequent in the 2000s, when the pace of the dizi industry began to increase. The leading writers of hit dizis, Ece Yörenç and Melek Gençoğlu began their careers working for Konduk, who wrote pioneering 'neighbourhood dizis' of the 1980s and 90s such as *Perihan Abla* and *Mahallenin Muhtarları*. Konduk remembers the circulation of his assistant writers during those years where the industry was not yet much structured (2014). Payments were irregular, and at times not made. Birol Güven and Gani Müjde developed their own teams from among humour writers. Meriç Acemi, now a leading writer, began acting and writing in those years, and continues to work with her own team. After graduating from the same department of dramaturgy, Sema Ergenekon and Eylem Canpolat began their careers by collaborating in the early 2000s, in time building

---

3 Writers such as Ayfer Tunç, Murat Gülsoy, Meral Okay and Gaye Boralıoğlu had relations with the press and publishing worlds, and produced works ranging from lyrics to novels in other literary circles as well.

their own team of writers to create many successful dizis in the 2010s. Kerem Deren and Pınar Bulut established Yazı Odası in 2014 and trained many writers. Some of the co-writers of the 2000s separated in the 2010s, writing alone or in partnership with their assistants or new co-writers.

In some cases, a whole group of story-finder, writer and director would work together during the production process, blurring the boundaries of cooperation. The collaboration of Selçuk Aydemir and Burak Aksak is a case in point. More recently, following their assistantships with the former generation of writers, Burcu Görgün-Toptaş and Özlem Yılmaz have taken the lead in writing their own hit dizis. 'Each scene requires the delivery of its sentiment through the depth of its dialogues,' states Murat Gülsoy, 'Those who establish the world, who write the treatments or the dialogues, may all be different people. Some, for instance, cannot give voice to the lower classes, others upper classes' (2012). Writing groups meet for brainstorming sessions, where new stories emerge, characters are drawn and research topics identified for upcoming episodes. 'Our meetings are rather tough,' Meriç Acemi maintains, 'I expect the most of their creativity there, this is where we examine the story in depth and reconstruct it' (2016).

Dizi-writing undoubtedly requires a literary and creative competence, but it is an interpersonal learning process as well. Over time, each writer builds a management strategy vis-à-vis producers, directors and actors, who directly affect their writing processes. Those who achieve harmony prefer to stay together, sharing risks. They often express how the 'team spirit' (*ekip ruhu*) is the key for successful projects, a state of mind, which all producers aim to establish.

'Let Us Not Fall Behind': In Pursuit of Foreign Consultants

During the 2000s, dizi writers became interested in learning about the success of foreign drama. Information platforms like *MediaCat*, *Alemetifarika* and *Digiturk* invited leading story consultant Robert

McKee, the author of *Story* (1997), known as the bible of script writing. Many writers joined the two-day lecture series McKee held in Istanbul in June 2007.[4] Some, like Meriç Acemi and Kerem Deren, attended McKee's intensive seminars in London as well. McKee's book was quickly translated and circulated, but many dizi writers also expressed reservations about adopting Western dramaturgical strategies that diverged from 'Turkish ways'. As one has confidently expressed, 'We often found our own formulas in our way, our dizi writing styles developed as we matured by experience.' Nevertheless, the desire to follow trends in global television industries endured and there were several conferences where different aspects of storytelling were discussed.[5] A panel organized at ITVF 2013, for instance, hosted discussions with BBC Academy's creative consultant Frank Ash on storytelling and the writer-actor John Pielmier on co-production. Likewise, at a roundtable event held at Boğaziçi University, American sitcom writers Sam Johnson and Julie Bean shared their Hollywood experiences and commented on the writing processes in their industries.[6]

---

4 Robert McKee came back in 2016 to give intensive seminars at the International Bosphorus Film Festival (17–18 November). I was among the attendees of the seminars, which were an interesting encounter between a 'Western script doctor' and the local players of the Turkish film industry. Many of us chatted in the breaks about how certain elements suggested by McKee would never work in the industry because of its speed and political context.

5 Kanal D hosted a Fresh MESH event on 17–18 January 2013; DISCOP was regularly organized during 2008–16; and ITVF, the Istanbul TV Forum and Fair, was launched in 2013—all aiming to enhance international encounters in the field, also organized panels and lectures given on site. For Fresh MESH, see *Hürriyet Daily News* (2013); for DISCOP see Clarke (2017); for ITVF see RTÜK (2013). Following the pandemic and its negative impact, there is a strong will to organize a global market in Istanbul, and interested parties, including the Ministry of Culture and Tourism, are taking professional guidance to organize one (TurkiyeTurizm 2021).

6 'Revisiting "Content": A Historical and Comparative Look at Screenwriting,' 26–28 November 2015, Boğaziçi University, Cultural Heritage Museum. Writer Sam Johnson, who also gave a lecture at the Mithat Alam Film Center of Boğaziçi

FIGURE 1 On the set of *Fatmagül'ün Suçu Ne?* on 12 November 2011 at the Zeytinburnu Municipality in Istanbul used as the site of Izmir Courthouse, because it had two palm trees at its entrance. This was the first dizi set I joined as an extra, invited by the Amargi feminist group. I stand with a poster in my hand waiting for the scene with feminist friends to be shot. Image courtesy of an anonymous feminist friend.

FIGURE 2 Visit of the foreign press to the set of *Paramparça* on 4 June 2015 in the Edib Efendi Yalısı, on the bank of the Bosphorus, organized as part of MIPCOM Country of Honour Year. In the picture are Nick Vivarelli (*Variety*), Mansha Daswani (*World Screen*), director Cevdet Mercan, Fahriye Şentürk (Global Agency) and me. Image courtesy of İpek Durkal.

FIGURE 3 The convoy of trailers along the Bosphorus for the shooting of *Karasevda* in Yeniköy, Istanbul, 29 April 2016. Image courtesy of the author.

FIGURE 4 The convoy of trailers along the Bosphorus for the shooting of *Hayat Şarkısı* in Yeniköy, Istanbul, 26 September 2016. Image courtesy of the author.

FIGURE 5 A shooting in Yeniköy, using the Bosphorus shores as a natural set, 29 September 2017. Image courtesy of the author.

FIGURE 6 Actress Tuba Büyüküstün waiting for a bicycle shoot for *Kara Para Aşk*. Küçük Bebek, Istanbul, 21 April 2014. Image courtesy of the author.

FIGURE 7 A garden shooting under rain for *Siyah Beyaz Aşk* at a 'remote set' in a villa in Polonezköy, a suburb of Istanbul, 22 May 2018. Image courtesy of the author.

FIGURE 8 Shooting of *Galip Derviş* in the balcony of a villa in Polonezköy, Istanbul, 3 May 2013. Sets in the suburbs are difficult to access, but they provide real, spacious and unhindered locations for shoots, where both cast and crew can fit. Image courtesy of the author.

FIGURE 9 Actors and crew getting ready for the shooting of the final scene at the set of *İstanbullu Gelin* at Beykoz Kundura, Istanbul, 29 May 2019. Image courtesy of the author.

FIGURE 10 Actress Elçin Sangu chatting with the crew in between shoots at Beykoz Kundura, Istanbul, 17 May 2016. Image courtesy of the author.

FIGURE 11 The set of *Arka Sokaklar* in Yıldız Kundura, a site used for action scenes, Beykoz Kundura, 30 October 2017. Image courtesy of the author.

FIGURE 12 A traditional street bazaar prepared for the shooting of *Ölene Kadar* in Beykoz Kundura, 6 February 2017. The set was temporarily constructed next to Demirane, the main restaurant of Beykoz Kundura. Image courtesy of the author.

FIGURE 13 Serpil Yıldırım, general manager of Beykoz Kundura, coordinating the arrival of a big boat to Kundura Port, for the shooting of *Vatanım Sensin*, 13 October 2017. Image courtesy of the author.

FIGURE 14 Timur Savcı, producer, and Serpil Yıldırım, general manager of Beykoz Kundura, at the 'Plato Adana Workshop', Adana, 22 April 2017. The workshop, supported by the city's Development Agency, aimed at promoting Adana as a promising city for the film industry. Image courtesy of the author.

FIGURE 15 TIMS&B Hadımköy Film Studio, built in 2015, on an area of 25,973 square metres in the industrial suburb of Istanbul. The studio includes replicas of historical buildings, including Topkapı Palace, constructed first for the filming of *Kösem*. A block of containers are piled up to obstruct the wind and provide a warmer environment for the shoots. 22 May 2016. Image courtesy of the author.

FIGURE 16 A dizi being shot in Yeniköy, Istanbul. The set is placed among the everyday crowd along the Bosphorus. 23 June 2014. Image courtesy of the author.

SETS IN REAL
NEIGHBOURHOODS

FIGURE 17 The team of the
director of photography preparing for a scene for *Çukur* in
Balat, 28 February 2019.
Image courtesy of the author.

FIGURE 18 Working overtime during night shoots at the set of *Çukur* in Balat, 28 February
2019. Image courtesy of the author.

FIGURE 19 Director of photography Aydın Sağıroğlu and actors Halit Ergenç and Okan Yalabık during the shooting of *Muhteşem Yüzyıl* in TEM Studios, Mahmutbey, Istanbul, 2011. Image Courtesy of Ayşe Özer.

FIGURE 20 Ensemble cast of *Çalıkuşu*, including Ebru Helvacıoğlu, Mehmet Özgür, Elif İskender, and the star Fahriye Evcen in the Reşat Paşa Konağı in Erenköy, Istanbul. Evcen visited the set that day to accompany the author to interview the other lead actor, Burak Özçivit, putting on his costume in the trailer at the back. 22 April 2014. Image courtesy of the author.

FIGURE 21 Extras acting as Crusaders in *Diriliş* taking a break at the Demirane restaurant of Beykoz Kundura, 7 June 2017. Image courtesy of the author.

FIGURE 22 Organizing the extras acting as janissaries (Ottoman professional soldiers) on the set of *Kösem* in the TIMS&B Hadımköy studios, constructed as a replica of Topkapı Palace and Ottoman neighbourhoods, 22 May 2016. Image courtesy of the author.

SET STATE OF MIND: WAITING FOR THE SHOOT

FIGURE 23 Crew members and actors Barış Arduç, Elçin Sangu and Esra Eron waiting for their scene at the set of *Kiralık Aşk* in Beykoz Kundura, 17 May 2016. Image courtesy of the author.

FIGURE 24 A break in the set of *Güldünya* in 2008, featuring director of photography Aydın Sağıroğlu, production coordinator Ayşe Özer and other crew members. Image courtesy of Ayşe Özer.

THE NARROW SPACE
OF INDOOR SETS

FIGURE 25 Technical crew discussing the positioning of the equipment for the next scene. The set of *Hayat Şarkısı* in Bebek, Istanbul, 8 June 2016. Image courtesy of the author.

FIGURE 26 Director of photography Aydın Sağıroğlu shows his shooting skills in the narrow living room of a real apartment used for *Bir Çocuk Sevdim*, Istanbul, 24 October 2011. Image courtesy of Ayşe Özer.

FIGURE 27 Typical outdoor set with UFO heater stand. In cold weather, cast and crew use heating patches during shots. Climbing onto rooftops is also common in order to find the best angle for shooting. Set of *Çukur* in Balat, 28 February 2019. Image courtesy of the author.

FIGURE 28 Director's position in front of the monitor, with a cup of Turkish tea, the indispensable drink of the sets. Set of *Çukur* in Balat, 28 February 2019. Image courtesy of the author.

FIGURE 29 Actors improvising for their own fun. Waiting for their next scene, the cast members of *Çukur* lined up with their chairs in the middle of the street in Balat, then moved up to the terrace of the building accross. 28 February 2019. Image courtesy of the author.

FIGURE 30 *Çukur* cast members Kubilay Aka, Cem Uslu, Erkan Kolçak Köstendil, Aras Bulut İynemli, Öner Erkan and Uğur Yıldıran on the terrace watching their colleague Berkay Ateş perform his scene. Their audience is the set crew, while they themselves form an audience for their actor friend. 28 February 2019. Image courtesy of the author.

FIGURE 31 A bird's-eye view from the Palais des Festivals, the space where MIPTV and MIP-COM takes place. The photograph is taken from the top floor of the Palais, overlooking the main garden and stands at the Riviera section. MIPCOM, Cannes, 16–19 October 2017. Image courtesy of the author.

FIGURE 32 Display of Turkish dizi content along the Riviera entrance of MIPCOM, Cannes, 17–20 October 2016. Image courtesy of the author.

FIGURE 33 Display of Turkish Dizis along the Croisette in Cannes, MIPTV, 13–16 April 2015. Image courtesy of the author.

FIGURE 34 The giant poster of actor Can Yaman on a wall overlooking the Croisette in Cannes, MIPCOM, 14–17 October 2019. Image courtesy of the author.

FIGURE 35 Promoting *Kuruluş: Osman* at the entrance of Carlton Hotel in Cannes, 13 October 2019. Image courtesy of the author.

FIGURE 36 Display of Turkish dizi content along the Croisette, by the entrance of the main hotels. MIPCOM, Cannes, 16–19 October 2017. Image courtesy of the author.

DISPLAY OF TURKISH CONTENT WITHIN THE PALAIS DES FESTIVALS

FIGURE 37 Display of Turkish dizi content on the walls and the information desk at the Palais des Festivals, MIPCOM, Cannes, 17–20 October 2016. Image courtesy of the author.

FIGURE 38 Display of Turkish dizi content on the walls at the Palais des Festivals, along the elevators, the busiest place of MIPCOM, Cannes, 16–19 October 2017. Image courtesy of the author.

FIGURE 39 Meeting with customers at the stand of Eccho Rights, MIPTV, 7–10 April 2014. Image courtesy of the author.

FIGURE 40 Meeting with customers at the stand of Global Agency, MIPTV, 4–8 April 2016. The scheduling of these meetings begin weeks before the MIP events. Image courtesy of the author.

TURKISH CONTENT FLAGS IN THE CAFETERIA

....

FIGURE 41 The main cafeteria of the Palais des Festivals in Cannes displaying flags of Turkish content at MIPTV, 4 April 2016. Image courtesy of the author.

FIGURE 42 The main cafeteria of the Palais des Festivals in Cannes displaying flags of Turkish content at MIPCOM, 17 October 2017. Image courtesy of the author.

FIGURE 43 Ahmet Ziyalar on the terrace of Inter Medya, which has operated as an informal hub for parties interested in Turkish content, including foreign press, researchers and other Turkish distributors. The Inter Medya terrace has been used as a site for communication, free food with socialization and relaxation. Cannes, 4 April 2016. Image courtesy of the author.

FIGURE 44 Preparations for the İTO stand at MIPCOM 2015 meant to host buyers and matchmaking meetings. Image courtesy of the author.

DIZI PROMOTIONS

FIGURE 45 Producer Timur Savcı, network director İrfan Şahin, actors Burak Özçivit and Fahriye Evcen with distributor of Turkish content İzzet Pinto, promoting *Çalıkuşu* at MIPCOM, Cannes, 10 October 2013. Image courtesy of Banu Savcı.

FIGURE 46 Producer Banu Akdeniz and Müge Akar, head of sales at ATV, at the special promotion panel for *Hercai* at MIPCOM, Cannes, 16 October 2019. Image courtesy of the author.

FIGURE 47 Timur Savcı, Burak Özçivit, Banu Savcı, Meryem Uzerli and Meltem Cumbul at the Hareem Al Sultan Exhibition in Dubai City Walk, 23 November 2016. Image Courtesy of Banu Savcı.

FIGURE 48 The TRT stand at DISCOP Istanbul, 6 March 2014, featuring Meltem Tümtürk Akyol, director of TRT programmes, sales and marketing. Launched in 2010, DISCOP Istanbul lasted five years before being discontinued in 2016. It targeted Turkey, Central Eastern Europe, Middle East and North Africa, and the former Soviet countries. Image courtesy of the author.

FIGURE 49 Traditional display of free television journals at the lower level of the Palais des Festivals during MIPCOM, Cannes, 17–20 October 2016. Image courtesy of the author.

FIGURE 50 The gala organized for watching live the last episode of *İçerde* (2016–17), Lütfi Kırdar Salonu, Istanbul, 19 June 2017. The event united the actors and fans for a special occasion, including a musical performance of the dizi's scores. Image courtesy of the author.

FIGURE 51 Actor Burak Özçivit and producer Mehmet Bozdağ, promoting *Kuruluş, Osman* at MIPCOM, Cannes, 15 October 2019. A medieval Ottoman tent decorated the garden of Ritz-Carlton Hotel for the occasion. Image courtesy of the author.

FIGURE 52 Virginia Mouseler, the CEO of THE WIT, presenting the trendy "Fresh TV" report at the Grand Auditorium of the Palais des Festivals. MIPCOM, Cannes, 19 October 2016. Image courtesy of the author.

FIGURE 53 Colourful booklets to captivate new customers, an important component of promotion costs. MIPTV, 4–8 April 2016. Image courtesy of the author.

FIGURE 54 Catherine Zeta-Jones at MIPCOM's Women in Global Entertainment Power Lunch, 16 October 2017. Her presence and speech was impressive for the general audience, while as Turkish guests we were amazed at her knowledge of Turkish cities, including Izmir. Image courtesy of the author.

FIGURE 55 The MIPTV panel to mark the world premiere of the remake of *Roots* from A&E Studios on 4 April 2016. The event which included executive producers Mark Wolper, son of the late David Wolper who produced the original 1977 series, and LeVar Burton, who played the original Kunta Kinte, turned out to be an oral history panel. The original series was broadcast on TRT, dubbed in Turkish, in 1981. Image courtesy of the author.

FIGURE 56 The MIPTV Medailles d'Honneur Dinner, where İrfan Şahin of Doğan Media received an award along with Cecile Frot-Coutaz (Fremantle-Media), Ricardo Scalamandre (Globo) and Ben Silverman (Electus), Cannes, 12 April 2015. The MIPTV Medailles d'Honneur were created in 2013, the 50th anniversary of MIPTV, rewarding industry leaders who have made an 'exceptional contribution' to the inter-national television business. Image courtesy of the author.

FIGURE 57 A scene from Inter Medya's fabulous parties that bring together members of the foreign press and Turkish participants alongside hosting leading stars who visit the event in that particular year. Parties are important components of promotion expenses in distribution practices, that lead to bonding and create common memories. Cannes, 6 October 2015. Image courtesy of the author.

FIGURE 58 Pelin Diştaş, Lale Eren and Özge Bağdatlıoğlu, hosting foreign journalists including Nick Vivarelli (*Variety*), Rhonda Richford (*Hollywood Reporter*) and Mansha Daswani (*World Screen*) in the headquarters of Kanal D, Istanbul, 5 June 2015. Image courtesy of the author.

FIGURE 59 Members of the MIPCOM Fair Executive Committee, Cannes, 5 October 2015. The group was hosted by the Istanbul Chamber of Commerce, including the vice president Dursun Topçu. Image Courtesy of the Istanbul Chamber of Commerce.

FIGURE 60 'Turkey: Home of "Dizi" Content' panel during the Country of Honour Year for Turkey, MIPCOM, Cannes, 6 October 2015, where the word 'dizi' was used for the first time in the global market. The panel was moderated by Ed Waller, editor of *C21*, and included Selin Arat, Halit Ergenç, Tuba Büyüküstün, Kerem Deren, Hilal Saral and the author. Image courtesy of the Istanbul Chamber of Commerce.

FIGURE 61 Aytekin Ataş, Toygar Işıklı and Burcu Yıldız at the 'Heroes of Content: Meet Turkish Film Musicians' panel in MIPCOM, 5 October 2015. Image courtesy of the author.

FIGURE 62 The author interviewing screenwriter Sam Johnson at Boğaziçi Univeristy, Mithat Alam Film Center, Istanbul, 27 November 2015. Image courtesy of the Mithat Alam Film Center.

FIGURE 63 Professor Christa Salamandra of the City University of New York, giving a lecture at Boğaziçi University on Syrian television and the reception of Turkish dizis in the Arab world, 14 June 2016. Image courtesy of the author.

FIGURE 64 Actress Canan Ergüder attending BLU TV's special gala for a new season of *Behzat Ç*, produced by Inter Medya, 24 July 2019. BLU TV is one of the first Turkish digital platforms.

FIGURE 65 A panel on Netflix, moderated by Pelin Diştaş, the director of Netflix's original content for Turkey, with participants Çağan Irmak, Ece Yörenç, Berkun Oya and Meriç Acemi. The event which was organized in Soho House Istanbul on 10 March 2020 for an exclusive audience was the last before Covid-19 pandemic restrictions were announced in Turkey.

FIGURE 66 Actors performing in hospital dizis took part in public service announcements for the Covid-19 pandemic. Timuçin Esen, who acted in *Hekimoğlu*, the Turkish adaptation of *House M.D.*, was among those informing the public about new rules of hygiene—cleaning door handles, armatures and bathroom sinks in this case. Broadcast on 17 March 2020. Image courtesy of the author.

These encounters helped familiarize dizi writers with global approaches to script writing. During my various interviews with writers, directors and producers, I observed that many use the term 'matematik' (mathematics) to describe the structuring of the stories (Küçükural 2011; Giritlioğlu 2013; Savcı 2014; Acemi 2016). Constructing a story involves imagining puzzles to be solved through different equations and with a matrix of characters and situations. The challenge of dizi writing is to deliver scripts under conditions of uncertainty, where the initial plots are subject to change or even termination. 'We work really hard,' states Özlem Yılmaz, 'Storytelling is mathematical in its essence, and it gets solved at the end' (Uras 2016).

What Turkish writers call 'mathematics' refers indeed to the issue of 'narrative structure'. In his seminal book *Story*, McKee emphasizes that a narrative progresses only through conflict and meaningful change. He offers a formula for storytelling on screen and suggests writers follow certain commandments in structuring their narratives. The story, he asserts, has to move from complication to complexity, converting expositions to ammunitions. Story design demands a grasp of the meaning, substance, limitations and inspiration of the story, whose structure encompasses a balance of rhythm, scenes, sequentiality and acts (McKee 1997). Similarly, creative consultant Frank Ash argues in his analysis of storytelling that it is a well-structured story that ensures the audience's attention: 'Without structure, stories are simply chaotic and will only confuse your audience. A story is a continuous development of characters, ideas and information. A good story will arouse, sustain and increase our anticipation about what will happen next and how it will turn out. Within 15 seconds, audiences decide to stay or leave . . . You have to intrigue them as soon as you can' (2013).

Ash calls this a 'firm thematic track', which is indeed the big challenge for dizi writers, given the need to alter storylines mid-process.

University, expressed his amazement at the detailed questions coming from young Turkish viewers on particular episodes of *How I Met Your Mother*.

However, as one dizi writer questioned, 'How can you structure your story if you don't know where it is going?' Some writers refer to the proverbial '*kervan yolda düzülür*' to best express the 'script-in-progress' phenomenon.[7] There are multiple facets to this endeavour, where writers face on-going demands from actors, directors and producers. Then there is happenstance as well—conflicts among actors, illnesses or accidents on set. *Leyla and Mecnun* is a case in point: the lead actress playing the protagonist Leyla experienced violence on the set that involved two actors from the ensemble cast. As they all left the project, writers wrapped up the story, killing off Leyla in a car accident, and casting two other women characters who owed their lives to her transplanted organs (Maro 2013). Writer Burak Aksak describes his experience:

> The change in cast affected us a lot. We had built a very nice team and we wish we could continue like this. But three of the leading roles were gone. On top of that, we had problems occurring every week. At times, actors had their personal problems and could not take part in an episode, or there were issues with payments. So, everything affects you while you are writing. (2015)[8]

Leyla and Mecnun was an absurd comedy from its very start. As its director Onur Ünlü notes: 'If you think about it, something very unusual happened to us, yet we survived it very well . . . We too really didn't know how the story would go. Another character could pop up in the next episode. Who knows, maybe İsmail Abi would fall in love' (2012). Because episodes are written in close proximity with the shooting, when an incident occurs, writers find themselves in the midst of a puzzle to be solved. Meriç Acemi offers her own account of the 'unexpected happenings:'

---

7 *Kervan yolda düzülür*, literally 'the caravan gets straightens on the road', refers to a situation where you make it up as you go along.

8 Director Onur Ünlü was diagnosed with cancer and operated on in October 2011 (*Hürriyet* 2011).

During such a long journey, you experience various things. Our leading actor had pneumonia. It happened all of a sudden while preparing the following episode! No leading actor! He does not exist! Solve it! I had left the former episode at such a point that there was no room to open a new story. We were all of course very sorry . . . Where would the character go? Accident, disappearance, hospital? This was an easy way. I proposed a flashback instead. The producer found it too extreme. We insisted. And I think at the end, it turned out to be a special episode. We also used technology, embedding a Skyped message from the actor, saying 'I am coming back like a lion,' a statement that referred to his specific health condition. Even if the sickness did not occur, I had in mind such a scene to use in the upcoming episodes, but it became necessary much earlier. (2016)

On Structuring the Dizi Stories

Coming from different backgrounds, dizi writers describe particular styles of developing and structuring their stories. 'Fikri bulmak'—'finding the idea'—is the key concept that many foreground. Finding the idea often means finding the conflict. Nilgün Öneş, who wrote hit period dramas in the 2000s, states, 'Writing is constructing a world, travelling and getting lost in it.' She relates: 'The most exciting moment of a work is certainly the moment when I come up with an idea. This moment comes after an already tough process of inquiry. It makes you feel, "Let me find a nice solution to this idea [conflict] and get started." Once the idea is there, the follow up stages moves faster' (2017b). In another interview, Öneş describes her journey of dizi writing:

First, there is something that triggers and aspires me to write a story. A piece of music, an event, a person, a situation, a memory . . . This is how the roof of the script begins to appear. Next come the characters. The pursuit of the depth of the characters enriches the main story. I begin writing the treatment, after past and future stories of the characters, their person-alities, their emotional domains are revealed . . . I think the treatment is the most important stage of the script. Everyone can write a dialogue following a well-organized treatment. But a bad treatment produces a chain of disasters. A treatment is almost like a map which gives you the opportunity to clear the structural mistakes. Fancy dialogues may sound nice, but they may be totally meaningless for that particular scene. You may see such weaknesses only at the stage of treatments. I write the treatment ten times from scratch before finalizing and making it public. Then comes the turn to write the dialogues . . . Writing a script is like walking on a tightrope. At any time, you can make a mistake and face the danger of being entranced by your own writing, not realizing it coming. The very charm of this job comes in fact from this uncertainty. Every script is another adventure and you never know how it will end. That's why a script is also like a poem; it is never complete. Nevertheless, you have to put an end to it. (2017a)

Melih Özyılmaz, who worked in the writing teams of many impor-tant projects, notes that characters guide him to find the conflicts of the story: 'To find the difficulty a character faces is to start creating his story . . . Once difficulties are found, the story reveals itself . . . The easiest part is to put it into writing, and in the dizi-writing business, to put the full stop is the hardest job' (2018). To keep postponing the writ-ing of the dizi finale is a huge challenge, Acemi confirms. The industry demands a 'long-lasting' performance from the writer: 'You may start with a story for ten episodes,' states Acemi, 'Then you come up with six to eight more, then the same thing once again . . . The script writer has a burden like this; 70 people get fed through this job! You have to make your story likeable and continuous. Dizi is a living world where there is always a problem. There is never only one ending' (2016).

Writer Gaye Boralıoğlu calls attention to another structural aspect of the dizi: the linearity of its narratives. 'For the Eastern mind,' Boralıoğlu states, 'narratives are predominantly linear, as opposed to Western fiction, where you can also start from the end . . . Our audience is flashback resistant, they don't like it' (2012). It is true that flashbacks have challenged a generation of audiences. Many of us grew up explaining to our elderly relatives, unfamiliar with such devices, how events unfold in movies and television dramas. Nevertheless, nowadays dizi writers seem to have found a solution to flashbacks: adding an extra scene to explain them. Likewise, to mark the passing of a few days, editors usually add some landscape scenes, moving from daylight to night.

Writer Nuran Evren Şit brings up another dimension of the dizi script: it being written as a component of a 'media text'. Trained in a cinema school, Şit stresses that the competence of the screenwriter lies in her ability to write a 'shootable story', using her audiovisual intelligence:

We have been trained by very precious directors, and graduated after writing scripts and shooting films under their guidance. I felt the benefit of this experience when I began working in the field. There, however, I faced many difficulties working with people who were not like them in terms of knowledge or experience . . . To be a scriptwriter, you need to have the ability of producing a shootable and audio-visually recordable story, and to have competence on script writing techniques, editing and dramaturgy. This can surface sometimes through instinct, or sometimes happen by experience, through trial and error . . . Give the same theme to ten different screenwriters and there will be ten different scripts. The script is the backbone of the film. It is the plan. It is the only guide and the only map when you are on set. That is why it should be strong like a rock; it is the script which carries the load of the whole film. (2011)

The Emergence of Dizis' Thematic Fields

Since the early 2000s, producers, project designers and writers have attempted to come up with themes that involve social and historical issues. Contemporary Turkish society has a complex fabric, embedding unsolved historical knots and issues of class and ethnicity that are often expressed in terms of relative deprivation (Başarır 2013). To Gaye Boralıoğlu, it is the 'Turkish value system' which determines the infrastructure of the dizi. 'This is why,' she notes, 'all our characters carry the motives of our value system, particularly on gender codes' (2012). Many dizis of the 2000s were indeed inspired by such social issues. Kerem Deren recalls the extensive research he made for his project *Uçurum* when he decided on the theme of human trafficking in Turkey: 'The story hit a wall at the network, which found it too hard to absorb. We were showing one-tenth of what we had found—the stories uncovered were so much more brutal. Television does not allow you to deliver such sensitive themes; we cannot always pursue an elaborate storytelling' (2014). Producer Gül Oğuz underlines the power of content in regard to thematic selection: 'Television is a very strong agent. If what I do will reach such large masses, I must have a message to deliver' (2007).

Writers have different views about dizi themes. For instance, Konduk opposes the 'Eastern drama' genre which focuses on the harsh conditions of gender and class in rural localities:

> You don't see people who get along well any more in television. They say, 'no one will watch if there is no intrigue' . . . Half of the country watches television. No one reads books, and opportunities to go to the theatre are few. In a country where the economy is very weak and the level of education very low, if you still numb people with these kinds of dizis just to make money, then I think maybe you don't love this country. (2012)

Acemi recalls how the notion that only 'tough themes worked' had changed over time, when softer but interesting genuine content emerged as new powerful dramedies. Her *Kiralık Aşk* offers a prime example, which began as a summer dizi to become a hit in 2016, a year in which many dizis were discontinued.[9] Acemi credits her success to a series of other preceding romantic comedies like *Limon Ağacı*, *Kiraz Mevsimi* and *Aşk Yeniden*: 'Ours was very successful, but there was considerable labour behind these other stories as well; they are the ones that paved our way' (2016).

Dizi writers proudly foreground the particularities of their own life stories as the main sources of their success. Many describe how their experience of certain communities, localities and social situations enriched their narrative repertoire. 'A writer writes up whatever she accumulated in life,' notes Nilgün Öneş:

> When my family was moving around in Anatolia, my dad decided that I should go to a boarding school in Istanbul. It was hard to separate from them, but life in a boarding school was a whole new experience . . . We collect and equip ourselves with information and emotions from the day we were born . . . After a while, we make our own choices based on these. What do we want to study? How do we perceive life? How do we see the country we live in? How sincere are we in our personal relation-ships? Differences are reflected in the work people do. When you are writing, you look inwards most of the time, and you change as you write. That's why writing is a therapeutic activity for me. As you change, what you write also changes. All emo-tions and situations like deep love, honest friendship, family love, ethics, hatred, sex and violence are human. Your priorities and reservoir of experience define your choices. (2017a)

Birol Güven, who wrote the pioneering dizi *Çocuklar Duymasın*, states that he wanted to break the habit of writing about the rich: 'I wrote of uninteresting ordinary life, which everybody else was writing as well.

---

9 *Kiralık Aşk* was the only dizi mentioned in the Eurodata survey at MIPTV in 2016.

Nevertheless, mine did not have the kind of charm that existed only in films. Viewers established an amazing empathy, they saw their own ordinariness reflected on television.' Güven names his genre *hüzünlü komedi* (melo-comedy), which he thinks characterizes the Turkish dizi. 'I place humour on side characters, keeping the main ones in the drama,' he notes, 'I catch the audience with humour, I take them by surprise carrying them to a dramatic situation, with melodramatic music in the background. This has no counterpart, it works well here because it is rooted in our Yeşilçam movies of the 1970s and 80s' (2014).[10] Actress Derya Alabora comments on the appeal of the class issue in dizi themes: 'Envied lives, or impossible loves, which do not at all correspond to real life, become objects of desire in a context where real life offers just the opposite' (2012).

Like many other writers, Konduk relates his selection of themes to his personal background, stating sarcastically: '*Ben de köylüyüm ama Kadıköylüyüm*' (I am also a peasant, but one from [urban] Kadıköy).[11] Referring to his Istanbul upbringing, he notes that he would sound awkward if he tried to write a rural dizi. He criticizes some urban writers who 'end up situating Nişantaşı's urban dialogue within a village context' (2012).[12]

Murat Gülsoy highlights the 'neighbourhood' as central to many dizis' content: 'Because we have a neighbourhood movie genre, our dizis follow the theme of family and neighbourhood. We are somehow xenophobic, [so] having enclosed social units looks safer' (2012). Gülsoy also emphasizes the challenge of finding 'interesting themes' under the confines of RTÜK, which strongly regulates primetime programming:

---

10 Güven later established his own production company MinT, the abbreviation of 'Made in Turkey.'

11 *Köy* means village in Turkish. But Kadıköy is a quintessentially urban neighbourhood on Istanbul's Asian side.

12 Nişantaşı is known as one of the fanciest neighbourhoods of Istanbul.

The red lines on sexuality, politics and many other conjectural issues push writers towards self-censorship. Then dizis' thematic fields narrow down. Conservatism emerges by itself, centring upon hospitals, police stations or prisons, giving more power to lead actors than the writers. There is usually no room left to construct dramatic characters, and it becomes more and more difficult to write as you wish. (2012)

Director Zeynep Günay-Tan expresses caution on the balance between the power of the story and its stars: 'To me the star of a dizi is always its story—everybody should serve it. This is the only time we can all shine . . . To me, calling a dizi after its acting stars is a scary phenomenon' (2019).

On the Writers' State of Mind and Style

Writers' styles vary; each tries to find their own personal path to survive their creative anxieties and meet strict deadlines (Aksak 2015). The pace of the Turkish dizi industry creates a mode of writing which puts the writers in a complicated position vis-à-vis actors and directors. Because many dizis are written at the same time they are filmed, writing processes can easily get affected by the set environment. In the last few years, I have seen some dizis collapsing with the sudden rising fame of the actors. The writers' relation to directors and actors greatly affects the content.

The phases of finding the story and writing the script have not been structurally segregated in the dizi industry. Hence, a single writer often produces both story and screenplay, with help from assistants or co-writers. Ali Can Yaraş confesses that he prefers chasing a story to writing it: 'I don't like writing much. Actually, I don't like it at all. If I didn't make this much money, I would not do it. I would not even write my name on a paper. I like to structure a story. I like to create a story in my mind' (2008). Writers also point out the physical demands of writing long scripts under pressure. Acemi describes the challenge of balancing creativity with labour:

My mind works 24 hours . . . When it is a holiday, the actors and actresses get a break, but not the scriptwriter. We too need a holiday. The producers ask for stocks. With your accrued knowledge, you can work as a doctor for 25 years, but as a scriptwriter you cannot. When imagining a world, you consume your own storage. We need to see and watch new things to refresh. (2016)

Melih Özyılmaz finds the dizi-writing process draining, taking the writer away from his family and private life: 'Life doesn't consist of just writing dizi for television. I enjoy writing, but not dizi writing. I wrote about 54 episodes of a dizi, and I spent a lot of time on one that wasn't broadcast. After writing 250 episodes, I do not want to write any more, I want to write a movie' (2018). To Eylem Canpolat, what the dizi writer achieves can be best described as a 'miracle': 'We wrote almost a movie-length episode on a weekly basis, for two to three seasons. This pace does not exist anywhere else, it is surreal and miraculous' (2015). The sheer volume of dizi writing is indeed remarkable. Emrah Serbes quips, 'You could pave the road from here to Ankara with all the pages I wrote' (2012). Likewise, Selçuk Aydemir remembers how he once delivered 600 pages in two weeks (2014). And finally, Birol Güven recalls how McKee was surprised at the number of episodes he had so far written: 'He asked me, "How many episodes did you write?" and I said, "1,500!" He had written 1,000. In fact, I had written the best-rated episode of *Çocuklar Duymasın* in three hours' (Güven 2014). Yaraş stresses how the pace and haste of dizi writing affect the writer's approach to the flow of stories and their characters:

At the beginning, like everybody else, you get to know the story and its characters. But then comes a certain point where, because you think and concentrate much more than anybody else, you begin moving on your own, just like while driving. At that point, a new process begins. You are competent and you are the master of the process. But after passing a certain number of episodes, you begin looking at it very much from within. Now you are inside the car and you cannot see the outside. I mean you cannot see the road as clearly as you did in the beginning. You even become blind to your own mistakes. You see something, but now what you see must be cross-examined by others. (2008)

Dizi industry has gone a long way to establish its writing mechanisms. Since the 1990s, when TRT's monopoly came to an end, collaboration models have varied. In the very beginning, writers, actors and producers developed common projects for networks. When the number of dizis increased, producers and network managers developed a more powerful stance vis-à-vis the writers. Following the models of established industries like Hollywood, some established writing rooms under the roof of their companies. However, many realized very soon how the dynamics of creative processes changed depending on the diverse working styles of writers. Today's dizi writers work mostly in private. Some have established their own writers' studios; some work with their team in their own homes; others prefer public spaces to deliver the best of their storytelling.

The World of the Art Department

Filming on Location: The Affective Component of Dizi Shooting

Shooting on actual location is an important component of filmmaking, enhancing a work's sense of realism. The authenticity of place contributes greatly to visual storytelling; many movies and television dramas owe their power to the picturesque places in which they were shot.[13] In film industries where studios are rare and expensive, shooting on location becomes a necessity producers have to abide by. In the old days of

---

13 For some British drama, for instance, see *Telegraph* (2018); Aryana Azari (2019). For *Muhteşem Yüzyıl* scenes shot in Topkapı Palace, see Mahmet Günsür (2012).

Yeşilçam, for instance, movies could only be shot in actual locations.[14] As the national broadcaster, TRT benefited greatly from state sponsorship during the 1970s and 80s, and used historical sites like the Sait Halim Paşa Yalısı or Topkapı Palace as the filming locations for TRT dizis like *Aşk-ı Memnu* and *4. Murat*. When the dizi industry began to take shape in the 1990s, many dizis were filmed in real locations as well, mostly because there were not many studios. For producers and directors, finding the 'right location' was the key to a project's success. Although many directors prefer shooting on location for the sake of 'realism', in the case of the Turkish dizi, the issue of location and place has further implications. To begin with, place in Turkish dizis come with a baggage of 'affect'.[15] The affective dimension is closely related to the concepts of *mekan* (place) and *yerellik* (localness), both terms having further emotional associations.[16] *Hemşehrilik*, sharing the same hometown, stands at the centre of one's identity in Turkey, as much as gender, class or national identity, often embedding ethnic and religious connotations.[17] For many Turkish viewers, the towns where the dizis

---

14 The images of these films offer invaluable ethnographic data for old Istanbul or many other towns and villages of Turkey. In the rapidly changing urban structure of Istanbul, dizis of a decade ago also earned such documentary value. *Fatmagül'ün Suçu Ne?*, for instance, includes scenes from Taksim Square, İstiklal Caddesi and İnci Pastanesi, which all changed substantially since the early 2010s.

15 For a review of the 'affective turn' and its impact on the research of sense of belonging and embodiment, see Patricia Ticineto Clough and Jean Halley (2007). For an example of the affective dimension of place, see Halide Velioğlu (2011). Affect studies approach is also extremely valuable for the analysis of audience reception, in terms of the embodiment of narratives told on screen.

16 Turkish language makes a difference between *yer* and *mekan* in reference to the concept of place. *Yer* usually refers to geographical location, while the term *mekan* embeds emotional meaning assigned to a particular place. Both location scouts and art directors use the term *mekan*, referring to different set venues.

17 See Ayşe Güneş-Ayata (1990); Harald Schüler, Yilmaz Tonbul and Tanil Bora (1999); Aynur Köse (2008); Benoit Fliche (2005).

are filmed evoke an ethnographic knowledge as well, accompanied by either a personal memory or a touristic curiosity.

The 1990s, when the dizi industry began to flourish, were also the years where debates over identity, place and memory surfaced in Turkey. This brought a novel gaze and a sense of 'place awareness', and assigned new meanings to old places.[18] By the 2000s, Istanbul in particular had become a top tourist destination; it joined many other locations in rediscovering long-disguised historical and geographical assets.[19] The launch of many dizis coincided with the gentrification of these cities and neighbourhoods, contributing to their revival and at times to their reconstruction.[20] One of the earlier example is *Perihan Abla* (1986), which greatly added to the recognition of the small Bosphorus neighbourhood of Kuzguncuk, helping it transform into a trendy hub for artists and intellectuals (Dursun and Atmaca Can 2019). *Süperbaba* (1993) followed with its impact on Çengelköy, another Bosphorus neighbourhood, and *İkinci Bahar* (1998) revived and reinvented the long-forgotten neighbourhood of Samatya. While these dizis benefited from the historical and cultural texture of these old neighbourhoods, *Bizimkiler* based itself upon another type of authenticity: the inescapable realism of the '*apartman*', the ultimate building unit of Turkish urbanization (see Gürel 2009). If one can talk about the assertion of realism in filming on location, *Bizimkiler* is indeed the prime instance. Filmed on location in two ordinary apartment buildings in the Kozatağı neighbourhood, *Bizimkiler* brilliantly captured the

---

18 See Çağlar Keyder (2000); Uğur Tanyeli (2005); Deniz Göktürk, Levent Soysal and İpek Türeli (2010). For some case studies, see S. Durmaz (2015); Özlem Sandıkcı (2015); Birol Güven (2011); Sezgi Durgun (2019).

19 For the anxieties of changing Turkey's image and the branding of Istanbul, see Arzu Öztürkmen (2005); Ülke Uysal (2013).

20 İpek Çelik Rappas and Sezen Kayhan (2018) thoroughly explore this era of reconstructing of Istanbul's neighbourhoods as a dialogue between the filming location and its urban space.

performance of quotidian life, captivating audiences for 13 years, from 1989 to 2002.

The *mahalle*, the neighbourhood, has in fact been at the centre of traditional Turkish traditional theatre. In the words of Yavuz Pekman, the *mahalle* is one of the 'the lead actors' in Turkish drama.[21] Both Karagöz and Ortaoyunu revolve around characters interacting in a neighbourhood environment. *Mahalle* opens up a performance platform linking characters from different social backgrounds, creating a certain situational comedy and uniting them in hard times. The warmth of communal space is often illustrated through the marketplace with its shopkeepers (*esnaf*) and residents from various walks of life.

Dizis were also set in provincial towns, centring on extended families living with their servants in big mansions.[22] *Asmalı Konak* (2002) was filmed in Cappadocia, making its original mansion one of the earliest dizi domestic tourism sites. *Yabancı Damat* (2004) was set and partially filmed in Antep, while *Sıla* (2006) brought a new visibility to Mardin-Midyat. In Istanbul, such big family stories unfolded in *yalıs* along the Bosphorus, like *Gümüş* (2005) filmed in Abud Efendi Yalısı, *Aşk-ı Memnu* (2008) in the Koç family's mansion, and *Paramparça* (2014) in Edip Efendi Yalısı. In all of these, family warmth was often transmitted through scenes taking place in the kitchen and the dining room. There is no film genre, one may argue, where food and its multiple modes of preparation and consumption take such a central place as in the dizi world.

The affect dimension of the dizis appealed to the collective memory of domestic audiences for sure, but it also touched the cultural affinities shared with the Balkans and the wider MENA region. This was partly

---

21 For a thorough analysis of the *mahalle*, see Hülya Uğur Tanrıöver (2002); Amy Mills (2007). On the literature of *mahalle*, see Yavuz Pekman (2007); Celil Civan (2013); Servet Dönmez (2019).

22 See Ayşe Öncü (2011); Murat Küçük (2013); Merve Tacirli (2017); Emine Köseoğlu and Denize Önder (2011).

related to the ethnographic curiosity on the part of neighbouring countries that had been distanced from Turkey after gaining independence from the Ottoman Empire. It is not very surprising that the first boom of Turkish dizis began in Greece with *Yabancı Damat* and in the Arab world with *Gümüş*. What was striking to international distributors from these regions was the authenticity of the sites and the modern and secular Turkish lifestyles depicted in them. The texture of the landscape and the cultural display of food and family soon captivated Latin American and Muslim Asian audiences. As one distributor says, 'The reception of our Mediterranean spirit illustrated the migration paths of the past and the present.'[23] The reference here includes the Middle Eastern migration to the Americas[24] in the nineteenth century as well as the flow of migrant workers to Europe. In this regard, dizis offered an ethnographic gaze to foreign audiences that had either entrenched prejudices or no former knowledge about Turkey. This was also true for the domestic realm, as dizis provided Turkish viewers from different classes and cultural backgrounds with a visual access to sites and lifestyles that they would not otherwise experience.

Last but not least, one should mention the cast and crew's bonding with—or hatred for—the place in which they work for weeks, months or years. In cases where the set is established in a given neighbourhood, actors and set employees develop a certain sense of attachment to the location. One of the actors of *Bir Bulut Olsam*, a hit dizi which used a historical *konak* in Midyat-Mardin, expressed resentment when he saw the same site being used for a meagre production with a modest story:

---

23 Many people in the industry are careful to talk about Turkey's imperial past in European encounters, as it may evoke tensions, and they choose to remain anonymous. Further research requires more in-depth analysis of the affective dimensions of international sales, where political concerns may often contradict with market demands.

24 See Christina Civantos (2006); Ignacio Klich and Jeffrey Lesser (1996); Cecilia Baeza (2014).

'It was such a unique site, and we had passed days and nights there over such a long time; this *konak* occupies a precious place in my memory. It hurts me now to see it being used for not-so-good projects.' During the filming of *Çukur*, actor Erkan Kolçak Köstendil expressed a similar sentiment. He noted how the long experience in Balat assimilated the entire cast and crew to the neighbourhood: 'You end up becoming a resident of the neighbourhood yourself. All of us come and mingle with this whole environment' (2019). For art directors who are involved in choosing the locations and designing the sets, the hardest moment comes when the dizi ends: 'However professional you are,' Nilgün Nalçacı says, 'you feel a sense of resentment in the aftermath of a long-lasting work. All the décor and props you prepared with such scrutiny and care, spending long hours, get demolished in one day. I usually do not go to see this' (Dağkıran 2016: 203–04).

'Passing the Feeling': Art Directors' Setting the Sets

Choosing a location is the first step to actually start the production process. This can be a real neighbourhood, a building or a reconstruction in the studio space. As philosopher Edward Casey (1997) argues, 'to be placed is *to be*,' and a dizi takes its first visual shape by determining the sites of its shootings. Besides their on-location shooting, many dizis also benefited in the initial years from the limited number of small studios in Istanbul. The TEM and Plato Film studios were indoor filming sites for music clips and commercials of the 2000s, and they were also used for television series. Beginning in the 2010s, new venues for film shooting emerged, including Beykoz Kundura, TIMS, MinT and Riva studios in Istanbul, and Sekapark in Kocaeli. Today, shooting practices are somewhat dispersed, and there is a wide array of places where dizi sets may spring up. Many dizis begin with a permanent site, either on location or in one of these new film studios. In many cases, apartments, houses or luxurious mansions are rented. Some dizis are set in neighbourhoods or locations with a particular texture marked by their class or ethnic identity.[25] For Istanbul, the shores of the Bosphorus and certain neighbourhoods regularly represent specific classes.[26]

Sets constructed outside of Istanbul have also been used as historical sites, including different dizis filmed in Adana, Ankara, Antep, Diyarbakır, Mardin and Nevşehir. Dizis that showcased natural beauty were located in Bodrum, Çeşme, or in the Cappadocia and Black Sea regions. Shootings also take place in nearby towns and cities in and out of Turkey.[27] Be it on a fixed spot or mobile, all shootings begin with the touch of the *sanat*, the art department. Whatever the dizi's period, milieu or mood, the art department immerses itself in architectural designs, inner decorations, dealing with the organization and control of the props.

In my interviews with art directors and their teams, I observed that many expressed their main concern as *duyguyu geçirmek*, 'passing the feeling'. This concept goes a bit further than conveying the feel of a time and place. It relates more to the notion of convincing the viewer to the enactment of emotions. As much as the script, art directors thought, it

---

25 The concept of 'particular texture' concerns mostly regional and historical values of towns or neighbourhoods, and also associates with particular classes. In Istanbul, for instance, one can cite Balat, Samatya, Çengelköy, Reşitpaşa, Büyükdere and Kuzguncuk as neighbourhoods with their own characteristics. Lately, modern villas are set in the suburbs of Istanbul like Zekeriyaköy, Çekmeköy, Polonezköy and Cumhuriyet köyü.

26 To give an example, Balat is often used to represent lower-income settlements. Traditional Bosphorus neighbourhoods like Kuzguncuk and Çengelköy were used as middle-class locations in the 1990s. Nowadays, *yalıs* along the Bosphorus, the Nişantaşı neighbourhood along with Maslak residences or suburban villas are used as sites of the upper classes.

27 In their initial episodes, *Fatmagül'ün Suçu Ne?* and *Sultan* began in Ildırı and Diyarbakır respectively, and then moved to Istanbul. Similarly, *Asmalı Konak* began in New York and moved to Cappadocia, while *Kara Para Aşk* and *Kiralık Aşk* had their opening episodes in Rome and *Gecenin Kraliçesi* in Grasse in the French Riviera.

would be the aesthetic quality that would 'pass' the sense of authenticity, and the feelings situated within it. The set's location and décor would therefore form essential components for creating a 'good-quality dizi'. Setting delivers the first visual impact, and many dizi producers take much time to construct an ideal physical context for their first episode, in order to hook their audiences for the weeks to come. As the dizi production and supply increased, the role of the art departments gained more importance in creating the image to publicize a new dizi. Before a dizi begins, comments in the press and social media begin to discuss, alongside the casting, its location, scope and the material investment made for it.

The development of art departments in the dizi industry is surprisingly new, and many of today's art directors learned on the job. Many emphasize their initial challenges in comparison with 'Western standards'; they note how their field has not yet been 'professionalized', and instead operates on the basis of 'individual effort'. Art director Deniz Göktürk-Kobanbay states that he greatly benefited from working in co-productions in which he was able 'to learn about job descriptions, division of labour and management'. He says 'such issues were solved years ago there', referring to the Western world (2017). He underscores the virtue of a longue-durée assistantship which helps attain in-depth experience on the path to art directorship. Mustafa Ziya Ülkenciler and Hakan Yarkın, however, emphasize the indispensability of formal training. As art directors who built long-lasting permanent sets for television industry, they both stress how skills in drawing techniques are fundamental for the profession (Ülkenciler 2019a, Göktürk–Kobanbay 2017). Ülkenciler, known as one of the doyens of the field, summarizes the key points of his profession as 'research' and 'expertise', emphasizing how art directorship requires a subtle combination of artistry and craftsmanship (2019a): 'Anybody who claims to be an art director needs to have a competence in all art forms, particularly in photography, sculpture and graphic . . . Nobody should aspire for art directorship if he lacks the skills to draw' (*Milliyet* 2015). All of these points may sound obvious for established film industries but they need to be spelled out continually in the dizi world.

As a former set photographer who worked closely with prominent Turkish film directors, Ülkenciler has observed the changes in film-industry art directing from Yeşilçam to the dizi industry.[28] Having designed important sets since the mid-2000s—including for hit series like *Avrupa Yakası*, *Karadayı* and *Diriliş*—he criticizes the dizi world in terms of budget distribution during the production processes. Looking at his profession from a historical perspective, he notes, 'Décor was an important component of early dizi making. Nowadays, producers prefer to use ready-made places because they are less costly, but often there occurs a discrepancy between the theme and the material culture one sees in such ready-made places' (2019a). He also feels that this may discourage one from working on dizi sets, not only because art-department budgets are constantly being cut but also because the audience does not seem to care for the 'artistic details' that art directors work so hard to find and apply (*Milliyet* 2015). Also, poorly trained assistants are used to meet the demands of the hectic pace of the industry. Given the shortage of qualified people, upward mobility from assistantship to directorship is not uncommon. As one art director put it: 'The boy I hired to carry stuff in the sets now moved to another project as an art director. They also use our names, saying that they learned the job from us.'

Constructing an Imagined World:
The Artistry and Craftsmanship of Art Directors

What Ülkenciler calls 'artistic details' are in fact the outcome of long research processes conducted by the production team. Research for period and historical dramas is compulsory, and preparations for their

---

28 Among others, Ülkenciler worked with directors Atıf Yılmaz, Yavuz Turgul, Ömer Kavur, Derviş Zaim, Ferzan Özpetek, Tunç Okan and Sinan Çetin.

set designs often begin even before casting is completed. Production researchers face a number of challenges. Access to visual imagery for the Ottoman or Republican era was not easy until the 2000s. Visual documents belonging to state and military archives involved time-consuming bureaucracy, and private archives were scarce. In the 2000s, the search for historical visuals coincided with the booming of digital visual data in social media, a development which called attention to the depiction of historical detail. Dizis of the 2000s and onwards began to invest more in research-based reconstructions on new sets. *Hanımın Çiftliği* (2009), *Öyle Bir Geçer Zaman ki* (2010), *Keşanlı Ali Destanı* (2011), *Muhteşem Yüzyıl* (2011), *Karadayı* (2012) and *Vatanım Sensin* (2016) were historical and period dramas for which art directors constructed whole new worlds. Some of these projects used the then-empty grounds of Beykoz Kundura while others were constructed in other towns. As an early example, one can cite the farmhouse in *Hanımın Çiftliği*, which was built by 50–100 construction workers in 33 days, on a 10,000-square-metre area (Yılmaz 2009).[29] *Muhteşem Yüzyıl* began in TEM film studios, then moved to TIMS Hadımköy studio where a replica of the Topkapı Palace was built. *Öyle Bir Geçer Zaman ki* is also a case in point. This dizi set was first established in the Zeyrek neighbourhood, situated in Balat, in the old city part of Istanbul. The art directors restored nine houses and painted 51 others, altering the window frames from plastic back to wood. Fatih Municipality also supported the project by restoring streets with old-style Albanian stones (Gence 2011).

Nevertheless, the everyday life of the neighbourhood continuously interfered with the shooting. The passing traffic, all kinds of costermongers, water distributors and garbage-collection vehicles also clashed with the period being depicted, a situation which began to affect

---

29 The farmhouse was reused for the dizi *Dila Hanım* in 2012 but burned down in 2014. A similar project was built for *Bir Zamanlar Çukurova*, TIMS & B production invested in the construction of a big farmhouse in the Karaahmetli village of Adana, using a team of 450 people in eight months (DiziSeti.tv 2019).

production efficiency.[30] Director Zeynep Günay-Tan recalls the decision to withdrawal from the neighbourhood: 'We had to have full control of the street that we were filming in because it was a period drama. We were using the real street vendor walking behind, or a kid passing by as extras. That's why what would normally take an hour of filming was taking us four hours' (Gence 2011).

As the dizi successfully moved into its second season, the set was transported to Beykoz Kundura, where a replica of the neighbourhood was constructed from scratch:

> We set up the neighbourhood, the streets parallel to it, Ali Kaptan's house, offices and some new places to be used later in Beykoz studios. These are 50 houses and around 20 shops. We first took the exact measures of the original houses in Balat. We rebuilt exactly the same neighbourhood here. There was a difference between rebuilding the single-storey and multi-storey buildings. We faced really hard times. Groundwork was done, concrete was poured, and 200 tons of iron was used. A space of 200 metres was paved with asphalt. Around 100 people worked for two months. The cost of this set was around two million Turkish lira. (Gence 2011)

In the earlier days, art departments frequently transformed real locations. Nilüfer Çamur, who worked from an early age as art director on many hit dizis, describes her profession as responsible for 'creating the atmosphere' of the dizi (2014). She remembers the desktop research that she had to undertake for *Hatırla Sevgili*, a period drama treating

---

30 *Öyle Bir Geçer Zaman ki* was not obviously the first to be filmed in a real neighbourhood, as many dizis like *Perihan Abla* and *Süper Baba* were also filmed in small neighbourhoods of Istanbul. But these dizis were produced before the growth of the television industry, when dizis were shorter in length and were shot at a slower pace. In that sense, *Öyle Bir Geçer Zaman ki* was perhaps the first to experience a new kind of encounter with real neighbourhood location.

the first military coup in 1960: exploring commercials, photographs and lifestyle magazines of that era. The 1950s and 60s were already depicted by Yeşilçam movies showing old Istanbul with its landscapes, lifestyle and costumes before its urban transformation in the 1980s. Nevertheless, with *Hatırla Sevgili*'s emotional political content—culminating in the execution of the prime minister Adnan Menderes—reconstructing a long-gone era demanded a wider exploration of the social and cultural memory of the characters during the coup in both Ankara and Istanbul along with the Princes' Islands. Thus far the topic had not been explored, with the exception of a documentary.[31] Çamur recalls the challenge of historical imagination and its reconstruction:

> We had four or five months. I spent two months before going to the field, reading like a student. I watched hundreds of minutes of documentaries and movies. I wasn't going anywhere but to libraries. I was speaking to witnesses. I spent a lot of time in Büyükada. Read a lot, read a lot, read a lot . . . I never considered it as a matter of 'did they have this object at that time or not?' I went after the emotions of the period and didn't bother with glasses and plates. There were political events, social life, and the concept of being from Istanbul [*Istanbullu*] and from the Island [*Adalı*]. How they entertained themselves, how much money they earned, how they spent their money. I went after these questions to catch the zeitgeist. For example, the patisserie: we built a building from scratch in Büyükada. Think about it, it was just walls. A completely empty building. But we created a patisserie by putting together every little detail including the floor tiles. It was a great pleasure to see it coming to life. (2014)

---

31 See *Demirkırat: Bir Demokrasinin Doğuşu* (1991), a serial documentary produced by TRT, written and directed by Mehmet Ali Birand, Can Dündar and Bülent Çaplı. See https://www.imdb.com/title/tt4077876/ (last accessed 1 July 2022).

Art directors operate under pressure to please all parties involved in the project, but they also work under the multiple eyes of the audience on the lookout for 'historical inaccuracies'. Viewers of *Hatırla Sevgili*, for instance, rapidly took to social media to question the gas pipelines featured in the dizi. Another issue was the characters wearing shoes inside homes, a habit which does not conform to Turkish tradition. The creators had to respond in social media with an entry explaining that these pipelines carried coal gas, and that the Istanbul elite of the period, adopting French manners, had in fact worn clean shoes in their homes (Çamur 2014).

Establishing the *mahalle*, the neighbourhood, is an essential first step for many projects. The 'Sineklidağ Mahallesi' for 2011's *Keşanlı Ali Destanı*, a period drama taking place in 1959, also took months of research and construction. Art director Hakan Yarkın describes the process:

> The construction of the neighbourhood took two and a half months. We spent the first week with 'polluting' the place, making a mess, making it look like it was lived in. People who worked in the construction were masters who built real slums. As many as 55 houses were prepared; 20 of them had their interiors designed. You could in fact live in these houses, even their roof wouldn't leak. We had everything in the set. Donkeys, wheelbarrows, copper vessels, 16 chickens . . . I had a team of 30 experts in designing period sets. If we count others like electricians etc., it makes 90 employees . . . In general, we didn't have big problems. But it was a problem to find cigars or bottles of the period. Never underestimate the bottles—we prepared a special mould and labels for them. (2011)

Ülkenciler, who was in charge of creating a 1970s neighbourhood in Süleymaniye for the set of *Karadayı*, recalls: 'Once I read the script, I quickly realized that Süleymaniye had greatly changed. We had to construct a set from scratch. I began exploring photographs and started drawing the market street, the passage, the coffeehouse and the inner space of the households' (2019a). Photographs revealed that the measurement of the wooden plates should be at least 20–25 cm, a detail among many others he particularly paid attention to while designing the set. Once the set design was completed, Ülkenciler remembers how it continued to change according to the requirements of producers, directors and even actors: 'New demands always come. The director can say, "Let us add one more room" or "Let this shop be a barbershop instead of a grocery."' (2019a). In reference to the set design of *Diriliş*, a medieval drama on the founding of the Ottoman state, Ülkenciler underlines the necessity for a full-time advisor in historical research:

> For older periods, the importance of these details increases . . . To make it convincing for viewers. It requires serious literature research and consulting historians. I believe that rather than ask about particular problems, one needs to have a full-time consultant. This issue is often left aside because of the budget concerns. But in my opinion, this is an issue that should never be neglected. (2019b)

Big projects require a close collaboration of art directors and set designers. For *Vatanım Sensin*, Soydan Kuş and Hakan Yarkın worked together to build the architectural design of different neighbourhoods in Izmir, including the famous Kordon Avenue. Preparations took about 25 weeks, and team of 250 people. A total of 70 façades, two mansions, a hospital, a garrison, a tavern, a prison camp and 20 shops were built; 3,000 square metres of Albanian stones were used to pave the streets (Tanrıseven 2017).

Location scouting has always been an important component of the production process. Ali Aktürk, now an executive director, remembers the beginning of his career when he searched for appropriate locations for new projects: 'There is probably no *yalı* along the Bosphorus whose door I did not knock on' (2019). In many cases, producers approach people with local knowledge of the neighbourhoods where they want to set up a permanent site for their new projects. Not all neighbourhoods are the same, however. Before the boom of the industry, filming in a real neighbourhood was a common practice. Nilgün Nalçacı recalls the friendly attitude of neighbourhood residents during the filming of *İkinci Bahar*. Whether a neighbourhood is receptive or not makes a big difference in smoothly conducting the shooting: 'The residents and shop owners in Samatya were so helpful and friendly. We still have a chat when we go there. In the later episodes of dizi, there were huge crowds flowing. It was interesting that we continued filming even when they were all around us, without having any problem' (Nalçacı 2016).

Some neighbourhoods with a rich texture appeal to producers but they can be difficult to manage as a community. Okan Akdemir, who has a local knowledge of the Balat neighbourhood, worked as a consultant for the set in the area for the dizis *İçerde* and *Çukur*. He distinguished himself from location scouts, as his job transcended the notion of just finding a 'real location' and involved managing a particular site, with his local knowledge:

Since the Balat-Fatih neighbourhood is very historical, it was to our advantage to have good knowledge of the locality, knowing people who live and work there. I was born and raised in Balat and I know everyone. When these kinds of productions come up, producers contact me directly. When we began this job, they brought me here. Last year, we did *İçerde*. If they had not approached me, it would be very difficult for them to manage things. You should definitely have a knowledgeable local person, so that even the smallest problem can be solved. Very simple things. For example, knowing the garbage man in the neighbourhood is an asset, or to know the shopkeepers here. When we go and work abroad, we also get the help of their production team. Indeed, at the beginning of this project, we had a shooting in France and we got local help. (Akdemir 2019)

Local knowledge of particular locations becomes more crucial when the production is set in the provinces or smaller towns (Geertz 1983). In the production processes of the films and dizis to be shot in Adana, for instance, producers usually contact Muhittin Elibol as an advisor or project coordinator. Since 2005, Elibol has assisted many movies and dizis—including *Beyaz Gelincik* (2005), *Hanımın Çiftliği* (2009) and *Dila Hanım* (2012)—choosing sites, obtaining necessary permissions and hiring local people for various jobs. He describes the difficulties he faced during the preliminary preparations for *Hanımın Çiftliği*:

We put a lot of effort into making the dizi reflect the 1950s, when Adana had dirt roads. We had to cover asphalt roads with dirt before the shooting. It is harder to create the conditions of 60 years ago than to film a story that is set in today's world. It wasn't hard to find extras in Adana. We received applications from around 15,000 people. Especially when filming in the villages, the kind of people and their natural looks made our job easier. We employed real peasants during filming, which was a financial support to them. This became a dizi that conveyed a natural feel. Because big cities cannot preserve their old texture, filming period drama gets harder there. In fact, we are not talking about a very distant past, but it is very rare to find places reflecting the spirit of 60 years ago. We had a really hard time during filming. We had to construct earth shelters, as part of the Teneke slum and the farm. (Elibol 2011)

Similarly, while filming *Sevdaluk*, Zafer Kanyılmaz started the preparations six months before in the Şen Yuva village of the Black Sea region. The hotel and the lead characters' household were built from scratch as described in the script, on a 1.5 billion-lira budget (Öz 2013).

During *Çukur*'s location planning in 2017, Akdemir recalled how they established a shanty cabin for the Aliço character under a highway bridge by the sea: 'We generally know all these sites, so we go and talk to people in charge. If the site belongs to the state, we make the necessary payments and get the official permits for the shooting' (2019). At times, searches fail. In *Fatmagül'ün Suçu Ne?* art director Nilgün Nalçacı and Ali Aktürk from the production team searched for days to find a dairy in Ildırı. Not satisfied with the 'real' dairies which were too dirty and small for the purpose, they decided to build one from scratch (Nalçacı and Aktürk 2011).

Many location scouts have a visual knowledge and memory bank of 'possible sites' from former research they have conducted. During my interviews on dizi sets, many expressed how they find most places by knocking on the doors of houses and asking if the residents would be interested in renting to them. Executive producer Ayşe Özer offers examples of such encounters:

> Location scouts used to knock on every door. There were also instances when we would suddenly need to shoot in a house that we have an agreement with. We would literally ask the owners to leave their own house. Sometimes the owner would not let us modify the house. We used to negotiate—sometimes we won, and sometimes they did. (2012)

In the early years of dizi making, many landowners were reluctant to rent their property; those who had agreed to do so at first could break their contract.[32] Therefore, location scouts need interpersonal skills for moments of crisis. Producers also keep a close eye on the locations, not only for their cost but also for providing a good and sustainable work environment for the cast and crew. The owner of Ay Yapım and the

---

32 This situation significantly changed in the 2010s, when expectation from rents increased, and formal contracts secured the transaction between production companies and landowners.

producer of many hit dizis, Kerem Çatay explained the great importance he gave to choosing the mansion for *Aşk-ı Memnu*. Believing in the dramatic power of real locations, he stated that 'Production quality should convince us all. In *Aşk-ı Memnu*, the mansion where the family would live was of key importance. This would be the location where they would pass all their time, both in the dizi's story as well as in real life' (2012).

Shooting in real houses may be problematic at times. During one of my set visits, I was approached by the landlady of a household who complained how the shooting harmed her house. In the filming of *Kara Para Aşk*, however, the set workers praised Feryal Gülman, a prominent high-lifestyle figure, for being a 'wonderful host'.[33] Sets in real houses are a fantastic merger of actual objects and props. In designing households, some sets are newly built; in others, props complement original objects belonging to rented households.[34] During the rush of scriptwriting and delivery, location scouts find themselves in search of a new site for the very next episode. For a shooting in *Fatmagül'ün Suçu Ne?* in 2011, there emerged a need for an underpass, a rather difficult setting in the crowded context of Istanbul. Following a week-long search, an underpass was found in Ataköy, a neighbourhood near Atatürk Airport. The location scout stated, 'It was a totally unnecessary underpass from the traffic-engineering perspective, but it was perfect for us.'

Art directors are responsible for the overall aesthetics of the project, and they need good construction team managers on a weekly basis. Given the pace of dizi production, the team must be prepared to deal with urgent demands. In shooting *Söz*, a dizi with a military theme, art director Erol Taştan had two days to prepare a 'swamp'. Construction took two consecutive days, with eight hours spent digging a hole with

---

33 *Kara Para Aşk* set visit, 5 June 2014.

34 As examples of sets for newly built houses, one can cite *Hanımın Çiftliği, Istanbullu Gelin* and *Bir Zamanlar Çukurova*. On the other hand, props serve alongside original objects in *Aşk-ı Memnu, Kuzey-Güney, Kara Para Aşk, Paramparça, Ölene Kadar* and *Hayat Şarkısı*.

a bulldozer, and using fifteen trucks of stones and soils and five tankers of water. The scene was finally shot with eight cameras, with many on hand to help in case of emergency (*Haberler.com* 2017).

Getting into the 'Spirit' of the Era and the Characters: The Mindset of the Art Director

Who is an art director in the dizi world? Nilgün Nalçacı describes her job as preparing places and costumes 'in the service of the script' (2016):

> With our director, we usually go over the script and the characters, and prepare a visual plan scene by scene. First, we find the places that suit the general scene and the characters. Then we design accessories and props that would convey the feel of the story and its characters. I see my job as composing a painting for each scene. (2020)

To Onur Tuğ, 'With the exception of the actors, anything that is visible in a certain scene is under the supervision of the art director' (2014). Nilüfer Ebru Çamur underlines how the 'wholeness' of the general picture is important:

> They are all under my umbrella—décor, costume, hair and make-up, all kinds of accessories, from cars to other props. They all serve a big picture, which is under my control. An art director should have the competence to situate every single scene in the grand picture and manage her team with her knowledge and skills. (2019)

Nalçacı remembers the problems she faced and had to resolve during the shooting of *Kurt Seyit and Şura* in Russia:

> We had to work under −30 degrees Celsius in the streets. We literally saw the crystal snowflakes, it was amazing. We had obtained work visas for the shooting, but there was a mistake: we were allowed only one entry for a stay of two weeks [. . .]. I was also in charge of constructing a décor for Istanbul's Istiklal

Road, and another in Çatalca for the scenes on a Crimean village. I had to travel in-between, but this was not possible. These sets were constructed online through the help of my assistants. (Dağkıran 2016: 203–04)

Art directors adopt different approaches to begin imagining the world they would construct in dizi projects. Çamur, who worked on many period dramas, stresses the importance of 'getting into the spirit of the era' at work:

The script comes, I read it, I reflect upon the world proposed. I usually visualize it through drawing or by making a collage. I describe how I can do this and what it makes me feel. The director and the producer agree or disagree. They say something, I respond. Through team work there emerges a world, and I claim every aspect of it . . . First, I try to understand the spirit of the period, its contemporaries, neighbours and interactions between these. I never began by researching whether they had spoons and forks at that time. For example, when I was working on *Bir Zamanlar Çukurova*, I started by asking how Turkey was in the 1970s, how the region of Çukurova was . . . Once I get this, you find all these props and accessories. But first, you have to discover the spirit and the colour of that period. (2019)

The characters often serve as guides for imagining the décor, costumes and props of the would-be set. Many art directors underscore how their starting point is usually the analysis of the story's main characters. Onur Tuğ notes:

First, we go over the character. You discuss this with the director from the very beginning. If the director has special requests, you evaluate them. I start with questions like 'What kind of house I would have if I were Ayşe?' 'What would be my hobbies?' 'What would I hang on my walls?' Happy-unhappy-depressed. These determine the colours and the props to be used. We keep on thinking about these details . . . With the colours you use, you convey the character such that there is no way the audience doesn't believe in him. Everything, even the tiniest details of the décor is there to serve the character. If you can also make the actor believe in this, there is nothing better. One of the best compliments I got from an actor was: 'My house was so much in accord with my character that my acting got stronger.' This shows that we have done the job the right way. (2014)

Similarly, costume designer Gülümser Gürtunca emphasizes how characters stand at the centre of art direction:

There is generally a subtext to the characters. The scriptwriter and director inform us about the characters' mother, father, where they grew up, which schools they went to, and the details that are not written in the script. Later on, we create visual charts to show how a particular character can be dressed. After drawing up these charts, we decide on light and colour together with the cinematographer and the director. We come up with a colour scale for the costumes, based on the general atmosphere of the film, the kind of light and the filter to be used. After these scales, we collect textile samples. If we have time—this is of course not always possible in Turkey—we make a screen test, and then move forward to purchase and sew. Screen tests of course offer the safest system. (Göktürk–Kobanbay 2017)

Naz Erayda, who has worked in the dizi world since the 1980s, notes that what counts most is the 'impact' that the décor and costumes create, rather than how 'beautiful' they look. She too pursues the path of the characters during her process of preparations:

Places, costumes and accessories—all these elements need to work together to create the required impact. I start working by reading the script several times, from different perspectives, and trying to discover the opportunities that the text provides.

Later on, I ask the director to tell me what she wants to do, what kind of an emotion and impression she is after. I ask questions about the details of the characters that are not included in the script. If she has never thought about this, I kindly ask them to think through and give me feedback. If possible, I try to ensure that the cinematographer joins this meeting. I learn what kind of light he is imagining, what kind of angles and scales are preferred, whether they plan to use a strong colour stabilizer in post-production. Later on begins a process in which I deconstruct and categorize the script, characters, places, scenes. I bring a series of regulations regarding the load of emotions, time, colour, social status, symbolic values and anything that the content necessitates . . . I form the colour, form and style scale of characters and places. I make lists of must-use and never-use. These make a guideline comprised of couple of folders with examples of colour, material and visuals. The actual design process begins after these preliminary preparations. (Erayda 2011)

Art director Murat Güney attributes the success of *Şaşı Felek Çıkmazı* to their detailed work in selecting 'convincing' costumes. 'We tried to form a special wardrobe for each character,' he says, recalling the small but effective items they got for the lead actresses, including a *hırka* (typical cardigan worn by a Turkish woman) and other costumes from Istanbul's street bazaars. 'We used that cardigan for 26 episodes,' Güney remembers, 'We had bought Füsun Demirel's costumes from the Salı Pazarı' (2009).[35]

---

35 Salı Pazarı (Tuesday Bazaar) is a quintessential street market of Istanbul, along with many others like Beşiktaş, Ulus, Beykoz and Çemberlitaş bazaars. Street bazaars are important *lieux de memoir* for Turkish women and a symbol of smart shopping. For an analysis of street bazaars and dress codes, see Arzu Öztürkmen (2008b).

Çamur notes, that the key to choosing costumes is the story of the dizi itself. Chief costume designers often find themselves caught between enthusiastic creative ideas and the 'right costume' for the story at hand:

> Throughout the filming, assistants come to us and say, 'We have found something very beautiful.' I ask, 'For which scene?' If the scene is very dramatic and tragic, then I explain to them gently that we cannot use this, because it would get ahead of the scene. We don't compete with the scene, we accompany it. Sometimes we enhance it, sometimes walk along side by side and sometimes stay behind. Nothing, including the actor, should get ahead of the story. Because that's where persuasiveness begins. For example, when [an audience] comes, watches and says, 'There is nothing here—they just filmed it in an already existing place.' This is the best compliment for me, for it proves that we built it right for that story. (Çamur 2019)

Güney also notes how art directors develop a certain gaze, scrutinizing every point and object surrounding them, and improvising on the spot:

> A place you enter, a book you read, a movie you watch begins to appear differently in your eyes. You begin to record everything in your visual memory. You begin to see everything from the perspective of cinematography. After a while, you begin recording in your mind what people wear, drink, how they travel and behave, without even realizing this. While you are reading a book, you visualize the characters and places in your mind. Think of this happening continuously and in extreme detail. This is such a process. This is how it happened with me. I don't know how it works with someone else. For example, when I enter an empty space today, if it is to be a cafe, after five minutes I know how it should be. Every little detail is visualized in my mind. (2009)

Negotiation between the Imagined Content and Its Production

Maintaining a balance between imagination and the budget is essential to the work of art direction. Çamur states, 'Budget control—to complete the job within the given budget—is very important to me; I would not call a work successful if it exceeds the budget' (2019). Nevertheless, in the rush to complete shooting, production teams end up constantly negotiating with producers. At times it relates to the use of a distant location, which is costlier in terms of money and time but promises a picturesque view: 'Sometimes they say: "Who will notice this?" but I still put that detail there. I know that you shouldn't spend money on things that won't be seen much. Producers sometimes resist, but I push back. Sometimes I even bribe them, promising a future concession' (Çamur 2019). Giving an example from the shooting of *Şaşı Felek Çıkmazı*, Güney reminds how directors can be picky on those props' details, which can contradict the story or the characters:

> I once prepared the table for the family to have breakfast. Before the scene, Mahinur Hanım pulled me aside and said, 'You put orange juice for everyone. Where have you seen a middle-class family in which everyone can drink orange juice? This is only Saadet's habit.' It is a little detail, isn't it? Small. Would the audience see this? If you say, never mind, they won't, then those little things will accumulate and destroy the world you are trying to build. (2009)

Çamur also acknowledges how important it is to cooperate with the director of photography: 'The cinematographer can destroy what I am doing, or light up something I have done poorly. Light is everything, frame is everything and cinematography is everything. My best companion is the director of photography and vice versa' (2019). Güney confirms this close collaboration: 'We work in parallel with the director of photography. We are like the right and the left arm, because we both have the duty to compose the closest image to what the director imagines' (2009).

In the case of period and historical drama, 'reflecting the historical truth' becomes an essential problematic. This debate was ignited during the filming of *Muhteşem Yüzyıl*. The criticism was based on Sultan Süleyman's portrayal as a lusty ruler rather than a conqueror, and the depiction of his harem and with its cleavage-revealing costumes (see *Haber7* 2011; *Milliyet* 2011). The fact that most criticism came from state authorities soon triggered nationalist demonstrations against the production company (see *Sol* 2013; Internet Haber 2011a, 2011b). From the perspective of the art department, however, there was a further factor to the issue. Çamur states that her primary loyalty was to cinematography: 'We need to stylize; we cannot be like a documentary. So we do stretch as much as we can. In the case of *Muhteşem Yüzyıl*, our producer was really brave' (2019). Tuğ, however, reminds us how the art director needs to be well equipped in designing a period drama project: 'This requires very serious preliminary research; you need to be in control of almost everything. These details convey the feel of the period, and achieving this is the art director's job. It necessitates deep historical knowledge' (2014).

Nalçacı underlines the importance of two keywords during the shooting of *İkinci Bahar*: 'realness' and 'sincerity' (2016). Convincing people is not that easy. In many cases, the assistants in the art team who come from modest backgrounds may lack the aesthetic knowledge needed for the project; as a result they can fall into the trap of clichés. Güney values experience and observation in the job of art directing:

> You know how people live. If you observe well, you develop knowledge about every walk of life . . . it is really important for an actor to carry well the accessory that you provide. Your accessory shouldn't be a burden on the actor, it must ease her acting. If an actor were uncomfortable with a costume, how would she act, right? You may attribute a certain quality to a costume, but if the actor cannot act in it, you are the one responsible for finding and providing another costume that she

can wear. You must know how to get rid of clichés . . . You may get a pair of black pants from a famous brand, but it may not look good; yet something you buy from the street market may look like a famous brand . . . You should know the difference between the rich and the tasteless. (2009)

One final aspect of art direction is related to the shooting of crowded scenes, where art directors may need to take the initiative to control the extras. 'The assistant directors may not always have time for that,' Güney states, 'then, I would start by checking the costumes. Because the director would be busy, focusing on shooting the scene, he does not deal with the grand picture you established. They do not care whether this man and this woman would stand side by side. At this point, it is your job to supervise all this' (2009).

Art direction has come a long way in the last three decades. When the dizi industry was blossoming during the 2000s, there were no established studio services except a few modest venues meant for indoor shooting. Location scouts were inexperienced and the logistics of running everyday shoots were poor. By the 2010s, though, many neighbourhoods, yalıs and even forested areas had been identified for location shoots. Large studios like Beykoz Kundura developed their services and began to offer permanent sites for sets such as prisons and hospitals. As for historical series, producers invested in new open-air studios with constructed medieval sites that were adaptable to different historical eras. The number of companies offering trailers to host stars along with catering, electricity and all other needs also increased. A whole generation of make-up, costume, décor and prop artists were trained by experience in the film sets. In turn, they shared their knowledge with their assistants, thereby grooming newer generations. By the 2020s, the art direction team of any dizi production was therefore beginning their project with substantial knowledge accrued in the last two decades of dizi production.

CHAPTER 7

Coping with Fame

The Joy and Curse of Acting in Turkey

On 15 April 2015, as a group of Turkish delegates, we attended the gala dinner for Médaille d'Honneur Awards of MIPTV, where İrfan Şahin, then the chief executive officer of Doğan TV, was also a recipient. The general editor of a global television journal who was sitting next to us, showed me on his cell phone an image of Fahriye Evcen and Burak Özçivit, then the stars of *Lovebird,* and asked 'Do you know these actors? Are they really famous?' Apparently, a video interview with them posted in the journal had received a considerable number of clicks. These young actors were unknown figures to him back then, but both Evcen and Özçivit have been among the new generation of Turkish dizi stars who had millions of fans from around the world.

Over the years, I had a chance of interviewing many of these actors and stars, and listened to their narratives of initiation, and their responses to the challenges in the dizi industry. Some became my close friends and helped me greatly to better evaluate the stance of actors in Turkey's film industry. The general framework of this chapter relies, to a great extent, upon interviews I conducted with them. Access to actors has always been a difficult aspect of film industry research. Transcending the gates of talent agents is almost impossible, and in the case of Turkey, the harshness of tabloid press also scares actors to give interviews to outsiders.

I had two good fortunes during my research on actors. To begin with, because my focus was on the historical development of the dizi genre and its industry, actors were not the first group of people I approached. Focusing on production processes, I had first interviewed writers, producers, directors, editors and cinematographers. These preliminary encounters provided me with a general ethnographic knowledge where I could situate the actors' input in the industry. In fact, I interviewed their talent and casting agents much before approaching them, and to distinguish myself from the journalists, I chose not to tape the interviews and only took notes. Thanks to the general respect for scholars and the good reputation of my university, I have been well received in most cases, while failing in a few. By the time I reached out to them, I was well equipped and had the preliminary knowledge to ask particular questions on the dizi industry and their experience in it. As an oral historian, however, I approached these interviews cautiously, as the front narratives reveal as much as they hide.[1] This is why I cross-examined what I heard with a pool of published interviews. I preferred to use these published accounts for most of the quotations in this book, keeping many sincere revelations anonymous as promised. One important venue to access actors' personal accounts has been the Mithat Alam Film Center at Boğaziçi University. As a devoted friend of the centre, I had the possibility to listen to, or sometimes moderate, many special interviews with actors, which were published, providing me with a great primary source for my research. Finally, preparing Turkey's conference sessions at MIPCOM 2015 gave me the opportunity to closely observe actors' relationships with their producers, friends, agents as well as with the international television press. Meeting many dizi actors in person in all these venues proved very valuable, giving me a chance to experience their energy and composure.

---

1 Eminent oral historian Alessandro Portelli states: 'Oral history tells us less about *events* than about their *meaning*' (1991: 50).

My second good fortune was personally knowing some actors, who greatly helped my understanding of stardom and acting in Turkey and abroad. I have known Mehmet Günsür since his childhood, and have proudly watched him grow into a powerful actor. To my surprise, Fahriye Evcen happened to be my student in the History Department at Boğaziçi, helping me as an assistant in 2014 to digitize part of my research data, and introducing me to another star, Burak Özçivit, whom I consulted many times. My close friend Şeyda Taluk was Yiğit Özşener's agent in the early 2010s, and I had a genuine and sincere input from both during my research. And finally, American actor and writer Eric Bogosian, whom I met through an event organized at City University of New York in 2012, has remained a friend since then, sharing his knowledge and experience of the American television world.

Today, dizi sets bring together a diversity of actors belonging to different generations, coming from backgrounds in theatre, cinema and modelling. Many of these actors are from educated, middle-income families; this gives them a wide range of instruments to use when acting. To begin with, I should underline how storytelling and performance in everyday life are important cultural forms of Turkish society.[2] Theatricality stands at the centre of Turkish daily life in many different forms, ranging from everyday gossiping or storytelling performances to women's 'gold days' (*altın günleri*), performances of public officers, bazaar sellers or minibus drivers.[3] Actors-to-be in Turkey, *alaylı* or

---

[2] For the anthropology of everyday life, see Erwing Goffman (1990, 1959); Richard Schechner (2006); for the genre of 'personal experience narrative', see Sandra Dolby-Stahl (1989). For everyday life studies in Turkey, see Deniz Kandiyoti and Ayşe Saktanber (2002); Nurdan Gürbilek (2011); Arzu Öztürkmen (2006a, 2006b); Ayfer Tunç (2001).

[3] *Altın Günü* (The Day of Gold) refers to a rotating afternoon gathering which combines both social entertainment and monetary savings among communities of women in Turkey, organized at set intervals to chat, eat, and give gold to the hostess. See Başak Bilecen (2019); Selda Tuncer (2018). For the performance of

okullu , find themselves in an ethnographic ground where they can be both the performers and the audience of these everyday life perform- ances. Growing up in crowded social environments, with extended families and large friend circles, they develop a keen knowledge of stereotypes, cultural codes, dialects and gender behaviour. As one said, 'We excel in depicting middle-class, neighbourhood, family domains, because we know this so well and from within. To act the elite, a real businessman, a real university scholar or an upper-class lady is more challenging; there we may need improvements.'

Indeed, class identity lies at the heart of the Turkish modernization experience, often analysed within the traditional (*alaturka*) versus Western (*alafranga*) continuum, which continuously produce conflict, humour and stereotypes used in dizis.[4] Eminent writer Orhan Pamuk calls '*salon*', the living room of the Turkish households, a 'museum sit- ting room', where modernity is on display. In his book on Istanbul's memory, Pamuk masterfully details how television altered the *salon* from a cold museum to a more theatrical space:

> Sitting rooms were not meant to be places where you could lounge comfortably; they were little museums designed to demonstrate to the hypothetical visitor that the householders were westernized . . . So it was not just in the affluent homes of Istanbul that you saw sitting-room museums; over the next fifty years you could find these haphazard and gloomy (but some- times also poetic) displays of western influence in sitting rooms all over Turkey; only with the arrival of television in the 1970s did they go out of fashion. Once people had discovered how pleasurable it was to sit together to watch the evening

---

public officers, see Catherine Alexander (2002); for bazaar sellers, see Özlem Öz and Mine Eder (2015); for minibus drivers, see Arzu Öztürkmen (2008a).

4 For the analysis of class issues, see Sencer Ayata (1988); Nazan Çapoğlu (2008); Çağlar Keyder (1987); Ferhunde Özbay (1999); Gul Ozyegin (2001).

news, their sitting rooms changed from little museums to little cinemas—although you still hear of old families who put their televisions in their central hallways, locking up their museum sitting rooms and opening them only for holidays or special guests. (Pamuk 2006: 10–11)

Many actors grew up in such households and continue to live among other forms of everyday life performances in public sites, including schools, hospitals and public offices, along with neighbourhoods, restaurants, coffeehouses, tea gardens or street markets. As citizens of modern Turkey, they also go through a centralized national education and carry a memory of *müsamere,* the ceremonial genre of national days and official events. The accrued knowledge of everyday life, its storytelling and performances provide them with a pool of images, gestures and sentiments that they later use as key instruments in giving life to dizi characters. Turkish dizis took their strength in their successful cinematic storytelling, where a new generation of motivated and hardworking actors made a significant contribution.

One must remember, however, that acting has been a problematic domain in Turkey since the Ottoman times. It is with the founding of the Republic that the approach to theatre changed (Tuncay 2007). To begin with, being a performer had low status, a matter illustrated in the proverb 'If you leave your daughter to her own will, she will elope either with a drummer or a horn player' (*Kızı gönlüne bırakırsan ya davulcuya varır, ya zurnacıya*). With the Republican reforms, theatre became a symbolic field in the establishment of modern Turkey, comprising multiple genres ranging from nationalistic plays to political theatre to adaptations of foreign plays.[5] After an evening at the theatre in 1930,

---

5 For a historical review, see Muhsin Ertuğrul (1963); Özdemir Nutku (1969); Metin And (1973, 1983a, 1983b); Turgut Özakman (1978); Rauf Tuncay (1968); Turgut Özakman (1988); Zehra Arslan and Kurt Güvelioğlu (2013); Tahsin Konur (1987).

Kemal Atatürk had praised the actors of Darülbedayi theatre, addressing his fellow officials: 'You may all be parliamentarians, you may even be a president. But you can never become actors' (see And 1973: 8).[6] People's Houses, the cultural centres of the Republican era (1932–51), had a special theatre section, which encouraged amateur actors but mostly trained provincial audiences in indoor viewing behaviour. The first state conservatory was established in 1936, under the supervision of German director Carl Ebert; and the first official state theatre in 1949. City and state theatres were subsidized, raising generations of talented actors who performed in various venues and received public acclaim (Akter 2014). In the 1970s, the general public would know by name many of these theatre actors, through radio drama and their dubbed voices in foreign television series.[7]

In parallel to theatre actors, Yeşilçam too had launched a series of movies stars, many of whom began their acting careers in front of the camera. The 1960s witnessed the rise of phenomenal movie stars, producing an enthusiastic domestic fan culture for cinema actors and actresses.[8] Beauty pageants, which had been encouraged since the early years of the Republic, became another source for new faces in

---

6 Darülbedayi was an Ottoman imperial theatre established in Istanbul in 1914, which continued to serve as Istanbul City Theatre under the leadership of actor and director Muhsin Ertuğrul.

7 Among many actors and actresses of city and state theatres, one can cite Kerim Avşar, Çetin Tekindor, Zafer Ergin, Ayten Gökçer, Tomris Oğuzalp, Işıl Yücesoy, Arsen and Can Gürzap. One can also add Yıldız Kenter, Müşfik Kenter, Şükran Güngör, Gazanfer Özcan, Gönül Ülkü, Nisa Serezli and Göksel Kortay as well-known actors who had their own private companies.

8 These would include Türkan Şoray, Filiz Akın, Hülya Koçyiğit, Fatma Girik, Cüneyt Arkın, Ayhan Işık, Ediz Hun and Murat Soydan, among others. Their fans would write actual letters to them. For an analysis of their image, see Seçil Büker and Canan Uluyağcı (1993); Pınar Çekirge (2014); Bircan Usallı-Silan (2004); Nigar Pösteki (2007); Burçak Evren and Bircan Usallı-Silan (2012).

cinema.[9] Nebahat Çehre and Selda Alkor, who became important character actresses of many hit dizis, made their way to acting in the 1960s through such beauty pageants.[10] One should also mention the rise of *fotoromans* beginning by the 1960s. *Fotoromans* were graphic novellas, first imported from Italy, where they originated, and later produced domestically with local stars (Tunç 2001; Topçu and Önürmen 2018; Narin n.d.). When the first television series were planned in the 1970s and 80s, TRT producers drew from each of these circles for casting. The first dizis of that era, like *Aşk-ı Memnu* (1976 version) or *Kartallar Yüksek Uçar* (1983), featured a cadre of actors from both cinema and theatre, in addition to new faces from modelling and beauty contests.

Becoming Celebrity: Growing Pains of a Dizi Career

During the 1980s, dizi actors enjoyed some popularity and many pursued their daily lives as usual. Those from the theatre would continue their regular stage activities. Although many would be occasionally interviewed in print media, broader coverage of actors came with the change in media in the early 1990s. These actors passed through a unique experience of 'becoming celebrities' at a historical conjuncture, where Turkish popular culture created its new domestic stars in film, music and sports. This historical conjuncture happened for different reasons. First, popular music production made a big leap in the 1990s, with the opening of private radio channels and television networks, leading to a boom of live concerts in big cities.[11] Music channel Kral

---

9 Turkish women's participation in international beauty pageants was also a Republican desire, an idea Atatürk promoted himself. For beauty pageants in Turkey, see Zoran (2019); Mustafa Arıkan (2015); Filiz Yıldız (2019); Ayşe Kocakaya (2009).

10 Nebahat Çehre was selected as Miss Turkey in 1960, and Selda Alkor became the winner of the beauty contest organized by *Ses* Magazine in 1965.

11 Pop singer Sertap Erener, for instance, who won the Eurovision Song Contest in 2003, made her debut in 1992. Pop star Tarkan, who had record-breaking sales

TV debuted in 1994, broadcasting for the first time video clips of newly emerging singers and bands. Second, there was a significant rise in the number of tabloid magazines. New entertainment programmes appeared on screen, along with emerging popular periodicals which focused on the rising film and music stars and the emerging socialites of an expanding nightlife in big cities, particularly Istanbul.[12] Media scholars called this development the 'magazination' (*magazinleşme*) of media in Turkey, which occurred not only through the increase in entertainment programmes but also through the content of other media, such as news, sports and talk shows.[13] News programmes *Siyaset Meydanı* (1994), *Ceviz Kabuğu* (1994) and *Teke Tek* (1995) launched Ali Kırca, Hulki Cevizoğlu and Fatih Altaylı respectively as the celebrity anchors of the 1990s. With the growing success of Turkish teams in European Cups, football shows also became popular, creating their own star discussants.[14] Third, the new genre of 'magazine shows' launched fresh television hosts who in turn became celebrities themselves. Cem Özer, Okan Bayülgen and Beyazıt Öztürk (Beyaz) produced novel talk-show formats, regularly hosting the rising stars of a new era.[15] Hülya Avşar and İbrahim Tatlıses, who became stars in the 1980s, began producing their own branded shows. For pop singers and dizi actors who started their careers in the 1990s, these platforms offered prestigious

---

in Europe during the 2000s, had also released his first album in 1992. For a review of the music industry in Turkey, see Michael Kuyucu (2014).

12 Following the trend-setter *Hafta Sonu Gazetesi* (1987), one can cite *Alem* (1993) and *Şamdan* (1996), among others.

13 See Hasan Çiftçi (2017); Ali Bayraktaroğlu and Ufuk Uğur (2011); Enes Bal (2007); Erdal Dağtaş (2006); Zeynep Karahan-Uslu (2002); E. Kurt (2001).

14 For a critique of the changing football media, see Ahmet Talimciler (2010).

15 The best-known shows included Rüstem Batum's *360 Derece* (1990), Cem Özer's *Laf Lafı Açıyor* (1991), İbrahim Tatlıses' *İbo Show* (1993), Yıldırım Benayyat's *Yıldo* (1994), Okan Bayülgen's *Gece Kuşu* (1995), Hülya Avşar's *Hülya Avşar Show* (1996) and Beyazıt Öztürk's *Beyaz Show* (1996).

visibility. To these, one should also add producer Can Tanrıyar's 'Tele-vole' genre, which in the beginning focused on the private lives of football players, evolving in time into a tabloid industry covering all types of celebrities.[16] And finally, 1990s were also when beauty pageants like Miss Turkey, Miss Globe or Best Model became widely visible with live broadcast in private networks and introduced many new faces that became the stars of the growing dizi industry.[17] Powerful talent and casting agencies were also established during these transitional years, branding many young actors in their initiation to a newly emerging dizi world.[18]

With the rise of the magazine media during the 1990s, dizi actors enjoyed a visibility they had not experienced before. Long-time theatre actors were used to face-to-face encounters with their audience, but to many who began acting in the early dizis, such popular visibility was a new phenomenon. Some had approached TRT in the 1980s, to adapt their staged performances for screen.[19] During the 1990s, producers formed their first casts from the state theatre circles, when the number

---

16 The tabloid industry got organized under their own association. Magazine Journalists Association (Magazin Gazetecileri Derneği) was founded in 1992, and since 1995 they have been organizing the Golden Lens Awards, which has become a well-attended domestic event.

17 Leading dizi stars Kenan İmirzalıoğlu, Kıvanç Tatlıtuğ, Burak Özçivit were launched through Best Model. In the footsteps of these contests, a one-time acting contest titled Türkiye'nin Yıldızları in 2004 introduced Engin Akyürek, Beren Saat and Cansu Dere to the dizi world.

18 Among others, one can cite Gaye Sökmen (1991), Rezzan Çakır (1995), Yasemin Özbudun (1995), Renda Güner (1996), Tümay Özokur (1999), Neşe Erberk (2000), Harika Uygur (2000), Ayşe Barım (2002) and Özlem Durak (2003), all of whom founded companies and shaped the careers of many dizi actors to come.

19 These were Cüneyt Gökçer's *Yedi Kocalı Hürmüz* (1983), Gülriz Sururi and Engin Cezzar's *Keşanlı Ali Destanı* (1988) and Haldun Dormen's *Hisseli Harikalar Kumpanyası* (1989). Comedian Perran Kutman was in the creative team of *Perihan Abla* (1986) for which she was also the lead actress.

of dizi projects began to increase. In the beginning, many actors were sceptical of television. The assistant director of *Aşkın Dağlarda Gezer*, a dizi shot in Urfa in 1999, recalled the resentful surprise of a senior actor, who was then in his early 50s: 'I was an actor all my life,' he stated, 'I never had anybody stop me and ask me for an autograph!' Similarly, theatre actor Erdal Özyağcılar, who was familiar with the film industry since the early years of his career, gained his popularity first in the ensemble cast of *Bizimkiler*, becoming later the indispensable face of many dizis to come.[20]

As the number of dizis increased in the 1990s, younger actors who made their way to dizis began to become the centre of attention in magazine media. The first breakthrough many of us remember is the emergence of Kenan İmirzalıoğlu as a male icon, after his first role in *Deli Yürek* (1998). One would also recall Memet Ali Alabora's sudden popularity during and after the shootings of *Yılan Hikayesi* (1999). A theatre actor and the founding chair of the Actors' Union, Alabora recounted his unease in being pointed in the streets as 'Memoli', the character he played in this dizi (Alabora 2011). By the mid-2000s, younger audiences began to be influential in organizing fan groups in the newly emerging social media. Turkish audiences adapted to Facebook, YouTube and other platforms very quickly, and became the passionate supporters of this first generation of young dizi actors. Nevertheless, the tabloid media continued to thrive, a conjuncture which put dizi actors under a harsh and critical gaze of the newly blossoming tabloids.

Today, actors who suddenly become big stars find themselves in a state of recognizability that surrounds them everywhere and at all times. Their privacy virtually disappears, and they are asked to cultivate and placate fans and the media. In the age of information, this experience

---

20 These included *Şehnaz Tango* (1996), *Yabancı Damat* (2004), *Elveda Rumeli* (2007), *Karadağlar* (2010) and *Sevdaluk* (2013).

is quite different from the star culture of former generations. Fan clubs are very organized; there is an aggressive tabloid press; and family or friends have their own demands. Not everyone has the social skills or the emotional capacity to deal with this radical change. The psychological adjustment is not always easy, and there are different responses to this heightened attention, ranging from narcissism to depression. Director Ayhan Özen calls attention to the importance of *kademeli oyunculuk*, referring to a gradually developing acting career. 'They need time to construct themselves,' he states, 'There is a big difference between getting famous at 20 and gradually gaining experience and celebrity status over time' (Özen 2014). Actor Yiğit Özşener confirms this by saying how important it was to protect himself from the lust of fame after he moved from theatre to television. After filming an effective commercial, his face suddenly appeared on TV screens and billboards: 'I was leery to approach fame,' he says, 'I took refuge back in theatre, like a reflex to protect myself' (Özşener 2012). Timuçin Esen also expresses that he had to take a four-year break after he first became famous with *Hırsız Polis*. He notes how fame deprives actors of the opportunity to learn from social settings: 'You are no more able to get lost in daily life—you move away from things that nourish you' (Esen 2019). Stepping into the visibility of the dizi industry was not easy even for Bergüzar Korel, who had a conservatory training and whose parents were both Yeşilçam actors. Korel had made her breakthrough with *1001 Gece*, but she remembers these early days of her career as a traumatic experience:

> I started at the age of 24. I knew nothing! The commentators first praised me . . . but they began to attack me after a few episodes. Frankly, I stopped enjoying life, laughing, felt as if in darkness. I thought a lot, what have I done wrong that these people react me as such? . . . They began to mock my teeth, my looks. I rebelled after a while. (2009)

Korel found herself in the midst of growing attention, which soon became a liability. A journalist called this a 'live broadcast from her life':

> People come to my door, give their card to my guard and tell him, 'Call me when Bergüzar comes out.' Then they begin to chase me, we survive accidents . . . I see this as a twist of the profession, but I am really bored of it . . . I've had enough of seeing myself on media, being compared all the time to my fellow actresses . . . There are times I feel like quitting acting. Settling in a village with my husband and living happily . . . If I was an ordinary viewer, I would be bored to see so much Bergüzar Korel, all the time. (Korel 2009)

Özcan Deniz, who was already a popular singer when he joined the dizi world, also resented media's judgmental approach towards his background in the early years of his career. His first dizi *Aşkın Dağlarda Gezer* (1999) was an 'Eastern Anatolian' genre (*Doğulu dizisi*). Although he played a lead role, it was difficult for him to break his image of traditional folk singer (*türkücü*) and convince critics that he was a promising modern actor. He made his breakthrough with *Asmalı Konak*, and remained in lead roles thereafter:

> There are some people who have curtain in their vision. They struggle with their prejudices, looking at you as 'yesterday's *türkücü*', or saying, 'He is the one with Anatolian roots trying to market himself to high society' . . . It really saddens me. Think of all the branded music around the world, they all are these countries' street music . . . After *Asmalı Konak,* they made an effort to get to know me. They said he is different from the one we knew. (Deniz 2010)

Many stars built up their reputation through a process closely followed by producers, fans and the tabloid press. As a leading male star of today's dizi industry, Kıvanç Tatlıtuğ remembers his initiation in a humorous way:

I began modelling to earn some money . . . but I didn't like it . . . I didn't have acting in my mind either. İrfan Şahin told me, 'We want you to be an actor, there is a dizi called *Gümüş*, read the script.' I immediately objected, saying that I'd never acted, and asked him, 'Do you really believe that I can be successful? The dizi may be cancelled after two episodes, and you will tell me how untalented I am.' But he told me that he believes in me and that he sees that light. He offered two roles: Mehmet and Mehmet's cousin . . . One is the leading character and the other is a side one . . . I go home, I am reading the script . . . I turn the pages: Mehmet, Mehmet, always Mehmet . . . Mehmet has so many scenes. I told myself, 'How can I do that!' I said, let me check the cousin Berk's character. He only had ten scenes in two episodes. I thought, 'That, I can do!' I can start with a small role, and learn the job from senior actors . . . And the dizi had the irreplaceable legendary actor Ekrem Bora in the cast. I had made a decision: if I have a hint of acting in me, I can proceed from there; if not, I will excuse myself after three episodes and forget about acting. I went to İrfan Şahin and told him I liked the Berk character better, and wanted to play him. 'No, no', he said, 'you will play Mehmet!' I will never forget my first scene, I was so nervous. (2013)

Barış Arduç, whose reputation grew dramatically after *Kiralık Aşk,* expresses his gradually changing perception and response to fame:

My life had a routine from home to work-out and back home. All changed in one day. I began receiving strong responses on the street. In the beginning, it was a novel experience, and I took it for granted; but over time it reached an extreme level. I heard the other day some girls kissed the bench I sat on the set. Having fans is nice, but when it comes to such dimension it is scary. (*Hürriyet Kelebek* 2015)

Sudden fame lead many actors to change their agents, which produces instant debates in tabloid media. Tatlıtuğ's separation from his first agent led to years of trials, while Elçin Sangu, who changed her talent agency, was sued by her former agent, claiming a commission from Sangu's new commercial contract (*Hürriyet Kelebek* 2011, 2016).

Dizi stars hold a memory of their own professional progress as well. Tatlıtuğ's career climbed up following his role in the ensemble cast of *Aşk-ı Memnu*, followed by his remarkable performance in *Kuzey Güney*. He recalls this leap as 'I got mature by then' (Tatlıtuğ 2013). Similarly, Burak Özçivit details how he began acting tentatively:

> I learned it all on the set. It was really hard the first few months. When you come from modelling, you face strong judgementalism, so you have to perform three times better. But acting also helped me learn more about myself. Kartal Tibet, who was the director in *Zoraki Koca*, my first dizi, encouraged me a lot. He believed in me; he is the one who made me come to like the job. (2014)

Beren Saat also warmly remembers the contribution of Tomris Giritlioğlu, who designed *Hatırla Sevgili*, in which Saat made her breakthrough in the ensemble cast:

> It is so important who shaped you in your first crossroads. With another producer or director, I could have been an actress obsessed with her looks. But Tomris put us into interesting challenges. She used to choose a painting, and show its colour scale and composition, relating it to our costumes, props and décor. I found myself in such a work, and thank goodness, I was there. (2019)

Ayhan Özen, who was the assistant director of many early dizis, observed the gradual development of many stars: 'If this is their first dizi, whom are they going to ask their questions? Us, the assistant directors, of course. They would check with me, "Am I standing in the right place? Is my voice tone all right? What about my hands?" In time, they grow to be who they are now' (2014). 'Our first generation of dizi actors grew up with us,' says a producer, 'We literally watched them learning how to act.' Neslihan Atagül recalls how she was launched in the dizi industry:

> I decided to become an actress when I was eight years old. When I said to my father, 'I want to be an actress', he said, 'You will, my girl', and caressed my head . . . I found a talent agency from the telephone directory. When they called me for an interview, I asked my mother if she would take me. My mother accompanied me to all my works, until I was 18. (*Sözcü* 2020b)

Leading stars keenly remember their gradual progress in acting. Engin Akyürek narrates the process that led him to stardom, acknowledging how each dizi brought a significant success to his career:

> *Bir Bulut Olsam* was my first leading role. Late Meral Okay wrote it. It's always had a special place in my heart. *Fatmagül'ün Suçu Ne?* made me a star; it was a distinctive project. It also launched me as an international actor. *Kara Para Aşk* sustained my international reputation; it was also a very special project, for which I was nominated for an Emmy, and received a prize from Seoul. (2018)

Beren Saat has a memory of how she literally grew up with the characters she embodied. She emphasizes her personal growth as an individual as much as her professional achievement as an actress:

> My personal progress in life is closely related to some projects . . . When I enacted Fatmagül, I felt like she was my own daughter . . . Acting the role of Bihter was a process of self-discovery. With Bihter, I experienced a very emotional process, concerning the nature of womanhood and love and pain. *İntikam* was a more physical experience, there were fighting classes every week . . . They asked me to hit someone for the

first time, to hurt him ... On that first day I left with my hands shaking. To hurt someone, causing pain, *İntikam* taught me that ... It prepared me for a situation where if someone attacks me on the street now, I can get into a physical fight, I can hit better, you know ... Each painful story in which I acted made me a better person. Characters have been my teachers, my parents over the years. They shaped me more than I did them. (2019)

Canan Ergüder approaches this issue through the implications that the concept of 'maturation' has for an actor:

I would rather call this a 'phase' than being restricted to the term 'maturity', as it is automatically associated with age. As a woman, as Canan, I pass through different stages of my life. I have very old aspects in me as well as childish ones. I choose to live them in different ways at different phases of my life. I therefore want all my roles have similar diversity. Instead of always playing the same role, it becomes more effective for me to search for an original aspect of a particular role. (Özcan 2015)

Dealing with instant fame is a heavy burden on the shoulders of young people, who get caught unprepared for the public-relations management they need to master. The notion of stardom is a matter they appropriate through time. I got an excellent view of stardom from a Turkish actress who shared a red-carpet event with a European movie star of the 1960s. She was taken by surprise observing the sharpness of the movie star's performance not only on the red carpet but at every moment under the public eye:

There was not a moment where she would let people look somewhere else; every gesture of her body language communicated her extravagance. Stardom to this generation is the life itself. We may have many more fans now, but for us, it is different. We separate acting from living. Our generation of stars would seek refuge in their ordinariness.

The interesting point about this statement was a frank assertion that new dizi stars, however globally acclaimed, had reservations about 'acting all the time'. In that, they differed from the senior actors of Yeşilçam, who too were perceived as 'extravagant' and 'eccentric'. One dizi actor recalls his early days with a former Yeşilçam star who had continued his career as a director: 'He would wear the most daring swimming suit, and laugh at my humiliation. "We are artists," he would say, "We are allowed to do crazy things, wear whatever we like. Never get embarrassed!"' Actress Derya Alabora, who joined the dizi industry in the early 2000s, finds this eccentricity a natural component of their profession: 'The idea that actors should be role models is not very viable. Artists are slippery (arızalı) characters, or even schizophrenic in a way. We like to be watched, on the one hand, but our real selves are so far from the characters we impersonate' (2012).

'Slippery character' refers to a certain unreliability, the changing attitudes of actors on dizi sets in regard to their relation to other cast members and the crew. An executive director openly states: 'I won't make friends with actors, because actors cannot be friends.' A director of photography details: 'You cannot expect them to be normal. People jump on them in the streets. It is difficult to keep a sense of balance. Moreover, if fame and money come in your 20s, forget about it.' Producers agree as well. One says, 'Famous people are unstable; I keep my relation limited to the set. I see very few of them outside, and if I meet them out of the set, I treat them all—from junior to senior—like stars.' Some production managers name their relationship with actors 'professional friendships'. Ayşe Özer recalls, 'We used to give feedback to actors after the broadcast, and they would appreciate this' (2012). Director Zeynep Günay-Tan states, 'The most essential rule to be a good actor is to be a good human being for me' (2019).

There are certain differences between the Yeşilçam style of stardom and the newly established dizi work culture. For instance, a 2012 project was discontinued because of such different working styles of the lead

Yeşilçam star and the younger but experienced dizi actresses. The fact that the cast could not 'cohabit' the set ended the project before it began (*Habertürk* 2012; *Medyatava* 2012). Media scholar Ece Özdikici-Duyal's research on the actors working at Istanbul City Theatres reveals the mutual perception of senior and junior actors. Based on a series of in-depth interviews, Özdikici-Duyal's research shows that senior actors perceived the younger generations as impatient, demanding, individualistic, too self-confident and poorly educated, and often looking at theatre as a transitional place. Young actors, in return, complained about the moralistic didacticism, sarcasm and self-indulgence of their seniors (Özdikici-Duyal 2015). Other senior dizi actors also confirm similar views. One complains that many young actors prefer social media to reading books, while another criticizes the lust for fame, contrasting them with previous generations of actors who had to wait long to be noticed (Özyağcılar 2014; Samancılar 2014). Some, however, situate young actors within the new conditions of the dizi industry, stating that there are many new actors who take their job very seriously, praising their collaboration (Çehre 2012), and acknowledging the difficult conditions under which they try to pursue their careers (Taylan 2016).

These encounters reflect how the dizi sets embed a merger of differently placed professionals and create a new social platform where actors from theatre, Yeşilçam and modelling backgrounds develop new social skills to cope with one another. In most cases, producers, experienced directors and actors would regulate these first encounters with preliminary meetings. Before the shootings of *Fatmagül'ün Suçu Ne?* began, producer Kerem Çatay arranged a special time and place for the four young stars to socialize (Çatay 2012). Director Zeynep Günay-Tan gives great importance to the interaction between the two generations:

Ensemble casts produce many stars through such interaction. Let's say a young actor has a scene with a charismatic senior actor for the first time. If the senior crushes the junior or the junior is too intimidated to act with him, nothing will come out of that scene. But if the senior approaches him and says, 'We will do a great scene together', this changes the energy of the whole set.

In most cases, young actors who began their careers with dizis greatly appreciate the presence of senior actors on the set. Cansu Dere, a leading star today, recalls fondly the support of many senior actors during the early steps of her acting: 'I was lucky to start my career with great actors like Uğur Yücel, Tuncel Kurtiz and Menderes Samancılar. You get a special training when you find yourself with such people on the set. You learn a lot during this face-to-face acting' (2013). Betül Durmuş, who coordinated the set of *Fatmagül'ün Suçu Ne?*, recalls how Musa Uzunlar and Murat Daltaban closely worked with some of the less experienced male actors during the shoots (Durmuş 2012). Theatre actress İpek Bilgin, who both acted in dizis and coached many future stars, explains her work with young actors:

> Actors need their instruments to be tuned. Imagine these young people who get noticed in one dizi, then suddenly get cast in a leading role in another. To provide them with an initial perspective is essential. It is important to motivate them, helping them to draw on experiences, memories from their own lives. Each actor has a problem of his own. Which instrument they need to be tuned differs in each case. One can be an exhibitionist, the other introverted—they all bring fears from their past which they need to face. Together we raise their awareness of senses, their relationships. Acting is, after all, transforming your deep personal senses into a public form. (2014)

Amid the traffic of the dizi sets in Beykoz Kundura, I have often witnessed young actors getting help and advice from experienced ones. This happened very often among actors who shared the same set, but also in the case of actors from different sets. Talent agents, and sometimes even directors, became key figures in pointing out the need for special coaching for actors and coordinating such training.

Being Cool but Down to Earth:
On Dizi Actors' Social and Local Backgrounds

Dizi actors come from diverse social and cultural backgrounds, bringing a different chemistry to the cast ensemble. Many emphasize how their modest backgrounds or provincial knowledge mark the authenticity in their acting style. Actor Timuçin Esen was born in Adana to a family who worked at the Keban Dam state enterprise compound, and later moved to Ankara. He sees his time in Keban having a particular influence, exposing him to both Eastern Anatolia and the cosmopolitan community of the compound with Italian and American engineers and their families:

> I spent a very nice childhood. We were like a colony. Because it was safe, parents were comfortable letting their kids go outside, and everyone knew one another. The compound had it all—a kindergarten, a social club, a guesthouse . . . There were engineers, lawyers, and people from all sorts of professions. There were also a lot of locals working there. Especially people from Elazığ and from Eastern Anatolia. We lived there together as a community. When we moved to Ankara, I used to make imitations for my friends, using my memory of characters with Eastern Anatolian accent, of old men and women I remembered. (Esen 2019)

Kadir Doğulu also refers to his local roots:

> I am from Mersin. We are five siblings—four brothers, one sister. My father is a retired worker. My mom is a housewife. It used to be a luxury to go to the movies in those years. There were theatres . . . But when I was a kid, there was no cinema in Mersin. Television came very late into our household. I first saw acting in theatre plays that came to Mersin and Adana; this is how my love for acting started. But life's circumstances led me to other things. One must never stop dreaming . . . My

childhood dream came true when a producer knocked on my door when I was 28. (Gence 2016, 2019)

Engin Akyürek, a leading star, underscores the virtue of local knowledge. 'Localities shape the actors,' he maintains, 'Growing up in Ankara or İzmir makes a difference in who we are and the ways we act' (2012). Long-time character actor Menderes Samancılar was a native of Adana, a city known for its devotion to cinema. He recalls this 'cinema city' inspired him to try his chances in movies: 'There were in average 20 movie theatres on one street in Adana; 20 movie theatres along 4 kilometres . . . Almost all the population of Adana was in movie theatres. I worked in these cinemas selling soft drinks, and working in the ticket office.' Samancılar decided to join a *fotoroman* contest in 1974, which he won while working as a factory worker (Samancılar 2014).

In some cases, local theatre establishments inspired young actors. Erdal Özyağcılar, who grew up in Bursa, enjoyed theatre and theatricality from his early school days. He recalls how the local and family culture had nourished him as an actor: 'We are locally from Bursa. I grew up within a very diverse and colourful environment. My parents, for example, were practicing Muslims. My grandmother was a member of a religious order; my uncle was a Bektaşi' (2014). Özyağcılar also remembers the impact of school shows (*müsameres*) on his growing interest in the stage:

> The costumes and the props of the year-end shows were stored in the attic. I liked to wander around there between the classes. Hoods, costumes, doors, etc. . . . You open the door of the décor, and see that there is no one behind it. The windows were shaky. It was like a shelter . . . I had developed a visual interest then. (2014)

Özyağcılar's parents were fond of theatre and regularly attended the newly opened state theatre. He pursued his training at the Istanbul City conservatory while performing at private companies until he stepped into the television series *Bizimkiler* in 1989.

Serkan Keskin, however, has a different memory of theatre from his locality. He recalls his deserted childhood in İzmit, where cinema was more of a passion than theatre that he had only seen at school shows. His idea of professional theatre was limited to the touring comedy companies. Everything changed when the City Theatre opened in his town in 1997, introducing him to classical plays: 'They played *Hamlet* for six hours and I was so impressed.' Keskin soon joined the theatre school opened by the İzmit City Theatre in 1998, later starting to work as a full-time actor there (2014).

The diversity in the life stories of actors brings a rich repertoire of cultural memory to the dizi production processes. As Diana Taylor reminds us, the repertoire of embodied memory is conveyed in gestures, words, movements, dances, songs and other performances (2003). Different social, regional, class and educational backgrounds of the actors reflect in how they act, and in how they cope with the relationships on sets. Yet they have to incorporate this cultural memory in their audition performance to be cast. For initial auditions, casting agents focus on talent than actors' backgrounds. Senior cast and talent agent Renda Güner states, 'We look at the conclusion; how they use their cultural memory is up to them' (2020). In time, agents accrue a valuable knowledge on the pool of actors, including their attitudes, discipline and social skills in different projects.

Actors' State of Mind: Enduring the Dizi World

Dizi acting has its own particularities. To begin with, it is the best-paying job in the film industry. If a dizi does well, it secures employment for the actors as well as the crew. Nevertheless, it is draining, with long hours of work and unexpected overtime. Actor Serkan Keskin expresses how exhausting it is to constantly wait for the shooting to begin, without knowing how long it will last, and what exactly one would do the next day:

As decision makers, networks' responses are so different now... They say December, but who knows, it may be January too. I don't know, it may start and be cancelled after three episodes. This means you will begin another project, go through the same experience, meeting new people again, have the common anxiety while waiting to see whether the project will be successful or not... I don't want to spend my life like this. (2014)

Many actors are aware that the general public perceives them as the 'privileged' of the industry. One lead actor complains about the general enmity towards actors, on sets as well as in the tabloid press. 'Our summer vacations become hell,' he states, 'reading what we did or ate the next day in the media.' Memet Ali Alabora, the founding chair of Actors' Union, commented on this perception: 'The actor seems like the one who does less but earns the most. But they don't know how hard it is to concentrate in front of the camera after waiting for a long time. And time is precious for us, as we usually run in-between theatre rehearsals, teaching or dubbing' (Alabora 2011). A leading actress of the industry, notes: 'Our presence is always under scrutiny once we step on the set. We get dressed, we try to get into the mood, and we too are always busy until the moment shooting begins, learning and rehearsing our lines'. While many actors greatly value the labour of the set crew, tensions emerge. Vying over whose work is more tiring and who leaves the set first never ends. As one actress stated, although everybody is exhausted, 'At the end of the day, it is the face of the actor which is most visible, and the actor's face cannot appear tired.'

Since the early days of the dizi industry, actors have been closely associated with the characters they enact for several seasons. Halit Ergenç, who has played many such long-standing characters, says: 'When you create a character, people identify you with that character as much as it is watched and liked, until you switch to another project and successfully adopt another character' (2014). Similarly, writer Gaye Boralıoğlu notes: 'Our audience don't detach themselves from what they are watching. They look for a character to identify themselves with' (2012). Passionate fan culture becomes increasingly intrusive, both on social media and on real locations. There are indeed fans who mourn the death of 'Bihter Ziyagil', the leading female character of *Aşk-ı Memnu*, every 24 June, the day her suicide scene was broadcast. In 2020, fans again made this a trending topic on social media (*Haber Global* 2020). Security guards at the gates of film sets often have to argue with fans who come from different towns; requests for photographs never end. At times, actors are confronted by angry fans who refuse to be rebuffed. As a lead actor puts it, 'They come and intervene, even sneaking into the set. Then they go back to their lives, probably cursing us behind our backs and blowing off their steam. We, however, stay on site and continue to work, with the emotion they left us with. It is unfair to expect that actors should please everyone all the time.'

Acting continues for actors, on and off the set environment, even when they are not shooting. On the set, all eyes are always on the stars, which proves to be a constant test of modesty, cooperation and congeniality. 'Producers would follow us from a distance,' a woman star affirmed, 'They would want us to embrace and protect the project. They inquire about how we behave on set, and how we talk about our work.'

The uncertainty of employment is also another challenge of acting in the dizi world. It is hard to wait for a project to show up, or to sustain one when it does. 'You feel like you're forgotten when there is no offer,' says Ozan Akbaba, 'You want to be remembered. And there are so many like you, waiting to be called. When you are feeling lost, people naturally go through anxiety. You think: "Is it always going to be like this?" Everyone goes through this' (2019). Yiğit Özşener sees the sustainability issue as a major problem of the industry as there is no job security: 'The psychological load of uncertainty is huge. You feel a big void when an intense project ends; but then you also learn to move along as you mature. In the end, you get used to the imbalance of things' (2012).

On Acting Styles: Encounters between Theatre, Cinema and Modelling

Turkish television stars today boast millions of fans around the world, an astonishing phenomenon which happened by the end of 2000s. Acting styles in the television world have changed a lot since the early years of dizi making. Aydan Şener, who won Miss Turkey in 1981, and became one of the first dizi stars, remembers her first encounters with experienced actors coming from state theatres:

> These were times when actors were very respectful of one another and caring. When someone else's scene was being filmed, we would stand across them so that they would act better. There were no acting schools back then, but I worked with all these state theatres actors like Haluk Kurdoğlu, Tomris Oğuzalp and Alp Öyken. After 2010s, new actors, digital cameras, new production companies came along, and the agency system began. The structure of the industry changed. We shied away. In fact, I may be the first to switch from dizi to theatre. I got an offer from a play directed by Abdullah Şahin in 2008. I was in Ankara, I read it and said: 'I am in!' Comedy was something I couldn't do in dizis, because they would always cast me in drama. I accepted right away. We toured a lot with that play for two and a half years. (2016).

In fact, what one today calls 'theatre acting' in dizi world is an over-generalization referring to a conservatory education and stage experience. Nevertheless, the difference in acting schools has been a complex issue of theatre training in Turkey, marking different approaches to theatre making and acting. Recent theatre history research reveals the intricacies of these different acting schools and their institutionalization in diverse venues.[21] By the mid 1980s, there were also new sites for

---

21 In their analysis of acting techniques of Turkish theatre actors, Yiğit Kocabıyık and Sibel Erdenk (2018) state how the Stanislavski methodology dominated the

drama training, opened as alternatives to the competitive state conservatories.[22] Theatre directors like Beklan Algan and Şahika Tekand, for instance, established their own circles teaching different techniques (Yılmaz-Karakoç 2015; Sünetçioğlu 2012). Algan invited acclaimed Italian theatre director Eugene Barba for workshops, while Tekand pursued an anti-realist approach, consistently training new actors (*Cumhuriyet* 1995). Acting techniques emerged as an important concept with the rise of dizi-making business in the 2000s.

As actors from all platforms—theatre, cinema, modelling—poured onto dizi sets, there emerged new encounters that evoked different emotions. Senior actors like Nebahat Çehre, Tuncel Kurtiz, Çetin Tekindor and Rutkay Aziz were charismatic characters themselves, bringing their aura to the set. Each had their particular style on how to approach dizis' working environment. Aziz, who has been a long-time director of Ankara Sanat Tiyatrosu (Ankara Art Theatre), used his directorship and managerial skills to cope with the film crew and actors from different backgrounds:

> My relationships have always been respectful and distant. I invite the others to care. In that sense, I determine how my relationships will be set. This partly comes from my directorship background. If you direct a theatre, you manage a set of relationships among people. So, you end up directing your own director as well ... I don't like to make people wait. I know from my young friends that they have variable moods ... My generation didn't grow up like that. We have believed in, respected

state conservatories for a long time. Deniz Başar's (2014) thorough review explains the 'Brechtian wave' of the 1960s and 70s, and its follow-up alternative theatre venues and approaches in the 80s. See also Cem Aykut (2016); Murat Usta (2018).

22 Among others, one can cite BİLSAK Tiyatro Atölyesi (1984), Şahika Tekand's STUDIO (1988), Müjdat Gezen Sanat Merkezi (1991), Sadri Alışık Kültür Merkezi (1997), Ekol Drama (1999) and Tiyatro Pera (2000).

and loved people's efforts. We knew how to thank people. I even thank the taxi driver, the shoeshine boy, my barber. (2016)

Over time, many young actors developed more awareness and interest in different types of acting. They were eager to improve their performances, and some attended special trainings or talent workshops abroad. Acting coach Anthony Vincent Bova, for instance, visited Istanbul several times since 2008, organizing workshops teaching Eric Morris techniques to Turkish actors.[23] Many more acting classes are now available for novices to the dizi world, in addition to conservatories and theatre departments of different universities. Nevertheless, some take pride that they developed their acting style on their own. A leading star, for instance, expressed her sense of freedom in building up her acting style without being influenced by a 'senior teacher' or an 'acting school'. Many young actors also state that they got their training on the set.

There is a general condescending attitude towards dizi acting, when compared with acting in theatre and cinema. It often struck me that many of my interviewees were sensitive to the term 'artistic'. A large majority of them were critical of dizis' hasty production processes but also their commercial vulnerabilities, which constrained artistic creativity. Be it a star or an extra, dizi acting means a commitment to overtime work in an industry with no strong unions. For many, the dizi world is essentially a way to make a living, or collect the necessary amount of money to invest in projects in theatre or cinema. Character actor Erkan Bektaş makes a clear distinction between his acting in theatre and the dizi:

If you act in dizis for three consecutive years without acting in theatre, and then decide to move to theatre, you lose a lot. Each year that you don't take part in a live play, you fall behind as an

---

23 The Eric Morris System offers an intimidating and challenging technique which requires actors to face their inner fears and weaknesses. See Eric Morris (n.d.). For Bova's visits, see Sadi Çilingir (2009); *Istanbul.net.tr* (2015).

actor. Because here in theatre, you discover new things every day . . . Whereas in dizi, you receive the role and the very next day they take you to the shoot. You can display your acting skills there as well, but you cannot improve your acting. You are consuming what you already have accrued, that's the thing. But in theatre, you are productive because you are rehearsing . . . There is always a flow. (2012)

As a character actor, Bektaş could develop a gradual balance in his career between the two arenas. Earning from the dizi industry and investing in the theatre company he founded in 2010, he notes:

> You cannot earn money from theatre, because you have to hire the stage; you always end up losing money. I established Tiyatro Baykuş in 2010, and I have been losing money in the last two years, but you have to earn the money to be able to lose it! I cannot earn that money from anywhere but dizi. Otherwise it would be a dream in Turkey. (2012)

The formally trained Demet Evgar acts in theatre, cinema, commercials and dizis simultaneously. She was a student in a conservatory when she first began acting for television. 'The world of acting is a lion's den,' she says, 'one needs genuine talent to survive' (2012). Birce Akalay values her theatre education from a different angle:

> Conservatory education gives you an additional opportunity; this is a boundless ocean . . . It is so incredible to get a chance for four years, to experience all these different characters that you may never act again in your lifetime. In a dizi or movie, they never propose you enact an 80-year-old if you are 20 . . . With my friends in the conservatory, we experimented tons of different roles. (2018)

Akalay makes clear that this is not about discriminating between those trained in conservatories and others who are not; rather on how the demands of the pace of dizis often cast actors in limited roles (2018).

Eminent actor Fikret Kuşkan points out to the risk of being 'categorized' from their conservatory years while being cast in film:

> [At the conservatory] a commission of 20 people evaluates how a student will perform in the coming two years. They make a proposition to you, 'We think that you should continue in that kind of acting. You will have higher chance of success if you pursue drama.' This is not an enforcement; it is a proposition. This may lead viewers to demand certain actors continuously play comedy roles. If you act in the same play for seven years, they end up associating you with that character. They, however, call me Fikret Kuşkan whatever character I play. I gave 35 years for that. Each of my steps was balanced and careful. I was hungry at times, but I did not play similar roles. This is a battle, a choice. There may be money there, but there is a choice here for artistic creativity. (2012)

The condescending attitude towards dizi acting also changed in time: 'I used to criticize my friends who played in dizis,' Serkan Keskin recalls,

> I had ideas like 'I will never go on television, never on advertisements'. I would even humiliate my friends acting on dizis and say silly things like 'You sold us'. This changed when I found myself penniless, in need of walking from my home in Taksim to Kocamustafapaşa where the theatre was located. Going there was okay but coming back was really hard. (2014)

Halit Ergenç similarly expressed his reservations about discriminating between acting on different platforms:

> Some of my actor friends used to say, 'I can understand, you may act in cinema, but why do you need to do that in dizi?' However, acting is the same everywhere, be it on stage, on big screen or in dizi. The profession is the same profession, the work you do is the same. The rigour should be the same as well.

People who understood this fact made a difference in taking dizi industry one level up. (2014)

There are various subtexts to the negative attitude towards switching to dizi acting from theatre. In the interviews I conducted with actors, the general belief that emerged was that acting skills do not improve in dizis owing to their length, and it also forces actors to repeat themselves. As many actors get cast in very similar roles in a row, it is thought that dizis confine the boundaries of their acting. Timuçin Esen, for instance, was turned down from many projects because he had an 'urban look'. (Esen 2019).

Acting in dizi and in theatre is often compared and contrasted in a moralistic discourse. There is a romantic idea that theatre experience is a continuous spiritual journey, while dizis are temporary even if they last a few seasons. Even if they are paid much higher rates in dizis, actors have to balance their budget, which is a difficult task. Serkan Keskin recalls how his mentor, theatre director Işıl Kasapoğlu, cautioned him, from the very beginning, that many good actors 'get lost' in television: 'I definitely believe that television can ruin actors. Many of my friends disappeared just because of television. That's why I will never quit theatre, this is my actual job. Television may end one day, cinema too; but theatre never will' (2014).

Birce Akalay, a theatre actress who also had a long career in dizis, says:

It is not possible to distinguish the two, but my first love is the stage . . . This is my play garden that I terribly miss and never want to quit. This is where I get healed, refreshed and rejuvenate. I can sleep in theatre, without acting at all; or I can do the décor. This is the place I belong . . . I love to act, of course, and the dizi set has a whole different aura, but the feeling you get when a play begins and ends, and you hear all this applause at the end is priceless. (2018)

A central issue brought up in many of the interviews I conducted with actors has been the distinction they made between acting for the stage and acting for the camera. There is a general belief that those who come from theatre tradition 'act big', meaning they put more emphasis on their voice and gestures in order to project their live performance. Some directors, however, favour a theatre background. One says: 'We often prefer actors who are trained in theatre, it is important that they have disciplined their body language.' Theatre actors have their own reservation about dizi acting. They are hard to please when it comes particularly to the use of language in dizis. Their Turkish is sophisticated with a rich vocabulary, and some do teach diction and pronunciation lessons in various venues. As senior actors, they take the liberty to correct mistaken expressions in the scripts. Occasionally, however, they too make mistakes or forget their lines while filming in haste. All actors from a theatre background have a memory of their first-time camera experience. Learning to be exposed to cameras requires a process of adjustment. Theatre actor and director Barış Falay recalls his first encounters with the camera:

> It was all about framing. The frame of the theatre is large; acting in front of the camera is different. You have to fill the frame. Otherwise the orchestration of acting, the managing of emotions, is the same in dizi, theatre and music video . . . The old generation used to have an exaggerated style of stage acting, but camera doesn't create any problems with the new generation of theatre actors. (2012)

Erkan Bektaş, who also hails from the theatre, developed a gradual balance between the two mediums. He began acting in short films and discovered acting for the camera. Meanwhile, he began dubbing for films, developing in time expertise to direct some dubbing sessions. On the dizi set, his best support were other theatre actors who worked on the same project (Bektaş 2012).

The relationship with the camera is quite different for those whose acting career started with the dizis. A leading woman dizi star explained: 'I was beamed in front of the cameras. My acting developed in conjunction with camera moves. I quickly learned where the director wanted me to stand, or to move according to the lights. I noticed in time that many senior actors lacked some basic tricks, simply because their acting was stage-oriented.' Beren Saat, who began acting at a very young age, approaches camera acting from a different angle:

> The reason that camera attracted me more than the stage is this idea that an unimaginable performance that you may give will be archived forever . . . I find it really magical that such a miraculous moment is selected to air, and will last there forever. This is why I decided that acting in front of the camera is the place where I should be . . . I am the most fascinated when even I don't know how I will act, and what I perform transcends my expectation. In *Kösem* there was this moment where [my son] Mehmet dies . . . Acting is all about struggling for months for that one miraculous scene to arrive. It is an extremely painful process . . . You tolerate many scenes so that you can reach this unique moment of acting. (2019)

I was visiting the set of *Kösem* when Saat performed that particular scene on 22 May 2016. It was an amazing experience to watch how the whole set, the cast and crew get ready for the shoot. In complete silence, Saat got out of the trailer in which she had locked herself to concentrate, then walked unflinchingly towards the marble floor where lay Mehmet's corpse. Facing death, loss and motherly pain, she began with whispers but rose gradually to a crescendo of screams. We felt like a true stage audience that day. The set was an open-air theatre with all the cast and crew, and myself, as viewers and witnesses to that 'miraculous moment' that Saat described a few years later. Television audiences watched the scene in its edited version on 26 May 2016, but the real performance was purely a theatrical experience (see *YouTube* 2016).

However fragmented dizi acting may be, actors do find moments of powerful performances. A director told me in 2012 how she had tears in her eyes watching her actors perform a most awaited scene in which they played a couple who are becoming physically intimate after a long time. The scene marked the climax of the story. She praised them: 'He performed so much more than I asked from him, and she was so good to respond—it was such a special work.'

Halit Ergenç, who has experienced both stage and camera acting since the mid-1990s, draws attention to generational differences in stage acting. Observing the exaggerated acting style of former generations, he felt more attracted to performing in a more 'natural' style: 'If you are in front of a camera, everything is normal, like in real life. Trying to catch this natural state, to give life to a realistic moment was more interesting to me. It was not possible to achieve this naturalness on stage' (Ergenç 2014). Demet Evgar, also trained in theatre, summarizes the distinction between acting for the stage and the camera:

> It is all about where and how you will project yourself. In ancient theatre, you had audience on four sides. In camera acting, you need the 'coordinates', you will determine your angles. It is like a mathematical code. I usually ask, 'Where are you going to focus?' Then I can interact with the camera, decide how much I will get closer, which angle should I adopt. (2012)

Erkan Bektaş distinguishes between the two in terms of the use of the body as an instrument: 'On stage, you have to use your whole body to transfer that energy. The camera usually focuses on your face—you just project a visual; but as actors we always have an awareness of bodily energy' (2012). A female star expressed her relation to the camera almost as an emotional interaction: 'Directors like working with me because I can feel the camera and am able to project the right visual. If the light moves and casts a wrong shadow, I know how to change my position on my own. Creating the image is essential—to cry but not to look ugly, to produce nuances for the viewers with a look, or to appear real even when you are acting.'

Small private theatres abound in Istanbul ever since the 2000s (Fişek 2018). Actor-director Haluk Bilginer, who runs the private theatre Oyun Atölyesi in the city, gives a very different account of acting for camera. While auditioning young actors for stage plays, he observed how camera acting had influenced their performance style. For him, this turned out to be 'bad acting':

> If you cannot use the camera in a smart way, or if you develop bad habits from the camera, you may have harmful outcomes in theatre. There is one thing the camera imposes on us: to be minimal. We understand doing nothing by being minimal; this is really dangerous. You need a different aura on stage, a different energy. Because you don't use this energy when you act for the camera, you lose it on stage as well; and I want that aura of the theatre . . . [In filming] some directors tell actors 'it is too theatrical'. I tell them 'don't say theatrical; don't insult theatre'. One should call this 'bad acting', not theatrical acting. (Bilginer 2013)

Bilginer has had a long dizi career since the 1990s and won the 2019 International Emmy Award for best performance by an actor. With his knowledge of both types of acting, he proposes an awareness of performative context:

> If the camera focuses here, act accordingly. Thinking about it is enough—this is simple reasoning. Camera will read your thoughts. Just think, that will do! But in theatre, thinking will not be enough. You have to deliver it with your body, your voice—because you have 500 people in front of you. How can those on the last row hear you? This is simple reasoning, a matter of intelligence. If you try to do on stage what you are used to doing in front of the camera, no one will be able to tolerate watching you, because it will be really absurd. (Bilginer 2013)

Canan Ergüder discovered another important aspect of 'camera acting' while enacting Gülfem, a complex woman character in *Güllerin Savaşı* (2014). The multifaceted performance of the character became challenging when she was all by herself. Ergüder describes how being alone in front of the camera affected her acting:

> The hard part of that role was the fact that this woman had many faces, and each was opening a gate for the other. When she was alone in front of the camera, the reality that she wanted to show to different characters in different ways transformed into its most genuine form. This enabled me to use the camera in different ways than usual. It improved my technical knowledge. Gülfem character contributed greatly to my personal and professional progress. I had accepted the project with a rather negative feeling, which in time turned into a positive one. (Özcan 2015)

The dizi industry's rise since the 1990s led to the development of a community of actors with its own codes of ethics and collegiality. When dizis last more than a season, actors bond with one another. Barış Falay says: 'You pass long hours together, develop a road companionship. Especially, imagine you are in a remote site, stuck in a trailer when it is terribly cold out there, you get to know people around you in a much much deeper way' (2012). Once the project ends, the cast gets dispersed, while technical crew often stick together for another project. Most stars point to the hardship of establishing friendships with other actors under the competitive structure of the dizi industry. A woman star expressed that such friendships develop mostly if they both work with the same talent agency, or spend a memorable time on the same set. For the first encounters, production companies organize preliminary gatherings, reading rehearsals or dinners. Falay tells that in some cases, producers even place senior actors as disguised leaders in the cast (2012). Although working in a very competitive industry, actors do cooperate on the set. Mustafa Avkıran reported how he assisted Kıvanç Tatlıtuğ during the shooting of a morgue scene: 'We came to a real morgue, we were walking around, sensing its smell and cold. Kıvanç told me, "Only a father can take this guy out of that kind of place, so you have to take the lead and help me"' (Avkıran 2012). Similarly, Halit Ergenç recalled the process of rehearsing for a scene with Okan Yalabık in *Muhteşem Yüzyıl* to imagine the body language and interaction between a sultan and his grand vizier in a historical context. After long hours of trial and error, they finally developed together a certain manner which convinced them and the directors (Ergenç 2014).

There are times, however, when actors encounter challenging situations. Gender codes of Turkish culture may sometimes cause social clashes, or even violence in daily life. Intimate moments in romance scenes in dizis often become a source of tabloid gossip, or inspire lots of reactions and responses on social media, especially when the actors are married or are in committed relationships. In one case, for instance, a male star made sure to meet his partner's husband in their house before the project began. In another, tabloid reporters triggered a dialogue between two husbands even before the dizi began. Unless they are not offensive to their personal feelings, many actors ignore such cases. Like the rapid pace of dizi production, clashes or gossips are also soon forgotten, replaced by other news from emerging new dizis.

Debates on Claiming the Character: The Strife between Writers and Actors

The encounter between the writers and the actors is one of the most delicate issues in the creation of a dizi. 'Written characters of course come to life through the interpretation of the actors who play the role. Because dizi episodes last over an hour, and seasons may continue for more than a year, this encounter turns into an ever-evolving relationship between writers and actors. As the scripts are also in-progress, written a few weeks before shooting, both sides have competing and altering claims on characters. One writer summarizes this, saying 'characters shape up on the way' (*karakterler yolda düzülür*). The attitudes of both writers and actors vary, depending on different approaches they adopt. Each dizi project has a life and chemistry of its own, and in the end, human relations on and off the set greatly determine the writing processes and the fate of the project at hand.

Writers' Perspective

Writer Meriç Acemi describes dizi writing as 'a companionship': 'Dizi is a living entity, which grows if all components work out well. We do write along with this companionship rather than heading towards an absolute end' (2016). Some sets create a sense of community, which can be interpreted in different ways. These dynamics and intimacy are what the cast and the crew refer in their testimonies as a 'family-like' environment. What Acemi calls a 'companionship', however, points to an individual dialogue with every member of the creative team. The creative process requires harmony among writers, actors and producers. Each group has its own priorities, which need to be 'smoothly' negotiated during the rushed course of dizis' production. Companionship combined with harmony is therefore a talisman that can be broken at any moment in this business of high egos. Over the years, there have been successful dizis which ended because of tensions among writers, actors and producers. Nevertheless, many dizis survived long years, thanks to the 'managed harmony' of these parties. Producer Şükrü Avşar openly narrates how he pays attention to the human values of the actors, before casting them in his projects:

> Let's say he is a good actor, and popular too. He may take us up, but I would check whether the project will proceed in a healthy way or not. If he is a defective type—and let's accept that many actors are defective—what would happen after the third episode? Where will the project go? He has to respect me, be someone who would not want me to get hurt or upset. I deeply care for the moral character of the actors. He must be

considerate, genuine and ethical. It doesn't work otherwise. I may work in the short run, but it gets worse and worse . . . I don't like pampering them and saying, 'Let the wheel spin.' If it won't work, let this be stopped from the very beginning. (2015)

In the early days of dizi making, maintaining this harmony was perhaps easier or it happened automatically. The experience was new to everybody; broadcast projects were rare; and television was a novel source of income. *Bizimkiler* (1989) is a case in point. Erdal Özyağcılar recalls having lived almost like a state employee in those days:

We used to go to the set as if we were going to a regular job. For nine years, I went there in the morning and came back in the evening. We used to work and chat, watch the episode with [writer] Umur Bugay and our writer friends . . . We would chat and discuss about it. Then we would go for dubbing . . . Those nine years were so beautiful. (2014)

During the 1990s, dizis were few, and producers mostly employed established actors. With private networks' growing demand for new programming, dizi production increased in the 2000s. This was the harbinger of a new generation of young actors who began their careers in dizis. They did not attain star status right away but many of them welcomed the attention of the print media and television talk shows. These were the years that launched numerous casting and talent agencies. Each agency had its own style and portfolio and they picked up actors. The 2000s saw the launch of dizis with powerful content, casting new actors in memorable roles that made them celebrities. These actors made up the first generation of dizi stars who received global fame and acclaim.[24]

---

24 Examples include Kıvanç Tatlıtuğ and Songül Öden (*Gümüş*), Kenan İmirzalıoğlu (*Deli Yürek*), Fahriye Evcen (*Yaprak Dökümü*), Bergüzar Korel and Halit Ergenç (*1001 Gece*), Beren Saat and Okan Yalabık (*Hatırla Sevgili*), Engin Akyürek and Engin Altan Düzaltan (*Bir Bulut Olsam*).

The interaction between writers and actors becomes stressful when it concerns claim on characters. Over the last two decades, both sides have developed strong ideas about one another, and one needs to explore them separately for an elaborate understanding of this important aspect of dizi production. Let us begin with the writers' perspective on how they approach the enactment of the characters they create. Following a series of interviews I conducted with writers, along with many others I collected from public media, my primary observation is that the determinants of this encounter has been the historical conjunction, the subgenre and the writer's subjectivity. The relationship between the actors and writers has changed through time, because the working style and conditions of dizi making have evolved. Writers of the early dizis benefited, for example, from the industry's 'age of innocence', when actors were not yet stars and their collaboration was stronger. Nilgün Öneş remembers how the actors' genuine interactions affected her writing of *Asi* (2007), a dizi filmed in Antakya in the southeast of Turkey:

When we visited Antakya for research, we passed quite some time with the actors who had begun shooting in the family house. This was a wonderful place, bordering Syria. Everybody was working with great harmony, belief and love. All these feelings reflected on the work as well. The unity, motivation and communal solidarity of the team affected me a lot. (2017a)

Meral Okay, the chief writer of *Muhteşem Yüzyıl*, details her relationship with real historical characters:

As a television writer, I cannot see the power of those dramatic heroes as a historian. It's not possible. Of course, we are inspired by history, we set out with a historical perception; but official history and ordinary battles and victories are all a background for me. What I want to put forward is the psychology of the characters who have made all those great achievements, their conflicts in life, their loves, their passions, their hatred, their power games . . . I'm fascinated by Kanuni's romance . . .

when I read his poems which he wrote under the name of Muhibbi, I could not gather myself for two days. Because I encountered a great romantic. Passionate, angry, in love, sad but a great romantic . . . It is in my hands how to construct the dialogues between Kanuni and Hürrem . . . I have Hürrem's love letters, Kanuni's poems. Those are my reference points. Other than that, I'm calculating what kind of fight might take place between a man and a woman in a power game. (Özkartal 2011)

The creation of characters forms the basis of a solid story; and writers embark on a journey of imagination in constructing them. They continue to nurture them as they mature through the season—or seasons. Every writer has their own way of constructing their stories and characters. Ethem Özışık states that the general frame of his script begins with the characters who build their own stories:

Most of the time, it is first the character that appears in my head. For example, once I had some free time and imagined a character by the name of Sönmez Alsancak. He was a detective in a homicide department, a figure similar you can find in Oğuz Atay's world.[25] He was in his 50s. I always had Haluk Bilginer on my mind while writing him. He was a reserved but witty character. (2017)

When a producer proposed he write an adaptation of *The Godfather*, he proposed back another story whose lead character Poyraz Karayel was similar to the detective he had imagined before:

When beginning *Poyraz Karayel*, I started with a blank page. Neither Zülfikar, nor Sefer, Taşkafa, Bahri existed. There was no overall story or character analysis . . . Poyraz opened with a scene that we had never seen before. He wakes up in the bed

---

25 Oğuz Atay (1934–1977) was a pioneer of the modern novel in Turkey. His novels pursued the controversies of Turkish society during modernization.

of a girl he doesn't know, and finds himself in thousands of funny situations. He has a kid that is taken away from him. With these at hand, later on, the main conflict of the story unfolded. (2017)

Dizi writers are also directors of their own scripts in their minds. Many write very detailed descriptions of the state of mind of their characters, the places where particular scenes should take place, or how they imagine a character's hair style. Meriç Acemi imagines her characters in real locations, suggesting sites where the scene should be shot (2019). Knowledge of the set is very important for the accuracy of the scenes. Before the writing of *Bir Zamanlar Çukurova*, Ayfer Tunç visited the newly constructed *konak* in Adana to better understand the inter-spatial relations of rooms and other neighbouring buildings, roads, gardens and walls (Karacakaya 2019). Gökçe Bilgin-Kılıç, who edited both *Aşk-ı Memnu* and *Fatmagül'ün Suçu Ne?*, provides an example from writers Ece Yörenç and Melek Gençoğlu: 'Their script is very detailed. Hair, accessories—everything is important. They write emotions in detail, too. For example, they write side notes like "they want to get closer, but cannot". What makes their scripts different is reading these side notes of the script as a novel' (Bilgin-Kılıç 2012).

The construction of characters in a comedy has its own dynamics. Humour writers say they particularly like to take the cue from comedians. Kandemir Konduk, one of the pioneers of screenwriting in Turkey, underlined the ease of working with comedians: 'If you know the actors, it is a great advantage for you as the writer, because you know how they can deliver a particular line, how they will look when they get mad. Once you know them, you develop an imagination of how they will act what you write, and you write accordingly' (Konduk 2014). 'They often tell me how good I am in casting,' says Birol Güven, the writer of hit dizis like *Çocuklar Duymasın* and *Seksenler*: 'I write indeed according to the actors I have in hand. Responding to the particular talent of an actor is like playing tennis. This is how I wrote for Tamer

[Karadağ] and developed further his character. It is so important to observe their performances. What comes out from the set gets restructured in the script' (2014).

Similarly, in *Leyla and Mecnun* (2011), where the ensemble cast and the creative team were very close, the set had become a site for many opportunities for improvisation. Writer Selçuk Aydemir narrates how his interaction with actors and the shooting process affected his writing: 'Sezai goes into auto-repair shop. What will happen? I don't know! I have to write something very different, so different that it amazes everybody . . . There are so many funny happenings on the set. When the actors bring up what they have in their bags, this also feeds our imagination' (Aydemir 2014).[26]

Ali Atay, who played the character of Mecnun, summarized this fact as 'It was like a division of labour. Our writer wrote it all on his own. Where he could not finish, we were completing the rest on the set' (2012). Burak Aksak, the co-writer and director of *Leyla and Mecnun*, confirmed how each actor contributed with their own style:

> When they all gathered together, there was a whole new energy. I began writing by hearing them act, using the jargon they produced among themselves. That was the fun part of it, and the fun came totally from this unique merger of these particular actors' talents. With different actors, the project would turn out to be something totally different. (2015)

Understandably, writers have a sensitivity regarding the casting, and they usually get actively involved in the process. As one lead writer

---

26 *Leyla and Mecnun* (2011) also had a large group of fans following them on sets and in social media. The team of actors, writer and director toured many cities for organized sessions meeting audiences and answering their questions. The project ended abruptly when members of the team commented on social media about the Gezi Park Protests of 2013, which later turned out to be a political breakthrough for the ruling party (see Öztürkmen 2014).

says, 'We must have a say in deciding who will give life to the characters we wrote.' In some cases, they scout out new talents themselves. The casting of Öykü Karayel as a partner to the leading star Kıvanç Tatlıtuğ in *Kuzey Güney*, serves as a case in point. The series writer Ece Yörenç proposed her name to the producers after seeing her in a theatre play (*Gecce* 2012). Yörenç also convinced the producers to cast Esra Dermancıoğlu in *Fatmagül'ün Suçu Ne?* after a series of auditions (Dermancıoğlu 2015). Both actresses, discovered by a writer, continue their careers in the field.

Ethem Özışık notes that although writers are inspired by certain actors while writing characters, there are times where circumstances do not allow them to be cast in these roles, and other actors are employed. How well or badly their written characters are performed also affects them deeply: 'Good, successful actors convince you, and the way they adapt to their characters is breath-taking . . . you see them embracing their characters. It looks as if they were waiting for these characters all along' (Özışık 2017). Meriç Acemi also occasionally takes inspiration from the actors. In *Kiralık Aşk*, she gave a new direction to the comic character of Necmettin, enacted by theatre actor Levent Ülgen. The moment she understood that the dizi will survive, she decided to give this character a stronger dramatic course, a move which enabled her to produce other side stories for script (Acemi 2016).

In certain cases, when a dizi continues for more than a season, the characters evolve through the actors' performances. Burcu Görgün-Toptaş, one of the writers of *Karasevda*, which won the 2017 International Emmy for best telenovela, explains how their dizi characters took new turns throughout the writing process. As the actors bring new flavour to them, the characters change while the dizi is broadcast:

> Three of our characters had come a long way from where they'd begun when we completed the 35th episode . . . Kemal, Nihan and Emir were very different people now . . . Kemal is a very special character. Burak Özçivit performs him wonderfully in

each episode. He puts forward all his spirit and intricacies. As he takes Kemal farther, we too pass through his honesty, truthfulness and conscience. He made this character one of us. For a full season, Kemal was never afraid of failure, and for that he never compromised in his virtues, fought for them, persisted and kept loyal to his beliefs. Nihan, on the other hand, fought her biggest battle against her own heart and loved ones . . . The fact that Neslihan Atagül gave life to Nihan's character was both our and the character's good fortune. As she excelled in that role, we loved Nihan all the more as writers and audience . . . She turned out to be a very valuable character for us with her love and state of mind . . . Like Kemal, and unlike most, she too chooses the hard path. Kemal's existence transformed Emir; Emir's existence grew and transformed Kemal. Of course, Kaan Urgancıoğlu's wonderful performance brought a whole different dimension to our story and character . . . When Kaan Urgancıoğlu's wonderful acting and interpretation enriched our script even further, we met Emir Kozcuoğlu whom we all enjoyed watching . . . Emir has a strong sense of humour and perceptiveness, an inner world of his own intertwined with naked truth. He is a bright man and Kaan crowns the character with wonderful acting. If we knit every knot carefully, he unties each of them one by one, as if he is solving an equation and deconstructing it, analysing the character, finding the correct answers and finally revealing it as a shining Emir Kozcuoğlu. And we end up watching him with admiration. (Görgün-Toptaş and Yılmaz 2016)

Writer's relation to actors vary depending on their subjectivities. Some writers enjoy the interaction with actors. Ali Can Yaraş, for instance, tells how he often talks with actors, and writes accordingly for them, even taking into consideration their physical characteristics.

'While writing, I like chatting with them,' he states, 'hearing their ideas and propositions.' He then asserts, however, his caution:

> What I mean by proposition is not that an actor asking, 'What will be my part?' I listen if he makes a suggestion about the character that he is playing, and I use it. Because when you are writing a script, you're creating 30–40 characters instead of 20. You think about all of them. But the person who plays a certain character thinks only about her own, and more deeply . . . I pay attention to the suggestion made by an actor who thinks deeply about her character and offers good input. Saying no to this would be silliness. Besides, I talk not only with the actors but all of the crew members. Lighting guy, cameraman, tea maker—I talk to everyone and listen to their ideas. Especially in long-lasting projects, everyone has an idea about the story. For example, in Serseri, the final line belongs to Recep Ağabey, the tea seller of the set. He worked in 65 episodes with us and wrote a poem. It was beautiful, and this is how we made the finale. (Yaraş 2008)

In some cases, writers like to cooperate intensively with actors and directors. During the writing of *Poyraz Karayel,* Ethem Özışık notes that he benefited greatly from the feedback of lead actor İlker Kaleli and director Çağrı Vila Lostuvalı. He appreciated Kaleli's reading and commenting on the entire script. This way, Özışık, states, they were able to 'solve' many problems during shooting without involving the producers. He also recalls a moment when he received a call from actor Burçin Terzioğlu about an abortion scene:

> Because I am a reserved person, I never believe that a certain scene, or the script in general, is good unless somebody approves of it. I always live with that uneasiness; the question 'Is it good enough?' regularly runs in my mind. Recently, Burçin talked about the abortion scene at a university panel.

I never forgot the moment when I wrote that scene. I had thought, 'Did I go too far; is it too much?', and had sent the script immediately to Burçin. I was driving that day and crossing the Bosphorus Bridge when Burçin called. She was crying her eyes out; she literally could not speak. I heard a 'God damn you, Edhem' that day. I would get rid of that scene if she had told me so (Özışık 2017).

Ece Yörenç and Melek Gençoğlu also remain in close contact with actors, exchanging ideas. They prefer actors to share their ideas with them, or inform them if they notice a mistake or if 'a word does not fit their mouth' (*ağzına oturmayan söz*). They are very sensitive about the mispronunciation or misuse of a certain word and usually ask for dubbing if necessary. Yörenç calls attention to fine semantic nuances: 'Once when an actor said *keşhane* instead of *kâşâne*, we sent him immediately to dubbing. The term *evladım* is not the same with *çocuğum*.' (Yörenç and Gençoğlu 2013). They also do not want any changes in dialogues: 'Things would go out of control,' Yörenç states, 'if they begin changing the script on the set. We make it clear to them why a certain character behaves the way they do in the current episode, informing them what will happen three weeks later. Each of our actors waits for the next script with the curiosity of a viewer' (Yörenç and Gençoğlu 2013).[27] For some writers, keeping in touch with the actors proves to be useful. 'We meet actors occasionally,' state Kerem Deren and Pınar Bulut: 'The request usually comes from them; we may discuss their characters, the feelings we find important to be delivered. They sometimes ask where to focus, or express their opposition to a particular line, which they say "does not fit them"' (Deren and Bulut 2014).

During my interviews with dizi writers, I also observed that some writers preferred to keep a distance, concerned that actors might

---

27 Yörenç and Gençoğlu ended their co-writing partnership in 2013 (see *Medya-tava* 2013).

interfere in the writing of the story. This was in fact how the creative teams worked in the early years of dizi making, when the episodes were shorter in duration. Actress Aydan Şener recalls how stars were more involved in the projects during the 1980s, having a say in the flow or the ending of the story. 'We could interfere in the course of the story or a particular dialogue,' Şener remembers. In *Kumru* (2000), for instance, she proposed switching the gender of the killer: 'I thought, very instinctively, perhaps also by experience, that it would be more effective if the wife killed the older husband, not the reverse. And it was very effective. In *Ay Işığında Saklıdır*, it was I who found the story, and the writer wrote the script' (2016).

In contemporary project design, writers, producers and casting agencies work closely together in selecting the actors who will enact the characters. Once the project takes off, however—and especially if it becomes successful—actors sometimes develop a desire to interfere in the script. 'I usually do not go to the sets,' a lead writer states, 'and I am careful not to be too friendly with actors, as they would, in the end, try to influence you.' Nihan Küçükural concurs, stating that writers should be kept off sets: 'We have to focus on characters in stories, not characters in real life. The actors want their parts enhanced, or they may ask for a smaller part because they need time for a movie project. If there is tension between the script writer and the actor, and if the director supports the actor, the actors may show off' (2011).

Other writers confirmed their prudence regarding actors' interference. 'Many have no idea about how literary plots work, and focus only on their own character's story line', notes another lead writer. 'Just because they enact their characters—and they do it very well—they claim the right to have a say in the story.'

Ali Can Yaraş likes to have a closer contact with the production team: 'I prefer to be present on sets as much as I can, I like it and I go there . . . To be able to talk one to one. To get comments. This is what feeds me. I often engage in this exchange' (2008). Gaye Boralıoğlu says it is the hardest thing to establish a relationship with the actor: 'Actors can sometime inspire you to pursue a detail in your text, but once a script goes to the set, it is always open for others' comments' (2012).

Actors' Perspective

While the writers imagine and pen the characters, actors are the ones who give life to them. Seminal Russian director Konstantin Stanislavski (1863–1938) underlined long ago how the subtext of the script is key to the actors' performance: 'Spectators come to the theatre to hear the subtext. They can read the text at home' (Moore 1984: 28). Subtext referred to the unspoken meaning of the text, which could only be interpreted by the actor through gestures, postures, pauses or intonation. It is through the actor's imagination that the subtext could 'speak' to the audience.[28] Richard Bauman's approach to verbal art as performance reminds us of the accountability of the performer: 'Performance rests on an assumption of responsibility to an audience for a display of communicative virtuosity' (2004: 9). For actors, this virtuosity refers to their skill in constructing their character. Nilgün Öneş explains how the writer's character shifts towards the actor's character, moving from the 'imagined' to 'enacted' in the context of the dizi:

> If you work for a dizi project, it is a long journey. As you carry on writing, the characters come alive and begin to move in front of your eyes. They become independent individuals apart from you and you sometimes feel that they confront what you write. At this point, I try to build a secret relationship with the characters. The actor doesn't know about it. The character they act and the character I write become conflicting. We succeed to the extend we compromise. I mean, after a while, we begin

---

[28] The literature on acting deconstructs 'subtext' in different ways, where the concept is used as a guide for actors-to-be. Among others, see Robert Barton (2011); John Gillett and Christina Gutekunst (2014).

to give direction to one another. Of course, I value speaking face to face with the actors, answering their questions about the characters, or solving any problems they may have. Both of us benefit from these kinds of interactions. At the end of the day, we are doing something together and we have a lot to learn from each other. (2017a)

Many dizi actors from a theatre background are familiar with different methods of acting, including Stanislavski's. Nevertheless, acting without having a knowledge of how the story will proceed is another challenge. Dizi acting is already fragmented and repetitive, as the same scenes are shot several times, from different angles. Many actors chase 'strong scenes' in the script, so that they can display a 'virtuosity' within a short span of time. There is also a difference between the preliminary preparations to weave a character, and acting it during the shooting. Many actors complain about 'acting within the unknown'. During the rush of the production process, actors do not usually have access to scripts until a few days before shooting. Their relation to the script is often a stressful one, as they are continually required to incorporate new material from the writers who are under pressure from producers and networks. With the change in ratings, producers may decide changing directors or even writers midway. In a recent dizi with two leading stars, for instance, a renowned director had coached the actors for a month in order to prepare them for their introverted characters. After the first two episodes, the ratings appeared much lower than predicted; the director quit, the writer changed, and the characters took on entirely new directions. The lead actress who played a reserved character dressed modestly in the first episodes was asked to wear stylish, colourful costumes. She expressed her concern: 'To stay on air, they pump up the characters; how I began has nothing to do with the character I now play.' The series could only survive for two more months and was finally cancelled. In such cases, many actors complain about the vulnerability of the dizis vis-à-vis the ratings, and accuse the networks of not sufficiently supporting the projects. 'This also affects our careers,' one star says, 'because when a dizi is cancelled, it is regarded as the failure of the stars, and also changing the character's profile midway makes us look as if we cannot act well.'

Cansu Dere, also a leading star, says it is difficult portraying a 'character-in-progress': 'In some cases, because of the rush of the production process, we follow our characters much better than the writers' (2013). Similarly, actress Esra Dermancıoğlu describes the difficulty of performing a 'character without a story': 'In cinema you act a settled character. In dizi, your character can take a totally new turn the following week to beam up the ratings' (2012). In the early years of dizi production, there were even times when shooting was delayed or rescheduled because of the belated delivery of the script. The assistant director of a project says, 'There have been days when scenes were shot literally "without a script".' The fact that the writer was also the director created this interesting performative platform, where the script was not read but delivered as spoken word.

As dizis are often written by a team of writers and in great haste, it is inevitable that sometimes discrepancies emerge in the flow of their narratives. In some cases, the hastily written scripts may include errors of logic that may occur owing to the haste of the fragmented writing process, or because of product placement, or for problems in finance or selection of location. In other cases, with the fall in ratings, producers or network managers may anxiously interfere to change the course of the story. Theatre actor and director Barış Falay has played in dizis since the early 2000s, and he comments on how actors have to at times react to the script:

> Sometimes, there emerge really absurd situations. Then, I even call the producer and tell them there is something wrong in the story. He checks and contacts the writer. But also, in a case where the writer, producer and the actor cannot arrive at a compromise, there's not much that an actor can do. The essence

of our job is to 'create moments'. We have to abide by the script and understand it very well, so that we can pursue the story and make choices on how to interpret it. (2012)

Once the characters are settled, actors feel more power to express their views on them. In a period drama adapted from a well-known Turkish novel, a male star who enacted the lead character was very uncomfortable about the rising number of fighting scenes. He stated, 'This character is a gentleman, fighting is not something my character would do. In those cases, I do the least I can do, so that they won't write me such a scene again.'[29] In *Fatmagül'ün Suçu Ne?*, the woman character played by Beren Saat was forced to move to the city from her small town. When she was asked to wear more urban outfits, Saat renounced, saying that she needed to stay in her provincial style to continue the character she had weaved through (Tunç 2012).

Stars are very sensitive in regard to the delivering the depth of their characters. For historical dramas, this comes with a particular baggage, as actors are expected to impersonate real figures from Ottoman history. In a country like Turkey where nationalism is strong and historical taboos dominate, this task is not easy. This is why *Muhteşem Yüzyıl*, a globally travelling dizi, was subject to harsh criticism and protests. However, it set a ground for many more to follow.[30] For actors, however, enacting a historical character is a memorable experience in their career. Mehmet Günsür, who acted the role of the son of Sultan Süleyman in *Muhteşem Yüzyıl*, recounts:

---

29 There is a growing literature on the portrayal of masculine charisma as heroism, family boyhood or romance in Turkish dizis. See Neslihan Sezgin (2006); Emel Baştürk Akça and Seda Ergül (2014); Yelda Yanat-Bağcı (2018). For men and romance, see also Katherine Byrne, Julie Taddeo and James Leggott (2018).

30 See *Hürriyet* (2011). Other dizis in the similar genre included *Diriliş: Ertuğrul*, *Abdülhamid* and *Kuruluş: Osman*, which were produced in a more conformist style. See *Cumhuriyet* (2016); Josh Carney (2018).

It gives you pleasure to act out someone who really lived. It is a great responsibility; and this responsibility is so exciting. Because you have so much data, and you make connections between today and 500 years ago. For example, in *Muhteşem Yüzyıl*, we filmed the sword-girding ceremony on real location in Topkapı Palace. We filmed it right where Prince Mustafa really took his oath. Imagine, the character you are acting out really took an oath there 500 years ago. (2012)

Engin Altan Düzyatan, who played the lead character in *Diriliş: Ertuğrul*, explains his relation to an important historical figure. Ertuğrul was the father of Osman Ghazi, the founder of the Ottoman Empire, and little is known of his life story (Kafadar 1995). Düzyatan details how he and the writers evolved his character in the script:

Ertuğrul Gazi, whom I play and we write, is very brave; he does whatever he wants to do instantly . . . As his responsibilities increase, his character shifts from someone impulsive to someone who behaves more consciously. He can stand by his decisions. I enjoy acting this season more than the other periods. Now the whole system has changed . . . It's pretty cool . . . We usually play clichéd roles on television. But Ertuğrul Gazi is not one of them. This is what I like in this character. (Ulusum 2016)

He also calls attention to the playful aspect of acting in historical drama:

They gave us a lot of toys and said, 'Take these and play!' There are too many toys in this series for an actor: swords, arrows, bows, horses, costumes . . . There is nothing more fun than that for an actor . . . We have been training really hard and we still do. There are battles all the time and we need to use swords. Now I can really guess where the next move will come from. If I have to ride a horse for hours, I can do that too . . . I believe I can also survive in deserted areas. (Ulusum 2016)

Fahriye Evcen, who studied history in college, also underlines how costume can be an advantage for getting into a historical character :

What you see as hardship becomes, at the same time, something helpful. You feel like entering a time tunnel where a different world is created with all the costumes and décor. You develop a deeper relation with the surrounding world, and it affects your acting. Researching the spirit of a period drama may become more interesting than playing a contemporary character. (2015)

'Historical imagination' is in fact a general challenge for historians, and both the description and the meanings assigned to the body and movement requires a deep inquiry.[31] Imagining the body and movement in historical context has been also a difficult task for filmmakers in all genres, as it involves a process of visual substantiation of historical ethnography. Eminent director Pier Paolo Passolini, for instance, is best remembered in his effective depiction of the medieval body (Mancini and Perrella 2017; Maggi 2009). The creative team of the BBC historical drama *Rome* (2005), for instance, imagined a more realistic portrayal of the city than its general glamourous depiction. Instead of Rome's pristine, marbled, noble image, they imagined a crowded and vibrant metropolis. The series' production designer Joseph Bennett stated, 'The buildings had colour, the streets were dirty, there were masses of multi-racial people living in very close quarters . . . We combined the academic research of what Rome was like with inspirations from places like Calcutta, Delhi, Cairo or Mexico City, where you have extreme wealth living alongside extreme poverty' (BBC 2005).

Halit Ergenç, who played Sultan Süleyman in *Muhteşem Yüzyıl*, gives a detailed description of the challenge they faced in how to

---

31 For an analysis of historical ethnography and historical imagination, see John Camaroff and Jean Camaroff (1992); Susan Foster (1995).

historically imagine the body language of the Ottoman state officials and their servants:

> History is a very interesting phenomenon . . . I read the works of many historians, but bringing the characters to life has been something different. I wish we could do a couple of months of rehearsals for all of these. I would like all the actors to come together and explore 'how we can do this'. I wish an expert came and told us, 'They would do it like this and that' . . . Indeed, historians came in, and we talked to them. They used to say, 'He has to salute when he enters'. Okay, the servant salutes when he enters, but how? 'He will just salute.' How? Does he bend, does he crawl, does he raise his head or not? . . . During the first episodes, we took the initiative to decide how to do it all. Where does he stand when he enters the room? How close can he get? Who can have an eye contact with whom? Who should look down when speaking to others? Whose hand should stay like what? Whose head should turn how? Because there was incredible hierarchy there [in the Ottoman state]. (2014)

The relationship between writers and actors is a fascinating one; it can be mutually beneficial or incredibly tense during dizi production. Writers construct the characters and situate them within the plot, a process in which actors have little say. Once the project starts, the issue of character becomes fraught as one writes it and the other gives it life. Actress Derya Alabora reminds us of the importance of division of labour in the hectic process of dizi making: 'Everyone has a different duty. No one can interfere with the other's job . . . Otherwise, it will be chaos, and no one can proceed. You cannot tell a screenwriter, "Write this or that way"' (Alabora 2012).

Even with all the respect they have for the written script, almost all dizi actors state that they slightly change 'certain ways of saying things'. One term I came across very often during my interviews was 'lafı ağzına *oturtma*', 'fitting the words to one's mouth'. Alabora considers this the moment of the text's transference to its enactment, 'a perplexing moment for both the writer and the actor' (2012). During the rapid writing and shooting, this may generate personal differences and disagreements as well as consensus. Esra Dermancıoğlu says she brings in certain lines to distinguish her characters from others. In *Fatmagül'ün Suçu Ne?*, for instance, to enact the cynical aunt she played, she added 'Allah Allah', an expression that communicates a sense of surprise and disbelief to her lines. 'As long as it fit my mouth, they would not object to it' (Dermancıoğlu 2012).

Character actor Mustafa Avkıran also gives us examples of how he contributed to written characters by adding specific expressions. He points to the dialogic relationship between the writer and the actor: 'Using certain ways of speaking offers new paths of writing for the upcoming episodes. In *Yaprak Dökümü*, I began using a particular term to address the senior woman character. The writers followed my shift from "*yenge*" (sister-in-law) to "*annem*" (mother), and began using the new term' (2012). This also happened in his recent dizi, *Yeni Gelin* (2017), in which he emphasized possessive pronouns, saying '*benim*', '*oğlum*', '*benim*' '*babam*', which the writers adopted in later episodes (Avkıran 2012).

Another important concept that actors frequently use is '*karakteri oturtma*', 'to settle the character', which refers to the encounter that determines the writer–actor relationship. To build characters, writers develop detailed fictional life stories to guide the casting and costume departments during production; and actors are usually very cooperative during these early stages. Tensions emerge once the shooting starts, when actors embody the written character, giving it flesh and spirit. Here they believe that they 'add' to the characters and, more importantly, to the overall success of the dizi. Nevertheless, dizis' instant success may sometimes be their misfortune too. When a dizi becomes a hit, the power relations within the set may quickly change, and the writing process may become more vulnerable to unexpected demands coming from rising stars. As one director states, 'I have seen that the lead actors sometimes takes too much credit for the overall success, which brings enormous management problems during the shooting. Because the ratings are high, producers want to continue, but life on the set often becomes a hell.' Similarly, a showrunner reminds us of the contribution of the editing department, which works hard to select the best 'cuts' for the emerging lead actors: 'Editors contribute greatly to the building of their image; they work for hours on that, so that audiences like them and the dizi survives.'

From the actors' point of view, however, each needs to develop their own acting style and working strategies in order to deal with the demanding conditions. A leading actor pointed to the emotional toll of dizi acting: 'After so many hours on the set, impersonating a character through deep and long focus, it is so hard to come home and sleep.' Unfortunately, the stress of production lead some actors to develop drug or alcohol dependencies. A star emphasized the potential of acting—impersonating characters they are curious about, or others with whom they would never associate themselves: 'While acting, you live certain moments which you would like to experience in real life, yet would be too shy to do so. Acting gives you a nice disguised comfort.' Similarly, Halit Ergenç states, 'When an actor gets the chance to play different characters, he will die with the memory of many people from different cultural backgrounds that he experienced in one lifetime. The actor may get to know their experiences not by really taking the same risks but by understanding their psychology' (2014). Engin Akyürek approaches the issue from another direction:

> Each role is a chance to know another person. I get a first-date anxiety each time I agree to play a character. It is a test of getting to know a new person, taking a journey with him, and experiencing emotions we never imagined. Acting is an interesting profession, giving you the chance of getting interested

and learning about things you never considered. Being a police officer, for example, was something I learned in *Kara Para Aşk*. (2014).

Belçim Bilgin, a leading star, expresses her dilemma in selecting her characters in movies and in dizis:

I am a person who establishes special relationship with the characters I play. They all make me grow, transform me. This is why I want the script that I have in hand to give me something I have not done before . . . I am ruthless to myself and always want to add more to what has been done before . . . The performance of the actor is closely related to the general performance of the project. In all the projects I take part in, I give to my characters all I have from my heart and body at that moment. I never say, 'Let me skip this.' Acting in dizis gets you closer to that feeling, and this is why dizis scare me and I have great reservations when I approach them. If you play the same role over and over again, you may turn up to be its merchant. (2014)

On the issue of actors' talent, Mehmet Günsür notes that, technically speaking, acting demands a very well-conducted preliminary preparation: 'Anybody who works hard enough can become an actor. The real talent is what kind of choices you make after reading a script' (2012). Timuçin Esen similarly expresses: 'In order to be relaxed on the set, you have to do your homework . . . Thereafter, you can perform with whatever technique you want.' He says how he makes preliminary research on the story's other characters as well, detailing their material and social life (Esen 2019).

Actors have a delicate relationship with dizi directors, especially if they are 'experienced stars'. Pressed for time, directors are in charge of finishing the scenes as planned in the best way they can. Mehmet Ada Öztekin, who has directed many hit dizis, touches upon the issue of holding the quality of acting under time pressure; he says 'If necessary, I put pressure on my actors, push them to perform better. Thereafter, each one of them gets offers from other directors of dizis, plays, commercials or movies' (2012). At times, power struggles emerge in the other direction, when actors presumptuously offer cinematographic advice. One actor emphasizes the need for delicacy and discretion in such exchanges: 'It is always better to offer your opinion when you are alone,' she states, 'if you propose a *mis en scène* that the director did not think of, and if this happens under the gaze of two assistants watching you, he will not accept it.' As one star eloquently expressed: 'Acting is also about communicating your own will and opinions as if these come from the director.' During the shooting of *Kösem*, Hülya Avşar, one of Turkey's most eminent film celebrities, interfered in a long and crowded scene that included several extras. Her sister recalled how she said to the young director: 'You can shoot this scene in five hours instead of fifteen.' Apparently, Avşar even suggested the placement of the cameras. 'The scene ended up being shot in five hours indeed,' her sister stated, and added, 'Experience! And no director can ignore her, especially if he is much younger' (Avşar 2016).

Mehmet Günsür expresses his belief in collaborative writing like in the old times, where the director and the writer worked together with the actors as a creative team: 'Not many people do this in Turkey. Analysing the story with the actors, allowing improvisations . . . I think both script writers and directors can draw inspiration from the actors and work together' (2012). Günsür experienced this kind of collaboration with *Bıçak Sırtı*, a project he designed with fellow actors Fikret Kuşkan and Nejat İşler, and with *Kanaga*, which he produced with his own family. Theatre director and actor Haluk Bilginer also believes in collaboration between actors and writers. As a theatre director, he suggests that it would be very useful if writers develop drafts to test them in rehearsals with actors, so that both parties benefit from it (2013).

Dizi actors develop different strategies for getting into their characters. Timuçin Esen, for instance, places the actor's contribution in-between a 'well-constructed script' and a 'masterfully managed directorship':

A good writer gives you an already completed world. When the script comes to the actor, it is obvious that the writer has already imagined and enacted it in their mind. This is the best thing for an actor, a marvel . . . All is there, ready! What you need to do is to only focus on your own job . . . Sometimes, however, actors tend to overdo things, to put everything they have on the table . . . They are enthusiastic people; they want to deliver everything they can do. This is where the director comes in. A good director is the person who sets the ground to take the substance out of the actor without scaring him, and from the cinematographer and the art director as well, so that each delivers their art freely, in the best way they can. (2019)

It is obvious that the story is the main axis of a project, and that a good director takes the best from their actors and gives a spirit to both cast and crew. What is particular in Turkish dizi industry is the long companionship of cast and crew under immense pressure of time. Dizis last sometimes a few seasons, and actors sail from one project to the other. Getting into the character needs preliminary preparations, but maintaining it through for one, two or sometimes three years requires a different state of mind. After more than a decade of dizi acting, Kıvanç Tatlıtuğ draws attention to how actors live alongside their dizi characters: 'However well a role is written, it is the actor who gives it flesh and bones. As you pass more time with the character you play, when you give life to him, you start talking to him. This is really interesting; like a reflex, like a habit of yours, it sticks on you' (2016). Engin Akyürek describes a similar state of mind, drawing attention to the threat of boredom:

When you decide to act in a dizi, you carry this character in your daily life as long as the dizi lasts. You have to make a very good decision not to get bored. If you join a project without being sure of what you will play, you can get bored in the eighth episode. Or you may say 'my character would not do that' and you may want to manipulate the story pulling it in another direction. Because life goes on, you end up living with the same hair and beard style for about two years. (2018)

The statement of the wife of a star who acted in a historical dizi confirms how characters may stick on dizi actors in different periods of their career. She humorously says, 'We have a king in our house, and we live with that king every day.'

As the dizis and their content change, actors' images also change in the public eye. One talent agent says: 'Our public identifies so much with the stars' characters that they literally forget their real persona.' Turkish dizi actors constantly face such responses to their changing characters. Experienced dizi actor Halit Ergenç narrates, for instance, how he takes the cue from the streets to understand whether his new character received public acclaim. Following his long-lasting dizi project *1001 Gece* (2006–09), where he enacted a businessman called Onur, Ergenç moved to playing a totally different character in 2011, enacting Süleyman the Magnificent in *Muhteşem Yüzyıl*: 'Instead of pointing at me as "Aaa Onur!", they slowly started to call me "Kanuni". I greatly care how people react to me at the street level' (Ergenç 2011).

Akyürek, who began his career with dizi acting, has now accrued a wealth of experience to explain the actor's state of mind during dizi making. Pointing to the parallel life an actor shares with his character, he illustrates how difficult it is to put a distance between the two:

Somebody imagined a character and you try so hard to give it a life. Getting to know the characters takes up as much time as getting to know a new person in real life. There are situations where you misunderstand, misinterpret. One cannot always approach himself objectively, and may prefer to disregard his weaknesses. If your character has these weaknesses too, you search for them from your own self, and you face them. A character therefore needs your feelings and details from your own life. But at the same time, you are not that character. You have to establish a sincere and direct relationship with the characters. If you try to go the easy way, or try to manipulate them, you will find yourself punished by bad acting. (2014)

Many dizi characters shine in unexpected ways through the powerful performances of the actors who enact them. Actress Hülya Duyar reminds how 'side actors' can move towards more essential roles over time: 'If you perform a certain side role really well, they begin writing more scenes for you' (2013). Barış Falay, who was recruited for a minor but important role in *Aliye* for only a few episodes, ended up staying until the end of the series after the success of his performance. This became a breakthrough in his career as a dizi actor (Falay 2012). The reverse is also true. In a hit comedy, a side story was planned based on a conflict between one of the main cast members and a new character. The poor performance of the new actress made the writer quit the storyline, leaving that character behind. In some cases, actors shine in particular characters, which helps them enhance their career opening up new and higher income opportunities; for this writers do not get much credit. For example, an actor whose career took off with a dizi in which he played a charismatic designer was soon invited to appear on a branded commercial as a pursuit of that character; the writer who created the character had no involvement in this process.

Theatre actor Yıldıray Şahinler, who has acted in dizis since the early 1990s, made his breakthrough playing the character of Alyanak in *İçerde* in 2016. As he was also acting in a play at the same time, he was worried about his voice. Hence: 'I thought it would be easier to use the whispering voice. Because I've done this job for the last 30 years, I can work with different types of voices, I have a quite large voice box . . . When I was cast for this character, I told to my manager that I would draw a "one-of-a-kind character". I felt this and knew this inside me. And indeed, it was how it happened' (Şahinler 2017). Şahinler remembers Alyanak as the most enjoyable character he played for the camera. The character soon became an anti-hero; even the writers who were planning to kill him after a few episodes kept Alyanak through the end. 'They really liked Alyanak,' Şahinler states, 'and I am really happy about this. I did not go the easy way, I acted very sincerely, and I have seen its reward. The love I see in the streets of Van or Eminönü is beyond a simple feeling of being admired' (2017).

Birce Akalay, a veteran of several different dizi projects, points to the time strains that actors face to mature their characters. Many actors begin a new project without being able to take a break. Although they are selective and only accept the best roles for them, they often lack ample time to develop their characters before the projects starts. Akalay says:

> When I read the story, it feels I am halfway through. It is like the first bite. If the story or the character moves and excites me, I begin to see the seeds sprouting. Thereafter, we all wish we had enough time to get prepared, but unfortunately, we don't have that time in our system. This is why we try to accomplish our work as if on an accelerated tour. On top of it, when we go to the set, we shoot episodes that are longer than a movie. Due to these circumstances, we have developed a reflex for adapting quickly. (2018)

And finally, actors must also acknowledge the role of audience reception in the way actors associate themselves with certain characters. Barış Arduç, for instance, stresses how the audiences found in the character he played in *Kiralık Aşk* a familiar face: 'I believe I gave an "our own boy" image with my good-hearted physiognomy. My character has

few deficiencies; he has a decent, hardworking, gentleman profile'
(*GQ* 2016).

Dizi actors have come a long way since the 2000s, adjusting to the changing dynamics of their creative industry. Dizi sets brought together a pool of actors from different backgrounds like theatre, music or modelling. As seniors or newcomers to that field, these actors grew to learn to co-perform despite disagreements and increasingly taxing working conditions. They also developed strategies to cope with fame at both domestic and global levels, protecting themselves while reaching out to a large number of fans from around the world. Talent agencies also progressed, diversifying their own professional profiles, and developing their unique styles of management. The stars of the first round of dizis that reached global acclaim are now very selective about their future projects. They have also achieved the comfort of delving into their hobbies or sustaining themselves through events and advertising. I will conclude this chapter by referring to *Menajerimi Ara,* the successful adaptation of the French series *Dix Pour Cent (Call My Agent),* in which many Turkish actors bravely accepted roles that deconstructed their own images. Nevertheless, as the number of dizi production increases, new actors continue to pour in, taking their chances in what is now a more established industry.

CHAPTER 8

Behind the Scenes, Behind the Sets
The Dual Performance of Cast and Crew

Sets are the cooking pot of the production process. This is where raw visual data is collected in the form of diverse fragments of scenes. The set is crowded, chaotic and frenzied, and it is in this environment that the dizi is shaped as a media text. During the many set visits I made over the last ten years, I have always felt equally interested in observing this crowd as much as the scenes which constitute the raw shots of an upcoming episode. In the early days of my research, I was usually seen as an outsider and kept under close supervision, being placed next to the directors' monitor, the safest place for everybody to keep the guest under control. The warning to switch off cell phones would come at the gate of the set. In time, as many producers, directors and actors got to know me and my research, I was allowed to be more mobile in the set environment. By then, I too had learned about the set rules, not only about keeping the cell phone silent, but also about going there with three kilos of baklava, and knowing where to stand and whom not to ignore.

My first dizi set visit, however, happened during the outside shootings of *Fatmagül'ün Suçu Ne?*, where I was among the invited guests from feminist NGOs, who would join the extras applauding and supporting Fatmagül outside the courthouse. In the middle of this crowd, I was trying to hide my face with the banner at my hand—'You will never walk alone'—and I was caught by the second director who warned me, 'Don't hide your beautiful face, honey, we need to see you!' A few years later, I had the opportunity to interview him at my university, and laughed about it, but the overall experience was a turning point for me to stay in the field and continue my research.

If one follows French film theorist Christian Metz's structuralist approach, then the 'scenes' constitute the smallest meaningful unit of the series, and 'the shooting moment' is how these scenes come into being through the collaboration of a large group of cast and crew (Metz 1974). Shoots are the prime time for the actors' performances; their first audience is the set crew. Sets therefore offer a layered performance ground where the cast and crew demonstrate their own performativity. Actors' performances in a given scene occurs within a much larger performance enacted by the other social players of the shoot: the crew members. This performance happens in the form of structured movement systems as well as verbal art like storytelling, punning and gossiping. This involves a double performativity, one that can be approached from a Schechnerian point of view as both *is* and *as* performance.[1] The whole set keeps an eye on the shooting of a particular scene, and the shot scene constitutes part of the final media text, which constitutes the episode that will be broadcast within a week. A distinguishing feature of the dizi industry is its pace of production. Because many dizis begin with no guarantee of remaining on air, they are written as they are filmed. The time frame between delivery of the script and broadcast may be as short as two weeks. This haste necessitates cast and crew to spend long hours in close proximity, with the intimacy and exhaustion generating various emotionally charged encounters. The performance of

---

1 In his book *Performance Studies: An Introduction* Richard Schechner distinguishes *is* performance from *as* performance: 'Any behavior, event, action, or thing, can be studied "as" performance', whereas, '"Is" performance refers to more definite, bounded events marked by context, convention, usage, and tradition.' The set environment embeds both forms, as actors deliver 'is' performance, while crews are engaged in 'as' performance (Schechner 2006: 40, 49).

these interactions takes place within a 'Turkish work culture', which is an important component of the overall ethnographic context in which dizis are produced.

Even if a dizi has a permanent site situated on real location, it may also use a studio or a backlot at times; filming thus travels in-between, and it moves quickly. In this regard, crews are like giant moving organisms with their own traffic and rhythm. Dizis makers are accustomed to mobility and quickly adjust to new environments. During dizi shoots, the set area consists of a momentary centre, in the periphery of which cast and crew members simultaneously circulate. The centre is the site of the actual shoot, which constantly shifts, redesigned for the following scene. Cast members usually prepare or rest in their trailers that are parked at the periphery along with other vehicles which house the transportation team, caterers and the costume department. The crowd, however, mainly consists of the crew, including the production and technical staff, and an army of assistants.

The interviews I have conducted since 2011 offer many narratives depicting how sets have evolved in time, culminating in today's excellent production quality and improved set conditions. My own first film-set visit in 1998, long before this research began, confirms these transformations. I had the chance to visit the set of *Cumhuriyet,* a TRT project on the founding of the Republic of Turkey. The 1990s was the decade during which competition between private networks and TRT had just begun, but the latter maintained an important upper hand in producing historical content.[2] The year 1998 marked the 75th anniversary of the Republic, which was celebrated in different venues.[3] *Cumhuriyet,*

---

2 Having easier access to real historical sites like Ottoman palaces and military zones, TRT produced *Kurtuluş* (1994) and *Cumhuriyet* (1998) as aspirational projects using best available technical equipment and logistic resources.

3 One of the events was *The 3x25 Years: An Exhibition on Turkish Republic,* organized by the Foundation of Social and Economic History, where I acted as the section director of 'Entertainment', 'National Days' and 'Education' (see Tanyeli 1998).

directed by Ziya Öztan, the eminent TRT director of historical content, was part of this commemoration (*Dailymotion* 2012a). As a pioneer of research on Turkish national days, I was involved in a series of these events. My dean, Professor Ayşe Soysal, who had friends working in the *Cumhuriyet* project, had kindly arranged a visit for my colleague Selim Deringil and me (see Öztürkmen 2001).

Cumhuriyet's set was constructed in a military garrison in Pendik, a place ordinarily inaccessible to civilians. I recall the experience as a 'time out of time', in an alienating, isolated atmosphere in this deserted military space. A large group of horsemen apparently brought all the way from Uşak,[4] waited for their part dressed in Ottoman military costumes. The set was strictly disciplined; Eda Liman, a woman assistant, was giving orders to another large crowd of extras. Trailers where the lead actors took refuge were parked here and there. Director Ziya Öztan and her assistant Pelin Esmer (a former student of mine who is now also an eminent director) greeted us, proudly pointing out the digital monitor, then a novelty on Turkish film sets: 'No more directors watching from the camera's eye,' Öztan said, 'Now you can follow the scenes as framed while they are being shot.' We were very impressed, as it looked like we were watching the episode long before it would be broadcast. One scene depicted the suicide of Fikriye, a character who was desperately in love with the newlywed Mustafa Kemal, the founder of the Republic of Turkey. We were all taken by the stars' presence, particularly the beautiful ballerina Hülya Aksular who played Fikriye and the charismatic theatre actor Rutkay Aziz enacting Mustafa Kemal.[5]

This account of the set visit is now historical ethnography, but it has served as an important reference point for many more dizi set visits

---

4 Uşak is an inner Aegean town in Turkey, known with its wild horses and traditional jereed (*cirit*) equestrian sport (see Çiftçi 2011).

5 I would like to thank Pelin Esmer in recollecting the exact time and place of the visit.

that I pursued over the years. Looking back, I realize how it encapsulated a transitional moment of the dizi-making process during the 1990s, merging elements of older modes of production with newer technologies. This experience has guided me in assessing the set milieus I have visited since 2011: more than 30 different dizi sets, most of them projects broadcast on private networks. By living in Yeniköy, a neighbourhood on the Bosphorus shore, and writing most of my book in Beykoz Kundura complex, I was able to observe additional outdoor shoots, and to meet several cast and crew members in Kundura's social venues. My primary observation was that each dizi set had its own particularities, depending on their production company, their location and the synergy usually driven by directors or lead actors. I also observed and collected interviews on the sets from different crew members in technical, transportation, costume and make-up departments.[6] The interviews revealed different types of narratives, which I could categorize both as a folklorist and oral historian. Some followed a historical comparative framework, depicting how the sets have evolved and reached today's production quality, and how set conditions improved over time. Others embedded anecdotes of recruitment and gendered experience. Perhaps the most striking were the 'bonding narratives' of crew members, who had built a committed team of their own, after working together in different projects over the years. I also came across narratives of 'know-how' that offered detailed job descriptions and labour divisions on dizi sets. The know-how of set labour is probably not much different in the rest of the world, but the desire to talk about it revealed an assertion of professionalism and a claim of competence. For many crew members, access to a dizi set offered an important source of cultural capital and professional status. As a folklorist, I also observed how some

---

6 The majority of the set workers and employees I interviewed asked me to keep their names anonymous, in order 'to keep their jobs'. I will not therefore quote their names nor the dates of these interviews.

narratives depicting incidents that happened during the shooting processes had a heroic, comic or tale-like component. What counted more, however, were the emotional meanings assigned to these narratives that rendered stories of solidarity, heroism or survival.

Memory of Past Dizi Sets: Between Nostalgia and Pride

Set milieus have evolved over time from humble conditions to the new high-powered dynamics that host the contemporary dizi genre. Today's set energy is nourished by a variety of factors rooted in past shooting practices in cinema, TRT and advertisement. Nevertheless, the written documentation of past experiences of filmmaking in Turkey is also limited. Actors and directors usually gave interviews or wrote memoirs, which often focused on their own performance, sharing only minor observations or comments about life on the sets. Oral history with a direct focus on labour practices and conditions of filmmaking therefore becomes an important way to collect the memory of these 'old days'. However nostalgic or disdainful, these narratives of filmmaking provide a key source for tracing the historical process through which set practices changed.

Since 2005, Boğaziçi University's Mithat Alam Film Center has been conducting oral history research on Turkish cinema: Turkish Cinema Visual Memory Project, directed by Elif Ergezer. The interviews this project has collected offer valuable data on the set experiences since the 1960s. Ergezer has made important observations regarding a certain sense of 'collective embodiment' in filmmaking during these years, which she describes as a 'classless' but 'authoritarian' experience. Working and travelling under difficult circumstances fostered bonding among actors, directors and the technical teams who all piled onto uncomfortable buses and journeyed to distant locations. Stories revealed a strong, genuine sense of collaboration, where stars helped carry heavy instruments and brought their own costumes and make-up. As imported film pellicles were costly and scarce, the set needed to be run strictly and authoritatively. Many remembered the stress on sets that required well-planned and carefully rehearsed groundwork, so that the scenes could ultimately be shot in a single take. To save on production costs, time efficiency was a priority; this required use of day and night-time shooting. Accidents or misfortunes often interfered. In these cases, either the director or the technical team would come up with practical solutions. Technical teams displayed creativity, building certain instruments which they knew about but could not afford. For instance, chariots were hand-made using soap and iron rails, and directors of photography produced additional lenses for their cameras (Ergezer 2019).

The set environment of the early years of television did not differ much from that of cinema. Aydan Şener, a leading star of the 1980s, remembers dizi shoots with affection:

> Sets were joyful and sincere. I would wake up and go there with pleasure. There would be storytelling, jokes and games in-between the scenes. We would not understand how time passed, but would not work too late as they do today. Humour and storytelling were at the centre. I was so young, yet working with all these senior directors. They would come very prepared, already knowing their shooting angles and breaks. It was like a school for me. (2016)

The warm, congenial but disciplined experience of 1980s dizi making is confirmed by other actors as well. Renowned theatre actors Perran Kutman, Tekin Akmansoy, Defne Yalnız and Gazanfer Özcan, who all launched their dizi careers under TRT's roof during this decade, report a sense of collegiality, a tradition carried to television culture from the theatre backstage. Memories of hardship, however, dampen their nostalgia for the old day. They remember, for instance, that the sets were often unhygienic, and that they spent hours dubbing their own scenes. Sitting up all night, working late hours, and surviving cold and hunger were also part of this shared professional experience. Actors of the 1980s also pointed to technological deficiencies, even if they worked with TRT, which had access to the best possible resources (*Alkışlarla Yaşıyorum* 2014).

Structuring the Sets from 2000s Onwards

What most marks the difference between earlier practices and contemporary dizi making is the expanding of episode 'duration'. A dizi's script is written in a particular week, shot the next, and broadcast the following week. Since the 2000s, the duration of dizi screening has grown from 50–60 to almost 180 minutes, raising costs and rendering work conditions evermore taxing. The new pace generates double-fold anxiety for all parties. To begin with, the dizi industry operates in a zone of precarity where productions begin without any assurance of survival. The vulnerability vis-à-vis the ratings is extremely high, and each dizi begins with a primordial survival anxiety. Second, the sets are where this pace is 'performed' in all senses of the word. The management of set traffic and the race against time are extremely stressful. The mobile sets are continually displaced between and within different locations. Director Mehmet Ada Öztekin summarizes this eloquently: 'Every day is a new *şantiye* [a site of construction] for us' (2012).

Historically speaking, dizi producing of the 1990s and 2000s also generated anxieties, but these involved situating and branding amid the fierce competition among private networks. It was important to make a breakthrough with a pioneering dizi that would dazzle audiences with its thematic and technical innovation. Although AGB Nielson has computed and provided TV ratings in Turkey since 1989, these ratings did not factor into programming decisions. Instead, it was often personal connections that secured successful broadcasting. In time, dizi production became more commercial, which necessitated much longer screening periods to accommodate commercial breaks. This engendered a labour-intensive process, with irregular, extended shoots, accompanied by the stress of deadlines. Elif Sönmez, who worked on the sets during this transition in the mid 2000s, experienced what they describe as an endless state of running around or standing up, calling cystitis a 'set illness' (Sönmez 2011). Art director Nilüfer Çamur remembers collapsing from fatigue on the set of *Hatırla Sevgili*:

> We were filming the scene for Yasemin's birthday party in the Büyükada.[7] We had rented a wonderful place, but the owners were very concerned. So, I was paying a lot of attention to avoid any harming . . . I was just sitting, and our tailor approached me. She said, 'Nilüfer, you look so bad. Why don't you go downstairs and take a nap? I will wake you up.' I hesitated at first, but I went down. Then I woke up. You know sometimes you wake up and you don't know where you are and what time it is. I was like that. Where am I? What is this place? I panicked. I couldn't understand where I was. I rushed, fearing that I was late. I was in a hotel room! I had slept 24 hours, and no one had woken me up. The scene had finished, they hadn't woken me up. When the shoot had finally wrapped up, they could hardly wake me up. And apparently, I had told them I could go by myself and walked ten minutes to the hotel, but I remembered nothing. I asked myself for the first time: Is this how I am going to spend my life? My body had collapsed. During the 14th and 15th episodes, I could hardly get out of bed; but I forced myself to do it. I don't know if I would have such energy now. I am not sure. (2014)

The initial reaction to the extended working hours employed the slogan '*Yerli Dizi Yersiz Uzun*' (Domestic Dizi Is Inappropriately Long), as a joint protest on 24 December 2010 by the Writers' Association and the Cinema Workers' Union. The second protest erupted on 31 March

---

7 Büyükada is the biggest Princes' Islands in Marmara Sea, a traditional summer resort for Istanbulites.

2017, when screenwriters published a declaration protesting the new dizi-episode length of 150 minutes. Nevertheless, neither the length of the dizis nor the exhausting work hours changed. The tradition of organized strikes had considerably faded since the 1980 military coup. Workers lacked the power to force producers and networks to change the structuring of the drama formats, and they also feared being instantly replaced by newcomers.[8] However, the protests did bring about improved set conditions. First, following the 2010 event, two important unions were established: The Writers' Union in 2011 and Cinema-Television Union in 2015. Director Zeynep Günay-Tan, who witnessed this transition, comments on the changes that followed the establishment of the unions:

> What unions ensured and what worked 100 per cent was the one-hour meal break. People don't compromise on this because this is the only right they achieved. One hour! Not 55 minutes! They don't even sacrifice their five minutes. They are insistent on this. They tightly hold on to this one hour. Because before, the sets were like this: 'Eat your meal quickly and go back to work . . . Quick quick quick!' Everyone would gobble down their meal. I am still the first one to finish among friends, when we go to a regular restaurant. It has become a habit now. I have this constant urge in me, 'Eat fast! Move on!' (2019)

Director of photography Tolga Kutluay links this issue to the general structure of the industry comparing it with the West:

> Abroad you work for eight hours per day, your overtime—if any—they inform you ahead of time. Preliminary preparations take 18 months, or 2 years. The rating system is not cruel, and the contracts are done over 8 to 13 episodes. Here, all is done on the run, and it is impossible to say no to overtime. (2019)

---

8 For how the strong union system changed following the 1980 military coup, see Hamza Kadah and Murat Pıçak (2017).

In the early stages of dizi making, irregular payment, lack of health insurance, and working for long hours under unsafe conditions emerged as the main problems (Başaran and Kurtulmuş 2016). As these issues became more visible, solving them became a priority, forcing producers to build sets that functioned better. Actress and writer Meriç Acemi, who has observed set milieus since the 1990s, calls attention to recent material improvements, like using trailers not only for stars but also to fulfil set workers' basic needs. It became obligatory to recruit health services on sets; inspections increased as well. Importantly, new regulations regarding the working time for child actors also added to these improvements (Acemi 2019). Nevertheless, when interviewed, set workers continue to share more hardship memories than opinions praising these improvements. As one of them openly stated, 'As long as the length of the episodes are two hours, we will continue to complain.'

Sets as Training Sites: Recruitment Processes in the Dizi Industry

The first generation of dizi actors, directors and technical crew members witnessed the transition to a much-improved work environment. As the late actor and producer Osman Yağmurdereli once noted, one thing that drove the changes was that a large number of set workers were trained throughout the 1990s (*Alkışlarla Yaşıyorum* 2014). The term 'training' carries a dual sense. This was the decade when a young generation of film studies graduates returned to Turkey from abroad and began teaching in media schools that turned out large numbers of young professional dizi makers (Bayrakdar 2016). But Yağmurdereli's statement referred primarily to the notion of *eleman*, the multi-purpose set worker who learned on the job. As noted in previous chapters, the television industry is today run by a community of people who have formally or informally developed a know-how and 'teamed up' in dizi sets.

Recruitment into the dizi world is rather informal. Many of my interviewees report that, especially in the early years, kinship connections often provided entry to the industry. As payments could be irregular, hiring relatives as crew members helped in dealing with finances and provided a social milieu where one could fully trust co-workers in demanding situations. But many crew members also began to work in the sets through acquaintances. Director Ayhan Özen recounts:

> A friend invited me to the set of a TGRT channel for a documentary film shooting in Eyüp [Istanbul]. As I watched from the side, I quickly learned how they operate the chariot, wheel chocks and cameras. Then I heard someone shout, 'Bring the camera here', but nobody heard. I jumped in and brought the camera. They asked me, 'Who are you?' I said, 'I am just a curious guy!' They told me to come back the next day. This is how I found myself in the dizi world. (2014)

Those who came from an *alaylı* background—that is, without any formal training—often started by undertaking small assignments in technical departments, costume, transportation or catering. For those lacking formal employment qualifications, sets appeared to offer a combination of work and fun. In time, although they developed significant know-how, the hardships of working under an authoritarian and exhausting work environment became evident. Many beginners remained in dizi making, either because 'there were not many other job opportunities out there', or because of the sense of accomplishment they felt, having gained valuable skills, stating that 'they knew it all now'. 'Learning the job' also raised their standing in the eye of the production team, which might pave the way to promotion.

Günay-Tan stresses the role of meritocracy in today's recruitment system. She states that newcomers now begin as trainees and are tested before being promoted. Kinship, acquaintanceship or references may be significant for initial access, but what counts most is always 'doing the job well'. This concept does have various semantic layers. First it refers to a certain sense of quick comprehension and mutual understanding, developed over time through common experience. Günay-Tan describes this concept as 'looking from the same perspective':

We have no bonds from the past. We are neither from the same hometown, nor from the same school. We have nothing in common but the tough experience of the set. We look from the same perspective. Rather than blood ties, what is important is to have someone paying attention to their job and sharing the same perspective. This is what's valuable. (2019)

'Doing the job well' also refers to a certain sense of endurance. Director of photography Tolga Kutluay touches upon a rather unfair aspect of the recruitment process. 'Many times, we end up hiring people with past experience,' he states. 'It is unfortunate that we often prefer them to well-educated new graduates from film schools, but time-tested endurance on the set is our priority' (2019).

Sets also function as schools. They offer training to incoming assistants in all departments. The directors and many crew members of today's hit dizis recall the mentorship of masters in the field. Günay-Tan, for instance, worked closely with directors Kartal Tibet, Ömer Kavur and Çağan Irmak. She deeply values the 'step-by-step' learning process they provided:

I was so young. Kartal Bey took me as his assistant with permission from my father. He told him, 'Trust me!' I worked both as his assistant on the set and during editing. I dealt with every little detail. Everyone wanted me to work with them because I was the youngest but the most motivated. I wanted a challenge, so I moved to editing. I was like the head of post-production, editing both the images and the music. I continued like this for five years. Then I went back onto the set as an assistant director. I started working with Ömer Kavur. His company was making Üzgünüm Leyla. He would host Danish filmmakers for a month in his production company Alfa. I closely worked with them because I was the only assistant who could speak English. Ömer Bey was a true gentleman, trained in Sorbonne. He was very supportive of me. He would deliberately bring me to places that

I could never reach at that age; we would go to script meetings, for instance, to social milieus where he would talk about cinema. We always had this special rapport while working together in four movies over these four years. (2019)[9]

Similarly, Ayhan Özen describes his training at the hand of director Tolgay Ziyal over many years. He remembers how he received professional training at his side, but also secured jobs in the initial years of his career (2014). Make-up artist Ebru Güleren feels privileged to have been trained by Derya Ergün and Neriman Eröz, two doyens of make-up art in Turkey at the Istanbul State Ballet and Opera. Güleren recalls these years as a school for her: 'I was their assistant during 1999–2003. I started with make-up for live performance, then moved to the dizi world . . . There is such a big difference between the two but being trained in live performance taught me the basics of this art' (2019).

Dizi sets as training grounds also produced 'informal teams'. The technical crew members, in particular, constantly bring new assistants into the industry. This is also true for directors, directors of photography and the managers of other departments. New crew members who come through connections of family and friend are tested on the set. If they are eager to work and quick to 'deliver', they are rapidly promoted. Many team members grow familiar with one another through working on the same projects and they share a repertory of common friends and memories. Director Ahmet Katıksız, on the other hand, underlines the importance of alumni groups during the professional initiation to the field. Today, a large number of media schools train new people for film sets. During the 2000s, however, there were mainly a few film schools which provided the majority of formal training: Mimar Sinan University in Istanbul, Dokuz Eylül University in Izmir and Anadolu University in Eskişehir. 'Graduates of both Dokuz Eylül and Anadolu Universities,'

---

9 Günay-Tan worked with other prominent directors including Orhan Oğuz, Atıf Yılmaz, Ziya Öztan and Türkan Derya (Günay-Tan 2018).

Katıksız notes, 'would come to Istanbul in search of jobs, and established alumni would lodge the younger generations during their first years and assist them finding a position' (2013).

Methodological Challenges of Set Ethnography

Despite the importance of technical expertise in the dizi world, ethnographic literature on set milieus is rather limited. The production process is not a domain which has been prioritized in film studies, partly because of limited access to its ethnographic ground. Many scholars who have written on television or film industries developed a knowledge of the sets, but few foregrounded the behind-the-scenes ethnographies in their writings. The work of Vicky Mayer, John Thornton Caldwell and Miranda J. Banks (2009) is an exception in which they delve into the production machine of Hollywood and provide insights from its work force, from technicians to writers. There is also some literature on how sets function, as professional guide for newcomers to the industry. Nicholas George's *Film Crew* (2010), for instance, approaches the production process as a bridge between the craft of storytelling and technical skill. Others approach the production process as a whole, like *The Complete Film Production Handbook* (2010) by Eve Light Honthaner, in which the author describes the complex structure of the production team working 'behind the sets'. Knowledge of the set is in fact the basis of educational curricula in media schools. Actor Timuçin Esen recalls how learning about cables and sandbags constituted an important part of his education at the California Institute of the Arts (Esen 2019).

There are also memoirs or oral histories of set experiences from particular shows and movies. For example, *Live from New York* is an oral history of the phenomenal *Saturday Night Live*, or *Movie Speak* is a compendium of terms and jargon from film sets (Miller and Shales 2015; Bill 2009). Turkish actors or directors published memoirs as well. Examples include those by Kemal İnci (2016), Leyla Özalp (2013), Halit Refiğ (2010) and Atif Yılmaz (1995). These memoirs focus on experience in the cinema world with some references to television. But they are important sources that give an idea about the set conditions in Turkey before and during television production.

The study of the 'behind-the-scenes' accounts appear more often in films than in published ethnographies. Early examples are François Truffaut's *La nuit américaine* (1973), a satire on filmmaking, and Tom Di Cillo's *Living in Oblivion* (1995), which portrays the frustration on a chaotic set. Television sitcoms such as *Murphy Brown* (1988) and mockumentary television series such as *30 Rock* (2006), *Call My Agent* (2015) and *Unreal* (2015) have focused on the behind-the-scenes chaos surrounding television production. In the Turkish context, *Yalan Dünya* (2012), *Jet Sosyete* (2018) and *Menajerimi Ara* (2020) have referenced dizi sets in a satirical way. Caldwell has underscored how 'industry self-analysis and self-representation now serve as primary on-screen enter-tainment forms across a vast multimedia landscape' (2008: 1). He calls this 'industrial narcissus', and analyses both the style and marketing dimensions of this industrial reflexivity: 'While film and television are influenced by macroscopic economic processes, they also very much function on a microsocial level as local cultures and social communities in their own right' (2008: 2).

There are also documentaries which treat this subject from a variety of different approaches. But the documentary film genre does not depict sets ethnographically; instead it usually celebrates the creative processes of writing and directing.[10] They often include edited excerpts which function as disguised promotion of the work they treat (see Bell 2013; Zamanian 2016; *Film Stage* 2015). Some even serve as direct advertise-ments of technological products (*YouTube* 2012). 'Behind-the-scenes'

---

10 Documentaries may cover the making of a particular film, such as in Vivian Kubrick's *The Making of 'The Shining'* (1980); a director's journey like in Keith Fulton and Louis Pepe's *Lost in La Mancha* (2002) and Liv Corfixen's *My Life*; or the history of filmmaking, like Mark Cousins' *The Story of Film: An Odyssey* (2011).

content is also covered in websites and blogs, which is intended to 'demystify' the process, commenting mostly on altercations among actors, writers or producers. These sites lend visibility to creative differences and disagreements as well as certain dramatic developments in the set environment. One such site summarizes, for example, how relationships sour over time when cast and crew work multiple seasons in close proximity, with swollen egos and competitive salaries.[11] General information regarding set milieus is also available in textbooks for film departments or individual publications on shooting practices for future directors or technical crew.[12] These books are important sources for newcomers to the field, introducing them to professional filmmaking practices. They also provide readers with the basic rules of the film production processes, advising new professionals on when to break the rules and when to abide by them. They usually target an audience of independent filmmakers, students enrolled in film schools, and even instructors of film departments. In short, whether printed or digital, most publications on 'set knowledge' are written for those new to physical production, informing them about the complexities of film sets and providing information about different staff positions and responsibilities. Brandon Tonner-Connolly and Alicia van Couvering, for instance, wrote helpful articles informing newcomers on 'set protocol' and 'set

---

11 See Lisa Waugh (2019). Also see Ally Abrams (2018); Ian Sandwell (2018); Evan Luzi (n.d.). There are also websites about the relics of film shoots, informing fans about auctions of props used in the film sets. One other genre of publication about the production processes concerns guidebooks on how to access certain crew members. Many of these reveal comprehensive production resources for film, television and media, including information on crew, equipment, location services, studios and production facilities. Many such platforms providing this information nationally are now in digital form and accessible online.

12 See, among many others, Eve Honthaner (2010); Nicholas George (2010); Blain Brown (2002); Sidney Lumet (1996); David Mamet (1992); Lynda Obst (1997); Robert Rodriguez (1996); Walter Murch (2001); Christine Vachon and David Edelstein (1998).

people' (2015a, 2015b). One can also mention actor Eric Bogosian's manual for actors, *Your First Day on Set*.[13] These publications or blogs usually approach the set milieu in a humorous style. Tonner-Connolly and van Couvering's articles give a glimpse into the greatest thrills and frustration that crew members typically encounter on set. These can range from inventing nicknames, observing non-actors eating prop food or having access to secrets, to having bruises as a constant companion or to learning how heavy a bag of clothes can be. During my set visits, I observed that most set people wanted and even enjoyed talking about their experiences, but they also expressed their wish to remain anonymous as their frankness could cost them their jobs. As I became more acquainted with set slang and behaviour, I also noticed my own performance of the 'insider ethnographer', a role that was acknowledged by both cast and crew.

Set Knowledge

Knowledge of the everyday life of sets is mostly circulated orally, gathered on the spot, and accrued over time, as experiences vary from set to set. During my set visits, I was often struck by how many crew members were willing to talk about the intricacies of their jobs, 'verbalizing' their roles and contribution to the overall production process. In the early years of my research, during set visits, I would concentrate more on the directors, actors and their performances. During breaks I would engage in small talks with different crew members. As I learned more about the routines of the set, my interest shifted towards the crew in terms of their behaviour, the display of their competence and performance. In addition to my own set visits, I had the opportunity to collect other set narratives. During the early years of my research in particular, many actors, writers, dizi directors, executive coordinators,

---

13 I am grateful to my friend Eric Bogosian for sharing this informative and humorous manuscript with me.

directors of photography, production assistants and costume, hair and make-up artists gave me detailed in-depth interviews. They all described the set milieu in general, but also situated themselves and spoke of what they do within it.[14] On the set ground too, cast and crew members would compare the present set with their past experiences. Since they hosted me as a guest, and particularly as a 'researcher', many would be driven to 'inform' me about aspects of the sets which they thought would surprise me. These narratives would be fragmented, as they were collected in a series of quick encounters. One could perhaps call them generally 'set narratives', which included the description of their jobs and the exploration of the nuances of the division of labour between different departments.

When I visited the set of *Çukur* in 2019, production manager Alara Hamamcıoğlu, described to me in five minutes the structure of the dizi sets as she had learned on the job. She also explained the division of labour in dizis' production team:

> The assistant director and production coordinator (*reji koordi-natörü*) prepare the programme for the cast and crew. They read the script, decide on the planning of which scene will be shot when and where. They decide on the whole team's time-table and control the time efficiency of the set. There is also a chief production assistant (*şef reji asistanı*), who is in charge of communication with the actors, coordinating the crowd of extras if there is a grand scene to shoot, following up on the flow of the script. A continuity assistant (*devamlılık asistanı*) would watch over the passages between the scenes in terms of

---

14 In that regard, my special thanks go to Fahriye Evcen (28 December 2011), Ayşe Özer (11 April 2012), Aydın Sarıoğlu (1 May 2012), Betül Durmuş (9 May 2012), Ahmet Katıksız (29 October 2013), Doğan Karaca (30 October 2013), Ayhan Özen (26 May 2014), Meriç Acemi (22 November 2015) and Zeynep Günay-Tan (6 March 2019) who enriched my understanding of dizi set milieus with their in-depth interviews.

sound, lighting and costume, while the time-code assistant would take notes on directors' remarks for the editing process. Finally, many sets now also have a preparation assistant (*hazırlık asistanı*), who makes sure actors get ready on time, checking upon their make-up and costume, even at times assisting them to learn their lines. (2019)

What she quickly summarized was in fact not much different from the content of 'What Everyone Does on a Film Set' (Tonner-Connolly and van Couvering 2015b). What everyone does on a film set may be pretty much the same all over the world, but what is more important here is perhaps to delineate how the work culture of an industry—in this case the Turkish dizi industry—distinguishes itself from others.[15] The general conditions of the sets affect the final media text which is produced. In the case of the dizi industry, one such condition is undoubtedly the duration of the episodes which require long hours of set labour. How Turkish sets evolved in time has definitely shaped the dizi as the genre we know today.

The subject of duration was brought up in many of the interviews I conducted. İrfan Şahin, former CEO of Kanal D, had told me how the duration of the episodes, a unique aspect of Turkish television industry, was in fact a key factor in the construction of the dizi genre (2015). Duration affected work conditions and environment, which brought a different pace and creativity to the dizi. Some of my interviewees approached the issue as a historical process that changed the structure of production in the dizi sets, and offered very valuable oral history of dizi making. Zeynep Günay-Tan, who began her career in the early 1990s, gave a thorough historical analysis of how directing altered over

---

15 In fact, several researchers have analysed the differences in the local conditions of industries from around the world. See Muriel Cantor (1988); Sylvia Martin (2012); Christa Salamandra (1998); Tejaswini Ganti (2012); Mayfair Yang (1994).

time, generating new units such as the 'second director' or 'production coordination':

> When I first entered the set, there would be three assistants. One would be the assistant director, and her job was reading the script and deciding on the locations. She would also be the person to whom the cast and crew would direct their questions; she was therefore the messenger between them and the director. She would help operate the day's programme, being present on the set all the time, while sometimes making creative suggestions to the director. The second person was the continuity assistant, who made sure that the actors follow from where they left off, and get ready for the next scene. The third assistant would be keeping the time code and prompt the lines in the scene, because we weren't recording the sound on set at the time. It was during 1994–99, when dizis were of 45–50 minutes' duration. I didn't have a minute when I wasn't on the set as the assistant director. On my off days, I was doing the schedule, and it usually went very smoothly. Dizis were filmed in five days. We never had to be up all night. If we had to, then it meant we were working with a bad director. (2019)

Günay-Tan vividly recalls the change brought about by the lengthening of dizi episodes from 50 to 90 minutes. This was how the structure of the shoots changed, generating a need for a 'second director'—a term used in Turkey that does not correspond to what the West would call the 'director of the second unit':

> While we used to film 9–10 pages per day with a single team, they started asking us to film 13–14 pages. This of course complicated the traffic! There emerged a need for another assistant. So we became two assistant directors on set. One would make the schedule and check on the actors and the actresses. The other would film when needed. Teams began to be split up to keep up with the schedule. For example, when the main team

was filming as planned, one camera assistant and an assistant director would go somewhere else to film another scene. It was like a cellular division. Eventually the duration of one dizi rose from 90 minutes to 120. Right now, it is 130–140 minutes. When we saw that they expected us to film this in five days, we realized that it would not be possible. How could this be formulated? So we had to split into two groups. When the team split up, the assistant directors who were able to film became the second director. This is how the concept of the 'second director' emerged. (2019)

The race against time also altered the way different units of the production team were coordinated. One assistant needed to stay on the set all the time, while another needed to follow the backstage preparations and inform all the related parties about the flow of or the changes in the programme. Hence a new unit emerged as 'production coordination', which Günay-Tan defined as a bridge: 'The set coordinator is in fact a director without any creative aspect, dealing with the coordination between the producer and set people at a crazy pace' (2019).

The lengthening of episodes had a direct impact on how sets are run in the dizi industry. In many of my interviews I observed that the issue has been raised mostly in comparison with Western industry practices, referring to European or American crew members with whom Turkish directors and other crew members collaborated in co-productions. Often expressed as a distinction between 'us' and 'them', these narratives revealed mixed feelings. On the one hand, there was a sense of envy towards matters such as decent working hours, salaries, credible rating systems and secure broadcasting time. On the other, many also believed that in terms of problem solving, fast delivery and warm collegiality, Turkish ways are unmatched. Over the years, I discussed these perceived differences in working styles with various producers and journalists from around the world at global markets like MIPTV, MIPCOM, ATF and DISCOP. But my exposure to foreign film sets and actors has been rather limited.[16] I will therefore not enter into such comparisons but will focus on how the dizi sets have been run in Turkey in the 2010s.

Short Passes in Confined Spaces:
The Crowd, the Traffic and Their Emotional Encounters

As a working space, the interior of a set area is crowded and messy by nature. On dizi sets, which usually use real locations, the cast and crew often squeeze into a few square metres. As mentioned above, beginning by the 2000s, dizis' episode durations increased and most dizis began to be shot simultaneously by two separate teams, each led by a director. Currently, a typical dizi set's ground would have a 'mobile centre', where scenes are filmed, surrounded by a periphery of administrative and logistic support. The centre is mobile in the sense that different scenes move in the same space, and the shooting of each obliges the director's monitor to be moved and placed accordingly. On each set, the mobile centre is built around its director, with the director of photography, cameramen and sound and light technicians being nearby. Stylists and managers from the art department for décor, costume, hairdressing and make-up closely watch the shooting from this centre. Each department has many assistants in their close proximity, intervening instantly when required. The set also requires accommodating cameras, monitors, light stands, foam boards, microphone booms and jib arms, all connected through countless cables. To give an example, let me cite the cameraman Gökhan Çınarlı, whom I interviewed on the set of *Çukur*:

---

16 I was allowed to briefly explore the shooting of a scene of the series *Person of Interest* in November 2013 on Fifth Avenue in New York, with the participation of Kevin Chapman. In 2015, I was hosted at the rehearsal of a read-through for the NBC sitcom *Crowded*. I have greatly benefited from the insider perspectives of my friends Sam Johnson, Julie Bean and Eric Bogosian in the US. I am most grateful to my scholar friends for our discussions regarding their regions: Christa Salamandra (for the Middle East), Carolina Acosta-Alzuru (for Latin America), Chen Xiaoda (for China) and to Virginia Mouseler for her feedbacks on the global trends she regularly explores at Fresh TV presentations at MIP events.

We have two cameras on the chariot, upon the Panther dolly. In addition, we have the jimmy jib operator and his assistant. We have two focus pullers for the two cameras and assistants for each. In total this makes six people for two cameras. We also have a separate DIT, the digital imaging technician, the lighting team with their chief is a separate group, the best boys and the two following assistants, and then of course a driver to carry all the lighting equipment. (2019)

IMAGE 8.1 Camera Skater Dolly located in the middle of the ordinary living room of a real apartment in Reşitpaşa, Istanbul, used as the set of *Ölene Kadar*, 6 February 2017. Image courtesy of the author.

Similar lists of people can be found in all the other departments, many of whom share the set space at the same time for different purposes.

The periphery surrounding the centre, which moves within the set ground, offers another 'domain of existence'. This is where the transportation and security teams, caterers, tea makers or at times executive producers sit or stand. They too have a view of the shoot, yet they usually do not 'crowd' the area, entering the action only when necessary. They are often warned to be careful. Although there is a formal security team, everybody at the periphery also controls the borders and zones, particularly when they see an outsider approaching—such as a fan, a curious passer-by, or the actual resident of a real location. In this sense, the periphery also functions as a fortress that bars unwanted intrusions. A final that must be mentioned is the cast and crew's 'invasion' of locations. In Bosphorus neighbourhoods like Yeniköy, Büyükdere or Beykoz, one often finds a long line of vans and trailers along the shore, separating passers-by from the cast and crew.

During shoots, directors usually sit behind their monitors, unless they need to give instructions to the cast. The rest of the directing department consists of the assistant directors, who are actively involved with the shooting, and other production assistants who are responsible for preparation of actors, followin up on continuity between scenes, timecoding and so on. Director Betül Durmuş, who worked as an assistant director and time-coder in the dizi world of the early 2000s, described how she coordinated the set crowd like an orchestra conductor of a social performance. Assistant directors closely monitor the pace of shooting, keeping track of time and place simultaneously: 'Sometimes we say "Keep them on the make-up table for half an hour",' Durmuş says, 'or at other times, "Send them down in three minutes"' (2012).

Some directors of photography like to be on the spot, 'in the field' with their cameramen. They often criticize others who prefer sitting with the director behind the monitor and giving 'digital directions'. Tolga Kutluay says: 'There are those who direct with cell phones or intercoms, I cannot take it! I must see it through the lenses, perhaps because I come from an old-school negative-film technique' (2019). As the decision makers on the quality of the imaging, directors of photography hold a key position and a respected status on the set. They manage the cameramen and delegate the implementation of the overall lighting design to the gaffer, the key grip, the best boys and electricians. Because the grip equipment includes a series of heavy instruments like stands, flags or gobos, the lighting team makes up the most visible part of the technical crew.

The ultimate goal is to construct the set in the best possible way for the day to come. Be it in a studio context or a real location, preparations must begin in advance, and it is the key grip (*set amiri*) who is responsible for preparing this zone. All assistants and costume managers, lighting chiefs, catering services and transportation professionals usually arrive to open and prepare the set about a few hours before the actual 'set time' begins. 'We sleep the last, yet it is us who are the early birds,' a wardrobe assistant told me while ironing the lead actor's white shirt at 8.30 a.m. Many set members try to overcome their lack of sleep with excessive consumption of tea, coffee or cigarettes. Key grips are often responsible for any physical help the set needs. This may include changing the place of the monitors or the director's seat, managing the dolly, crane or the jib, making sure disposable overshoes are used for sensitive indoor areas, blocking the road with parking cones or pouring the 'rain' when needed. They are, in a way, the foremen of the sets who make sure that all is run 'properly'. They are also the hardest to interview because, as one puts it, 'The job is schizophrenic; you forget what you did a minute ago, as you constantly run to deal with another problem.'

Dispersed on location, the set space belongs more to the crew than to the lead actors who take refuge in their trailers. Trailer vehicles were a luxury back in the 2000s, but they are now routine—a right that workers and actors have earned. Many of the actors need trailers to prepare for scenes when there are no other available spaces on location;

they also need them for privacy or for receiving guests. As an ethnographer, I conducted some of my interviews in these trailers.[17] But for the crew, particularly in real locations 'away from civilization', as they say, trailers were most necessary for providing bathroom services.[18]

Shooting Practices: 'Action!' and Beyond

At the time of my first exposure to dizi sets, I was fascinated by the crowd of people and their constant and rapid displacement and adjustment. It was interesting to observe the army of assistants from different departments running around to support both cast and crew while maintaining a symbiotic relationship with their superiors. The costume and make-up departments were most visible, as their artists would circumambulate the actors in-between scenes. The set crowd further swelled with visiting guests, or with those accompanying child or baby actors, including parents, coaches and teachers. In addition to this circulation, unforeseen incidents might happen anytime, and require instant solutions, at times spawning new heroes. Timur Savcı, now a leading producer, joined the television industry by pragmatically solving an unexpected problem during a visit to a friend who was working for a film set (Savcı 2017). With its crowds, traffic and heavy equipment, the set environment at first appears chaotic and complex. In due time, however, one learns to distinguish the specifics of divisions of labour among crew members. It took me numerous set visits, to begin differentiating between the layers of this complex structure of shooting practices.

---

17 These happened usually when the actors had no other available time. To give a few examples, I interviewed Kenan İmirzalıoğlu during the shooting of *Karadayı* in Balat; Burak Özçivit on the set of *Çalıkuşu* in Erenköy; Mete Horozoğlu on the set of *Kösem* in Hadımköy; and Fahriye Evcen on the set of *Ölene Kadar* in Reşitpaşa.

18 Beren Saat humorously recalls how the cast and crew used to call these trailers *kakavan* (a van for pooping), a punning for *karavan*, the word for trailer (2019).

As a media text, each scene that is screened in a dizi is constituted by different 'shooting moments' (Metz 1974) of the same scene, taken from different angles—close-up, medium and long shots—to be later edited. In the rushed pace of production, dizi scenes are shot many times and often with mistakes, which directors and actors do not stop to correct. The 'shooting moment' comes into being with the collaboration of a large group of cast and crew (Metz 1974). It is the high time for the performance of actors, whose first audience is the set crew. Actors who wander around the set, in costume and ready to act, embody the scene to come. Lead actors are accustomed to a continuous gaze; their good will and behaviour are constantly tested. They also need to endure the continuous interference of costume and make-up artists. Racing against time, directors are often hard pressed to complete many scenes in order to provide the editors and musicians enough material to work on. And the real set time, which means the shooting time, literally begins when the director arrives and lead actors filter in. Directors are addressed as *Hoca*, meaning 'teacher', a common term used in many different circumstances in Turkish etiquette.[19]

Although 'acting' stands at the centre of the shoots, I have often observed actors' solitude within the crowd on set. As Memet Ali Alabora puts it, 'Actors' labour is usually invisible, as we often wait for the director's command for action. But while the crew do their last check-up, we seem to hang around as if doing nothing. Nobody sees us repeating our lines in our minds while hanging around. And once "action" is uttered, we are the ones on the spot to deliver the performance perfectly' (2011).

Despite the number of workers, as soon as shooting begins, the set requires absolute silence. It is a common practice that whoever phone

---

19 The original meaning of the term is a religious figure, as the priest of a mosque. But friends can also call one another *hocam* to show their sincerity or respect. Students call their professors *hocam,* and professors can call their colleagues *hocam.* IIn its different usages, the term acknowledges respect for knowledge.

rings during a shoot must buy *baklava* for the whole crew. Since the mid1990s, dizis have been shot with synchronized sound recording. But because most are filmed on location or open-air studios, sets are disrupted by, for instance, calls to prayer or passing airplanes, as was the case for historical dramas like *Muhteşem Yüzyıl* or *Vatanım Sensin*. For dizis shot in *konak*s or *yalı*s, old wooden mansions of the Ottoman era, directors may ask for absolute immobility except among the cast to avoid the creaking of floors, as was the case on the set of *Çalıkuşu*. Shooting in real locations also requires constant adjustments of furniture, old and new alike. Technical issues like running out of camera battery or needing to adjust décor or make-up necessitate brief interruptions. Sometimes, the post-production department has urgent requirements. For instance, director Ahmet Katıksız had to stop in the middle of shooting *Kara Para Aşk* to watch the first version of a teaser and suggest revisions to the post-production team so that it could be broadcast that day.[20]

Post-production usually occurs away from this crowded realm as editing, colouring and sound mixing are all done in labs. Editor Gökçe Bilgin-Kılıç who once had an opportunity to observe conditions on a set, said:

> *Fatmagül'ün Suçu Ne?* was going to be shot in Ildırı, a small Aegean town. Director Hilal Saral wanted the whole team nearby during the shoots of the first episode. So we set our post-production lab near the set. That's when I witnessed the traffic. You deal with so many people on the set. Here, in my lab, I am only reporting to my director. Most of the time, I am all alone with my machines and monitors. (2012)

---

20 Set visit to *Kara Para Aşk*, 5 June 2014.

Layers of Performativity on Set:
Parallel Performances of the Cast and Crew

As a researcher, I often joined the sets through a reference, which afforded me a place next to the director, behind the monitors. This way, I was able to follow the 'set traffic' in real time and observe the performance of the cast and crew from a privileged vantage point. In-between shoots, I also had time to engage in small chats with crew, extras and members of the production team like time-coders or location scouts. Given production gets squeezed in-between writing, shooting and post-production, dizi sets are as dramatic as the scenes that are being shot. Sets are like organisms which have their own rhythm, temporality and frequency, with a continuum from 'resting time' to 'camera action'. The rhythm is set by the peak moment—that is, the shooting of a scene. Like sprinters warming up for a race, the whole cast and crew focus and prepare in their own pace and style for the particular scene to be shot. To an outsider, it is difficult to discern who is who at first sight, as many would appear to be just hanging or running around. But once the shooting starts, they suddenly form a composite unit, taking the collective action required of them.[21] From a movement studies perspective, sets have an improvised choreographic flow of their own. Every moment of break is used for a 'time out of time', a micro-leisure, a chat, a zip, a puff of cigarette.

The performances of the cast and the crew therefore take place simultaneously, offering encapsulated cultural data, which reveal a great deal about the dizi industry in general. Different crew members engage in a performance of skill, competence and efficiency. When the cast focus on the enactment of the script, they are in fact making the absent

---

21 To me they often resemble *tulumcu*s of the Ottoman imperial festivals, who served as security guards and used various instruments, gestures and ribald humour to control the crowds (Öztürkmen 2011). The movement and choreography in the set environment will be a fascinating domain of research in years to come.

writer visible. Set performances resemble festival parades—'public enactments in which a culture is encapsulated, enacted, placed on display for itself and for outsiders' (Stoeltje and Bauman 1988: 585). The set milieu is an assembly of performances, where cast and crew perform concurrently on their own stage situated in the same workspace. To any outsider, including the ethnographer, the crowd and action of the set ground is overwhelming, where the concept of 'participant observation' elides with that of 'participant performer'. The moment a researcher joins the set, his or her actions are subject to the gaze of the whole set audience. As an ethnographer she finds herself to be both performer and audience member alike.

From an ethnographic point of view, the performativity of the 'behind-the-scenes' is indeed as striking as the shooting of scenes. Like festive grounds embedding different performances, sets offer a variety of performances not only in front of the camera but behind it as well, enacted by various crew members. In the dizi set milieu, one can very easily spot the cast and crew as the *is* and *as* performers of the shooting event (Schechner 2006). With their costume and make-up, any actor— be it a star or an extra—can be distinguished at first sight from set workers who appear in their jeans and t-shirts, with mostly unshaven, tired faces.

The movement systems of the cast and crew are also remarkably different. Amid the intense traffic of 'setting the set', one can observe how the technical crew members dominate the *as* performance. To cameramen, boom and jimmy-jib operators, their instruments—equipment that consists of heavy machines which require subtle handling— are like extensions of their bodies. Strong, athletic, swift, skilful and practical, crew members constantly move within the shooting site. Like weight-lifting acrobats, they must cooperate and assist each other while respecting production hierarchies. They set up and disassemble their dollies, monitors, booms and jimmy jibs with amazing speed. In many of my set visits, I would often find myself deserted as the crew disassembled around me as soon as the shot was completed. By the time I collected my bag and coat, the director would already be standing next to the actors giving them instructions for the next scene and the monitor moved to the next location. I always felt overawed by the physical agility of the crew.

As a dispersing yet connected group, the crew develops various communication skills to cope with the crowded and hectic set environment. Part of this is their lingo, designed to condense communication and also to assuage boredom and exhaustion. This jargon developed over decades, drawing on an oral tradition in filmmaking. To give a few examples, *kakavan* refers to the trailers with toilets; while *bizden*, literally meaning 'from us', refers to taking the blame for repeating a shot. Sometimes directors are not satisfied with the acting, but to reshoot they tell the actors that the mistake was technical, a *teknik kaza*. Directors may also say to their assistants to *aşağıyı uyandır*, 'wake up those downstairs or in trailers', in order to prepare the cast for the next scene to come. Similarly, *sıfırdan gel*, 'come from ground zero', means to warn the actor to come from behind the camera; and *bulut bekliyoruz*, 'we wait for the clouds', refers to waiting for better light during open-air shoots. The language of the set also displays the tacit hierarchies among cast and crew.[22]

Günay-Tan gives great importance to the special language developed on the set because it helps save time:

Everything is easier with someone who knows you. Speaking the same language is important. For example, when I say to my art director: 'Make this room a cold place', they get what I mean because of all the time we have spent together in previous projects. But if I were to work with a completely new art director, I would end up with a different concept from what I meant. In fact, I am after this: reducing the number of the words and

22 For a general analysis of slang on film sets, see Tony Bill (2009).

questions; and seeing things from the same perspective. I've worked with my art director since *Öyle Bir Geçer Zaman ki*. We rarely speak. We have codes. He asks, 'Do you want *cıngıllı?*', I say 'Yes, *cıngıllı*'.[23] You can never say to someone else, 'Make a *cıngıl* here and put *pıtpıt* there.' It is like a whole other language we have between us. Same thing applies to the actors and actresses. For example, I have worked with Salih [Bademci] for seven years. We get along easily with very few words. What I value most is 'fewer words'. If we had time, I would talk for 45 minutes and get the emotion I want from any actor. But I usually have only 5 minutes to get this emotion. I have to get what I want instantly and move on, because we have no time . . . Same thing with my scriptwriter, we are a perfect match. This is so important for the speed of the industry. (2019)

Generally speaking, crew's performance is a spectacle to watch, and showing how well you do the job is a crucial matter for junior assistants, and is perhaps one of the best examples of performativity on the set. Those who have just begun to work are closely evaluated by their peers and managers on the criteria of being 'harmonious', 'hard working' and 'practical'. In this sense, sets are also a ground for 'performance at work', where being 'indispensable' helps secure future jobs.

Alongside these professional performances, unexpected encounters happen as well. Shooting in real locations surrounded by fans and curious passers-by creates challenging situations. During the scenes filmed among the real crowd on a street, crew members often assume extra roles surrounding the actors, allowing them to act uninterrupted. But the untrained extras are often the most fun part of set performance. When I was among the extras in *Fatmagül'ün Suçu Ne?*, I had a chance to interview many women playing a crowd of feminists gathered to sup-

---

23 *Cıngıl* refers to 'jingle', meaning ornamented or beaded in Turkish. In the context of art direction, it refers to the idea of 'making something shinier' with glitter.

port the protagonist during her first trial. The agencies providing extras improved since the early 2010s, but before this, roles of extras were filled by everyday housewives and unemployed men who joined sets for amusement and free food, or even in the hope of being 'discovered'. New extras were not paid until they proved their viability. Some might escape after lunch, start an argument with an assistant, or disturb the set by giggling. They would have a leader, an *ekipbaşı*, a term used mostly for the lead dancer of a folk-dance group. On that particular day on the location of *Fatmagül'ün Suçu Ne?*, extras were all told to wear purple, the colour associated with feminism, though none had an idea about this connection. Ayhan Özen, the second director, was in charge of preparing the extras in such a way that they would deliver what the directing department wanted. 'Now you are very good people,' he started, 'You are a good crowd.' The crowd would need to act as a feminist protest group but he had no time to explain the real story, so he gave them a short scene casting them as 'good people':

> Once you see Kerim and Fatmagül getting out of their car, you all pull back a little bit to open a path for them. They have to pass through the corridor you open. But remember, they are not Beren Saat and Engin Akyürek [the stars]. So, you don't smile at them, nor wave hands or shout.[24]

In order to break the ice, Özen then himself began to act, saying, like an acting coach: 'Look at me now, I am Fatmagül.' As a man impersonating a woman, he prompted laughter which encouraged him to pull an extra from the crowd as Kerim, and he said 'This is how we come!' The rest of the crowd held banners with feminist slogans. As I was trying to hide my face, he picked on me: 'Hey honey,' he said, 'Put this over your head; let people see your beautiful face!'

In one of the *Kara Para Aşk* sets I visited, I witnessed a scene shot on Bebek shore, a rather busy road by the Bosphorus during summer

---

24 *Fatmagül'ün Suçu Ne?* set visit, 12 November 2011.

evenings.[25] The passers-by did not like being stopped, some swore, some wanted to appear in the film, while others honked their horns near the cameras. The set in their eyes was a stage, and they wanted to act on it. Finally, the crew who were kept from their task became nervous and shouted back at them. They quickly retreated when their director Ahmet Katıksız warned them not to interfere in any way: 'No such conversations. We need to be calm, we are the ones who are responsible and mature.' During the shooting, the director of the second team joined the set with his own story of stress. Apparently, they had this scene in a boat, but Bosphorus had been choppy, and an inefficient captain sailed for three hours instead of one. His crew got seasick and the shooting got unexpectedly extended.

The set also offers a platform for exchanging stories and other forms of verbal art. Like slang, gossip is also widespread, along with the frequent dropping of proverbial sayings and cracking of jokes. Gossip is a survival outlet on the set, and harmless gossip prevails at all levels—directors gossip about actors, actors about other actors, and crew about all of them. Admission to a set milieu also means access to confidential information about the dizi being filmed. In this sense, the set produces its local knowledge, which becomes a fringe benefit and can easily turn into cultural capital. Insider information from the set, however confidential, empowers every crew member in their personal social circles.

Emotional Encounters *alla Turca*

Because of the long hours of work under tight deadlines, dizi shoots need to be emotionally regulated. 'This factory is indeed a wheel,' writer Gaye Boralıoğlu states, 'When there is an error at one point, it affects all the other units' (2012). Given this rush, both cast and crew pour all their blood, sweat and tears to finish their tasks and go home. Who or

---

25 Set visit to *Kara Para Aşk*, 5 June 2014; and to *Hayat Şarkısı*, 8 June 2016.

what scene will have the priority may sometimes cause conflict. Since creators work in close quarters, their tolerance is strained in time, and emotionally charged encounters often occur. Anxiety may be called the primordial feeling of the set, affecting all members of the cast and crew. At the same time, close proximity fosters a sense of 'family intimacy'. Surviving one set after the other as a team creates a sense of bonding. Some of these feelings can be associated with emotional aspects of Turkish work culture, best expressed by the concepts of *yakınlık* (closeness) or *samimiyet* (sincerity). Developing a sense of belonging to a real location is not uncommon. One can add to this how shared tea, food and cigarettes create small comfort zones.

Any researcher who is engaged in set ethnographies would observe and experience these emotional dimensions. Following a visit to the set of *Çocuklar Duymasın* in the early 2000s, my colleague sociologist Nükhet Sirman had remarked, 'It was like you are beamed into a family's intimate living room.' Günay-Tan deconstructs this concept of intimacy:

> The set milieu is so conspicuous; you are all naked there, you open up your inner self. This is such an intimate place. To tell you the truth, we don't like outsiders. How are you going to treat an actor under the gaze of a stranger? As usual, or not? The set is an organism with its own mechanism. It has an ethos, and it is this openness and exposure which makes your work shine. (2019)

The sets are structurally organized, yet they need to be socially regulated. As actress Fahriye Evcen explained, 'The mood of a set takes its cue from its director' (2011). Günay-Tan agrees that dizi directors function like orchestra conductors to manage the emotional traffic of the set, which is an unavoidable aspect of working in challenging conditions:

> My primary role, of course, is to get the right feeling from my actors as they play their roles. But I have a second invisible duty,

which is not cited in my job description, but for which I spend an extra amount of time: to be in control of the emotional state of the set. This is something I prioritize while building up the project—to keep and protect this discipline under this umbrella of care. This is when you have a successful end product. Then you don't have capricious behaviour, competition or conflict. Sets are generally like a family, and this directly reflects on screen. The audience cannot know what happens on the set, but I really believe that the good energy of the set is something which communicates itself on screen. (2019)

Many directors use the 'family-like' (*aile gibi*) metaphor for their cast and crew. But Memet Ali Alabora, the founding chair of the Actors' Union in Turkey during 2011–14, dismisses the idealization of the set as a 'family' setting, calling it a 'memorized cliché'. Alabora had reservations about the notion of 'having great fun together which naturally reflects upon viewers'. He also calls attention to the conflicts of interest on set. Actors, for instance, always argue with the production team over scheduling, since their time is divided among other activities like dubbing or rehearsing for theatre (Alabora 2011). Dizi sets build up their own synergy, but overtime labour becomes an exhausting experience for both cast and crew; and this sometimes leads to accidents (see *TV Aktüel* 2014; *Haberler.com* 2016). During our interview on set conditions, Elif Sönmez (2011) spoke about her own injury during the shooting of a dizi in Kayseri in 2001, which necessitated a year-long break from work.

The state of the set is indeed a different state of mind. Sönmez, who had an opportunity to observe work habits during the late 1990s, expressed some reservations on the matter: 'Every set has an invented notion of "set ethic" (*set etiği*), which literally means "to work under all circumstances."' In reference to women crew members, she also mentioned a notion of 'set manners' (*set adabı*), which required 'dressing up accordingly': 'You must dress appropriately, that's the rule. Your clothing must cover you up as you bend and get up. And no cleavage please!' (2011). The clothing issue was also brought up by Günay-Tan, who spoke about how her style changed over the years:

> During my first experience of directing, I was wearing cute dresses and shorts. But what I experienced on set showed that I had to compartmentalize this. When you are like this on the set, you are seen primarily as a woman. I was very young and pretty. In Turkey, it is difficult to be both smart and beautiful. You don't have a chance. If you are smart, you have to be ugly; if you are pretty, you should be silly. If you are both, it is a bit too much. I didn't experience any harassment or anything, but my words were not taken seriously. This was one of the problems that I had with the teams at that time. Later on, I realized that I had become more masculine. You had to wear postal boots to become a woman whose words were heard. The way I am on set now is very different. I still pay attention to my outfit, put on my jewellery and so on, but I rarely come to a set wearing a dress. (2019)

Although guests, particularly scholars, spark curiosity by their mere presence, they are also perceived as short-lived acquaintances. Following a series of warm and long conversations on the set of *İntikam*, a crew member frankly told me: 'It is nice to have a different person to talk to here in the middle of a boring day, but you know and I know, you will go and we will stay!'[26] It is of course possible to do longer ethnographies on particular dizi sets. There, the dynamics will be much different, as the researcher will be part of that synergy in due time.[27]

---

26 *İntikam* set visit 23 May 2013.

27 In such cases, the experience of the researchers will be limited to that particular dizi project, but because of the *longue-durée* exposure, they will be able to develop the set knowledge of that project. It will also be interesting to see the growing network of relations among the cast and crew, during and after the ethnography.

There are obviously other visitors to the set, who come and go through connections of the cast or crew. On the set of *Kara Para Aşk*, a young woman, who also happened to be one of the sponsors credited at the end of the episodes, told me she visited the set regularly, and was now friends with some of the cast members. The same day, two fans of actress Tuba Büyüküstün were visiting. They came a long distance, and stayed on set all day long. Apparently, they were granted this privilege because of their efforts in promoting the dizi on social media. At times, journalists or researchers like me join the set with permission from producers or by invitation. Lately, with the rising awareness of academic research, producers are more open to welcome ethnographers into their sets, a matter which promises more scholarship in coming years.[28]

Many crew members join film sets through connections of relatives or friends, and therefore have an awareness of whom they 'represent'. Sets also foster romance. Given the long working hours, cast and crew tend to socialize on the set in a confined space. 'There are set lovers at all levels,' a crew member at the set of *İntikam* confided. Romance is more tolerated when it happens at peer level. Many actors date and marry one another, and set workers may often flirt or become involved.[29] However, rumours of romance between directors and actors may sometimes create trouble in the set environment concerning fair and equal treatment.

Like romance, the notion of *kankalık* (to be buddies) is an important affective category, and an inevitable social consequence of the set milieu. Yet, close friendships may be subject to discipline. In a hit dizi

---

28 For long-term set ethnographies of other genres like talk shows or news programmes, see Zeyneb Feyza Akınerdem (2015); Deniz Tansel-İlic (2015); Emek Çaylı-Rahte (2017). Ethnographic approach to dizis have been pursued mostly in audience studies; among many others, see Sinan Yörük et al. (2015).

29 Star couples who met and got married after working in the same dizis include Fahriye Evcen and Burak Özçivit, Halit Ergenç and Bergüzar Korel, Tuba Büyüküstün and Onur Saylak, and Neslihan Atagül and Kadir Doğulu, among others.

set I visited in 2011, the director reprimanded two set workers in my presence: 'Don't hug and giggle like this,' she said, and then felt the need to explain: 'They get so close and intimate with one another that they stop seeing each other's mistakes; or worse, they sometimes cover them up.' Similarly, the executive director of another hit dizi explained her harsh treatment of assistants, saying, 'I rather prefer they fear me than love me!'[30] In this highly demanding environment, directors claim they need almost military-level discipline 'to control problems' and to solve them. In the words of another executive director, set workers are the *erat*, the privates of the set milieu. The military analogy is not a coincidence, as running against time requires strict policing for the common interest of 'finishing and going home'.

Set narratives also include accounts of each production department's activities and achievements. During all my set visits, I heard many narratives of efficiency, functionality and pragmatism. Some were delivered as short and swift accounts of job descriptions or taxonomies. As the social players of the overall set performativity, crew members claimed 'the accountability to an audience for a display of communicative competence' (Bauman 1989: 175). The narratives may seem obvious, even boring, but if one approaches them in their performative context, they serve as accounts of 'solemnity' or 'responsibility', which embed stories and anecdotes of solidarity, heroism and survival in the set milieus.

It would be useful here to note some of the distinctive features of Turkish work culture. The 'Turkish style' of work has been a frequent subject of business studies literature.[31] These studies highlight the importance of sentiment in Turkish business culture, advising outsiders

---

30 *Muhteşem Yüzyıl* set visit, 23 May 2012.

31 This literature has grown in recent decades as part of 'cross-cultural management' studies, with the rising global impact of Turkish entrepreneurs who began to invest in Central Asia at the end of Cold War.

to take 'emotion' as seriously as 'reason' in work relations. They often describe the Turkish work environment as a setting where the use of expressive gestures and speaking out loud are considered ordinary, in contrast to the supposed restraint of Western or Asian business cultures. Foreign businessmen are often warned about the social distance they put between them and their junior employees, since too much formality may be read as arrogance or condescension. This literature also underlines how work and social life merge in Turkish culture. Generally speaking, most Turkish employees prefer a multitasking working style to a sequential one. And the ability to 'adapt' to changing hierarchies and new material conditions emerges as an important skill of Turkish business culture (see Öğüt and Kocabacak 2008; Parlar and Menekşe 2016; Aksoy 2013).

Given this framework, Turkish codes of sociability on dizi sets reflect a concept of *samimiyet* (sincerity), which in this case refers to solidarity. Covering or filling in for one another, sharing food, chatting during breaks and socializing after work are essential survival mechanisms. Order, however, needs to be maintained. As executive director Nermin Eroğlu puts it: 'No set can be run without hierarchy or discipline. There have been times when we have had to formally check the arrival and departure times of our set workers.'[32] This statement may sound unusual for the established film industries of the West, but Turkey's the work culture has its own hidden faces.

Regulation of emotions in the workplace is also a significant challenge for management. Senior assistants often train juniors on set behaviour, or many newcomers learn such social codes through observation. Although humour is a helpful, even indispensable part of set life, at the end of the day, workers understand how knowing one's limit (*had bilmek*) is essential for a successful career. The concept of sincerity also involves 'closeness' (*yakınlık*), with an implied transcending of

---

32 *Muhteşem Yüzyıl*, set visit, 23 May 2012.

IMAGE 8.2 Director of photography Münür Gürsoy taking a break with his team in-between shoots at the set of *Siyah Beyaz Aşk* in the garden of the villa in Polonezköy, 22 May 2018. Image courtesy of the author.

power relations on set. How warmly a director or a star behaves with crew members is also a test of their modesty. Stars in particular, but all actors in general, are the centre of attention on set, regardless of whether they are in front of the camera. Their presence creates its own magnetic field, and they perform not only in front of the camera but behind it as well. Dizi stars affect the mood on set as much as directors do.

Early his career, actor Cahit Gök worked on a dizi filmed in Mardin, a town in south-eastern Turkey. Given the remote and isolated location, the cast and crew grew intimate, and one day a crew member suddenly patted his neck as he was moving towards the camera. This took Gök by surprise: 'I was so concentrated on my role that it totally interrupted my acting. But because we were so close, we could also get over it' (Gök 2012). Interactions are a mutual learning process. As they gain experience, crew members learn how to handle the stars. But a general reservation about approaching them remains. Some crew members, and even directors, openly say that they prefer to stay away from actors. As a director of photography put it, 'I don't make friends with the actors;

I am friendly with them, but I would not rely on their friendship.' Actors, on the other hand, complain that they are sometimes subject to unfair treatment. As one star recounts:

> Once, shooting was delayed for almost an hour because of a technical issue. But the key grip told the rest of the cast that they were waiting for me. I was, however, ready and waiting in my trailer memorizing my lines. The impact of this lasted for a few days, and I was so puzzled as to why people were treating me weirdly. In the end, I understood why, but the feelings remained.

Director Şenol Sönmez approaches the issue from another angle, where the actors can also set the mood of the set. Having worked on *Hayat Bilgisi* (2003), he remembers how the set revolved around lead actress Perran Kutman's energy. Kutman would come in and chat with everybody; she had a delicate way of questioning who was feeling what and regulating emotions on the set accordingly (Sönmez 2016). Kutman's comportment was rooted in her theatre tradition. Today's stars, however, are more concerned with image management; they know that anything that happens on set may appear on social media and in the tabloid press. Nevertheless, once they come out of their trailers in make-up and costume, they become the centre of attention and attract the gaze of the crew. These are valuable moments for all set people that emerge in the stories they relate.

Günay-Tan approaches the concept of 'closeness' by giving examples of her different on-set selves. She distinguishes 'doing the job well' from 'being friendly', a matter which can generally be misunderstood in Turkish working environments. Her team calls her a 'true professional', a statement hardly heard in contexts of sets in the West, where all directors would be assumed to behave professionally. In the Turkish industry, however, this evokes her authority over the cast and crew. Günay-Tan explains her principle:

> I have two faces. When I am working, I can be really grim and focused, closed to communication, expecting everyone to do

their best. I won't care even if my father or my brother visits the set. I speak very directly and abruptly if an actor or actress is not doing a good job, if they don't have proper make-up, if the camera movements are not correct. But when we say stop, we may have all kinds of conversations. Is my director of photography's kid sick? Is the make-up artist getting married soon? Or, looking at photos from a party last night, how beautiful her blouse is, did someone get a haircut, or did someone buy something new, what is going on in everyone's life? I become very good friends with every one of them and know everything that's going on in their lives. I try to break the hierarchy by having conversations during breaks. But during the filming, I became the kind of person who says 'Move away! There is only one president here, and it is me. Behave!' This way people understand what I say during filming is about the way they work, not something personal . . . For me, everyone on my set is worthy and special. I don't have any sense of superiority. We are all equal human beings. But everyone needs to be extremely professional during the shoot. I never mix these two. We may have eaten together three minutes earlier, but I cannot ignore a mistake during filming, because I am doing my best, without any mistakes. (2019)

There are many projects which fall apart when human relations are not well managed on set. Since the 2000s, the dizi industry created its own stars, as actors, writers and directors. Many actors value the creators or agents who helped them launch their careers.[33] However, certain dizi projects may get hampered by emotionally charged altercations between

---

33 Beren Saat, for instance, talks highly of Tomris Giritlioğlu, who cast her in *Hatırla Sevgili* where she made her breakthrough (Saat 2019). Similarly, Engin Akyürek, a leading star of the dizi world, acknowledges and honors writer Meral Okay, saying 'playing the character she wrote, carried me to a totally other level' (*Dailymotion* 2012b).

actors and writers, where the lead actors gain power as a dizi becomes a hit, which from the writer's perspective happens thanks to the plot and characters of the story. Tensions arise when actors want to interfere with the script, and alter their characters' journey in the narrative. In other cases, co-stars may not get along well over time, or directors may fall in love with actors or vice versa. In any case, the longevity and the success of a promising dizi lie in its affective management. If not well handled, there comes a moment where team members run out of patience, get bored or alienated, a situation which can cause a well-rated project to come to an end.

The cast and crew develop certain strategies to survive the stress on sets. Tea-time is central to Turkish culture in general, but in the set environment, it has a particular symbolic meaning of warmth and hospitality. The set tea maker of is known to all by name, and a *çay ocağı*, meaning literally the 'tea hearth', remains continually open throughout the shootings. The name of the *çaycı*, the tea server, appears among the dizi credits at the end of each episode.[34] Many of my interviewees note that food constitutes a 'breath' on the set, and that the calibre of the catering represents the 'quality' of the production company. To set workers, the notion of 'quality' refers more to 'generosity' as a human value, while to extras, set food is a fringe benefit. Extras 'making crowds' receive very modest payments, so food is an essential motivation for participation. As one expressed in the shootings of *Fatmagül'ün Suçu Ne?* 'We will see if they serve a meal or not; if not I will not stay for the afternoon shooting.' Another stated, 'We are paid so little, let us at least fill our stomachs before going home.' In the 2000s, there were no set times for meals; food was delivered only when the director or set coordinator decided to give a break. Nowadays, sets are obliged to monitor work and break times, and ensure a one-hour lunch break.

Given the difficult working, the sets are perceived as sites of deprivation, where any piece of food has great value. As one director put it,

---

34 See *Bir Zamanlar Çukurova* by TIMS & B production, ATV 2019.

'Just give us any food during the set, we would eat everything!' 'Food time' is also an opportunity for cast, crew, extras and guests to converse. In the early days of my research, I learned that the best way to cheer a set is to bring them *baklava*.[35] In fact, all Turkish sweets are welcome on set, as they bring what the crew calls source of 'instant energy'.

The set milieus also have some departments which operate as 'tranquilizers'. The costume, hairdressing, and make-up artists see themselves as the 'soothing agents' or even 'therapists' on the set, setting the mood of the actors, energizing them many times by 'just listening to them'. 'We "degas" them', hairdresser Metin Tektaş told me: 'Sometimes they come here in a depressed mood, or sometimes, in between the scenes they get uneasy. We are the ones who take away their negative energy'.[36] Costume manager Nehir Arıcı confirms this calming function:

Actors may have a bad day before coming to the set. Once they are here, they first prepare, get their hair, make up and costumes ready. We cheer them up as they arrive on set, so that nothing is reflected while filming. This aspect of our job is not visible. They rapidly get into a new mood, and start filming . . . We even help the extras. In one case, I had to convince an extra not to leave the set, as she did not know that she would impersonate a B-girl. I wanted them to wear shiny dresses, and she refused. I talked to her for 15 minutes, like a therapist. 'Look', I said, 'this is what our director wants. They didn't tell you this and I am sorry about that, though I warned the agency to inform you'. So, from time to time we have to be their therapists (Arıcı 2019).

Erkan Bektaş comments from a different perspective, giving an example on the actors' role of tranquilizer. While filming *Fay Grim* in

---

35 I should thank my friend Ayşe Özer to teach me the difference between the 'salted pastry' and sweets like *baklava, tulumba* or *şöbiyet*. Salty pastries would fill the stomach but would bring sleep. This is why the crew always preferred the sweets bringing instant energy.

36 Metin Tektaş, *Çalsın Sazlar* film set visit, 20 August 2014.

Germany, he observed how German set workers were joyful. 'We are often exposed to depressed set workers,' he stated, 'they are so tired working for long hours. Many times, it is me who try to be easy going and smiling on the set' (Bektaş 2012). Make-up artist Ebru Güleren, however, sees affective communication as an important part of her job. Noting that her department is in continual contact with the actors, she believes that one becomes a good make-up artist by learning how to deconstruct actors' personalities and habits:

> Firstly, you have to get the hang of the actors. What do they like, what they don't. Some don't like their faces to be touched a lot, so you finish their work fast. Some don't let you put on any eyeshadow. You need to learn the habits of each one of them. You develop a common understanding over time. This is a mutual learning process, as you learn from one another. After a few rehearsals, once the set is open, time flies by. (2019)

Betül Durmuş, who worked on production teams for many years, calls attention to the functionality of these teams: 'Sometimes set directors hold the actors' hands like parents do. Make up rooms always offer comfort with tea and coffee, and we would be in touch with the hair dressers or makeup artists, sometimes saying "keep them busy the next half an hour", or "send them here in three minutes"' (Durmuş 2012).

There is no set worker who does not complain about the exhaustively long hours, or stress the sacrifices they make in their private lives. However, despite the frenetic pace of production, dizi sets can be also addictive. Once captivated by the excitement of hard work, intimacy and the public success that comes after broadcasting begins. Many crew members concede that they prefer working on dizis to advertising or cinema. For instance, makeup artist Ebru Güleren relates that she has been tempted to leave the dizi world many times: 'I tell to myself many times "I will quit it," but I never do. It has been years and years. I continue because I like this rush, I guess. When we take summer breaks, we all miss here. One turns into a workaholic' (2019). What Güleren explains refers indeed to a saying in Turkish theatre terminology, that 'once you swallow the stage dust, (*sahne tozu yutmak*), you can never get away from it'. Costume manager Nehir Arıcı gives another angle why she prefers dizi sector over advertising:

The advertising industry is quite nice. But it is very simple. What advertisers do in four hours; we do it in 15 minutes. Dizi teams are very pragmatic. They get organized just in one day. There had been times, I also worked in the advertising world, filming four commercials in one month. But I missed making dizi. In fact, the working conditions are more humane in advertising industry. But in dizi world, there is a continuity; you are taken into a story. The costume you make always have a story. Whereas in advertising it begins and ends, just like that! (2019).

Teams (*ekip*s) develop over on the basis of reliability, quick delivery and harmony. They share the same language and other communicative skills that increase their efficiency. Department managers endeavour 'to protect their crew', which means helping them obtain future jobs in the industry. These teams consolidate through the shared memory of past projects, but they do not have a formal contract binding them. Director Zeynep Günay-Tan explains this bonding:

Because we do not have strong unions to look after us, we have our own professional groupings with people who share similar perspectives. There are some friends in the industry I worked with very closely in the past while we were in more junior positions. We all feel very close to one another; we exchange assistants and technical teams. These are old relationships that are rooted in past friendships and co-working. Let's say one of my former assistants looks for a job. Let say, I don't work at that moment and cannot employ her. So, I call my old friends and let them know that they can hire her. I would not want her to go and work elsewhere. Once she starts there, I would know that she is in good hands (2019).

Be it a woman or man, many directors follow a Turkish style of management, recalled as 'babacan patron' (fatherly boss) who is at the same time authoritarian and protective (see Aycan 2006; Gerçek 2018).

Last but not the least, it is important to note that sets' cast and crew bond not only to each other, but also to locations. In cases where the set is established in a given neighbourhood, both actors and set employees develop a sense of attachment to that place. One of the actors in *Bir Bulut Olsam*, a hit dizi which used a historical *konak* in the Midyat-Mardin district, expressed resentment when he saw the same site being used for a meagre production with a weak story: 'It was such a unique site,' he stated, 'and we had passed days and nights there for such a long time that the *konak* occupies a precious place in my memory. It hurts me now to see it being used for not-so-good projects.' Actor Erkan Kolçak Köstendil notes the attachment he and the cast and crew developed to the neighbourhood of Balat while filming *Çukur*: 'You end up being a resident of the neighbourhood yourself,' Köstendil told, 'all of us come and mingle with this whole surrounding' (2019).

The sets mirror the industries in which they are constructed. Obviously, they all share some universal features, like the load of the equipment, the traffic or safety rules. However, the performance of the sets also encapsulates the work culture in which they are situated (Stoeltje and Bauman 1988). The study of particular dizi projects as in-depth ethnographies will bring a much profounder understanding of the diverse performances on sets. So far, dizis have been studied more on the basis on their content and we have seen more ethnographies on dizi audiences than on sets. As I tried to emphasize in earlier chapters, we can better comprehend each dizi project by approaching them as media texts. The study of set performativity will greatly contribute to elaborate the intermediality of dizi as a genre, and it will certainly receive more scholarly attention in the future.

CHAPTER 9

The Wonderland of Global Markets

International Distribution of Turkish Dizis

Global markets for television content are vital platforms for television industries. Their impact has grown over the years, making these fairs acquire a festive character of their own. For many decades, television programme flows travelled one-way from the US—and to some extent the UK—to the rest of the world (Varis 1974; Tracy 1985; Alvarado 1996). This situation changed, however, when globalization opened up new possibilities for production collaborations, which reached wider audiences in multiple screening venues. With the rise in demand for imported programming, there is today a vibrant world market for television (see Havens 2003). Until the Covid 19 pandemic, producers, distributors, sales agents, broadcasters and national agencies of different countries used to come every year to such international television content markets as MIPTV (1963), NATPE (1964), MIPCOM (1985), DISCOP (1992) or ATF (2000).[1] Although some of these markets have a regional focus, they all target a global flow, creating a transnational community whose members develop strong ties through their market

---

1 MIPTV: Marché International des Programmes de Télévision; NATPE: National Association of Television Programme Executives; MIPCOM: Marché International des Programmes de Television or de Communication; DISCOP: Discount Programming; ATF: Asia TV Forum and Market. For more, see Justin Malbon and Albert Morsan (2006).

exposures. MIPTV and MIPCOM, which were held in Cannes, France, have been known as the most attended markets, while NATPE has a focus on Latin America, DISCOP on Africa, and MIPASIA and ATF on Asia. These dynamics changed greatly since MIPTV 2020 was cancelled and transformed into the first online television market, to be followed up in later years in a hybrid form.

My initial interest in visiting these fairs was to understand the scope of Turkey's presence. The timing of my research coincided with the boom of Turkish content in the MENA and the Balkan regions, and I was really curious about how this phenomenon was visually reflected in the global marketplace. The first global market I ever visited was Berlinale, the Berlin Film Festival, which I attended in 2013 to celebrate my friend Köken Ergün receiving a Special Mention Prize for his short film *Ashura*. My filmmaker friends who observed my fascination with the market and its national pavilions insisted that I should attend the MIP events to observe the display of various television industries.[2] Access to MIP events, however, was not an easy endeavour for an academic, as they were expensive commercial fairs. Through a short research, I found out that the Istanbul Chamber of Commerce (İTO), was Turkey's official representative at these global fairs. Luckily, Murat Yalçıntaş, the chairman of İTO, happened to be my childhood friend, and he directed me to the protocol team that made my first visit possible to MIPTV in 2013.[3] Thereafter, I joined İTO's Film Industry Coordination Committee and visited such events in Cannes, Istanbul, Johannesburg and Singapore.

2 Visiting Berlinale was a turning point in my research. I am indebted to my friends Ayşe Özer and Köken Ergün for making this possible. I would also like to thank Belçim Bilgin, Sevilay Demirci, Önder Çakar and Murat Akagündüz for their valuable insights during this trip.

3 I would like to thank Aysun Yılmaz, the then director of İTO's Exhibitions Department, who shared her experience with me and lent great support to my research during its early stages.

Television markets are 'gated events' that are strictly monitored. Until the pandemic, the MIP markets in particular were crowded, vibrant and impressive with huge posters, national and corporate stands, and their little niches for negotiation meetings. During my first visit to MIPTV 2013, my first impression was surprise. The domineering visual presence of Turkish content was striking, displaying a variety of dizis' posters within the Palais des Festivals, but also along the streets of Cannes. As an academic, I found the series of conferences, presentations and screening events as interesting as the visual display of the market. My first observation was how their structure differed from academic conferences. There was a strong impressive performative aspect of the conference, hosting many CEOs, talents and stars, with well-rehearsed and well-regulated interviews and panels. These conference events were much shorter than academic ones and followed a very focused and to-the-point style. They were moderated by leading journalists of the field and had a terminology of their own with abbreviations which took some time for me to decode. Nevertheless, they were most useful for me to understand the scale and scope of the global markets and situate the Turkish industry and dizi distribution processes.

A turning point for my research was the start of preparations for MIPCOM 2015, where Turkey was announced as the Country of Honour, which meant a series of conferences and events were to be organized that year. İTO included me in the preparations, and I joined the MIPCOM 2015 Executive Committee in 2014. The committee soon entrusted me with organizing the Country of Honour conferences, as I had closely followed the panels and events and accrued a certain knowledge on how they operated. While distributors were all very busy with their sales, I had more time and interest in following the conference events, which constituted a core part of my ethnography. Moreover, as a scholar of performance studies, the festive frame and structure of the panels, interviews and screening caught my special attention. Some of these conferences were sponsored events, with invited speakers, some

IMAGE 9.1 Arzu Öztürkmen, Ahmet Ziyalar, İdil Belli, Dilek Telkes and Emirhan Emre at the 'The Success of Turkish Content: Reaching Out to Global Markets' panel discussion at DISCOP in Johannesburg, 15 November 2018. Image courtesy of the author.

others were sold to national official representatives or private corporations. Their organization encompassed a negotiation between the participants and the market organizers.

In the case of Turkey, beginning with the 2015 MIPCOM event, the process required a collaboration between the public and private sectors of the Turkish television industry, which had never had such an experience. The development of the Executive Committee for the MIPCOM event was a mutually informative experience for all parties, and the committee still continues as the Executive Committee for Film Industry, thus renamed in 2017. Under the auspices of the Istanbul Chamber of Commerce, other conferences followed at ATF in 2016, MIPCOM 2017 and DISCOP–Johannesburg in 2018.[4] These experiences have greatly contributed to my research, vis-à-vis my access and collaboration with different social players of the dizi industry along with the executives of the global markets.

---

4 For the list of these events and corresponding participants, see Appendix 4.

Deconstructing the Myth of Cannes:
The Global and the Local Aspects of the MIP Events

Each market has an aura, a feeling which dominates its overall atmosphere. A book fair is different from a tourism fair; food fairs nowadays have ecological connotations, reaching out to new-age philosophies. Until the Covid-19 pandemic, MIPTV and MIPCOM have been known as the twin events organized each year in April and October in the glamorous city of Cannes, hosting 'television content' industries. (Both were organized as online events in 2020.) During four days of networking, many buyers, sellers, commissioners, distributors, broadcasters and producers engaged in a creative exchange. These markets also offered screenings and conferences with talents, content creators, marketing executives, along with stars who attended to promote their new projects. Spread over 20,000 square metres, they were attended by more than 10,000 people each year, to trade a diverse selection of programmes ranging from series and documentaries to factual formats, game and reality shows. Although MIPTV was founded much earlier than MIPCOM, the latter had grown more in its scope in later years and was recognized as 'the largest television market in the world, bringing together every year the most influential television and digital content executives' (MIPCOM 2020).[5]

The MIP markets were also where new technologies were displayed as a supportive component of the content. The UHD and 4K venues, for instance, were thought to enhance the sense of 'realness' in delivering the content (Forrester 2019). Experiencing technologies like how 8K resolution works, for instance, would become an event in itself, as

---

5 One should note here that Reed Midem Company, which organized MIPCOM and MIPTV in 2020, had announced before the Covid-19 pandemic that beginning by 2020 MIPTV would reduce its size and space, and will be centralized across the three floors within the Palais des Festivals, giving up the its surrounding space (Ravindran 2019).

IMAGE 9.2 Megasession panel on 'Dialogue with the Americas', MIPCOM Country of Honour: Turkey, 5 October 2015. Participants are Kerem Çatay, Pelin Diştaş, Kim Moses, Can Okan and Juan Vicente, with moderator Anna Carugati, group editorial director of *World Screen*. Image courtesy of the author.

IMAGE 9.3 Writers Sema Ergenekon, Eylem Canpolat, Ece Yörenç, Ayfer Tunç and Pınar Bulut at the 'Heroines of Content: Meet Turkish Women Screenwriters' Panel at MIPCOM, Country of Honour: Turkey, in Cannes, 6 October 2015. Image courtesy of the author.

companies which specialized in these technologies displayed their products in separate trailers. Nevertheless, trading creative content was the primary goal of many participants, where producers and distributors were both chasing for captivating stories, and trying to sell them to territories not explored before.

MIPTV and MIPCOM take place in Cannes at the Palais des Festivals et des Congrès, where the Cannes Film Festival and many other events like advertising, music, property, games or yachting are organized. These fairs are crucial to the economy of this city, whose aged population lives with this continual influx of visitors. Because of its glamourous reputation, many participants approach Cannes cautiously, and develop in time a certain 'knowledge of Cannes', finding affordable places to eat and stay. The glamour of Cannes is rooted in its nineteenth-century discovery as a European holiday destination. The city carries historical and contemporary layers of urban space, which combine the fashionable front with more European middle-class presence and the migrant cultural domains of the city. The 'image' and 'experience' continuum of Cannes offers a complex awareness of the 'Mediterranean' to its visitors.

Since 2013, I have several times visited the MIPTV and MIPCOM events in Cannes and observed how they differ from other markets like DISCOP, ATF or ITVF organized in other cities. Given its unique location, Cannes's contribution to MIP markets is indisputable. As I observed through my visits, the city has a 'front', hosting the traffic of tourism, fairs and festivals. Thousands of non-residents occupy the front, which mainly consists of three layers—namely, the Croisette, Rue d'Antibes and Place de la Gare. Le Boulevard de la Croisette, along which line up many expensive shops (Prada, Gucci, Hermes, Chanel, Bulgari, Louis Vuitton) and hotels (Carlton, Majestic, Marriott, Martinez), gives an impression that only those who can afford such luxury can visit the town. Rue d'Antibes, however, offers more down-to-earth venues where visitors can find more affordable hotels and restaurants, and mingle with residents consisting of a mostly retired and well-off population. In the third circle of the 'front' stands Rue Jean Jaurès, where one can find a series of much cheaper fast-food restaurants and 'Asian' markets owned mostly by Muslims selling halal meat. Tekin, a young Kurdish man from Muş, who works in Diyarbakır Kebap House, says that many celebrities from the Croisette come to their restaurants. He states, 'They are curious about the down-to-earth places. They give us tickets for public screenings, so we too often go to the Palais for festivals' (2017). Catherine, a souvenir shopkeeper along the Rue Meynadier, the cheap side of Cannes, calls attention to seasonal differences in demography and the 'receptivity' of the town. She says, 'Les Cannois n'acceptent pas les nouveaux' [People of Cannes do not accept newcomers]. You do not realize this in the summer, but when winter comes they start noticing you' (2017). The real residents of Cannes consist mostly of retired people today, along with a sizeable group of European expats, and entrepreneurs. Nevertheless, Cannes' economy survives with fairs and festivals like the MIP events and many more, a matter which brought serious challenges after the pandemic hurt (Dimitrova 2020). Now the city is trying to catch up with its pre-pandemic spirit by reviving fairs and festivals.

Building a MIP Space, Community and Memory: Aesthetics and Performance of Content Showcase

Until 2020, MIPCOM and MIPTV took place within a gated area at the Palais des Festivals et des Congrès, its surrounding open-air space, and the terraces overlooking Cote d'Azur. The first post-pandemic MIPTV was organized as a digital meet in April 2020, and thereafter in a hybrid form in which the festival space shrank to a much smaller size. Many physical attendees of the hybrid markets expressed their sadness and nostalgia for the old glamour, even though their business was not greatly affected.

It has often amazed me how the market is constructed almost within 48 hours, from a mess to an amazingly set up wonderland with glamorous images, posters, and video screenings. The 'before' and 'after' of the Palais under construction for the MIP events constitutes a performance of labour and organization in itself. The staff of participant companies arrives in Cannes a few days earlier to set up their stands. Teams of interior design, decorators, constructers, cable men, florists and cleaners fill up the Palais, and accomplish an amazing job creating the festive space, which officially opens the following morning.

Thereafter begins a traffic of people running between meetings and appointments, screenings and conferences in the midst of the mini-booths which offer functional social space. One can learn a lot simply by taking a promenade between the stands. Each stand has a life of its own. Each has a front, displaying eye-catching posters or screens and a well-decorated meeting space, and a back space where many material objects are stored. These storage closets are fascinating compilation of objects stuffed one on top of the other. They are like the props of a stage play, ranging from promotion gifts, bags and booklets to water bottles, patisserie, tea, coffee and daily left coats or bags. Flowers are like fake fragrances of the market; some are real, others are not. The day before the market, they travel in pushcarts through the corridors of the Palais, distributed to stands, sometimes waiting for their turn in the midst of all the dust and noise of the preparations.

Stands and tents are priced depending on their location on the map, and where and how companies are located has a symbolic meaning. Some countries are organized under a national pavilion, like the Korean, French or Chinese. Global media companies (the 'big heads', as they say) have their own kingdoms, taking up the best spots of the Palais overlooking at the Riviera. They settle on the same spots over the years, and are usually landmarks to guide newcomers to other stands: 'Take a right after FOX,' 'It is right across Disney,' etc. Turkish companies are not organized under a national pavilion, except the Istanbul

IMAGE 9.4 Producer Timur Savcı and actresses Beren Saat, Hülya Avşar and Anastasia Tsilimpiou at the launching gala of *Kösem* in Villa Domerguein, Cannes, 7 October 2015. Image courtesy of the author.

Chamber of Commerce, which since 2015 gathers smaller companies that cannot afford a space of their own. Turkish broadcasters and distributors who could afford their own stands searched and found good spots in time. The dispersed location of Turkish distributors and broadcasters reflects, in fact, how the television industry is self-financed, each company following a strategy of its own.

Time is always the most respected dimension of business meetings; it is all the more so in MIPCOM and MIPTV as an expression of professionalism. The traffic and pace of the events are pre-set months ago; and once the fair starts, appointments, meetings and conferences take place strictly on time. Participants run from one meeting to the other, attending panels or screenings in-between. MIP events offer more social space than other television markets, turning acquaintances into friendships over the years. The social bonding is visible, with hugging and passionate small talks on the stairs, in the cafeteria or the VIP room and along the streets of Cannes. For four days, everybody becomes a Cannois/e, developing a knowledge of the city, and sharing their expertise of where to eat, stay or shop. MIPCOM and MIPTV primarily take

IMAGE 9.5 Kerem Çatay and Nicola Söderlund at the Eccho Rights party at MIPCOM, Cannes, 17 October 2016, to introduce the remake of *Son*, an Ay Yapım drama. Image courtesy of the author.

IMAGE 9.6 Producer Kerem Çatay and Fatma Şapçı from Ay Yapım in a discussion with Fredrik af Malmborg of Eccho Rights during MIPCOM, Cannes, 16–19 October 2017. Image courtesy of the author.

place in the gated area of the Palais des Festivals, but their presence dominates the Boulevard de la Croisette and all the hotels of the city. I remember my surprise when I first saw the giant ads of Turkish dizis along the streets of Cannes and on the walls of big hotels.

MIP events are networking hubs with matchmaking sessions, conferences, social events and parties, which all perform a spectacle of their own. During the organization of Turkey's Country of Honour year, I found the opportunity to closely experience the preparation process for these events. Conferences stage leading professionals as keynote speakers and offer panels on new trends and strategies, and world-premiere screenings launch the content, cast and creative talents of upcoming series. There are also some special features, which include 'Personality of the Year', 'Women in Global Entertainment Lunch' or 'Diversify TV Excellence Awards'. All of these platforms undoubtedly help participants to build an effective knowledge of the global film industry, but they also operate as platforms to celebrate the key figures of the industry. Each year, the Country of Honour and the Focus Country programmes promotes a particular national industry. There are also regular market overviews, often presented by WIT and Glance (formerly Eurodata). Virginia Mouseler's conference genre of Fresh TV, which includes Fresh Fiction and Fresh Format, is among the most attended overviews.

From a folklorist point of view, I find the festive elements of these events very significant in understanding the institutionalization of the global film industry. As aptly expressed by Beverly Stoeltje and Richard Bauman, most performances, but predominantly festive forms, are 'public enactments in which a culture is encapsulated, enacted, placed on display for itself and for outsiders' (Stoeltje and Bauman 1988). Exploring the festive components of the MIP events will be helpful in revealing the essentials of the industry and the meanings assigned to them. The happy hours, galas or parties embed the obvious morphological aspects of festivals, combining food, music or dance. Nevertheless, the 'festive' component of the conferences offers perhaps a more powerful impact. MIP events take their glamour not from film stars, but from high-level executives of media groups, senior writers and creative producers, whose staged interviews become a content to be watched live. Even the generic titles of these conferences imply their allure, as 'Personality of the Year', 'Media Mastermind Keynote', 'Super-panel' or 'Mega Session'. Over the years, I had an opportunity to attend several such exclusive interviews with the creative and executive stars of the industry. To cite a few examples, in MIPCOM 2016, we had the opportunity to hear renowned writers Andrew Davies and Shonda Rhimes giving memorable interviews on their writing career. The panel for Davies was a tribute to the writer's 80th year, where he told anecdotes on his transition from being a literature professor to one of the writers who excelled on literary adaptations for television. In MIPTV

IMAGE 9.7 A panel in tribute to writer Andrew Davies, who is interviewed by executive producer Rebecca Eaton at MIPCOM, Cannes, 16 October 2016. Image courtesy of the author.

2017, I was very touched to attend the screening of the remake of *Roots* (1977), the phenomenal miniseries that had aired in TRT in 1981. The follow-up panel brought the cast and the creative team together as an oral-history platform, where executive producer Mark Wolper talked about his state of mind imagining the efforts of his father, who was the executive producer of the original.

Stars also show up to promote their new projects. MIPTV 2014 hosted Kim Cattrall for her series *Sensitive Skin*; award-winning actor Kiefer Sutherland delivered a keynote talk about his series *Designated Survivor* in MIPCOM 2016; and finally at the MIPCOM 2017's Women in Global Entertainment power lunch, I got the pleasure of shaking hands with Oscar-winner Catherine Zeta-Jones, who was in Cannes to promote her new show *Cocaine Godmother*. Very recently, in MIPCOM 2019, former NBC Entertainment chairman Robert Greenblatt was hosted in the Grand Auditorium of the Palais as the Personality of the Year to talk about his his transfer to Warner Media.

Because of the high profile of the guest speakers, these conferences and panels are negotiated months before. To bring them on stage requires a bureaucratic journey ranging from reaching them through their acquaintances, assistants or agents to multiple correspondence and technical rehearsals. Once the interviews and panels are set, they are matched with moderators who are often top editors or experienced journalists of television periodicals. These publications differ greatly from television entertainment magazines by focusing mainly on the international media business. They pursue the news on global trends of the media industry and include exclusive interviews with the leading executives of the international entertainment industry.

A Brief History of the Transnationalization of Dizis

The MIPCOM and MIPTV markets have a festive framework, but the ultimate aim of these global markets is to sell or buy new content. Today, contemporary circulation in global markets undoubtedly transcends the one-way travel of the 1980s, where we all fell for the addictive American serials such as *The Fugitive and Dallas*. Despite the dominating US-based content, contemporary television dramas today travel in different directions, in different forms.[6] Many hit American series like *Homeland, Hostages* or *In Treatment* were first produced as Israeli series, and then remade in the US. Korean dramas are widely watched, while they are globally exported as content for remakes. Most European dramas are co-produced, and circulate as such within the European borders on many streaming platforms.[7] The Turkish remake of *Desperate Housewives* reached 40,000 US dollars in the Arab market, while the original was sold for 8,000 US dollars. In many cases, the original content is sold from one country to diverse markets as it is, or after reformatting.

Since the late 2000s, dizi sales have become an important part of these markets, and research regarding this transnational move and its impact is rapidly increasing.[8] Nevertheless, Turkish broadcasters and distributors have been following global television markets since the 1970s, primarily for buying new content and formats for TRT's national broadcasting. In the early years, it was compulsory to physically go to the Cannes market and watch the films. Faruk Bayhan, then the acquisition director of TRT, reminds us that 80 per cent of the imported films would come from American scripted content.[9]

---

6 For the role of distribution in the consumption and purchase of television content, see Albert Moran (2009).

7 For a review of European fiction production and circulation, see Gilles Fontaine (2017); Gilles Fontaine and Marta Pumares (2018).

8 Among many others, see Pınar Aslan (2018); Deniz Özalpan (2017); Bilge Yesil (2015); Dilek Özhan-Koçak and Orhan Kemal Koçak (2014).

9 See Chapter 2, pp. 53–55.

Although acquisition had been the primary goal of the TRT managers in attending these global markets, Turkish productions like *Aşk-ı Memnu* (1975) and *Çalıkuşu* (1986) were also sold abroad in the 1980s.[10] When private networks emerged in the early 1990s, they also began attending television markets to search for shows to fill their programming. Many TRT directors and managers, who now worked for new private companies, already knew these international markets and their content. The trade of the early 1990s followed the one-way flow of foreign content that small distribution companies or networks were buying for the newly opened private television channels. One may call them the 'mobile merchants' of a global market, as many lacked a stand of their own in the marketplace. Although they would know one another, it would be difficult to say that they had a sense of 'belonging to an industry'. They focused mainly on acquisition; but some like Avşar or TMC companies were also involved with production for the domestic market. Sales from Turkey were very rare, limited to a few shows that TRT sold to nearby regions in the 1980s.

The history of the new trend in Turkish content export can be traced back to the sales of *Deli Yürek* (1998) to Kazakhstan in 2001 in a rather tentative way by Fırat Gülgen, the owner of Calinos Entertainment. Gülgen was then marketing Latin American telenovelas to the Central Asian countries. He thought that dizis were similar to these telenovelas, particularly in terms of romance, family and class relationships. He began marketing the dizis at the same unit price in Turkic Central Asian countries: 30–40 US dollars per episode (Gülgen 2012). A few years later, a more effective turn came with the broadcasting of *Yabancı Damat* (2004), first in Greece in 2005, then spreading in the region via satellite broadcasting, in many cases without subtitles. Produced by Türker İnanoğlu, the doyen of the Turkish film industry, *Yabancı Damat*

---

10 Russian Turcologist Apollinariya Avrutina has spoken about the impact of the 1986 version of *Çalıkuşu* on Soviet audiences, which led to the development of a keen interest in Turkish culture and literature (*Haberler.com* 2014; Başlamış 2010).

depicted the story of a young Greek man falling in love with a Turkish girl, touching the memory of cultural affinities as well as conflict between the Turkish and non-Muslim communities. This coincided with the era of Turkish–Greek rapprochement, giving the Turkish dizi its first emotional bonding with foreign audiences.[11] The genesis of the international 'boom' of the dizis is, however, often marked by the 2008 sales of *Gümüş* (2005) to the Arab world. Fadi Ismail, then the group director of MBC, the Middle East Broadcasting Center, discovered the dizi at a trade show in Istanbul (Salamandra 2012; Al Saeid 2015) and approached İrfan Şahin and Özlem Özsümbül from Kanal D, who recalled this experience in amazement during a MIPTV event that they had mainly attended for acquisition (Özsümbül 2017).[12]

Thereafter, Turkish dizis began to be sold through two streams in the market: the Middle East and the Balkans. Sales in the Balkans were mostly based on bilateral agreements, but for the MENA region MBC was the main network holding the distribution rights.[13] The golden age of this transaction coincided with the simultaneous success of newly consolidating production companies like Ay Yapım and TIMS, which produced the highly rated dizis such as *Ezel, Karadayı, Aşk-ı Memnu, Kuzey Güney, Fatmagül'ün Suçu Ne?* and *Muhteşem Yüzyıl,* and established the dizi genre alongside the primetime American series, soap, telenovela and *musalsal*.

---

11 Although broadcast in Kanal D, *Yabancı Damat* was then directly sold by Erler Film, with the initiation of Türker İnanoğlu, without using a distributor (Özsümbül 2019).

12 Both Şahin and Özsümbül left Kanal D in 2015 and 2018 respectively. Şahin established 1441 Productions; Özsümbül currently serves as the director of international sales at Madd Entertainment.

13 MBC is a Dubai-based broadcaster which also has an in-house production unit, broadcasting dizis via satellite in their own region, dubbing them in Arabic. They also began to distribute dizis to other MENA countries and Arab-speaking countries of Middle Africa.

Following the initial success of the late 2000s, Turkish distributors who mainly focused on acquisition before, developed more interest in joining the sales market. Distribution companies like Inter Medya, Calinos and Global Agency began to be more actively involved, along with Kanal D, ATV and TRT networks, who opened their distribution departments. Özsümbül remembers these early days of the market:

> We did not even have a 'distribution' unit in our network, as we did not expect any revenue from such a sale. We had acquisition, production and programming departments, but not a distribution one . . . Once the department was set up, we began to learn how to proceed. We were observing the flyers and tapes that circulated, and we too began producing such material, making suggestions to our superiors on how to technically improve them. We were providing the material, and beginning the promotion processes, spending money on it, visiting fairs, setting up our own stands, reaching out to new territories through aggressive phone calls, intensive mail, exploring their broadcasting venues. In fact, we learned many things as we walked with baby steps. (2017)

Turkish distributors brought a new energy to the market, where the dominant flow was one-way. Handan Özkubat, director of Turkish Drama at Eccho Rights, remembers how in these early days Turkish distributors accrued a valuable knowledge of international sales, through many face-to-face encounters at the markets and follow-up communication in a 'Turkish style': 'My first sale was to Afghanistan. The customer could not speak English but knew some Turkish. Nobody took him seriously. Thanks to our communication skills, I prepared and sold a big package to him. Turkish dizis were just on the rise; there was some interest, but it did not reach its highest point yet' (2020).[14] Müge Akar, ATV's

---

14 Müge Akar (2020) also points out to the issue of 'packaging' as a sales strategy, combining various dizis, movies or documentaries.

content sales deputy manager, calls attention to how continuity of this transaction between distributors and customers establishes a genuine relationship: 'I had a customer with whom I worked for years, made dozens of transactions, without having a face-to-face meeting. One day, we finally met when he visited Istanbul, talking as if we were old friends' (2020). These encounters established a new platform in time, where sales took on a new direction and created a new profile of customers who developed a know-how on the dizis. Özkubat notes: 'Our customers developed an expertise on our dizis and industry in a very short time. Today, none of them asks the questions they used to ask before. They now have an idea about which dizi can fit which time slot, or work better on which channel. They know all of our successful stars and love them' (2020).

Sales with the MENA region were simultaneous with those in the Balkans. With the memory of cultural affinities rooted in Ottoman past, the Turkish dizi had become a new venue of encounter in the region, after long years of separate nation-building processes. Due to the appeal to Balkan countries, dizis also reached many migrant communities of Europe via satellite channels and emerging websites. The rapid success of dizis offered a win-win situation in the beginning, when relatively cheaper and good-quality products made many international broadcasters earn more than what they had expected. Like the MBC network in the Arab world, the rather modest Russian Domashny channel earned well during this process, leading the Turkish distribution companies to raise their unit prices in time. The preference for the dizi genre became more visible, when the Turkish remake of *Desperate Housewives* was sold at a higher price in the Arab market than its original American version. This trend continued with *Kösem*, which was sold for 275,000 US dollars. İzzet Pinto, the CEO of Global Agency, refutes the idea that dizis are now overpriced. He states that 'If one compares the actual prices of the dizis to the sales in the initial years of the market, they do look high. Nevertheless, if one considers that each dizi episode is long enough to be cut into half, its rate is reduced by 50 per cent. Assuming the income to be earned from reruns, the overall pricing is reasonable' (Pinto 2013).

Dizi sales moved in time to other regions as well. The transforming political context in the Middle East after the Arab Spring and the 2013 coup in Egypt[15] changed Turkey's political stance in the region, and consequently led some Arab countries ban dizis on MBC. Egyptian and Saudi opposition was foremost, and was justified on the basis of 'cultural differences' in the depiction of lifestyles. Many distributors believe that current resistance to Turkish content is also related to limiting its rapid rise as a soft power in the region. This sudden change in the Middle Eastern market led distributors to revise their sales strategy. Many began to sell directly to individual companies in the region. This was indeed a significant shift. In the first place, they needed to invest rapidly in developing their post-production skills, in the domains of dubbing and editing. As newcomers to the Middle East market, they lacked the contacts for barter that local broadcasters like MBC maintained. Getting used to the Arab business style in collecting revenues was also a challenge. Today, some distributors think that problems in the MENA region could have been better handled, if competition between distributors, broadcasting networks and individual companies had been better managed. Distributors see sales as their exclusive domain.

The owner of Calinos, Fırat Gülgen, strongly opposes the networks' foray into 'distribution': 'Distribution is not the networks' business,' Gülgen notes, 'Producers produce, networks broadcast, distributors sell . . . This is how it goes in all parts of the world. Now anybody who grabs a business bag gets out saying "I will sell the dizi"' (2012). As one distributor notes: 'As distribution companies, we are merchants of a

---

15 On 3 July 2013, the Abdel Fattah el-Sisi, commander-in-chief of the Egyptian Armed Forces, led a coalition to depose elected Egyptian president Mohamed Morsi; following this coup, the Egyptian constitution of 2012 was suspended.

bazaar—we see, notice, read the situation quickly and respond to it right away.' To him, networks do not always hold a solid attitude as partners of the same industry, and they disregard their own long-term interests. As network directors change rapidly in the industry, their decisions also concern short-term interest. Handan Özkubat has also reservations in combining production, broadcasting and distribution under the same organization:

> To operate separately would be beneficial to all parties in the long run. When you link production to distribution, or broadcasting to distribution, you lose your motivation for sales, and it becomes more difficult to be impartial and objective. And at the end these units usually get separated. The in-house production units of broadcasters, for instance, do not exist anymore. It is so much better in the long run that each one of us pursues her own expertise. (2020)

Independent distributors nickname the network people as 'institutionals', meaning they operate through elaborate layers of bureaucracy. While independent distributors share a gentlemen's agreement among themselves, networks are usually reluctant to cooperate. Broadcasters are also often seen as a threat to lower the market prices of the dizis. However, Şenay Filiztekin-Turan, head of drama acquisitions at Global Agency, reminds us that price lowering is sometimes a necessary strategy to approach new markets (2018). Many factors determine the scope of a dizi's export, but as Ahmet Ziyalar states, what counts as a success in distribution processes relates more to how high the dizi's price is, rather than how high the number of countries where that dizi is sold: 'Once you lower your price, you can sell anywhere, and you will brand your dizi at hand as a cheap product' (2017).

Sharing Revenues: Rising Conflict of Interest between Distributors and Producers

The relationship between distributors and producers is multifaceted. Both Ahmet Ziyalar and Özlem Özsümbül remind us how producers welcomed earning the additional revenue that the sale of dizis abroad generated. While the production budgets did not have an item like 'foreign sales revenue' in the 2000s, many producers now include it in their forthcoming projects' budgets. Whether independent or network affiliated, distributors gradually became important actors in decision making. Bringing professional knowledge collected from various markets, distributors are now consulted in the early stages of pitching and project design. Özsümbül explains: 'Earlier, when they decided to buy a dizi to broadcast, the network director or manager used to sit and estimate the ratings, number of episodes, commercial revenues, and sponsorships. Now they add a fifth component: distribution . . . This is why now we are as important as the content during the negotiation processes between the producers and networks' (Özsümbül 2017). Şenay Filiztekin-Turan expresses how she values being included in the production process: 'We have now reached the point where we have begun having an impact on the content. I really appreciate this—they come and ask us whether the project lacks an aspect in regard to sales abroad. They sometimes consult us on casting, requesting a list of the top best-selling actors' (2018).

Distribution had another impact on dizi production: it improved its technical quality. Özlem Özsümbül remembers how shooting techniques had to evolve after this first sale:

> When we first sent the tapes to MBC, they sent them back to us, because the sound recording was done on a single channel, including the music, dialogues and the effects. We spent more money than we earned for these unexpected technical revisions, which required separating the sound channels in *Gümüş*. This lasted about three months and it cost us a lot of extra

money. This was a turning point for further production. Thereafter, dizis began to be shot in such a way that one would not face such discrepancies and inconveniences. Using multi-channel sound recording began to be a new criterion that came with the distribution processes. (2017)

Today the alliances between producers, network directors and distributors vary, as each relationship has its particularities. Different models prevail in different cases, as there may exist strong bilateral ties or individual alliances. While business interests engender strong links, bonds strengthen with 'binding' relationships. For instance, a network director may be a board member in a distributor's side company. This position makes it harder for that network to switch to another distributor, whatever the cost of loyalty. Alternatively, the owner may have a very traditional way of doing business, with collaboration based on a simple handshake and personal trust. The relationship between the producers and distributors is also a complicated domain, which altered over time. In the early years of international sales, this was an interaction which empowered the producer over the distributor. The head of acquisitions for a leading production company once stated in a clearly condescending way: 'These are, after all, people making money on the projects "we" produce.' Convincing a producer to grant the distribution rights to a new season of promising dizis required serious preparation, which had a strong performance aspect that resembled pitching negotiations. Ahmet Ziyalar of Inter Medya explained the seasonal flow of this process experienced as of 2017:

We prepare presentations for the producers, to explain to them how we work, and also to show the performance of various products in the market. We generally do it in August–September before the winter season begins, and then in January for new series that are just about to start. By September, we begin hearing about the launch of new dizis and we approach producers, making presentations on what kind of promotion we will do for each particular dizi, and what would be the expected revenue. Then again, the same thing happens for launches in January. We are not chasing the summer season so much, as they are usually 'light'. If the successful summer series continue during the fall, we deal with their negotiation in September as well. (2017)

This pattern of negotiations has altered since 2017, as former collaborations changed and new distribution models emerged by 2020. To give one example, Ay Yapım, which closely worked with Eccho Rights and Inter Medya during the 2010s, founded Madd Entertainment in 2018 in partnership with another important production company, MED Yapım. In the past, some production companies had tried distribution, but their attempts were short-lived. Some distributors confirm this fact, but add that producers usually came back to them after a year or two, following their distribution experience. As one distributor put it:

Looking from outside, they have no idea of the promotion expenses in the beginning. We spend a great and continual effort in these promotions. We purchase advertisements in magazines, prepare giant flyers to be posted all over, throw great parties in the markets, and open and maintain well-decorated, captivating exhibition stands for their dizis. At the end of a year-long cycle, they end up preferring our services to dealing with the complexities of this new domain. They usually end up surrendering to our proficiency.

The actual cost of distribution is difficult to ascertain. The end product is the signed contract, which has no visibility. The process, however, has its own creative dimension. Many distributors list similar expenses. Some are regular ones like the travel costs or the salaries of sales people with different language skills. Some, however, demand more aesthetic approaches, including items like designs of stands, gifts and visual aids, stylish happy hours, cocktails and party organizations, along with creative investments in dubbing and editing (Özkubat 2020; Akar 2020). Özlem Özsümbül recalls how distributors acquired this proficiency through a *longue durée* experience in the market. Switching from acquisition to sales requires true research and fieldwork. She remembers the physical labour required in these early years to develop market know-how and a network of contacts. She recollects strolling through different exhibition stands at every occasion, collecting piles of flyers and filing them to explore after returning from the trade show. She remembers how this global market knowledge and networking skills could impress her senior managers in Istanbul.

Part of the physical labour Özsümbül describes involved finding new sites in the market area for display. In the early days, Turkish distributors opened exhibition stands wherever they could find an available spot. The most sought-after sites (like outside the Palais or the front stands of main corridors) belonged to 'established oldies'. These included national industries that gathered their companies in one area, or global firms that returned to the same spots for years. In time, by chasing down vacated spaces and using their 'Mediterranean' human relations, they moved to more desirable venues. Özsümbül attributes this successful penetration of the market to what she sees as a characteristic of Turkish culture, assigning a great meaning to the 'representational appearance':

> As Turkish people, we like to show off and exaggerate. We also know how to produce a 'bazaar effect'. When I took my boss İrfan Şahin to the site where our exhibition stand was opened in 2011, he saw on his way the flags displaying images from our productions hanging in a circle on the top of the Grand Café at MIP. He was literally shocked. 'When did we do all this?' he said. I had discovered and wanted that display area for us for a long time. I had finally hooked it for us, but more than that, with all these hanging flags, I had reinvented the display platform with a colourful new visual impact. (2017)

As producers developed an interest in taking a share from the realms of distribution, distributors also noticed their growing expertise in successful content in global markets, and developed an interest in getting involved in production. This began with unscripted content at first. Besides the game formats *Yarı Yarıya* (2016) and *El Poder del Amor* (2021), Inter Medya had also produced two dramas for digital platforms, *Behzat Ç* (2019) and *Saygı* (2020). The interdiscursivity between the domains of production and distribution offers a developing platform where professional expertise are traded. This trend appears to be promising in the years to come.

Expanding Markets: New Regions and Strategies for Distribution

Distribution involves mutual learning between sellers and buyers through long-term correspondence and face-to-face meetings in global markets. Interest in Turkish content was a regional one in the beginning, coming particularly from the Balkans and the MENA region. This trend shifted later to Latin America and to some countries in South Asia (Gülen Oarr 2016; Özkubat 2020; Akar 2020). Müge Akar proudly states:

> We now sell to almost 100 countries. We have several customers with whom we became friends after long years. We now actively sell to Asia, Latin America and Europe. Good results in a country usually attracts the attention of its neighbouring countries as well. The Latin American breakthrough began in Chile, for instance, and spread in the region with a snowballing effect. (2020)

The global market was reached with further focus and hard work on the part of distributors. First and foremost, this included establishing new contacts with other regional distributors and journalists. To do so, distributors began locating new exhibition stands at strategic points so that they could display their content on screen in crowded public areas and catch the eyes of established buyers in a market dominated by Western content. Özsümbül recalls these early encounters with Western buyers:

> It took time for them to see the production quality of Turkish dizis, with a set of incredibly handsome actors, beautiful women, about modern lives, telling contemporary stories on contemporary issues. They had no idea of Turkey after all. In the beginning, we were knocking on their doors to show our stories, emphasizing the locations where they were shot, with well-produced teasers and commercials. This process was really hard, tiring, even draining at times. Now everybody knows the places we use in the dizis. They see how we interpret stories from a different perspective, with amazing actors and actresses, with beautiful landscapes of Istanbul and Turkey, and most importantly, modern lifestyles. They had no idea in the beginning, and they approached Turkish productions as 'low-calibre content'. In time, they too discovered and began asking 'Is this really Istanbul?' or 'Is he really Turkish?' (2017)

Distributors began to approach the Latin American (LATAM) market in the early 2010s. This was a period after they had proved their success in MENA, the Balkans, Central Asian countries like Kazakhstan, and Pakistan and Afghanistan in South Asia. Like Fırat Gülgen, Ahmet Ziyalar emphasizes that they were encouraged by the fact that telenovelas had worked well on Turkish television (2017). The passionate reception of the telenovelas during the 1990s, often referred to as 'pink series', inspired them to think that there may indeed be a certain reciprocity, and that dizis could work well in Latin America.[16] Approaching

---

16 A considerable amount of research emerged in the early 1990s trying to understand this passion. Among many others, see *Beyazperde* (1989); Şebnem Kadıoğlu (2010); Asuman Taçyıldız (1995); Mutlu Binark (1997); Fatma Gözlükaya-Tütüncü (1998a); Mehemet Mete (1999).

the LATAM market required new investments, like hiring native speakers as salespeople and establishing friendly relations with Latin American journalists. Both Inter Medya and Kanal D sales departments opened their first exhibition stands in 2013 in the region, and retained them even if they sold nothing for three years. Once they launched the first dizis in the LATAM market, others sold easily. Handan Özkubat states that in the early years, the sales to the MENA region made up half of the total sales. This trend has now shifted to the Latin American region, which now constitutes 60 per cent of the total (Özkubat 2020).

Today, the reception of the Latin American market is more enthusiastic than had been imagined.[17] This success encouraged many distributors to move into other regions like South East Asia and Africa. 'No market lasts forever,' Ahmet Ziyalar argues, 'One needs to be prepared' (2017). Turkish distributors' success in reaching these markets soon caught the attention of other global companies, like Sequoia, Red Arrow, Mediaset, Netflix and Iflix, who began working with them, using their 'regional expertise' in markets where Turkish content is successful.

Özkubat evaluates the early stages of the industry in terms of production and distribution costs, and highlights the changing trends: 'There were fewer distributors, and similarly fewer producers. Dizi budgets were affordable in the old days, but today's producers count more on export revenues. On the same lines, digital platforms and copyrights also became important. Now, with the entrance of Netflix and foreign SVOD platforms, the form and style of content production has also changed' (2020).

---

17 For an analysis of the rise of the dizi in the Latin American market, see Victor Falcón Castro (2018); Pınar Aslan (2018).

The Invisible Labour of Disguised Distributors

The other social players of dizi production, such as the actors, writers, directors, editors or cinematographers, have been largely unaware of the labour and entrepreneurial efforts of distributors. Many of them are connected to one another through pitching, production and post-production. Producers try to keep leading stars and successful writers in-house, to secure the success of their next projects. Executive producers and set managers keep an eye on set workers or location scouts, testing them on how they perform under stress. Directors form their own technical teams through experience, developing silent agreements enlisting assistants, cinematographers, and editors to collaborate with them for their future projects. However, neither actors, directors nor writers have access to the distribution processes, while distributors hold the memory of how their dizis made a breakthrough in global sales.

Today, many Turkish distributors are well-known figures in the global television market, receiving invitations to serve as jury members in important competitions like Emmy International, Seoul Festival or MIP Screenings. When I asked about their invisibility in the dizi world, each distributor offered a different account. Şenay Filiztekin-Turan of Global Agency emphasized that they indeed have a growing visibility and recognition in the eyes of dizi producers and writers (2018). To Inter Medya's Ahmet Ziyalar, it would be beneficial to the industry if dizi stars cooperated more in publicizing new productions and were more visible in the foreign press. Özsümbül expressed a sense of pride at the distributors' achievement, the fact that their labour has paid off well and established new professional communities. 'Going to MIP is now coming home,' she says. Özsümbül also points to the growing official interest from the state, which she sees as a satisfactory development:

> In every official encounter with an ambassador, a minister and so on, we hear how much the success of the dizis reflect on them. If Netflix is considering producing a drama fully based on Turkish content today, if Sony wants to invest in Turkish

production, if we exchange content with different countries for remakes, this is all a consequence of our promotions, of the impact of distributors. That is enough satisfaction and visibility for me. (2017)

Yet she recalls a funny moment when her boss introduced her to Kıvanç Tatlıtuğ, the star of *Gümüş* (*Noor*), when she found herself telling him instinctively: 'Hi, I am Özlem, I am selling you!' Tatlıtuğ and everybody else present responded with laughter, but she stresses the truth in her outburst:

Imagine the actors: their taped performance is archived; we are the ones who take them out, polish them, and pay the promotion expenses. They do not see us or hear about us. These tapes are not sold to the rest of the world by themselves. We are the ones who attract the global attention. But at the end, we also know that we do so thanks to their talent and beauty and their branding. So no need to complain much. (2017)

To conclude, let me mention the sense of collegiality that has emerged over a decade-long experience in these markets. It is easy for a researcher of the dizi industry to observe a sense of rivalry among those who work in similar places. This is understandable, as each writer, producer, director and actor competes with their counterparts every season for limited number of jobs. In our discussions, directors and actors usually avoid referring to their colleagues' contributions to past or current projects, although they generously mention those from other fields with whom they collaborated successfully. Compared with other social players of the dizi world, distributors have a more collaborative, sincere and open discourse in sharing their experiences with one another. They are like the pragmatic, efficient merchants of an old bazaar, openly and humorously interacting and negotiating with one another. Although conflicts arise, they are rapidly forgotten by the time of the next interaction. As the dizi trade evolved, there emerged a mutually constructed history of collaborations, a common memory of the market in which distributors experienced first-hand the success of the dizi. I myself observed this collaboration in 2015, when Turkey was hosted as the Country of Honour at MIPCOM in Cannes. As part of the preparation committee, different parties came together around a table for the first time, and had to cooperate with one another. This was not a romantic encounter, where each party had their own aesthetic and business approach. But the encounter proved at the end an eye-opening experience, one that forced all parties to make concessions. It was, as Özlem Özsümbül puts it, a 'bonding experience' (2017).

As for the global market, the new energy that Turkish sales generated has met with various responses. The market organizers readily acknowledged what they call a 'Mediterranean spirit', a vigour that Turkish distributors have brought to their trade fairs over the last decade. As one distributor asserted, 'We fuelled a rather stagnant market. With the coming of Turkish dizis in the picture, competition heated up, the inertia of many global markets changed into liveliness.'

Revisiting Global Markets: The Effect of the Pandemic on Dizi Distributors

After two years of Covid-19 pandemic, both the organizers of the global markets and the distributors have been trying to adapt to the evolving conditions. The major Turkish companies exhibiting at these trade shows are convinced that reviving the 'old times' will be difficult, simply because they experienced that business can be conducted online in an 'equally efficient but less costly manner'. There are, however, different approaches to the changing conditions of the market. There is a strong sense of nostalgia that prevails. Attending the fairs, particularly the MIP events in Cannes, has been the joy of the profession, offering in-person meetings with customers and helping develop a vision of how the general trade progressed. Nevertheless, while some participated in MIPTV 2022 by putting up their usual stands, others—including TRT— 'attended' only with their badges. İTO decided not to have their stand, because many companies were concerned whether they would be able to cover their own costs despite İTO subsidies. Inter Medya's Ahmet Ziyalar thinks that global markets are losing vigour with low participation rates: 'Markets have never been the same after the pandemic, and I am afraid they never will have the former zeal. When participation is low, the market becomes not worth investing in' (2022). Ateş İnce, the managing director of MADD, had a more positive approach: 'The pandemic has increased the importance of face-to-face relationships. Markets are very important in this respect and I do not think that they can be replaced'. Similarly, Şenay Filiztekin-Turan expressed that attending MIPCOM in October 2021 felt good in terms of raising the mood and motivation of the participants (2022).

The pandemic also encouraged distributors to use their budgets more carefully. Attending the MIP markets with big teams was a tradition that is now likely to change as companies discover considerable savings in representing their firms through a core sales group. There was a significant increase in markets organized online, which created the opportunity for exploring specific regions or themes. Many distribution companies also organized their own online meets and events, a process Ayşegül Tüzün, the managing director of MISTCO, considered to be functional in the beginning but not sustainable in the long term: 'People's motivation decreases; physical markets are still important for face-to-face communication' (2022).

There is indeed a strong will among many to organize a global market in Istanbul, and interested parties are taking professional guidance to organize one. In 2021, the Turkish minister of culture and tourism, Mehmet Nuri Ersoy, stated: 'Using the power of our television series . . . we plan to make Istanbul the centre of the television content market and organize the "Content Istanbul Fair" in 2022, bringing together the world's most important film, television series, animation and format producers. With this breakthrough, we will be attracting the market to Turkey.' (Erdem 2021).

Despite the low profile of participation, those who can attend target the best of these global markets. Reed Exhibition, the new organizing company for MIPCOM and MIPTV, has confidently announced that MIPCOM 2022 will be revived in October in its a 'super-sized format' (Keslassy and Barraclough 2022). The upcoming years will reveal how the pandemic will have affected business models in negotiating between old habits, digital opportunities and financial strategies.

CHAPTER 10

Concluding Remarks

The first steps of this book began in 2011 when dizis were rapidly rising in global markets, while many of us had reservations about its sustainability. The global reception had come as a surprise to both the Turkish television industry and the international content markets. My fascination, both as a folklorist and as an ordinary viewer, was primarily with the genre, which had matured by then and was being watched across the world. The first MIPTV event I attended on 8–10 April 2013 was an eye-opening experience, an opportunity to observe the scope of the dizi industry's presence in a global scale. As a result of a particular historical process, which benefited from a variety of creative fields, the dizi industry had constructed itself with its own social and creative energy, raising a large number of filmmakers and producing its own expertise. The industry had developed a unique interactive production process, where the genre of the dizi was shaped as a media text. It also owed a great deal to the aspirations, entrepreneurship and flexibility of Turkish working culture. The creative and production processes working hand-in-hand led to a close interaction between the two fields and ensured mutual impact. This enabled an effective reflexivity: writers handing over their scripts to the sets to be shot right away, with episodes broadcast the following week. This pace is often branded as the curse of the industry, but it is also its gift—this is what generates the distinctive value of dizi as a genre.

The surprising growth of the dizi triggered both popular and academic curiosity about the origins of its appeal. There is a growing scholarship exploring the transnationalization of dizis (Bilge 2015; Kaptan and Algan 2020; Arda, Aslan and Mujica 2021; Yanardağoğlu 2022). *Kısmet,* a popular documentary that aired in 2013, was among the first to explore this transnational enthusiasm (see Paschalidou 2014). Newspaper and academic articles followed, attempting to explain different aspects of the phenomenon. In the beginning, the rise of the dizis in the Balkans and the Middle East was linked to a certain 'cultural affinity' rooted in the Ottoman past of these regions (Berg 2017; Karlıdağ and Bulut 2014). The argument was that after a century-long experience of being separate nation-states, many countries in the region remembered the common cultural codes, like words but also body language, humour and sentiments of family ties, friendship and romance. But when the dizi reached Latin America, Muslim Asia and even Europe, the surprise was even greater (Pınar 2020; Berg 2020; Aksoy and Robins 2000; Roxborough 2013; Marshall 2018). One may see this as part of the general global waves (Bhutto 2019). While the world was watching Turkish drama, Turkish youth streamed Korean content (Chong-Jin and Young-gil 2013; Khan and Yong-Jin 2020; Öztürkmen 2019). Regional-historical common heritage might be confined to geographical boundaries, but even so one could still talk of 'cultural proximities' across borders. The Latin American communities, for instance, shared many similar Mediterranean cultural codes displayed in the dizis,[1] as much as the migrant communities across Europe, which find a similar value system in them. Nevertheless, it would be too simplistic to confine our understanding of the dizis' appeal to cultural affinities; international fans must have been taken up by some other structural features of the genre.

---

1 One should also remember that there was a wave of Middle Eastern migration to Latin America, which began in the mid nineteenth century and continued in a second wave after the 1950s (Civantos 2016).

A recent article in the *New York Times* cites Nahid Akhtar, a viewer from London, who expresses her attachment to dizi by saying that 'it calls to your soul' (Marshall 2018). Akhtar's view reflects the general idea that dizis' appeal is rooted in their success in 'delivering emotions'. Constanza Mujica, an academic at the Pontificia Universidad Católica de Chile, gives credit to the acting techniques in this process:

> In Latin American telenovelas, the actors say what they think, what they are doing and what they are going to do. In Turkish television series, they are sober and concise with the dialogue, the actors look at each other and this way they tell each other everything. The leading pairs are linked deeply on an emotional level. The emotion is felt and that is important. It is what captivates the people. (Sepúlveda G. 2017)[2]

Peruvian writer Víctor Falcón Castro called this 'the Turkish alchemy', and explained the dizi wave in its relation to the particular stance of telenovela genre: 'Turkish fictions entered Latin America at a time when narco-novellas had distanced the ordinary viewer, with their emotionally damaged characters. Turkish dizis reunited Latin American audiences with the melodrama that they narrated for decades' (2018).

Dizis are valuable in showing characters engaging in non-verbal communication, using looks, facial gestures or small actions that deepened the reading levels of the story. Silence has the same narrative importance as the word. This situation differs from the Latin American telenovela, Falcon Castro reminds us, where expressivity is usually sharp (2018). Fredrik af Malmborg, managing director of Eccho Rights, one of the main distributors of Turkish content, underscores the resistance from France, Germany, United Kingdom and the United States, although Netflix began showing Turkish dramas in 2016 and has recently begun making its own shows (Marshall 2018). *The Protector, The Gift* and *Love*

---

2 I thank my friend and colleague Dr Pınar Aslan for her translation from Spanish to English.

101 have been successful projects, moving into their second seasons. Handan Özkubat expresses her confidence, asserting that the success of 'Turkish content abroad' is a very 'valuable asset' and that there is no similar content to compete with 'Turkish drama' (2020). What global audiences appreciate in the dizi genre will certainly be the subject matter of new studies to come.

During my visits to international television markets, I often heard sceptical comments on whether the Turkish television industry will sustain the vaulting success it achieved through the 2010s. The general argument was that Turkey's achievements in football, for instance, were short-lived; and the rise of Turkish pop music stars did not last long. The precarious sociopolitical context of Turkey may justify such reservations, and frankly, the dizi industry of the early 2010s was still an industry-in-progress. Like many other creative industries, however, it went through the harsh trials of Turkey's politics in the last decade, including the Atatürk Airport attack and the failed coup event, both in 2016. Each time, our friends from the international press called us, sincerely expressing their concerns about whether the dizi industry would be affected. In such cases, after consulting a series of industry players, I would respond that filming continued uninterrupted, producers designed new projects, and distributors planned their next visit to global fairs. In fact, political attacks were now a global phenomenon, and Turkey had a long history of coping with political stress.[3]

How the dizi industry faced the Covid-19 pandemic reveals the long way it has come since the 2000s. The pandemic reached Turkey on 11 March 2020, and the first confirmed death was announced on 15 March. The next day, all channels began to broadcast two public-service announcements from the Ministry of Health, using the fictional

---

3 Statements are from the email correspondence dated 19 July 2016 with reporters from *Variety, World Screen, MIP Daily News* and *Hollywood Reporter.*

characters from two different medical dizis.[4] Organized under their professional unions and associations, industry players rapidly responded to the emerging situation. Actors' Union, Cinema and Broadcasting Workers' Union and Art Directors' Association called for the suspension of on-set activity (İdil 2020). Meanwhile producers' associations gathered, taking the common decision to close the sets right away (Savcı 2020).[5] Leading production companies continued to pay their actors and staff;[6] while some other public and private support mechanisms emerged to secure the jobs of crew members whose sets were closed down (Savcı 2020).[7]

During the curfews and 'shelter in place' phase of the first weeks of the pandemic, networks continued to broadcast the few episodes they had in storage, which were rapidly consumed by the end of March. In mid April, different models of production began to be developed in order to keep the dizi industry alive with diverse strategies. Despite the general agreement to close the sets, some production companies returned to the sets and continued their filming, including for the dizis *Eşkıya Dünyaya Hükümdar Olmaz, Kuruluş-Osman* and *Arka Sokaklar*. The set crew of *Eşkıya Dünyaya Hükümdar Olmaz*, for instance, was

---

4 The actors were Taner Ölmez, who plays the character of Ali Vefa in *Mucize Doktor*, *and* Timuçin Esen, who plays Ateş in *Hekimoğlu*. Both dizis are adaptations from American series: *Mucize Doktor* from *The Good Doctor*; *Hekimoğlu* from *Dr. House* (see Yener 2020).

5 Timur Savcı is the Chair of TESİYAP, the Association of Television and Motion Picture Producers, and a founding member of Yapımcılar Derneği, the Producers' Association. Turkish producers responded in a very prompt and organized way to close the sets, compared with some other industries such as Hollywood (Press 2020). One should also remember that the production processes are very different in these industries.

6 There were, however, some reports of delayed payments (*NetHaber* 2020).

7 Netflix, Istanbul Foundation for Culture and Arts (İKSV) and Cinema and Broadcasting Union established a 'Film and Television Relief Fund' for employees working behind the scenes (İKSV 2020).

divided into three groups of 40 people each, cleaning and sterilizing locations and trailers three times a day, and handling transportation with private cars instead of service vans. Ambulances waited outside and set workers wore protective masks and medical coveralls. Because of restrictions for people above the age of 65, some actors could not perform and new scripts had to be written accordingly (*Hürriyet* 2020a; *TV100* 2020). *Arka Sokaklar* incorporated Covid-19 in its content, with a sneak peek on 1 May 2020 showing police officers wearing medical masks. The episode involved the case of an infected character on 15 May, almost enacting real-time information seen fresh on news channels (*Haber7* 2020; *Sözcü* 2020a; *Vatan* 2020). Since its set was built in a vast open-air film studio in Riva, *Kuruluş-Osman* had more space and lodging facilities to host its cast and crew. Nevertheless, production was reduced to a minimum. Writers wrote the new episodes; keeping in mind the evolving situation with the pandemic, they wrote scenes allowing social distancing and minimizing those with crowds.

The industry's flexibility offered new creative models for production during the pandemic. In a special case for the dizi *Tutunamayanlar,* the production team sterilized the filming locations, set up costumes and robotic cameras from a day before. Actors came the next day, dressing themselves up and doing their own make-up. Directors communicated with them—one from Istanbul, the other from the central Anatolian town of Yozgat—each directing the episode online with the help of the actors who both acted and operated the technical equipment set up for them (*Avrupa* 2020). In another case, a special 'Corona' episode of *Jet Sosyete* was produced as a 'stay-at-home actors' shoot' in which actors recorded their parts in their homes, and footage was combined and edited afterwards (Birsel, Bozkurt and Eren 2020). Similarly, *Çukur* also produced a special episode in which actors performed from their own homes, semi-improvising on the emotional turns of earlier episodes, adding an element of humour to the online interactions (*Mynet* 2020).

Covid-19 restrictions coincided with Ramadan between 24 April and 23 May 2020. Even though dizis differ from the Arab *musalsalat*, which are particularly produced for that month (*Mynet* 2020), Turkish television networks also offer some special programming during Ramadan.[8] For 2020, *Kuşlarla Yolculuk*, a project inspired by Fariduddin Attar's Sufi story collection *Conference of the Birds*, had been planned for TRT. The series began to be shot in TRT's new film plateau in Çekmeköy with extensive precautions (TRT Haber 2020b; *Hürriyet* 2020b). Director Sedat İnci expressed his own amazement to see the number of trailer vehicles: 'I could not believe my eyes. I immediately thought how unique this experience would be for us all' (2020). The set consisted of fifty trailers, housing both the cast and crew who quarantined themselves. Filming began in early April, completing the 30 episodes meant for each night of the month of Ramadan. In fact, on 19 May 2020, before the Ramadan holiday began, the Association of Television and Motion Picture Producers and the Producers' Association had already issued an advisory on the precautions for filming during summer (*Box Office Türkiye* 2020). By June, sets reopened to film their seasons' end or launch their summer dizis. These models displayed the foremost characteristic of the dizi genre once again: its tightly paced and interactive production method in which the narrative content reflected the real-life issues at the time the script was written and subsequently broadcast the following week. This gave dizis an almost live-performance feel, which has always been a hallmark of the genre.[9] There has been growing

---

8 In Egypt, for instance, many sets continued to work through the pandemic to finish their intended projects, taking the risks but also securing jobs for the seasonal economy (TRT Haber 2020a).

9 One should add how audiences find in this interaction a ground for meta-stories: the snow of a week ago may appear the following week in a dizi episode, or an actor's hand injury reflects on screen, each such occasion leading fans to engage in heated after-screening chat.

literature on the reflection of actual politics in dizis,[10] but the industry's response to the pandemic illustrated the flexibility of Turkish work culture.

One important feature of the dizi industry is that it derives its energy from private entrepreneurship. Television in Turkey began as a state enterprise and monopolized public broadcasting obviously shaped the taste and habits of television consumption. As the official network, TRT set the earliest models for Turkish content. Nevertheless, given the painful democratization processes of Turkey, it always reflected a precarious stance, and was challenged by its own ideological constraints for creativity, despite its advantages of better funding and technical resources. Today's dizi genre sparkled more in the hands of a blossoming private sector from the 1990s, whose entrepreneurs saw lucrative business opportunities in commercial television. Turkish content improved amid the competition that rose among them, benefiting from filmmakers' desire for better cinematic storytelling in 'world technical standards'.

State officials' attention turned on dizis only by the late 2000s when dizis began to receive some international acclaim. The first promise of 'state support' for the private dizi sector came only in 2010, when Zafer

---

10 I had touched upon this issue during the Society for Cinema and Media Studies conference in 2017 with a paper entitled 'On Politics of Political Expressivity in Turkish Television Series'. Since the 2011 elections, political critique in Turkish media has become an increasingly constrained and state-controlled issue, obstructing a tradition of political debates and humour in Turkish television. Rising sociopolitical tensions found new expressive and performative forms, including the genre of dizi, where some screenwriters used their scripts as an opportunity to drop a few lines about responses to daily political events. These came as posing a subtle critique of rising corruption, the contestation of secularism, human rights violations, threat to freedom of expression or women's status. This strategy differed from the earlier use of political drama, which depicted the memory of the coups or supported state nationalism. See, for instance, Sule Altın (2018); Nesrin Demir (2007); Çağdaş Günerbüyük (2009); Fulya Şen (2018).

Çağlayan, the minister of foreign trade, acknowledged that dizis greatly contributed to the promotion of Turkey's image as well as its export products (*Kanal 46* 2010). Situating dizis among the 'foreign currency earner, trade in service', the Ministry of Finance developed a subsidy model for participation in global fairs in 2011, which was issued as a decree in 2015, offering partial state funding for dizi producers and distributors' visits to global television fairs (Ticaret Bakanlığı 2015). In 2004 a law (No. 5224) was passed to provide state support for film-makers (Binatlı 2005; TCCMBS 2004), but dizi production was not included in this law until 2019. This new law (No. 7163), which was passed on 18 January 2019, does not provide any project-design grant as is the case for cinema, but rewards dizis that have been exported to at least 'three continents' and broadcast at least one season (*Resmi Gazete* 2019; Kültür ve Turizm Bakanlığı 2020). Some dizis seem to have benefited from public promotion funds (Erturan 2018; *Finans Gündem* 2019). Both the state officials and representatives of the private sector have recently come together in a workshop organized by the Presidential Directorate of Communications and Istanbul University, discussing the role of dizis in 'public diplomacy' (TCCİB 2020).

Given these circumstances, the dizi industry grew into self-financed one, operating through negotiations between producers and network directors, and dependent on market conditions. As explained in previous chapters, there have been leading individuals, private companies and cultural-creative clusters which contributed to the historical development of the dizi industry. Its growth also coincided with the rise of political Islam under the rule of AKP (Justice and Development Party), which has been in power since 2002. With AKP's more conservative cultural policies, the creative industries began to take a different shape over time.[11] Through the 2000s, there grew a discrepancy between

---

11 See Tuğba Öztürk (2014); H. Ayça İnce and Serhan Ada (2009); Banu Karaca (2012); Begüm Kösemen (2015). For the rise of conservative content, see Hikmet Kocamaner (2017).

government-controlled content of state-subsidized artistic institutions—State and City Theatres, State Ballet and Opera—and that of the
newly opened private artistic venues that brought important exhibitions
and performances to Turkey. The opening of Sakıp Sabancı Müzesi
(2002), Istanbul Modern (2004), Pera Müzesi (2005), Garaj Istanbul
(2007) and SALT (2011) brought a new energy to the already established art NGOs, including İKSV founded in 1973 and BİLSAK in 1984.
It was a similar story for TRT and private television networks. Although
TRT continued broadcasting dizis, its programming gradually changed
after 2002. With many constraints to keep up conservative content, TRT
fell behind the creative leap produced by the private networks during
the 2000s. The content which drew the initial international acclaim
came from private producers and distributors, who by the 2010s had
established themselves as the effective players of the dizi industry. It
must be noted, though, that these dynamics changed by the mid 2010s,
as TRT invested more resources in historical content and expanded its
film plateaus.

The mid 2010s formed also a decade where state bureaucracy and
public institutions began to give more attention to the dizi industry,
organizing formal meetings to better understand its system and explore
its potential benefits.[12] As a researcher of the field, I often contributed
to their preparation as a voluntary adviser, and attended some of the
meetings. My general observation was that these meetings served more
to inform state and public authorities than determining or solving the
problems that the main players of the industry expressed. These
encounters also revealed several challenges of communication. To begin
with, there was a temporal difference between the pace of the dizi
industry and the state bureaucracy. Second, knowledge on the industry's

---

12 These included Istanbul Chamber of Commerce, Turkish Assembly of
Exporters, the Ministries of Economy and Development, Ministry of Culture and
Tourism, and the Institute for Strategic Thinking.

financial operation was often weak or misperceived. The high turnover in the industry often labelled dizi making as a 'rich' enterprise, while expenditures were high and investment swallowed the earned profits for future projects. And finally, the glamour aspect was perceived differently from the two sides: while state officials would be surprised to see Turkish dizis mentioned in their international encounters, to industry players, this was a common phenomenon experienced for years.

One institution which developed a significant know-how through this process was İTO. As the official representative in global fairs, İTO closely followed the dizi industry figures in its global context, and observed first-hand the domestic and global mechanisms of the dizi economy. Since 2014, the İTO's Film Industry Coordination Committee has worked closely with the players of the dizi industry. Originally established for the 2015 MIPCOM Country of Honour preparations, the committee continues to meet regularly to organize visits and conferences for dizis' representation in global television markets. Recently, the Ministry of Development raised interest in the dizi industry, writing a report based on a meeting they organized with industry players. Ministry officials also began to join the regular meetings of İTO's Film Industry Coordination Committee (TCKB 2018). However well intentioned, 'planning' obviously requires a deeper knowledge of the industry, which the state bureaucracy, particularly the Ministry of Culture, neglected for a long time.

As mentioned earlier, TRT began to invest in new historical drama productions in the 2010s. In fact, historical drama has always been part of the TRT focus, but following the success of *Muhteşem Yüzyıl* (2011) in global markets, this subgenre attracted more attention, and the newly established production companies wanted to produce historical content reflecting a neo-Ottoman conception (Çevik 2019; Emre-Çetin 2014; Kraidy 2019; Erdem 2017; Ergin and Karakaya 2017). Today, *Diriliş, Filinta, Mehmetçik Kut'ül Amare, Abdülhamid, Uyanış* and *Alparslan*, which all aired on TRT, are often shown as an attempt towards governmental soft power (Carney 2018; Çevik 2020). *Kurtlar Vadisi,* which aired not on TRT but on Show TV and Kanal D, has also been associated with intended soft power owing to the similarities between its content and real-life politics (Carney 2014; Yanık 2009).

Nevertheless, one should always remember that dizis earned their initial global acclaim without any intention of making propaganda. The first round of dizis—*Gümüş, 1001 Gece, Aşk-ı Memnu, Fatmagül'ün Suçu Ne?, Ezel* and *Muhteşem Yüzyıl*—which created the initial global impact were indeed intended for the domestic market. In that regard, they naturally strolled through Istanbul and other cities, while trying to develop their cinematic content and style. For global audiences, this was obviously a new encounter with contemporary images from Turkey, with its natural beauty, modern looks yet traditional values.

Distributors often underline the surprise of initial buyers who would ask questions like 'Is this really Turkey?' or 'Is she really a Turkish actress?' (Özsümbül 2017; Ziyalar 2017). Pınar Aslan's research on the dizis' impact on Latin American audiences illustrates the first-hand expressions of initial surprise that dizis created (2018). Many of her interviewees were impressed by the way characters dressed, the general landscape and architecture, and women's visibility in social life. Some had no preconceived idea about Turkey; they began researching about it. Later they expressed that dizis made Turkey appear closer to them than it geographically was. This era coincided with the rise of Istanbul as a new brand, replacing the negative *Midnight Express* public image that Turkey had long suffered.[13]

Whether intentionally or not, dizis certainly contribute to Turkey's public image. Yet there has been a significant change in content, which

---

13 For the impact of Alan Parker's 1978 film *Midnight Express,* see Geoffrey Macnab (2016); Arzu Öztürkmen (2005); Dilek Mutlu (2005); Maria Alvarez (2010). For Istanbul's branding, see Ülke Uysal (2013).

has lost its original energy. Eccho Rights' Handan Özkubat underlines how dizi sales would suffer from censorship which seriously challenges writers and their storytelling at a time when production quality excels (2020). State impact on content is exerted through RTÜK, Turkey's Radio and Television Supreme Council, which has the power to penalize broadcasters in case they show a scene considered contrary to the 'national' and 'moral' values of Turkish society. Recently, censorship of political issues have increased, and the representation of sexuality and alcohol has been curtailed while scenes of violence have been tolerated as representing 'heroism'.

The breakthrough content of the late 2000s used thematic diversity that enabled appealing narratives. With the change in ratings panels, content has had to be constrained within the limits of standard melodrama, dramedy or fierce action. Lately, the creative teams of leading production companies have shifted to digital platforms, where they can pursue creation of unrestricted content. In his *New York Times* article, Alex Marshall shares his perception of the dizi industry from a bird's eye view:

> *The Protector* is the latest evidence of how Turkish television drama is spreading worldwide. In Turkey, several drama series compete for viewers every night, each episode two hours or more filled with romance, family strife and gangsters . . . Some have been associated with rising nationalism in the country; others have angered conservatives by showing historical figures drinking and philandering. The shows are a phenomenon in the Middle East and Latin America . . . Now the shows are spreading across Europe. (2018)

Streaming platforms will certainly grow more important in the Turkish dizi industry. Kanal D had first tested its digital content *Ulan Istanbul* in 2015 (Taylan 2015). That same year, actor Mehmet Günsür was announcing at MIPCOM the series *KANAGA,* the first independent web series that he produced, which was eventually broadcast on 4

March 2018 on the web platform Onedio. The pioneering digital portals, BluTv and puhutv have been broadcasting their original content since 2017, and new platforms will continue to emerge—like Foxplay, Fox TV's online platform and Gain Medya, both established in 2019, and Exxen, launched in 2021. TRT has announced that their own digital platform is on its way (*Bosphorus Film Lab* 2020).

One important change that the entry of global digital platforms will bring to the Turkish dizi industry will be in distribution patterns. The rise of dizis owes a lot to the entrepreneurial wisdom and energy of independent distributors in the 2010s. Global platforms like Netflix, HBO or Disney however, distribute the original content they produce. Foreseeing this narrowing in the market, distribution companies in Turkey began to invest in production as well, using their expertise they accrued over the years on successful content. Inter Medya, a leading distributor, for instance, invested both in the production of games and dizis.

However much digital platforms develop, many industry players still prioritize mainstream television broadcasting. Ateş İnce, who was the founder of Doğuş Digital, creating puhutv in 2016, asserted a few years ago his strong belief that television watching habits are hard to change in Turkey:

> Television will never die in Turkey, simply because this is the evening fun for Turkish people. In the last ten years, our notion of entertainment is going home and watching dizi. As the alternative won't come so easily, television business will never die. This is due to our social structure. But the television industry will grow … With the introduction of digital monitors into the definition of television, total views will increase with the new measurement system. The penetration pace of smart devices, the proliferation and fastening of the internet, and the stance of our established dizi industry show that digital viewing will follow an increasing trend in the upcoming years. There is also

the fact that multiple dizis are being broadcast simultaneously on primetime . . . We also have a young population. Our students cannot stay up late to watch dizi . . . How are they going to watch what they missed? We are patriarchal too; our fathers control the remote. The rate of our night-time workers is also high . . . How will all these people be able to watch these dizis? (2007)

İnce's observations make us consider how widespread television watching is in Turkey. I have often observed that men tend to deny that they watch dizis. But when asked what their family members watch, they do cite the title or characters of popular dizis. I also believe that watching television is a central activity in the social life of a family even if the members do not agree on its content. My students at Boğaziçi University report how their taste deviates from their families' taste of content; they have little option but to seek refuge in digital platforms for their own choices. As the recent pandemic has put us all in a heavy digital-communication milieu that we have not experienced before, our relation to these platforms are being redefined and recontextualized. In 2021, Can Okan, the CEO of Inter Medya, underscored the launching of another genre of Turkish drama, 'New Generation Turkish Series', which he claims will change the game in Turkish production:

Following the popularity of streaming platforms, mini-series have been on the rise in general. Mini-series is our new shining category and we call them 'New Generation Turkish Series'. We want to create this new generation perception because these series are bringing different and new interpretations to long running, traditional dramas. They are produced more specifically for streaming platforms. They count between 6 and 10 episodes per season, with durations varying between 25 and 60 minutes per episode. In regard of traditional Turkish dramas, they tell their stories in bolder, edgier and braver ways.

They have efficient storytelling and character developments. (*Formatbiz* 2021)

At this point, I would like to make a few remarks on future scholarship. My research took me into a number of different fields, ranging from anthropology to economics, folklore to media studies, to develop a better understanding of Turkey's television industry and the dizi genre that emerged from it. A particular challenge was explaining the historical course in which different individuals and institutions played a determining role. When as cultural historians we explore creative industries, we are naturally inclined to study their 'creative' aspects. The same industries, however, are also analysed in business studies with a different focus, which could be useful for cultural studies. Management and organization studies, for instance, offer us a beneficial perspective in exploring how industries are organized in terms of clusters, path dependencies or critical junctures. Similarly, the 'historical institutionalism' approach shows how both public and private institutional constraints and responses affect policy making in the long term (Thelen 1999).

As part of a globalized economy, creative industries look very contemporary and market-driven. However, they are deeply rooted in historically and geographically specific social networks and clusters, which strongly affect the paths they take. The works of Ivan Turok (2003) and Allen J. Scott (2005), for instance, look at film industries through the tools of economic geography and show how the agents of production are organized. Their focus is on the clustering of creative companies, but their research gives important clues on the history and ethnography of the industries they explore. The economic and business approach could benefit greatly from the anthropological approach to film industries, in which Lila Abu-Lughod (2005), Christa Salamandra (2013b) and Tejaswini Ganti (2012a) investigated the emotional and social aspects of the main players, like writers, producers and viewers, displaying clearly the forces behind the social and economic clusters. One should acknowledge here John Thornton Caldwell's 'integrated cultural-industrial method of analysis' (2008), which invites us to a synthetic approach that combines analyses of texts and artefacts, interviews with industry players, ethnography of production spaces and professional gatherings, along with economic analysis.

I have observed similar dynamics while studying the growth of dizi as a genre, where different fields had different focuses in exploring the boundaries and interactions between the concepts of intertextuality, intermediality and interdiscursivity. To explain how dizi emerged and consolidated itself as a genre, the works of two distinguished scholars, Richard Bauman (1986, 2004) and Vijay K. Bhatia (1993, 2017) offer very important insights. Bauman's approach enlightens us on how cultural forms go through an entextualization process, interacting with other genres and enabling the emergence of new ones. Bhatia's work on the promotional genres in professional life has been a model to contextualize television genres in their business context, where distribution dynamics affect production, casting and even writing, like in the case of dizis. In the footsteps of Mikhail Baktin (1981) and Jacques Derrida (1980), genre studies have developed its own critical literature that examined in depth the structure of cultural forms and their relation to social context and communicative performance (see Fishelov 1993; Miller 1984; Orlikowski and Yates 2002; Stewart 2005). However, media genres receive relatively little attention compared with literary ones, and the general interest in media studies is more on new social media than film genres (see Jousmäki et al. 2013; Kelly and Miller 2017). Film genres are often categorized in terms of their literary content, as romance, thriller or fantastic, rather than as media texts, which involve other cinematic and musical elements which contribute to the genre. In that regard, I find it very useful to approach television genres in their historical interdiscursivities and as media texts with their intermedialities.

Last but not the least, understanding the similarities and contrasts between diverse regional industries has been another demanding task. Industry ethnographies were not only scarce but also involved different international experiences in diverse regions. Ivan Turok writes on Ireland, Allen J. Scott on Hollywood, Christa Salamandra on Syria, Tejaswini Ganti and Vijay Kumar Bhatia on India. All of these industries have their own dynamics but they are also part of a global market. The dizi as a genre, for instance, has been often compared to the American soap opera and the Latin telenovela, rather than to geographically closer Middle Eastern *musalsal*. In that regard, Salamandra's studies of the Arab media landscape were of particular importance to my research for situating the dizi in its regional context (see Salamandra 2004, 2008, 2013a, 2013b, 2015). Understanding *musalsal* also helps us to apprehend the fascination with dizi in the MENA region. New comparative perspectives are on their way, particularly with Latin America and Asia (Acosta-Alzuru 2020; Aslan 2018; Özgökbel-Bilis, Bilis and Sydygalieva 2018). Many scholars also focus on the different impacts of the dizis' transnational movement (Algan 2019; Bilge 2015; Özalpman 2017; Khan and Won 2020). Research on the dizi industry will undoubtedly flourish in the years to come. The 1990s' research interest in 'pink series' has faded fast, but contemporary dizi research is developing in many different directions.

I would like to conclude by emphasizing certain points that this book tried to express. The success of the dizi industry is not a coincidental phenomenon. It is deeply rooted in the Turkish Republican cultural institutions and modernization project. Turkey has a complex demography, conflicting historical legacies and aspirations for modernization while keeping up with its traditions. With its continuous challenges to democracy, its history of secularization and often contested cultural and ethnic diversity, it has its own texture and identity in its surrounding region. Despite authoritarian politics, it has also produced a tradition of self-criticism that is well reflected in its academia and research journalism. Artistic production followed this line of content, producing its own theatrical and cinematic traditions. Republican reforms promoted theatre since the 1930s, establishing state theatres and conservatories. But theatre in Turkey benefited more from the diverse theatrical trends, including classical, political and comic, which mostly blossomed in the hands of private enterprises. In terms of cinema, despite the long-dominant devotion to melodrama, passionate film-makers had always kept an eye on world cinema while bringing to screen their local stories. 'Turkey: Home of Content' has been the slo-gan of the 2015 MIPCOM, but in fact, the search for original content had first begun in cinema and trained a community of filmmakers who took the challenge of reflecting many domestic issues on screen, and generating generations of cinephiles. 'Issues' in Turkey are endless, and standing on the academic side of many debates, I have observed the tensions but also the strong will to pursue them. Looking from that angle, dizis have indeed caught global audiences by surprise, showing visual glimpses of a Turkey they were not interested in before or only knew through its negative image. Turkish content was sometimes criti-cal to social issues like gender and poverty, or reflected a traumatic political memory. In other cases, it consisted of historical or political eulogy, or of simply written, light but glamourous modern tales. In all of these, the distinct and often uncompromising cultural backgrounds of characters, found refuge in the familiar concepts of Mediterranean culture as food, family, and neighbourhood. From a folkloristic point of view, dizis encapsulate, in all its intensity and heightened imagery, the culture in which they are embedded (Stoeltje and Bauman 1988).

Finally, I should point to a rather paradoxical aspect of mainstream Turkish culture, where extreme enthusiasm for novelty goes side by side with a conservative value system. Reaching out to the updated technol-ogy has been a strong aim of the Turkish state and society. Since the early years of the Republican era, Turkish audiences connected with Western forms of telecommunication.[14] Quickly adapting to cellular

---

14 The Ottomans got access to telegraph in 1855, and to telephone services in 1909, while the first radio broadcast took place in Istanbul in 1927 (Çelik and Eldem 2015; Öztuncay 2011).

technology, Turkey ranks second in the world in the use of the Internet and social media via smart phones (*Habertürk* 2015; Özcan and Koçak 2003). It has a young population which is eager to sustain global digital developments, and follow television content in all its global variety. A bright new generation is now stepping in as the new social players of the dizi industry. The last face-to-face social occasion I attended before being locked down in our home was a Netflix event in Istanbul, launching their original content produced in Turkey on 10 March 2020. Very recently, I moderated an online panel, which showcased Turkish content in global markets, and one other where industry players discussed the digital future of the industry.[15]

Digital content will continue to trend, perhaps in many such platforms, offering more freedom for both writers and producers. As of today, despite many structural and conjunctural problems it has to deal with, one can firmly state that the dizi industry has developed its own structure; that its creative potential is high and goes far beyond what today's mainstream broadcasting allows. There is growing investment in new film sets and studios, along with post-production services. Turkish dizi stars have millions of fans around the world. Obviously, much improvement is needed in the domain of working hours and conditions, for the well-being of the many players who depend on its economy. All these developments will continue to spur academic interest in the dizi, producing new research and new ethnographies on areas that have been highlighted, or perhaps neglected, within the scope of this book.

---

15 Prensario International, 'VS Showcase: Turkish Content Rises' Panel, 17 September 2020; and Bosphorus Film Festival 'The Transformation in Television and Digital Content' Panel, 25 October 2020.

Acknowledgements

This book is a homage to a series of encounters that I had with television, and the performativity that surrounds it. The first of these was my personal journey, as a member of the first generation of TRT viewers and growing up in a house with a television set permanently switched on. I should probably begin by thanking my mother, who set up our relationship with television. Having grown up in a Black Sea town in the 1930s, where access to entertainment was rare, she greatly appreciated the availability of television broadcasting. As a college student, she had visited Istanbul Technical University television studios, and bought her first television set in 1963, when she was reporting from Beirut as a journalist. When TRT's national television broadcasting began in 1968 in Turkey, I had enjoyed with my sisters the first children's programmes produced for us.

Second, the book is an outcome of the academic scepticism about, and personal passion for, television drama in general, and for the dizi in particular. After 10 years of research, it is also a salute to the labour and creativity of a vibrant industry, constructed by enthusiastic social players and entrepreneurs. I am most grateful to Richard Schechner, whose friendship, human values and academic style influenced me deeply. Being in his classroom in New York, Istanbul and Abu Dhabi was a true experience each time, a performance of teaching in itself. His unique editorial approach to creative research and writing is what made this publication possible. I would also like to salute at this point my publisher Naveen Kishore and editor Bishan Samaddar for their creative and poetic approach to the art of the book at Seagull.

In Turkey—and perhaps elsewhere—academics are labelled as 'serious' people rather distant or aloof from popular culture. I have been a shameless consumer of popular culture since my childhood, and following my training in folklore and history, I learned how genres encapsulate the culture of the communities that surround them. My former work consists extensively of the history and ethnography of performances, including the ethnography of two culture-related industries, namely, folk dance and tourism. When I naively began this research, my original idea was to interview a few representatives from each segment of the dizi industry. In the aftermath of a series of interviews with screenwriters, directors, cinematographers and editors, the challenge was to make sense of the diversity of experiences and opinions I had listened to. I quickly realized that such research needed more exposure to the industry players and its institutions than predicted.

Show business is a gated arena where interview requests require 'contacts', which I totally lacked in the beginning. My advantage, however, was that I taught about performing arts from the early years of my academic career, and I was familiar with performance studies and practices. Many of my former students had come of age, and were actively involved in different fields of theatre, music, dance and cinema. This is how my research literally began when my former student Merve Eken put me in touch with Toygar Işıklı, my first interviewee. Toygar was the chief musician of *Fatmagül'ün Suçu Ne?*, composing a musical narrative which complemented the text. I am grateful to him for his patience that day, taking the time to explain the dizis' post-production processes. This interview inspired me to engage in a more ethnography-based research.

My former students and their circle of friends have been my first supporters in this journey, sharing their experiences, offering me further contacts. I owe greatly to the initial encouragement and help of Aytekin Ataş, Fahriye Evcen, Beyza Gümüş, Ulaş Özdemir, Burcu Yıldız and Altuğ Yılmaz. Fahriye Evcen has been my greatest support since the early days of my research giving me an insider perspective of the dizi world and helping me to interview other people. I admired her acting for sure, but mostly, her managerial skills in gracefully handling her student identity and stardom.

Aytekin, Burcu, Ulaş and Beyza have been my initial teachers on the intricacies of dizi production. They too connected me with their friends from the dizi circles, and, more importantly, gave me the encouragement I needed at the beginning of the research. Similarly, Şebnem Aksan, Serdar Biliş, Gurur Ertem, Zeynep Günsür and Köken Ergun from the performance art circles introduced me to other acquaintances that opened gates to new friendships. This is how I first interviewed Ayşe Özer, Aydın Sağıroğlu and Nermin Eroğlu, who since then became my dear friends and consultants. As the early witnesses of the growth of the dizi, Ayşe, Aydın and Nermin helped me enormously to articulate the memory of the past through the present state of ethnography. Ayşe took me to Berlinale at an early stage of my research. I will always fondly remember this miraculous trip with a plane full of celebrities and key figures of the Turkish film industry.

I presented my preliminary findings for the first time at City University of New York in 2012. This lecture introduced me to two valuable friends, Christa Salamandra and Eric Bogosian, through the help of Anny Bakalian. Christa, who had mastered the labyrinths of the Middle Eastern studies, had already written extensively on the Arab *musalsalat,* the Syrian film industry and the reception of the dizis in the Arab world. I learned greatly from her work and her knowledge of media studies, which she generously shared with me. Christa's interest in my ethnographic approach to the dizi has also been a great encouragement. I am greatly indebted to her for being a close reader of this book; the time we spent together in reviewing the manuscript at INZVA in Beykoz Kundura will remain a most treasured memory.

Since our first meeting in 2012, Eric Bogosian, who is a renowned actor and writer, answered my questions on the Hollywood industry and the ethnography of film sets. Both Eric and his director wife Jo Anne Bonney are creative minds, from whom I continue to learn and be inspired. I should also mention producers and screenwriters Sam Johnson and Julie Bean, whom I also consult on different occasions about Hollywood practices. I am thankful to my dear friend Justine McGovern for putting us in touch again. Sam generously hosted me and my students at the NBC

Studios in Los Angeles in 2015. A month later, we both cherished him meeting Boğaziçi University students in Istanbul, surprising him with meticulous questions at Mithat Alam Film Center.

Boğaziçi University has been my home since I became a student there in 1983, then a professor in 1994. As an academic institution, Boğaziçi gave us a unique training, where we were able to set up a new paradigm studying the complexities of our own history, while developing a critical approach to Eurocentric and orientalist discourses of the academia. The final stages of this publication crossed with the unfolding of a series of unfortunate events, which we continue to face and protest as an academic community (Bounbaki 2022). I fondly thank all our former rectors and deans who provided us with a fruitful work environment, among them Üstün Ergüder, Ayşe Soysal, Gülay Barbarosoğlu, Gülen Aktaş, Taylan Akdoğan, Nilgün Işık and Özlem Berk-Albachten. I am particularly grateful to Ayşe Soysal for having arranged my first dizi set visit in 1997. I would like to thank all my colleagues at the Department of History for the invaluable academic environment, and our staff Oya Arıkan, Ali Dağıdır and Buket Sargan, who helped me many times with the logistics of my research. My warmest thanks are particularly to Professor Selçuk Esenbel, with whom I shared every stage of this book. It has been a privilege to have her wisdom, love and friendship in my life. My dear colleague Peter Campbell has been the first person to whom I confided with my manuscript. I am most grateful to him for kindly copyediting the text; his comments were the first valuable responses I received on the content. My good old friend Nükhet Sirman was among the earliest researchers of dizis. We have many memories, but the best is when she told me one evening either 'to leave or stay', because she had 'a date with Sıla!' With our common passion for cinema, I had a warm film companionship with my friend Aslı Göksel over the years. I am most grateful to her for kindly taking me to the set of her director son Yusuf Pirhasan; I know that it was not an easy job for a mother. Boğaziçi had other eyes on dizis, including Ayşe Öncü and Belgin Tekçe, who pursued their research since the 1990s, and Murat Gülsoy, who was among the writers' teams of the early dizis. I learned greatly from the entertainment industry analyses of Özlem Öz and Mine Eder, and from Ceren Özselçuk's research on the affective modes of consumerism. I hope to collaborate more with them in years to come. I also always greatly appreciated the comments of Nilgün Işık, who joined me at the Asian Television Forum (ATF) in Singapore, and of Suraiya Faroqhi, Huricihan İslamoğlu and İsenbike Togan, who are all great historians and also have a deep understanding of the different facets of Turkish high and popular culture.

My former assistants and students at Boğaziçi also lent me a hand throughout this project with their wit and energy. Yasemin Baran, Sevinç Çalhanoğlu, Yeliz Çavuş, Yeliz Çelebi, Sarp Çölgeçen, Jale Karabekir, Derya Karabulut, Yener Koç, Enno Maessen, Saadet Özen, Elif Kevser Özer, Uğur Özkan, Defne Özözer, Burcu Özkaçar, Sinem Erdoğan, Simge Erdoğan, Cafer Sarıkaya, Melis Süloş, Naz Vardar, Demet Yıldız and Altuğ Yılmaz have all helped me in different ways. They assisted me during the preliminary library research, directed me to new contacts, supported me during my set visits, hosted me at their institutions, and helped as translators during the MIPCOM 2015 preparations. I will always cherish the memory of the moment when Sinem rushed from the real Topkapı Palace Library to the fake Çinili Köşk set up for the *Muhteşem Yüzyıl* exhibition at UNIQ, to translate Timur Savcı's interview for the foreign press. Last but not least, I am also indebted to the assistance of the staff of the Faculty of Arts and Sciences, the Research Fund Office (BAP), the Computer Center (BİM), the Aptullah Kuran Library, the Pandora Bookstore, the Transportation office (Garaj), the Kennedy Lodge Faculty Club, the Gift Shop and Nazar Kırtasiye, which all contributed to my research process in different ways.

The Mithat Alam Film Center at Boğaziçi University was our jewel before I started this research. Mithat Alam's friendship is a precious memory that I treasure. The institution he established has been my right arm in exploring the past and the present of the film industry in Turkey. My research bonded us with the centre's team, opening doors to many collaborations with Zeynep Ünal, Elif Ergezen, Sadun Başer and Özcan Vardar, along with Yamaç Okur who is now a dizi producer himself. Although the centre is primarily founded for cinema, their 'Visual Memory' project comprised interviews that I benefitted from as much as their 'Interview Series' with actors, writers and directors of the Turkish film industry, including television production (https://mafm.boun.edu.tr).

My other home has been Beykoz Kundura, a site which I witnessed grow and prosper while my research continued. The Yıldırım family in general but Serpil, Buse, Tarık and Aslı in particular have been generous hosts throughout my research and writing process. Since 2014, their friendship joyfully accompanied my daily life. I am grateful for their sincere love, good humour and support. Beykoz Kundura is a palimpsest estate which served in the past as a shoe factory, privatized in 2003 (www.beykozkundura.com). It became a favourite site for filming since 2005, eventually growing to be one of the main sites of the dizi industry. Sharing the everyday life of Kundura has also been a tremendous contribution to my research project, offering me an ethnographic site to observe production processes. The institutions set up by Buse and Tarık, Lita, INZVA and Famelog, also offered me other beneficial venues during my research. The industrious INZVA team and staff hosted me several times at their place, while Famelog's Şule Bilgiç and Fahriye Şentürk organized exclusive events with important dizi industry players.

My visit to Berlinale convinced me that I should engage in research on global television fairs. As an official representative of these fairs, İTO, the Istanbul Chamber of Commerce, kindly included me in their protocol, and this is how I paid my first visit to MIPTV in 2013. I am grateful to İbrahim Çağlar, Murat Gürbüz, İsrafil Kuralay, Mahmut Özden, İlhan Soylu, Dursun Topçu, Murat Yalçıntaş and Aysun Yılmaz for their initial help during this process. Later, I closely worked with the İTO teams, organizing conferences in MIPCOM, ATF and DISCOP as a member of the Film Industry Coordination Committee. I learned greatly from the committee's members including Müge Akar, Selin Arat, Alev Aydın, Mustafa Aydoğan, Özge Dumlupınar, Emir Düzel, Şenay Filiztekin-Turan, Emre Görentaş, Handan Özkubat, Özlem Özsümbül, Yeşim Sezdirmez, Fahriye Şentürk, Fatma Şapçı, Beşir Tatlı, Meltem Tümtürk-Akyol, Rıdvan Şentürk, Ziyad Varol and Ahmet Ziyalar. During the MIPCOM 2015 preparations, I closely worked with Aysun Yılmaz, Mine Güneş, Begüm Ece, Sanem Onat, Banu Çağlak and Aylin Odabaş of İTO's Exhibitions Department. I am thankful to all for their help and collegiality. The everyday life of MIP events required another expertise. Şebnem Şahin and Özlem Özsümbül have been my first guides, followed up with a long-standing companionship with Can Okan and Ahmet Ziyalar of Inter Medya, and their wonderful team. Since then, they have been my dear friends with whom I can discuss the main issues of the industry and everyday life. I had the opportunity to closely consult producers İdil Belli and İnci Gülen Oarr in the global markets in Johannesburg and Singapore; I thank them for sincerely sharing their experience with me. My conversations with Xavier Aristimuno, Ted Baracos, Samira Haddi and Virginia Mouseler were particularly inspiring and helpful for me to understand the different aspects of the global television industry. I learned a lot from our conversations, both in Istanbul and in Cannes, and I greatly value their friendship. International journalists reporting on television business have also greatly helped me to contextualize Turkish dizis at the global stage. I wholeheartedly thank Diego Alfagemez, Gün Akyüz, Mansha Daswani, Fabricio Ferrara, Andy Fry, Julian Newby, Sebastian Novacovsky, Alejandro Sanchez, Rhonda Richford and Nick Vivarelli, all of whom became friends I followed and consulted along the way. My visits to the MIP events would be impossible without Sonia and Haygaram Bakar, Ayda Tanikyan and Mateos Saint Yrian, who hosted me several times in Nice. Ayda Teyze and Sonia have been close dizi viewers, giving me genuine insights from abroad. In Cannes, I am also thankful to Yves and Zilia Deranlot, Fatimata Diop and the amazing Patric Bastiani from Hotel de France, who shared with me their local knowledge over the years.

As my research evolved, the support that I received from the industry increased, leading me to new friendships. Inter Medya has embraced me as a researcher since the first year of my research; later giving me a home in a field where I was a total stranger. My path crossed with Meriç Acemi in 2015, when I first interviewed her at Boğaziçi and was impressed with her intelligence, analytical mind and perceptiveness. Since then, she has been a companion and a close consultant throughout my research, but mostly a friend with whom I now share my daily worries. I deeply cherish our friendship with her, Murat and Ferzan, whose sense of humour and energy kept me going. I took my first 'formal lesson' on production and distribution processes from Elif Dağdeviren. We shared our Ankara memories as both of us had grown up there. As the daughter of a TRT director, Elif had also developed her own perspective on the transition to private networks. She has been one of the early supporters of my research, for which I am most grateful. I could not organize the Country of Honour preparations without the help and assistance of producers Kerem Çatay, Pelin Diştaş, Birol Güven and Timur Savcı, who mobilized their own resources and helped a successful organization to take place at MIPCOM 2015. I am also most thankful for working in synergy with Kanal D, then under the direction of İrfan Şahin, along with an active input by Pelin Diştaş, Lale Eren, Özlem Özsümbül and Özge Bağdatlıoğlu.

It was very important for me to conduct in-depth interviews with Kerem Çatay and Timur Savcı, as two leading creative producers of the industry with an eye to inquisitive content. I am wholeheartedly grateful to Timur who, after two short interviews at TIMS, proposed to come to my office at Boğaziçi and told the sincerest producer story I ever collected. Since then, we have been in touch on different occasions, including a collaborative project in Adana. As one of the founding members of TIMS, Banu Savcı has gracefully assisted me in reaching out for visual resources I needed for this book. Similarly, I will always remember gratefully the morning Kerem Çatay accepted me and Andy Fry from *MIP Daily News* at AY Yapım—then in Beşiktaş—on the day when he had a newborn at home. This in-depth interview was also a very sincere and informative resource for both Andy and me. From the very early stages of my research, Pelin Diştaş has generously helped whenever I needed a contact or support. I knew Birol Güven and his talented musician wife Burcu years before I began this research. Knowing his sense of humour, neither I nor Nükhet (Sirman) were surprised to see him captivating audiences with his phenomenal *Çocuklar Duymasın* in 2002. I sincerely thank Pelin, Birol and Burcu for their hospitality when we visited them with foreign journalists in 2015.

The day I interviewed Türker İnanoğlu in his Kavacık office will remain as one of the most memorable experiences of my research. It was a privilege to hear a first-hand narrative from him, as the quintessential doyen of Turkish filmmaking, which turned out to be a breakthrough moment for understanding how producers differed in their approach to dizi making. Combining his Yeşilçam style with his vision on the international content, İnanoğlu developed a sustainable model of his own. I would like to salute at this point the memory of my journalist friend Selahattin Duman who kindly organized my meeting with him. Two other journalists, Ferhat Boratav and Umur Birand kindly sponsored my visit to the Antalya Television Awards in 2012. I passed three phenomenal days with reporters of tabloid press, an experience which taught me a whole new angle to look at the dizi world.

My access to the early players of the industry was an important challenge of the research process. I am indebted to other senior players, including Arzu Akmansoy, Faruk Bayhan, Yılmaz Dağdeviren, Mustafa Karahan, Moris Sarfati and Beşir Tatlı, with whom I conducted in-depth interviews that proved to be an invaluable oral history data for my historical analysis. It is with their help that I could fill in the gaps that I could not find in written sources. I am also most thankful to Dursun Güleryüz, who explained in great detail the change in the rating system, a consultation I value deeply. A moment I really enjoyed during my research was an interview request I received from a network manager. Puzzled by the fact that many people knew me at the McKee seminars I attended, she approached me with a visit request. The encounter between us turned out to be a 'double-sided interview', a unique experience I now use in my oral history classes.

On the creative side, I am also grateful to the screenwriters, directors, art directors, cinematographers, actors and editors who have understood and valued my research inquiries. The talented directors of the dizi world, Zeynep Günay-Tan, Doğan Karaca, Cem Karcı, Ahmet Katıksız, Ayhan Özen, Mehmet Ada Öztekin, Yusuf Pirhasan, Hilal Saral, Yağmur and Durul Taylan, Barış Yöş, and acclaimed cinema director Nesli Çölgeçen accepted me on their sets. I will always cherish the memory of the whispering conversation we had with Hilal on the stage of the MIPCOM panel 'Turkey, Home of Dizi Content', and Doğan joining me at my performing arts class at Boğaziçi. I also warmly thank production managers and coordinators Orhan Demirci, Yavuz Ertüm, Alara Hamamcıoğlu, Emrah Karacakaya and Irmak Yazım, who kindly hosted me during my visits to their sets. International Bosphorus Film Festival also organized visionary workshops and events from which I greatly benefited. I warmly thank dizi editors Haluk Arus, Gökçe Bilgin-Kılıç and Aykut Yıldırım, who have been my first teachers of post-production processes, and Nilgün Nalçacı, who has been my first guide in deconstructing the illusionary aspects of dizis' art direction.

. My sincere thanks go to screenwriters who generously opened gates to their inner world for me. My talk with Kandemir Konduk, one of the pioneering dizi writers, was an important oral history interview, revealing many details from the earlier years of dizi production. I am most thankful to Meriç Acemi, Deniz Akçay, Selçuk Aydemir, Cenk Boğatur, Gaye Boralıoğlu, Pınar Bulut, Eylem Canpolat, Kerem Deren, Özge Efendioğlu, Sema Ergenekon, Melek Gençoğlu, Murat Gülsoy, Uğraş Güneş, Nihan Küçükural, Yılmaz Şahin, Ayfer Tunç and Ece Yörenç. Nihan and Gaye were the first writers who explained to me the dynamics of the dizi-writing processes. Meriç hosted me several times at her writing environment, which was a true privilege. I will always fondly remember the special time we passed with Sema and Eylem, chatting and shopping in Kuala Lumpur at ATF. I never had an opportunity to formally interview Deniz, but I learned a lot from the conversations we had with her in Cunda. Our paths crossed several times in our neighbourhood cafe in Yeniköy with Pınar and Kerem; they also hosted me several times at their Writers' Room, then in Arnavutköy; I am grateful for their hospitality. Yılmaz Şahin rushed to my help during the preparations of MIPCOM 2015 to give an interview to the foreign press. I first met Ayfer Tunç, while organizing the special MIPCOM panel 'Heroines of Content'; I am grateful to her and all the other participants, namely Pınar Bulut, Eylem Canpolat, Sema Ergenekon and Ece Yörenç, for agreeing to be part of this panel.

Actors are the recognizable face of the dizi industry, but they are the hardest to access. It is often difficult to transcend the rightful blockage of their agencies, but also many fear being interviewed, because of the association with aggressive tabloid press. As my research's priority was the ethnography of the industry and the rise of the dizi genre, for a long time interviewing actors had not been my priority. I was more interested in interviewing the talent and casting agents to better understand their role in the industry. I warmly thank Ayşe Barım, Rezzan Çakır, Özlem Durak, Mine Güler, Renda Güner, Ahmet Koraltürk, Sonay Özbal, Ali Sabuncugil, Gaye Sökmen, Cem Tatlıtuğ and Gözde Yılmaz for sharing their perspective with me. The first actor I interviewed was Memet Ali Alabora, who was then the chair of the Actors' Union, and now working as an actor and activist in the UK. I am most thankful to him for his initial encouragement for my research. I was really lucky to have known some actors in person. I knew Memo, Mehmet Günsür, since he was four years old, watching proudly his career evolve and prosper. Fahriye Evcen was my student at Boğaziçi, and remained my friend, while Yiğit Özşener was closely working with Şeyda Taluk, one of my old friends. With their help, followed by that of other actors, musicians and friends, I was able to arrange interviews with actors, for which I am deeply thankful. I had a chance to chat on their dizi experience with actresses Hülya Duyar, Çiğdem Selışık and Deniz Türkali in private occasions. I was able to host some actors at Boğaziçi University. I sincerely thank Engin Akyürek, Derya Alabora, Memet Ali Alabora, Özge Borak, Cansu Dere, Esra Dermancıoğlu, Demet Evgar and Yiğit Özşener who came and shared their experiences and exchanged ideas about the industry. I interviewed Mustafa and Övül Avkıran, Erkan Bektaş, İpek Bilgin, Barış Falay and Cahit Gök in diverse cafes of Istanbul, and learned a lot from their comparative perspectives on acting on stage and on camera. I will never forget the moment when Aydan Şener entered Tribeca Café in Yeniköy, making all heads turn to her, as the unforgettable star of the early dizis. I am deeply thankful to her for giving me an invaluable interview of a transitional era of our television history. Kerem Alışık, Belçim Bilgin, Caner Cindoruk, Fahriye Evcen, Engin Hepileri, Kenan İmirzalıoğlu, Erkan Kolçak Köstendil, Burak Özçivit and Aytaç Uşun gave me interviews in their set environment, granting their precious time to talk about acting, while acting. It was also a great pleasure to host and moderate many other actors at the Mithat Alam Film Center, along with my friends there, who, in the first place, made these interviews possible.

I was taught the study of performance by great scholars. Although I have not been formally his student, Richard Schechner's writings have guided many of us in the analysis of performativity. Richard Bauman, Beverly Stoeltje and Margaret Mills have been my mentors in the semiotics of performance. Richard Bauman's approach has been my inspiration to study the ethnography of communication in both historical and contemporary cultural domains. I am most grateful to him for his support since the early stages of this research, and for his invaluable comments on the interdiscursive modes that historically shaped dizi as a genre. Beverly Stoeltje and Margaret Mills have greatly affected my thinking with their feminist approach; their continuing friendship enriches me every day. They have been my role models in teaching and conducting fieldwork. For my formal training in folklore and cultural studies, I am also grateful to my dear professors Roger Abrahams, Dan Ben-Amos, Hasan El-Shamy, Henry Glassie, Kenneth Goldstein, John McDowell, Robert St George, and Don Yoder in giving me the key of a folkloric approach in the study of cultural forms and communities. They all have paved my way in academic research and teaching. Besides Indiana University and the University of Pennsylvania, New York University has been an academic venue teaching me new aspects of performance. My friendship with Evelyn (Timmie) Birge Vitz has been a blessing both academically and personally. Although we mostly collaborated on medieval performances, I learned greatly from her on the intermediality between historical texts and performances, and the role of belief systems in everyday life. I owe my knowledge on the 'theatre of the real' to Carol Martin. I am fondly thankful for the great conversations we had on dance, performance and urban space both in New York and in Istanbul. My dear friend Deborah Kapchan hosted me many times at her place, where we had long discussions on performance, Sufism, academia and family.

My discussions and collaborations with my colleagues and friends Beth Baron, Regina Bendix, Heather Companiott, Lisa Gilman, Lynne Hamer, Jane Hathaway, Deborah Kapchan, Nathan Light, Ulrich Marzolph, Dorothy Noyes, Joan Savarino and Bill Westerman continue to enrich my perspectives on the different realms of folklore and history. I also deeply appreciate the friendship of the following scholars, who shaped how I research and write: Egil Bakka, Dieter Christenson, Anca Giurchescu, Adrienne Kaeppler, Irene Loutzaki, Mats Nilsson, Barbara Sparti and Judy Van Zile from the ICTM circle; Joanna Bornat, Alessandro Portelli, Paul Thompson and Mercedes Vilanova as oral historians; Feroz Ahmad, Ahmad Baydoun, Azza Baydoun and Badia Baydoun, Hasan El-Shamy, Samar Kanafani, Mary Martin, Margaret Mills, Walid Sadek, Hawry Talabani and Peri Talabani as my guides about the Middle East; and Metin And, Pertev Naili Boratav, Aptullah Kuran, Şerif Mardin and Şirin Tekeli as our influential Turkish cultural and social historians. To know them in person has been a privilege of my life.

My research also directed me towards media studies, a field with which I was not much familiar before. As folklorists, we are trained in the ethnography of artful communication, but media studies had developed its own approach, introducing me to new scholarships in Turkey and abroad. I learned greatly from the scholarship of Ece Algan, Savaş Arslan, Deniz Bayrakdar, Melis Behlil, Feride Çiçekoğlu, Nezih Erdoğan, Yeşim Kaptan, Levent Soysal, Hülya Uğur Tanrıöver, Aslı Tunç and Eylem Yanardağ on Turkish filmmaking and media. Over time, I also discovered the growing pace of this field through the works of Feyza Akınerdem, Pınar Aslan, Şebnem Baran, Fatma Gözlükaya-Tütüncü, Devrim Karagöz and Ayşegül Kesirli Unur among many others. My historian colleagues Günhan Börekçi, Esra Danacıoğlu and Akşin Somel have shared with me their experiences as advisors for the historical dizis.

The dizi research also connected me to new international scholars. Since we first met in 2016, I have cherished the friendship and collaboration with my dear friend Carolina Acosta-Alzuru, whose knowledge of telenovela helps us better understand the dizis' narrativity, which now she explores and situates in its transnational context. Barbara Villez, of Université Paris 8, was among the brave hosts of the first international conference on the dizis, which gathered a rather dispersed group of scholars and industry players in Paris in 2014. I learned greatly from her analytical vision, in making sense of the transnational travels of television genres. With Víctor Falcón Castro (1979–2018), an untimely loss, I had a short but powerful friendship. Víctor's enthusiasm for the dizi genre consisted mostly of its transnational success, which, looking from Peru, he thought was a miraculous experience. I hope that I can honour his memory soon in a conference on Turkish–Latin American genres, as we had planned back in 2017.

The decade in which I conducted my research and writing was not an easy one. It was a politically straining era, which interrupted our order many times, including the unexpected Covid-19 pandemic, the arrests of many academics and the sudden change we experienced at Boğaziçi University. We also went through a difficult test as a family during the illness and untimely passing of our dear Defne, to whom I dedicate this book. Defne was an excellent dancer, singer, chorister, storyteller and a wise friend, whose spirit continues to accompany us. While passing through these hard times, personal and political, my research process has been a 'time out of time', which in retrospect I deeply appreciate. I could not survive these challenging years without the help of my close friends and family, who shared with great patience and grace many of the hardships I experienced along the way. I wholeheartedly thank my good old friends Figen Adıgüzel, Rüya Atamer, Sonia Bakar, Vivyan Behar, Karin Çizmeciyan, Aylin Gözübüyük, Dalia Kandiyoti, Didem Kocataşkın-Doğruol, Füsun Külahlı, Nejla Osseiran, Çiğdem Özyürek-Azizof, Eda Pekelman-Karakullukçu, Ayda Şirin-Manukyan, Şeyda Taluk, Meltem Türköz, Aylin Vartanyan and Müge Yelekçi, along with my NDS83, BÜFK and BÜ İşletme groups. We are connected through our childhood and youth memories, but also with the sharing of everyday life joys, including the dizis.

My family experienced all the emotional stages I passed through while writing this book; I am deeply thankful to each of them for their patience, love and support. Watching the dizis with Hakan and Nihal has been a performance in itself; regardless of what we watch, the way we watch and comment makes up the real entertainment. We have long shared our passion for television dramas with my sisters Ayşe Mudun and Ahu Yıldırmaz; our dizi gossips will continue ever after, with endless cross-examinations. Three of us owe our television-watching habit to our amazing mother, Neriman Malkoç Öztürkmen, who will not be able to read this book, but who gave us the affective frame behind it. I am thankful to all the other members of my family, Baki Mudun, Rasih and Özce Öztürkmen, who shared with me their ideas and comments along the way, and also to Rıza, Ülkü and Figen Yılmaz and my cousins in Tirebolu, whose television knowledge continually taught me different perspectives about audience reception. As we were all watching the diverse dizis of our own taste, our children Ayşe Nihal Yılmaz, Lara and Deniz Yıldırmaz, Ömer and Ayşe Öztürkmen, and Oğuz Kaan Yüksel were engaged in their own relations with social media; I continue to learn from their curious minds and joyful hearts. Last but not least, my warm thanks are for Gulnar Reyimova and Gülten Şimşek for their help and support at home.

Like all research, this book is also partial and incomplete. I fondly apologize to people I could not thank in name. My hope is that it inspires many more research to come on this amazing experience that we have all gone through in the last two decades.

List of Interviewees, 2011–2022

A number of interviewees were not included in this list. Some were set workers and crew members who asked to be anonymous.

Toygar Işıklı, Musician	5 July 2011
Elif Sönmez, Production Assistant	6 October 2011
Nilgün Nalçacı, Art Director	16 November 2011
Nihan Küçükural, Screenwriter	12 December 2011
Canan Candan, PR Advisor	16 December 2011
Memet Ali Alabora, Actor	22 December 2011
Fahriye Evcen, Actress	28 December 2011; 26 October 2013; 22 April 2014; 6 February 2017; 14 March 2017; 9 April 2017
Aytekin Ataş, Musician	12 January 2012, 25 August 2015
Özlem Durak, Talent Agent	19 January 2012
Ayşe Barım, Talent Agent	2 March 2012
Selin Kılıçarslan, Director	6 March 2012
Taylan Kadığlu, Art Director	6 March 2012
Kerem Çatay, Producer	8 March 2012
Deniz Türkali, Actress	12 March 2012
Renda Güner, Casting	21 March 2012
Gaye Boralıoğlu, Screenwriter	23 March 2012
Erkan Bektaş, Actor	23 March 2012
Demet Evgar, Actress	28 March 2012
Engin Akyürek, Actor	29 March 2012; 1 June 2012; 6 February 2017

Ayşe Özer, Line Producer   11 April 2012
Cevdet Mercan, Director   12 April 2012, 4 June 2015
Ulaş Özdemir, Musician   18 April 2012
Sercan Kısmet, Reporter   21 April 2012
Gündüz Sevgi, Reporter   21 April 2012
Yusuf Bülbül, Reporter   21 April 2012
Samet Altay, Reporter   21 April 2012
Kürşat Demirhan, Cameraman   21 April 2012
Mahmur Pas, Reporter   21 April 2012
Barış Falay, Actor   25 April 2012
Haluk Arus, Editor   26 April 2012
Aydın Sarıoğlu, Director of Photography   1 May 2012
Mehmet Ada Öztekin, Director   2 May 2012
Sonay Özbal, Talent Agent   7 May 2012
Betül Durmuş, Director   9 May 2012
Gökçe Bilgin-Kılıç, Editor   10 May 2012
Cahit Gök, Actor   10 May 2012
Yiğit Özşener, Actor   11 May 2012
Hüseyin Tunç, Director of Photography   23 May 2012
Nermin Eroğlu, Line Producer   23 May 2012
Mine Güler, Casting   24 May 2012; 14 January 2013
Beyza Gümüş, Post-Production   28 May 2012
Hilal Saral, Director   29 May 2012; 4 June 2015
Yağmur Taylan, Director   12 June 2012
Durul Taylan, Director   12 June 2012
Murat Gülsoy, Screenwriter   15 June 2012
Özge Özkan, Actress   3 July 2012
Derya Alabora, Actress   10 September 2012
Mustafa Avkıran, Actor   11 September 2012
Övül Avkıran, Actress   11 September 2012
Türker İnanoğlu, Producer   19 September 2012
Rezzan Çakır, Talent Agent   25 September 2012
Esra Dermancıoğlu, Actress   3 October 2012

Ece Yörenç, Screenwriter	7 January 2013
Melek Gençoğlu, Screenwriter	7 January 2013
Özlem Havuzlu, Screenwriter	14 January 2013
Hülya Duyar, Actress	15 January 2013
Belçim Bilgin, Actress	8 February 2013; 20 August 2014; 5 September 2014
Elif Dağdeviren, Producer	23 February 2013
Selim Başarır, Psychiatrist	6 March 2013
Şebnem Şahin, Distributor	7 March 2013
Cansu Dere, Actress	19 March 2013
Özlem Özsümbül, Distributor	20 March 2013
Yılmaz Dağdeviren, Network Director	22 March 2013; 3 April 2013
Armağan Çağlayan, Producer	25 March 2013
Ezel Akay, Director	27 March 2013
Erdal Tuşunel, Producer	28 March 2013
İpek Durkal, Journalist	3 April 2013
Samira Haddi, MIPTV/MIPCOM Manager	7 April 2013
İzzet Pinto, Distributor	8 April 2013
Can Okan, Distributor	8 April 2013
Ahmet Ziyalar, Distributor	8 April 2013; 2 June 2022; 14 November 2017
Mehmet Demirhan, Distributor	9 April 2013
Fırat Gülgen, Distributor	9 April 2013
Xavier Aristimuno, Telemundo/HBO Executive	10 April 2013; 4 April 2014
Fredrik af Malmborg, Distributor	10 April 2013; 4 April 2014
Mete Horozoğlu, Actor	10 May 2013
İlksen Başarır, Director	20 May 2013
Özge Borak, Actress	24 May 2013
Kenan İmirzalıoğlu, Actor	30 May 2013
Nevin Ayaz, Line Producer	11 June 2013
Canan Çayır, Costume Director	12 June 2013
Cengiz Özdemir, Producer	19 July 2013
Ahmet Katıksız, Director	29 October 2013; 5 June 2014
Doğan Karaca, Director	30 October 2013

Timur Savcı, Producer	6 February 2014; 21 April 2014; 28 May 2014
Birol Güven, Producer	13 February 2014; 22 August 2015
Burcu Güven, Musician	22 August 2015
İpek Bilgin, Actress	20 February 2014
Nasima Boudi, Media Analyst	4 April 2014
Selin Arat, Director of International Operations	21 April 2014; 28 November 2015
Kandemir Konduk, Screenwriter	22 April 2014
Burak Özçivit, Actor	22 April 2014; 30 October 2017; 21 January 2018; 16 January 2020
Arzu Akmansoy, Director	12 May 2014
Ayhan Özen, Director	26 May 2014
Pınar Bulut, Screenwriter	27 May 2014;18 June 2014
Kerem Deren, Screenwriter	27 May 2014;18 June 2014
Selçuk Aydemir, Screenwriter	30 June 2014
Akşin Somel, History Advisor	30 June 2014
Gaye Sökmen, Talent Agent	1 July 2014
Nesli Çölgeçen, Director	22–23 August 2014; 5 September 2014
Caner Cindoruk, Actor	5 September 2014
Engin Hepileri, Actor	5 September 2014
Sema Ergenekon, Screenwriter	15 June 2015
Eylem Canpolat, Screenwriter	15 June 2015
İrfan Şahin, Network Director	11 February 2015
Lale Eren, Drama Director	5 June 2015, 5 October 2019
Deniz Akçay, Screenwriter	18 August 2015; 28 November 2015
Cenk Boğatur, Screenwriter	24 August 2015
Berkun Oya, Screenwriter	25 August 2015
Yılmaz Şahin, Screenwriter	25 August 2015
Meriç Acemi, Screenwriter	22 November 2015
Uğraş Güneş, Screenwriter	29 November 2015
Özge Bağdatlıoğlu, Drama Director	29 November 2015
Aykut Yıldırım, Editor	17 December 2015

Mehmet Günsür, Actor	31 December 2015
Ahmet Koraltürk, Talent Agent	8 April 2016
Evrim Doğan, Actress	13 April 2016
Barış Yöş, Director	12 May 2016
Selman Kolcu, Production Coordinator	17–18 May 2016
Irmak Yazım, Executive Producer Assistant	22 May 2016
Cem Tatlıtuğ, Talent Agent	31 May 2016
Nilüfer Kuyel, Format Director	10 June 2016
Özge Efendioğlu, Screenwriter	7 October 2016
Bülent Turgut, Producer	10 October 2016
Muhittin Elibol, Executive Producer	28 October 2016
Hasan Gündüz, Director	28 October 2016
Aydan Şener, Actress	29 October 2016
Pelin Akat, Producer	18 November 2016
Şebnem Aksoy, Network Drama Director	22 November 2016
İnci Gülen Oarr, Producer	8 December 2016
Günhan Börekçi, History Advisor	20 January 2017
Çiğdem Selışık, Actress	2 February 2017
Faruk Bayhan, Producer	14 February 2017
Beşir Tatlı, Distributor, former Network Drama Director	7 July 2017
Dursun Güleryüz, TIAK (TV Audience Measurement Committee) Director	27 November 2017
Mustafa Karahan, Producer	2 February 2018
Yavuz Ertüm, Production Coordinator	3 May 2018; 22 May 2018
Sinan Çetin, Director-Producer	23 May 2018
Alara Hamamcıoğlu, Production Manager	28 February 2019
Tolga Kutluay, Director of Photography	28 February 2019
Gökhan Çınarlı, Cameraman	28 February 2019
Aytaç Uşun, Actor	28 February 2019
Mehmet Öztekin, Drone Operator	28 February 2019
Erkan Kolçak Köstendil, Actor	28 February 2019
Ebru Güleren, Make-up Artist	28 February 2019

Nehir Arıcı, Costume Director	28 February 2019
Okan Akdemir, Location Advisor	28 February 2019
Zeynep Günay-Tan, Director	6 March 2019
Emrah Karacakaya, Line Producer	8 November 2019
Nilüfer Çamur, Art Director	8 November 2019
Kerem Alışık, Actor	8 November 2019
Ali Sabuncugil, Talent Agent	6 November 2020
Mehmet Bozdağ, Producer	16 January 2020
Metin Günay, Director	16 January 2020
Orhan Demirci, Production Coordinator	16 January 2020
Sedat Yücel, Director of Photography	19 May 2020
Sedat İnci, Director	26 May 2020
Handan Özkubat, Distributor	2 May 2020
Müge Akar, Distributor	2 June 2020
Mehmet Eryılmaz, Producer	16 October 2020
Sarp Kalfaoğlu, Producer	1 December 2021
Ayşegül Tüzün, Distributor	10 March 2022
Şenay Filiztekin-Turan, Distributor	4 March 2022

Public Interviews Attended

In the interviews marked here with as asterisk, the author acted as the moderator.

Deniz Türkali, Actress (Mithat Alam Film Center)   8 March 2012

Nazan Kesal, Actress (Mithat Alam Film Center)   8 March 2012

Fikret Kuşkan, Actor (Mithat Alam Film Center)   15 March 2012

Nebahat Çehre, Actress (Mithat Alam Film Center)   21 March 2012

Mehmet Günsür, Actor (Mithat Alam Film Center)   3 May 2012

Emrah Serbes, Screenwriter (Mithat Alam Film Center)   28 March 2012

Tomris Giritlioğlu, Producer (Mithat Alam Film Center)   22 February 2013

Nur Sürer, Actress (Mithat Alam Film Center)   28 February 2013

Rezan Yeşilbaş, Directo, (Mithat Alam Film Center)   14 March 2013

Nilay Erdönmez, Actress (Mithat Alam Film Center)   21 March 2013

Nihal Yalçın, Actress (Mithat Alam Film Center)   21 March 2013

Haluk Bilginer, Actor (Mithat Alam Film Center)   20 May 2013

Deniz Akçay, Writer-Director (Mithat Alam Film Center)   30 October 2013

Menderes Samancılar, Actor (Mithat Alam Film Center)   20 February 2014

Erdal Özyağcılar, Actor (Mithat Alam Film Center)   13 November 2014

Serkan Keskin, Actor (Mithat Alam Film Center)   19 November 2014

Halit Ergenç, Actor (Mithat Alam Film Center)   27 November 2014

Burak Aksak, Director (Mithat Alam Film Center)   11 March 2015

Nesli Çölgeçen, Director (Mithat Alam Film Center)   18 March 2015

Farah Zeynep Abdullah, Actress (Mithat Alam Film Center) 26 March 2015

Ali Atay, Actor (Mithat Alam Film Center)   3 November 2015

Sam Johnson,* Screenwriter (Mithat Alam Film Center)   27 November 2015

Julie Bean, Screenwriter (Mithat Alam Film Center)   28 November 2015

Zafer Algöz, Actor (Mithat Alam Film Center)   11 February 2016

Abdullah Oğuz, Director-Producer (Mithat Alam Film Center) 3 March 2016

Özcan Deniz, Actor, Singer (Mithat Alam Film Center)   16 March 2016

Meriç Acemi, Screenwriter (Senaryo Yazarları Derneği)   5 June 2016

Rutkay Aziz, Actor (Mithat Alam Film Center)   9 November 2016

Robert McKee, Writer (International Bosphorus
Film Festival)   16–18 November 2016

Timur Savcı,* Producer (Mithat Alam Film Center)   30 March 2017

Ülkü Yılmaz, Retired teacher   17 June 2017

Selim Bayraktar, Actor (Mithat Alam Film Center)   7 February 2018

Perihan Savaş, Actress (Mithat Alam Film Center)   22 February 2018

Rıza Kocaoğlu,* Actor (Mithat Alam Film Center)   28 March 2018

Timuçin Esen,* Actor (Mithat Alam Film Center)   7 February 2019

Beren Saat, Actress (Famelog Academy
Sunday Conversations)   17 February 2019

Ayfer Tunç, Writer (Mithat Alam Film Center)   20 March 2019

Nilgün Öneş, Writer (Famelog Academy
Sunday Conversations)   24 March 2019

Okan Yalabık, Actor (Mithat Alam Film Center)   28 March 2019

Caner Cindoruk, Actor (Mithat Alam Film Center)   19 February 2020

APPENDIX 3

Set Visits

Cumhuriyet	12 October 1997, Istanbul
Fatmagül'ün Suçu Ne?	12 November 2011; 1 June 2012; 13 June 2012, Istanbul
Bir Çocuk Sevdim,	18 April 2012, Istanbul
Muhteşem Yüzyıl	23 May 2012, Istanbul
Kuzey Güney	28 May 2012, Istanbul
Galip Derviş	3 May 2013, Istanbul
İntikam	23 May 2013, Istanbul
Karadayı	30 May 2013, Istanbul
Öyle Bir Geçer Zaman ki	11 June 2013; 12 June 2013, Istanbul
Çalıkuşu	26 October 2013; 22 April 2014, Istanbul
Person of Interest	10 November 2013, New York
Karagül	4 February 2014, Gaziantep
Bugünün Saraylısı	26 May 2014, Istanbul
Kara Para Aşk	21 April 2014; 26 May 2014; 5 June 2014, Istanbul
Çalsın Sazlar	22–23 August 2014; 5 September 2014, Istanbul
Paramparça	4 June 2015, Istanbul
Kara Sevda	1 October 2015; 29 April 2016; 14 February 2017, Istanbul
Crowded	14 October 2015, Los Angeles
Kiralık Aşk	17 May 2016; 18 May 2016; 19 May 2016, Istanbul
Hayat Şarkısı	8 June 2016, Istanbul
Vatanım Sensin	4 November 2016, Istanbul
Cesur Güzel	6 November 2016, Istanbul
Kösem	22 May 2016; 5 November 2016, Istanbul
Ölene Kadar	6 February 2017; 14 March 2017; 9 April 2017, Istanbul

Siyah Beyaz Aşk	3 May 2018; 22 May 2018, Istanbul
Ufak Tefek Cinayetler	29 November 2018, Istanbul
Çukur	28 February 2019, Istanbul
Istanbullu Gelin	6 March 2019; 29 May 2019, Istanbul
Bir Zamanlar Çukurova	8 November 2019, Adana
Kuruluş-Osman	16 January 2020, Istanbul

APPENDIX 4

Conferences Organized for Global Markets

With Istanbul Chamber of Commerce, Film Industry Coordination Committee

MIPCOM, 'Turkey: Home of Content', Country of Honor Conferences, Cannes, 5–8 October 2015.

ATF, Asia TV Forum and Market, 'The Charm of Turkish Content: A Road from Writing to Distribution', Panel at Asia TV Forum and Market, Singapore, 8 December 2016.

MIPCOM, 'A New Era for Content and Partnership in Turkey', Panel at MIPCOM Cannes, 17 October 2017.

DISCOP, 'The Success of Turkish Content: Reaching out to Global Markets', Panel at DISCOP–Johannesburg, 15 November 2018.

APPENDIX 5

Media Markets and Events Attended

2012

Antalya Television Awards, Antalya, 21 April 2012

Akdeniz University, *Leyla and Mecnun* Team Panel, Antalya, 21 April 2012

Altın Kelebek Awards Ceremony, Istanbul, 11 June 2012

2013

Berlinale, Berlin Film Festival, Berlin, 9 February 2013

Kadir Has University, Psikeart Meeting, Istanbul, 30 March 2013

MIPTV 2013, Cannes, 8–11 April 2013

ITVF 2013–Istanbul TV Forum and Fair, Istanbul, 20–22 June 2013

2014

DISCOP-Istanbul 2014, Istanbul, 4–6 March 2014

MIPTV 2014, Cannes, 7–10 April 2014

Kurt Seyit ve Şura, Launching Gala, Cannes, 7 April 2014

ITVF 2014–Istanbul TV Forum and Fair, Istanbul, 12–14 June 2014

MIPCOM 2014, Cannes, 13–16 October 2014

2015

DISCOP–Istanbul 2015, Istanbul, 24–26 February 2015

MIPTV 2015, Cannes, 13–16 April 2015

MIPTV 2015, Médaille d'Or Award Ceremony, Cannes, 15 April 2015

MIPCOM 2015 Preparation Meeting, Boğaziçi University, Istanbul, 17 September 2015 (with the participation of Timur Savcı, Selin Arat, Halit Ergenç, Tuba Büyüküstün and Pelin Diştaş)

MIPCOM 2015, Cannes, 5–8 October 2015

Kösem, Launching Gala, Cannes, 7 October 2015

Altın Kelebek Awards Ceremony, Istanbul, 29 November 2015

2016

MIPTV 2016, Cannes, 4–7 April 2016

MIPCOM 2016, Cannes, 17–20 October 2016

International Bosphorus Film Festival, Istanbul, 10–18 November 2016

Sumru Yavrucuk Acting Workshop, International Bosphorus Film Festival, Istanbul, 11 November 2016

ATF, Asia TV Forum and Market 2016, Singapore, 6–9 December 2016

2017

İçerde Final Gala Event, Istanbul, 19 June 2017

Blu TV *7Yüz* Gala Event, Istanbul, 22 September 2017

MIPCOM 2017, Cannes, 16–19 October 2017

MIPCOM Women in Global Entertainment Power Lunch with Catherine Zeta-Jones, Cannes, 16 October 2017

2018

Çukur Final Gala Event, Istanbul, 11 June 2018

DISCOP–Johannesburg 2018, Johannesburg, 14–16 November 2018

Altın Kelebek Awards Ceremony, Istanbul, 9 December 2018

2019

Çukur Final Gala Event, Istanbul, 26 May 2019

Blu TV *Behzat Ç* Gala Event, Istanbul, 24 July 2019

MIPCOM 2019, Cannes, 14–18 October 2019

2020

Netflix Turkey—Content Roadshow Panel, Istanbul, 10 March 2020

Prensario International 'VS Showcase: Turkish Content Arises' Panel, Online, 17 September 2020

MIPCOM 2020, Cannes, 12–15 October 2020

International Bosphorus Film Festival 'The Transformation in Television and Digital Content' Panel, Istanbul, 25 October 2020

2021

'The Institutionalization of the Dizi Industry in Turkey: From Past Experiences to New Directions', Film and Dizi Production and Export in the Pandemic Process, UNESCO-Turkey National Commission, Online, 11 May 2021

'*Üç Kuruş*: Confronting the Racist Within Us', *Brand Week Istanbul*, Zorlu Center, Istanbul, 10 November 2021

APPENDIX 6

Attended and Organized Academic Meetings on Media

2012

'The World of Our *Dizi*s: The Rise of Turkish Television Drama as a New Genre', Middle East and Middle Eastern Americans Center at the Graduate Center of the City University of New York, New York, 6 December 2012

2014

'Dizi as a Genre: A Historical Review in Comparative Perspective", Turkish Television Series (diziler): Production, Representations and Reception in the Mediterranean, Paris, 17–18 October 2014

2015

'Television Industry in Turkey: A Historical Ethnographic Approach', 12th International SIEF Congress, Zagreb, 21–25 June 2015

'MIPTV as Wonderland: The Aesthetics of a Vibrant Market', American Folklore Society, Long Beach, California, 13–18 October 2015

'Revisiting "Content": A Historical and Comparative Look at Screenwriting' (Organizer), Boğaziçi University, Istanbul, 26–28 November 2015

2016

'Historical Drama in Turkish Television', *Glimpses of the Past in the Cultural Expressions of Greece and Turkey,* Lectures in Gennadius Library, Athens, 20 September 2016

'Historical Research on Television Content', Boğaziçi University, Istanbul, 4–7 November 2016

'A Roundtable on Chinese Media' (Organizer), Boğaziçi University, Istanbul, 2 December 2016

2017

'On Politics of Political Expressivity in Turkish Television Series', Society for Cinema and Media Studies Conference, Chicago, 22–26 March 2017

2018

'Disguised Impact of the Distribution Processes in Turkish Television: Domestic Strategies for the Global Dizi', The Society for Cinema and Media Studies Annual Meeting, Toronto, 14–18 March 2018

'Historical journey of the *dizi* genre in Turkey', A Roundtable on the Historical Development and Reception of Television Genres (Organizer), Boğaziçi University, Cultural Heritage Museum, Istanbul, 15 May 2018

'Kore Dalgası ve Türk İçerikleri: Televizyon Dizileri Arası Diyaloglar' (Korean Wave and Turkish Content: Dialogues between Television Dramas), Uluslararası İpek Yolu Sempozyumu, Türkiye ile Kore Arasında Uygarlıkların Etkileşimi (International Silk Road Symposium, Civilizations' Interaction between Turkey and Korea), Istanbul, 2–3 July 2018

'Remembering Political Humor in Turkey: An Oral History of Television Genres', Oral History Association Annual Meeting, Montreal, 10–14 October 2018

'Turkish Television Dramas: An Historical Reappraisal', Ohio State University, Columbus, 5 November 2018

2019

'The Historical Rise of the *Dizi* Genre: Memory and Politics of Television in Turkey', ARTES Seminar, Amsterdam School for Regional, Transnational and European Studies, University of Amsterdam, Amsterdam, 5 April 2019

2020

'The Emergence of Turkish Content: Situating the Dizi in Global Markets', *The World Is Watching 'Musalsalat'* Exhibition Preliminary Meeting, Media Majlis at Northwestern University, Doha, 19–22 January 2020

2021

'Consolidating the Dizi Industry: The Changing Content and Social Players', *The Turks Are Coming! The Popular Outreach of Turkish TV Series* Conference, Lorentz Center, Leiden University, Leiden, 6–10 December 2021

2022

'Domestic Priorities and Global Impacts: Turkish Television Explained', Roundtable Discussion on Turkish TV Series at Ottoman and Turkish Studies Department, New York University, New York, 28 January 2022

Les écrans turcophones: l'industrialisation de l'audiovisuel (Turkish-Speaking Screens: The Industrialization of the Audiovisual Sector) Conference (Moderator), Galatasaray University, Istanbul, 23–24 June 2022

Works Cited

Unless otherwise mentioned, all weblinks last accessed on 15 June 2022.

ABANOZ, Enes. 2012. 'Using Twitter's Hashtag in Television Series to Create a Social Capital: Season Finale Episodes of Turkish Television Series'. *AJIT-e: Bilişim Teknolojileri Online Dergisi* 3(8): 75–85.

ABRAMOVICH, Paulina. 2014. 'Turkish Soaps Invade Latin America, Land of "Telenovela"'. *Middle East Eye*, 23 December. Available at https://bit.ly/2Jn7FWn

ABRAMS, Ally. 2018. 'The Drama behind the Scenes of Your Favorite TV shows'. *Kiwireport*, 9 July. Available at https://bit.ly/3c7Xn8O

ABU-LUGHOD, Lila. 2005. *Dramas of Nationhood: The Politics of Television in Egypt.* Chicago: University of Chicago Press.

ACEMİ, Meriç. 2015. Interview by the author, 22 November and 31 January.

ACEMİ, Meriç. 2016. Interview by the author, 5 June.

ACHILLI, Giulia. 2016. 'Turkish Dramas Conquer the World'. *Middle East Eye*, 1 February. Available at https://bit.ly/2WQK605

———. 2018. 'Turkish Drama is Expanding around the World. How?' *Prensario Internacional*, 16 May. Available at https://bit.ly/2JrS4Vu

ACOSTA-ALZURU, Carolina. 2017. 'Telenovelas: A Looking Glass into Media, Culture and Society'. Museum Lectures, Boğaziçi University, Istanbul, 27 July.

ACOSTA-ALZURU, Carolina. 2018. 'Ratings or International Sales? Local and Global Market Tensions for Telenovela and Turkish Dizi Producers'. SCMS Annual Meeting, Toronto, 14–18 March.

———. 2020. 'Türk Dizileri Duygularından Utanmayan Bir Kültürü Yansıtıyor'. Interview by Zafer Yılmaz. *Sineblog*, 31 March. Available at https://bit.ly/3g7vhwt

ADORNO, Theodor W. 1991. *The Culture Industry: Selected Essays on Mass Culture.* New York: Routledge.

———, and Max Horkheimer. 1972. *Dialectic of Enlightenment* (Gunzelin Schmid Noerr ed.; Edmund Jephcott trans.). Stanford, CA: Stanford University Press.

AHISKA, Meltem. 2010. *Occidentalism in Turkey: Questions of Modernity and National Identity in Turkish Radio Broadcasting.* London: Tauris Academic Studies.

AHMAD, Feroz. 1977. *The Turkish Experiment in Democracy, 1950–1975*. Boulder, CO: Westview.

AKALAY, Birce. 2018. 'Tiyatro Hiç Ayrılmak İstemediğim Oyun Bahçem'. Interview by Bade Çakar. *Şamdan Plus*, 27 December. Available at https://bit.ly/2WOE66e

AKAR, Müge. 2020. Interview by the author, 6 February.

AKBABA, Ozan. 2019. 'Eşkıya Dünyaya Hükümdar Olmaz'ın İlyas'ı Bir Zamanlar Aşçı Yamağıymış! EDHO'nun Ağır Abisinin Meşhur Olma Hikayesi'. *Yeni Asır*, 27 February. Available at https://bit.ly/3cox5Q6

AKDEDE, Sacit Hadi, and Şansel Özpınar. 2016. 'Political Economy of Turkish State Theatres and Cultural Development' in Halil İbrahim Aydın, Bryan Christiansen and Elif Akgün (eds), *Economic Development: Social and Political Interactions*. London and Istanbul: IJOPEC, pp. 129–38.

AKDEMİR, Okan. 2019. Interview by the author, 28 February.

AKGÜL, Birol, and Ebrar Feyza Kılıç. 2019. 'Gazete İşletmelerindeki El Değiştirmelerin Ekonomi Haberlerine Etkisi: Hürriyet Örneği' in *Online Proceedings of the 6th Yıldız International Social Sciences Congress, 12–13 December 2019*. Istanbul: YTÜ Sosyal Bilimler Enstitüsü, pp. 88–94. Available at https://bit.ly/3xYT5x8

AKIN, Rojin Canan, and Funda Danışman. 2011. *Bildiğin Gibi Değil-90'larda Güneydoğu'da Çocuk Olmak*. Istanbul: Metis Yayınları.

AKINERDEM, Feyza. 2005. 'Between Desire and Truth: The Narrative Resolution of Modern–Traditional Dichotomy in Asmalı Konak'. MA thesis, Boğaziçi University, Istanbul.

———. 2012. 'Yerli Dizi Anlatıları ve İzleyici Katılımı: Uçurum Dizisini Ekşisözlük ve Twitter'la Birlikte İzlemek'. *Folklor/Edebiyat* 72: 77–90.

———. 2015. 'Marriage Safe and Sound: Subjectivity, Embodiment and Movement in the Production Space of Television in Turkey'. PhD dissertation, City University of London.

———, and Nükhet Sirman. 2017. 'Melodram ve Oyun: Tehlikeli Oyunlar ve Poyraz Karayel'de Bir Temsiliyet Rejimi Sorunsalı'. *Monograf* 7: 212–45.

———, and Nükhet Sirman. 2019. 'Kadın Cinayetlerinin Sorumlusu Diziler midir?' *Reçel*, 29 August. Available at https://bit.ly/2MVvwy3

AKMANSOY, Arzu. 2014. Interview by the author, 12 May.

AKSAK, Burak. 2015. Talk given at Mithat Alam Film Merkezi, Istanbul, 11 March.

AKŞİT, Bahattin. 1998. 'İç göçlerin Nesnel ve Öznel Toplumsal Tarihi Üzerine Gözlemler: Köy tarafından Bir Bakış' in İbrahim Sirkeci (ed.), *Türkiye'de İçgöç*. Istanbul: Tarih Vakfı Yayınları.

AKSOY, Asu. 2000. 'Implications of Transnational Turkish Television for the European Cultural Space' in J. Behnisch Becker (ed.), *Zwischen Ausgrenzung und Integration. Türkische Medienkultur in Deutschland*. n.p.: Rehburg-Loccum, pp. 63–85.

——, and Kevin Robins. 1997. 'Peripheral Vision: Cultural Industries and Cultural Identities in Turkey'. *Environment and Planning A* 29: 1937–52.

——, and Kevin Robins. 2000. 'Thinking across Spaces: Transnational Television from Turkey'. *European Journal of Cultural Studies* 3(3): 343–65.

AKSOY, Erol. 2014. 'Kurtlar Vadisi-Destan İlişkisi Üzerine'. *Electronic Turkish Studies* 9(6): 1308–2140.

AKSOY, Metin (ed.). 2002. *Tek Başına Orkestra: Mahmut Tali Öngören*. Ankara: Türkiye İnsan Hakları Vakfı Yayınları.

AKSOY, Temel. 2013. 'Türk usulü şirket kültürü'. Kigem.com, 30 January. Available at https://bit.ly/2XzOP6q

AKTER, Turgut A. 2014. *Genel Kaynak Kitabı: Devlet Tiyatroları Tarihi (1936–1991) Araştırmacılar El Kitabı*. Mitos Boyut Yayınları.

AKTÜRK, Ali. 2011. Interview by the author, 16 November.

——. 2019. Interview by the author, 25 April.

AKYÜREK, Engin. 2012. Interview by the author, 29 March.

——. 2014. 'İstanbul Geleni Bırakmıyor Beni de Bırakmadı'. Interview by Sonat Bahar. *Sabah*, 31 August. Available at https://bit.ly/2WSIm4E

——. 2018. 'Tuba da Beren de İşinde iyi'. *Hürriyet Kelebek*, 17 March. Available at https://bit.ly/3cqfYh4

AL SAIED, Najat. 2015. 'Walid al-Ibrahim: Modernizing Mogul of MBC' in Donatella Della Ratta, Naomi Sakr and Jakob Skovgaard-Petersen (eds), *Arab Media Moguls*. London: I. B. Tauris, pp. 97–112.

ALABORA, Derya. 2012. Interview by the author, 10 September.

ALABORA, Memet Ali. 2011. Interview by the author, 22 December.

ALANKUŞ, Sevda, and Eylem Yanardağoğlu. 2016. 'Vacillation in Turkey's Popular Global TV Exports: Toward a More Complex Understanding of Distribution'. *International Journal of Communication* 10: 3615–31.

ALEXANDER, Catherine. 2002. *Personal States: Making Connections between People and Bureaucracy in Turkey*. Oxford: Oxford University Press.

ALGAN, Ece. 2003. 'Privatization of Radio and Media Hegemony in Turkey' in Lee Artz and Yahya R. Kamalipour (eds), *The Globalization of Corporate Hegemony*. New York: State University of New York Press, pp. 169–92.

ALGAN, Ece. 2017. 'On the Value of Longitudinal Media Ethnography and a Response to John Postill'. *Moment, Journal of Cultural Studies* 4(1): 44–51.

ALGAN, Ece. 2019. 'The Transnationalization of Turkey's Television Industry' in Shawn Shimpach (ed.), *The Routledge Companion to Global Television*. London: Routledge, pp. 445–57.

ALLEN-ROBERTSON, James. 2013. *Digital Culture Industry: A History of Digital Distribution*. London: Palgrave Macmillan.

ALVARADO, Manuel. 1996. 'Selling Television' in Albert Moran (ed.), *Film Policy: International, National and Regional Perspectives*. London: Routledge, pp. 62–71.

ALVAREZ, Maria D. 2010. 'Marketing of Turkey as a Tourism Destination'. *Anatolia* 21(1): 123–38.

AMERICAN FOLKLORE SOCIETY. 2019. 'New Directions in Folklore Section'. Available at https://bit.ly/3dFWA0v

AND, Metin. 1973. *Elli Yılın Türk Tiyatrosu*. Istanbul: Türkiye İş Bankası Kültür Yayınları.

——. 1983a. *Cumhuriyet Dönemi Türk Tiyatrosu*. Ankara: Türkiye İş Bankası Kültür Yayınları.

——. 1983b. *Türk Tiyatrosunun Evreleri*. Ankara: Turhan Kitabevi.

ARCHER, Anne. 2017. 'Showrunners Talk about Their Jobs'. *Manchester Journal*, 17 October. Available at https://bit.ly/3Qg9tBD

ARDA, Özlem, Pınar Aslan and Constanza Mujica (eds). 2021. *Transnationalization of Turkish Television Series*. Istanbul: Istanbul University Press.

ARI, Bilal. 2008. 'Gırgır ve Leman Dergileri Örneğinden 1980 Sonrası Mizah Basını ve Muhalefet Anlayışı'. MA thesis, Marmara University, Istanbul.

ARICI, Nehir. 2019. Interview by the author, 28 February.

ARIK, Bilal. 2006. 'Kemal Sunal, Levent Kırca ve Cem Yılmaz'ın Mizahına Teorik Bir Bakış'. *İstanbul Üniversitesi İletişim Fakültesi Dergisi* 14: 111–29.

ARIKAN-SALTIK, Işıl, Yeşim Coşar and Metin Kozak. 2010. 'Televizyon Dizilerinin Destinasyon Pazarlaması Açısından Olası Sonuçları'. *Anatolia: Turizm Araştırmaları Dergisi* 21(1): 41–50.

ARIKAN, Mustafa. 2015. 'İnkılaplar Devrinde Bir Millî Mesele: Beynelmilel Güzellik Müsabakası'. *Journal of International Social Research* 8(41): 360–70.

ARSLAN, Savaş. 2011. *Cinema in Turkey: A New Critical History*. Oxford: Oxford University Press.

ARSLAN, Sinem. 2015. 'Tüketim Toplumu ve Televizyon Dizileri: Medcezir Dizisi İncelemesi'. MA thesis, Istanbul Ticaret University.

ARSLAN, Zehra, and Gülşah Kurt Güvelioğlu. 2013. *Türkiye'de Devlet Tiyatrosu'nu Yaşatmak*. Istanbul: Sahhaflar Kitap Sarayı.

ARUS, Haluk. 2014. Interview by the author, 26 April.

ARYAY, Barış. 2019. 'Üyelerimize Sorduk'. *Vizyon*. Available at https://bit.ly/3oef3HV

ASENA, Duygu. 1994. 'Senin Rating'in Kaç'. *Milliyet*, 14 May, p. 18.

ASH, Frank. 2013. Talk given at ITVF Storytelling Panel, 20 June.

ASLAN, Pınar. 2018. 'Bir Uluslararası Halkla İlişkiler Stratejisi Olarak Kültür ve Yaratıcı Endüstri Ürünleri: Latin Amerika Pazarında Türk Dizileri Üzerine Bir Araştırma'. PhD dissertation, Istanbul University.

——. 2020. 'Digital Fandom Overseas: How Do Turkish Television Fans in Latin America Do It All?' in Robert Andrew Dunn (ed.), *Multidisciplinary Perspectives on Media Fandom*. Hershey, PA: IGI Global, pp. 118–31.

ATAŞ, Aytekin. 2019. 'Müziğin Filmlerdeki Önemi–2'. *Vizyon*, October. Available at https://bit.ly/3zl5nBC

ATAY, Ali. 2012. Panel discussion with the *Leyla ile Mecnun* team. Akdeniz University, Antalya, 21 April.

ATV. 2019. 'Bir Zamanlar Çukurova', 16 May. Available at https://bit.ly/2V1zeLq

AVKIRAN, Mustafa. 2012. Interview by the author, 11 September.

AVKIRAN, Övül. 2012. Interview by the author, 11 September.

AVRUPA. 2020. 'Tutunamayanlar Çevrimiçi Ekrana Gelecek, Robot Kameralarla Çekildi'. *Avrupa*, 18 April. Available at https://bit.ly/2zOjK5D

AVŞAR, Şükrü. 2015. Talk given at Mithat Alam Film Merkezi, Istanbul, 14 October.

AYATA, Sencer. 1988. 'Statü Yarışması ve Salon Kullanımı'. *Toplum ve Bilim* 42: 5–25.

AYÇA, Engin. 1994. 'Türk Sinemasının Periyodizasyonu: Engin Ayça ile Söyleşi'. *Görüntü* 2: 43–52.

AYCAN, Zeynep. 2006. 'Paternalism: Towards Conceptual Refinement and Operationalization' in K. S. Yang, K. K. Hwang and U. Kim (eds), *Indigenous and Cultural Psychology: Understanding People in Context*. New York: Springer, pp. 445–66.

——. 2015. 'Paternalistic Leadership' in C. Cooper (ed.), *Wiley Encyclopedia of Management*. Boston, MA: Wiley and Sons, n.p.

AYDEMİR, Selçuk. 2014. Interview by the author, 30 June.

AYDOĞAN, Filiz. 2005. 'New York'tan Nev Şehir'e Asmalı Konak'. *Ege Üniversitesi İletişim Fakültesi Yeni Düşünceler Hakemli E-Dergisi* 1: 173–83.

AYDOS, Serpil. 2013. 'Muhafazakâr Milliyetçi Muhayyilede Kanuni: Muhteşem Yüzyıl'a Yönelik Tepkilere Dair Bir Okuma'. *History Studies* 5(1): 1–16.

AYERİ, Burhan. 2011. 'Kuzey Güney Dizisi Çalıntı mı?' *Akşam*, 9 September. Available at https://bit.ly/2UybpcM

AYKUT, Cem. 2016. 'Bertolt Brecht Estetiği ve Türk Tiyatrosuna Etkileri'. MA thesis, Yakın Doğu University, Nicosia.

AZARI, Aryana. 2019. 'The Real-Life Places behind 6 of the BBC's Best Recent TV Shows'. *Matador Network*, 14 November. Available at https://bit.ly/39uXidq

AZIZ, Rutkay. 2016. Talk given at Mithat Alam Film Merkezi, Istanbul, 9 November.

BAEZA, Cecilia. 2014. 'Palestinians in Latin America: Between Assimilation and Long-Distance Nationalism'. *Journal of Palestine Studies* 43(2): 59–72.

BAKHTIN, Mikhail M. 1981. *The Dialogic Imagination: Four Essays* (Michael Holquist ed.; Caryl Emerson and Michael Holquist trans). Austin: University of Texas Press.

BAL, Enes. 2007. 'Televizyon Haberciliğinde Magazinleşme Olgusu: TRT, NTV ve Show TV Örneği'. MA thesis, Selçuk University Social Sciences Institute, Konya.

BALCI, Murat. 2019. 'Interrelations between Family, Divorce and Crime in the Context of Criminology'. *Dokuz Eylül Üniversitesi Hukuk Fakultesi Dergisi* 21: 3197.

BARANSEL, Nil. 2003. *Eli Acıman: Sevmediği Sözcük Reklam, Aşık Olduğu Mesleği Reklamcılık*. Istanbul: Doğan Kitapçılık.

BARTESAGHI, Mariaelena, and Chaim Noy. 2015. 'Interdiscursivity' in K. Tracy (ed.), C. Ilie and T. Sandel (assoc. eds), *The International Encyclopedia of Language and Social Interaction*. Boston, MA: John Wiley, pp. 1–7.

BARTON, Robert. 2011. *Acting Reframes: Using NLP to Make Better Decisions In and Out of the Theatre*. London: Routledge.

BARUH, Yakup. 1968. 'Agency Structure in Advertising Industry in Turkey'. MA thesis, Robert College Graduate School, Istanbul.

BAŞAR, Deniz. 2014. 'Performative Publicness: Alternative Theater in Turkey after 2000s'. MA thesis, Boğaziçi University, Istanbul.

BAŞARAN, Altan, and Meryem Kurtulmuş. 2016. 'Türk Film Endüstrisinde Çalışma İlişkileri ve Sendikalaşma'. *Çalışma ve Toplum: Ekonomi ve Hukuk Dergisi* 1: 199–228.

BAŞARIR, Selim. 2013. Interview by the author, 6 March.

BAŞCI, Pelin. 2017. 'Television Searches Deeper and Farther: Remember, My Darling' in Pelin Başçı (ed.), *Social Trauma and Telecinematic Memory*. London: Palgrave Macmillan, pp. 203–40.

BAŞLAMIŞ, Cenk. 2010. 'Ruslar Tayfur'u unutmadı'. *Milliyet*, 17 January. Available at https://bit.ly/3bI7lNQ

BAŞTÜRK AKÇA, Emel, and Seda Ergül. 2014. 'Televizyon Dizilerinde Erkeklik Temsili: Kuzey Güney Dizisinde Hegemonik Erkeklik ve Farklı Erkekliklerin Mücadelesi'. *Global Media Journal: TR Edition* 4(8): 13–39.

BATEMAN, John. 2014. 'Genre in the Age of Multimodality: Some Conceptual Refinements for Practical Analysis' in Paola Evangelisti-Allori, Vijay K. Bhatia and John A. Bateman (eds), *Evolution in Genres: Emergence, Variation, Multimodality*. Frankfurt: Peter Lang.

BAUMAN, Richard. 1977. *Verbal Art as Performance*. Long Grove, IL: Waveland Press.

———. 1986. *Story, Performance, and Event: Contextual Studies of Oral Narrative*. Cambridge: Cambridge University Press.

———. 1989. 'American Folklore Studies and Social Transformation: A Performance-Centered Perspective'. *Text and Performance Quarterly* 9(3): 175–84.

——— (ed.). 1992. *Folklore, Cultural Performances and Popular Entertainments: A Communications-Centered Handbook*. New York: Oxford University Press.

———. 1993. *Folklore and Culture on the Texas–Mexican Border*. Austin: University of Texas Press.

—. 2004. *A World of Others' Words: Cross-Cultural Perspectives on Intertextuality.* Malden, MA: Wiley-Blackwell.

—, and Charles L. Briggs. 1990. 'Poetics and Performance as Critical Perspectives on Language and Social Life'. *Annual Review of Anthropology* 19: 59–88.

—, and Charles L. Briggs. 2003. *Voices of Modernity: Language Ideologies and the Politics of Inequality.* Cambridge: Cambridge University Press.

—, and Joel Sherzer (eds). 1974. *Explorations in the Ethnography of Speaking.* Cambridge: Cambridge University Press.

BAYAR, Armoni. 2019. 'Digital Media Consumption of Children in Television Series: Çocuklar Duymasın with Conversation Analysis' in Gülşah Sari (ed.), *Handbook of Research on Children's Consumption of Digital Media.* Hershey, PA: IGI Global, pp. 72–88.

BAYHAN, Faruk. 2013. *İkonoskop: Televizyon Dünyası ve Sevgili Dostlarım.* Istanbul: Doğan Kitap.

—. 2017. Interview by the author, 14 February.

BAYRAKDAR, Deniz. 2016. 'Türkiye'de İletişim Fakülteleri, Sinema-TV Eğitimi: Başlangıcından Bugüne Bakış ve Gelecek Önerileri'. 'The Charm of Turkish Content: A Road from Writing to Distribution', Asia TV Forum and Market Panel, Singapore, 8 December.

BAYRAKTAROĞLU, Ali M., and Ufuk Uğur. 2011. 'Televizyon Haberciliğinde Magazin-leşme Olgusu'. *Art-e Sanat Dergisi* 4(7): 1–47.

BBC. 2005. 'Rome—This Autumn on BBC TWO: Authentic Costumes and Props Add to the Realism of Rome', 26 August. Available at https://bbc.in/3Hgkyi6

BEHLİL, Melis. 2010. 'Close Encounters: Contemporary Turkish Television and Cinema'. *Wide Screen* 2(2). Available at https://bit.ly/3RPrKXp

BEKTAŞ, Erkan. 2012. Interview by the author, 23 March.

BELGE, Murat. 2009. 'Nationalism, Democracy and the Left in Turkey'. *Journal of Inter-cultural Studies* 30(1): 7–20.

BELL, David Christopher. 2013. '8 Honest Behind-the-Scenes Documentaries That Show Both Sides of Movie Making'. *Film School Rejects*, 17 January. Available at https://bit.ly/2UXrfPq

BEN-AMOS, Dan. 1972. 'Toward a Definition of Folklore in Context' in Americo Paredes and Richard Bauman (eds), *Towards New Perspectives in Folklore.* Austin: University of Texas Press, pp. 3–15.

BENJAMIN, Walter. 1969[1935]. 'The Work of Art in the Age of Mechanical Reproduction' in Hannah Arendt (ed.), *Illuminations.* New York: Schocken Books, pp. 217–52.

—. 1999[1934]. 'The Author as Producer' in *Walter Benjamin: Selected Writings, Volume 2, 1927–1934.* Cambridge, MA: Harvard University Press, pp. 768–82.

BERG, Miriam. 2017. 'The Importance of Cultural Proximity in the Success of Turkish Dramas in Qatar'. *International Journal of Communication* 11: 3415–30.

——. 2020. 'Cultural Proximity or Cultural Distance? Selecting Media Content among Turkish Diasporic Audiences in Germany'. *Diaspora* 20(3): 354–71.

BERKENKOTTER, Carol, and Thomas N. Huckin. 1994. *Genre Knowledge in Disciplinary Communication: Cognition/Culture/Power*. London: Routledge.

BERNHART, Walter, and David Francis Urrows (eds). 2019. *Music, Narrative and the Moving Image: Varieties of Plurimedial Interrelations*. Boston, MA: Brill.

BETANCOURT, Manuel. 2018. 'Turkish Novela "Madre" Is a Huge Hit in Chile'. *Remezcla* (7 August). Available at https://bit.ly/2UuF5sz

BEYAZPERDE. 1989. 'Latin Amerikan TV Dizileri'. *Beyazperde* Special Issue 2.

BHATIA, Vijay K. 1993. *Analysing Genre Language Use in Professional Settings*. London: Longman.

——. 2017. *Critical Genre Analysis: Investigating Interdiscursive Performance in Professional Practice*. London: Routledge.

BHUTTO, Fatima. 2019a. 'How Turkish TV Is Taking over the World'. *Guardian*, 13 March. Available at https://bit.ly/3e4soM8

——. 2019b. *New Kings of the World: Dispatches from Bollywood, Dizi, and K-Pop*. Columbia Global Reports.

BIANCOROSSO, Giorgio. 2016. *Situated Listening: The Sound of Absorption in Classical Cinema*. Oxford: Oxford University Press.

BİLECEN, Başak. 2019. '"Altın Günü": Migrant Women's Social Protection Networks'. *Comparative Migration Studies* 7(1): 1–17.

BİLGİN-KILIÇ, Gökçe. 2012. Interview by the author, 10 May.

BİLGİN, Belçim. 2014. 'Yakında Oscar alırız'. Interview by Şenay Aydemir. *T24*, 23 March. Available at https://bit.ly/3csnWWH

BİLGİN, İpek. 2014. Interview by the author, 20 February.

BİLGİNER, Haluk. 2013. Talk given at Mithat Alam Film Merkezi, Istanbul, 20 May.

BİLİS, Ali. 2013. 'Popüler Televizyon Dizilerinden Muhteşem Yüzyıl Dizisi Örneğinde Tarihin Yapısökümü'. *İstanbul Üniversitesi İletişim Fakültesi Dergisi*, 45(December): 19–38.

BILL, Tony. 2009. *Movie Speak: How to Talk Like You Belong on a Film Set*. New York: Workman Publishing.

BİNARK, Ferruh Mutlu. 1992. 'Televizyon Gündüz Seriyalleri ve Etkin Kadın İzler-Küme'. MA thesis, Ankara University.

——. 1997. *Ben-Bir Kadın Özne-ve Benim Sabun Köpüklerim ya da Pembe Dizilerim*. Ankara: Ankara Üniversitesi Yayınları.

BİNATLI, Ömer Cüneyt. 2005. '5224 Sayılı Kanuna Göre Sinema Filmlerine Devlet Desteği'. *İstanbul Ticaret Üniversitesi Sosyal Bilimler Dergisi* 4(7): 133–37.

BİNGÖL, Ulaş. 2017. 'Peyami Safa'nın Romanlarında Doğu-Batı Meselesi Bağlamında Değerler Çatışması'. *İdil* 6(31): 891–921.

BİR, Ali Atıf, and Kerem Ünüvar. 2000. *Bir Reklam Ajansının Öyküsü*. Istanbul: Cen Ajans Grey.

BİRSEL, Gülse, Hasibe Eren and Cengiz Bozkurt. 2020. 'Interview-Turkey: Stay-at-home Actors Shoot Episode of TV Show'. Interview by Salih Şeref and Hilal Uştuk. *Anadolu Ajansı*, 30 March. Available at https://bit.ly/3dmDUkW

BOLUS, Michael Peter. 2019. *Aesthetics and the Cinematic Narrative: An Introduction*. London: Anthem Press.

BORA, Tanıl, and Aksu Bora. 2010. 'Kurtlar Vadisi ve Erkeklik Krizi: "Neden İskender" i Öldürmüyoruz Usta'. *Birikim* (August–September): 28–37.

BORALIOĞLU, Gaye. 2012. Interview by the author, 23 March.

BORATAV, Korkut. 2018. *Türkiye İktisat Tarihi 1908–2015*. Istanbul: İmge Kitabevi Yayınları.

BOSPHORUS FILM LAB. 2020. 'TV ve Dijitalde İçeriğin Döngüsü'. *YouTube*, 25 October. Available at www.youtube.com/watch?v=GM_-nulW4YE

BOUNBAKI. 2022. *Boğaziçi Ayakta*. İstanbul: Ayhan Matbaası.

BOURDIEU, Pierre. 1983. 'The Field of Cultural Production, or, the Economic World Reversed'. *Poetics* 12: 311–56.

———. 1984. *Distinction: A Social Critique of the Judgement of Taste*. Cambridge, MA: Harvard University Press.

BOX OFFICE TÜRKİYE. 2020. 'TESİYAP ve Yapımcılar Derneği, Film ve Dizi Yapım Sürecinde Covid-19 Salgınına Karşı Tedbirlerin Yer Aldığı Bir Kılavuz Yayınladı'. Box Office Turkiye, 19 May. Available at https://bit.ly/2BrR16Z

BRIGGS, Charles L., and Richard Bauman. 1992. 'Genre, Intertextuality, and Social Power'. *Journal of Linguistic Anthropology* 2(2): 131–72.

BROWN, Blain. 2002. *Cinematography: Theory and Practice; Image Making for Cinematographers and Directors*. Waltham, MA: Focal Press.

BUCCIANTI, Alexandra. 2010. 'Dubbed Turkish Soap Operas Conquering the Arab World: Social Liberation or Cultural Alienation?' *Arab Media and Society*, 30 March. Available at https://bit.ly/3frSBop

BUDAK, Leyla. 1993. 'Televizyon Yayınlarında Soap Operalar'. MA thesis, EGE University, Izmir.

BÜKER, Seçil, and Canan Uluyağcı. 1993. *Yeşilçam'da Bir Sultan*. Istanbul: AFA Yayınları.

BULUT, Ergin. 2010. 'Dramın Ardındaki Emek: Dizi Sektöründe Reyting Sistemi, Çalışma Koşulları ve Sendikalaşma Faaliyetleri'. *Galatasaray Üniversitesi İletişim Dergisi* 24: 79–100.

BULUT, Pınar. 2014. Interview by the author, 27 May.

———. 2016. 'Pınar Bulut Deren: Global Bir Başarı Yakalamanın Yolu Lokal İçeriklerden Geçiyor'. *Ranini.tv*, 10 April. Available at https://bit.ly/33JqYSR

BURROUGHS, Benjamin. 2018. 'House of Netflix: Streaming Media and Digital Lore'. *Popular Communication*, 26 February. Available at https://bit.ly/2B4gVhg

BYRNE KATHERINE, Julie, Anne Taddeo and James Leggott. 2018. *Conflicting Masculinities: Men in Television Period Drama*. London: I. B. Tauris.

ÇAKIR, Hamza. 1996. 'Türkiye'de Reklamın Tarihçesi'. *Istanbul Üniversitesi İletişim Fakültesi Dergisi* 3: 251–60.

ÇAKIR, Ruşen. 2013. 'Prof. Şerif Mardin: "Mahalle Baskısı, Ne Demek İstedim?"' *Rusencakir.com*, 29 May. Available at https://bit.ly/2JeMpCd

ÇAKMAK, D. 2012. 'Göç ve Kent Yoksulluğunun Toplumsal Görünümleri: Van Bostaniçi Örneği'. MA thesis, Van Yüzüncü Yıl University, Tuşba.

CALDWELL, John Thornton. 2008. *Production Culture: Industrial Reflexivity and Critical Practice in Film and Television*. Durham, NC: Duke University Press.

CALHOUN, Craig (ed.). 1992. *Habermas and the Public Sphere*. Cambridge, MA: MIT Press.

ÇAM, Aydın, and İlker Yüksel Şanlıer. 2021. 'Adana Sinemalarının Haritalanması: Yeni/Yerel Sinema Tarihi Çalışmalarında Çoklu Yöntemlerin ve Coğrafi Bilgi Sistemlerinin Kullanımı'. *Moment Dergi* 8(1): 289–310.

CAMAROFF, John, and Jean Camaroff. 1992. *Ethnography and the Historical Imagination*. Boulder, CO: Westview Press.

CAMPSALL, Steve. 2002. 'Analyzing Moving Image Texts: "Film Language"'. *Media–GCSE Film Analysis Guide*. Available at https://bit.ly/3yin704

ÇAMUR, Nilüfer Ebru. 2019. Interview by the author, 8 November.

ÇAMUR, Nilüfer. 2014. 'Dönemin Bardağını Çanağını Değil Ruhunu Yansıtmaya Odaklandım'. Ranini.tv, 1 November. Available at https://bit.ly/39oby80

CANKAYA, Özden. 2015. *Bir Kitle İletişim Kurumunun Tarihi: Trt-Özden Cankaya Bir Kitle İletişim Kurumunun Tarihi: TRT, 1927-2000*. Istanbul: İmge Kitabevi Yayınları.

CANPOLAT, Eylem. 2015. 'Heroines of Content' rehearsal meeting with the author, Boğaziçi University, Istanbul, 12 September.

CANTEK, Levent. 2010. 'Yalancı Dünyanın Yalancı Hikayeleri: Gündelik Hayat, TV Dizileri ve Popüler Kültür'. *Birikim* (August–September): 84–9.

CANTOR, Muriel G. 1988. *The Hollywood TV Producer: His Work and His Audience*. New Brunswick, NJ: Transaction Books.

ÇAPOĞLU, Nazan. 2008. 'Home as a Place: The Making of Domestic Space at Yesiltepe Blocks'. MA thesis, Middle East Technical University, Ankara.

ÇARKOĞLU, Ali, and Kemal Kirişçi. 2004. 'The View from Turkey: Perceptions of Greeks and Greek-Turkish Rapprochement by the Turkish Public'. *Turkish Studies* 5(1): 117–53.

CARNEY, Josh. 2016. 'Turkey's TV Business Booming Despite Domestic Woes'. *Variety*, 4 April. Available at https://bit.ly/3O0wuY8

———. 2018. 'Resur(e)recting a spectacular hero: Diriliş Ertuğrul, Necropolitics, and Popular Culture in Turkey'. *Review of Middle East Studies* 52(1): 93–114.

———. 2019. 'ResurReaction: Competing Visions of Turkey's (proto) Ottoman Past in Magnificent Century and Resurrection Ertuğrul'. *Middle East Critique* 28(2): 101–20.

CARNEY, Joshua. 2014. 'Reality (TV) in Wolves' Clothing? Valley of the Wolves'. *Arab Media Report* 4 (The Turkish Touch: Neo-Ottoman Hegemony and Turkish Television in the Middle East) (October): 37–42.

CASEY, Edward. 1997. *The Fate of Place: A Philosophical History*. Berkeley: University of California Press.

ÇATAY, Kerem. 2012. Interview by the author, 8 March.

CATHERINE. 2017. Interview by the author, 17 October.

ÇAVLIN-BOZBEYOĞLU, Alanur, Ece Koyuncu, Filiz Kardam and Altan Sungur. 2010. 'Ailenin Karanlık Yüzü: Türkiye'de Ensest'. *Sosyoloji Araştırmaları Dergisi* 13(1): 1–37.

ÇAYLI-RAHTE, Emek. 2017. 'Medya ve Kültürün Küresel Akışı: Türk Dizilerinin Kosova'da Alımlanması'. *Milli Folklor* 29: 114.

ÇEHRE, Nebahat. 2012. Talk given at Mithat Alam Film Merkezi, Istanbul, 21 March.

ÇEKİRGE, Pınar. 2014. *Başrolde Filiz Akın*. Istanbul: Altın Bilek Yayınları.

CELASUN, Merih, and İsmail Arslan. 2001. *State-Owned Enterprises in the Middle East and North Africa: Privatization, Performance, and Reform*. London: Routledge.

ÇELENK, Sevilay. 2010. 'Aşk-ı Memnu'dan Aşkı Memnu'ya Yerli Dizi Serüvenimiz'. *Birikim* (August–September): 18–27.

ÇELİK RAPPAS, İpek, and Sezen Kayhan. 2018. 'TV Series Production and the Urban Restructuring of Istanbul'. *Television and New Media* 19(1): 3–23.

ÇELİK, Fatma. 2015. 'Özel Televizyonun Babası, Mehmet Turan Akköprülü'. Haberler.com, 27 August. Available at https://bit.ly/2UmgtAR

ÇELİK, Filiz. 2011. 'Modernleşme Serüvenimiz ve Yeşilçam'. *Sanat Dergisi* 17: 31–8.

ÇELİK, Zeynep, and Edhem Eldem (eds). 2015. *Camera Ottomana: Photography and modernity in the Ottoman Empire, 1840–1914*. Istanbul: Koç University Press.

ÇELİKTEMEL-THOMEN, Özde. 2018. 'Regulating Exhibitons at Cinema-Houses in Imperial Istanbul'. *SineCine* 9(1) (Spring): 81–112.

———. 2019. 'Film/Cinema (Ottoman Empire)' in Ute Daniel, Peter Gatrell, Oliver Janz, Heather Jones, Jennifer Keene, Alan Kramer, and Bill Nasson (eds), *Online International Encyclopaedia of the First World War*. Berlin: Freie Universität Berlin.

CEM-ERSOY, Nevra, Marise Ph Born, Eva Derous and Henk T. van der Molen. 2011. 'Antecedents of Organizational Citizenship Behavior among Blue- and White-Collar Workers in Turkey'. *International Journal of Intercultural Relations* 35(3): 356–67.

CEM, İsmail. 2010. *TRT'de 500 Gün: Bir Dönem Türkiye'sinin Hikayesi*. Istanbul: Türkiye İş Bankası Kültür Yayınları.

ÇETİN, İhsan. 2015. 'Defining Recent Femicide in Modern Turkey: Revolt Killing'. *Journal of International Women's Studies* 16(2): 346–60.

ÇEVİK, Senem B. 2014. 'Turkish Soap Opera Diplomacy: A Western Projection by a Muslim Source'. *Exchange: The Journal of Public Diplomacy* 5(1): 78–103.

———. 2019. 'Turkish Historical Television Series: Public Broadcasting of Neo-Ottoman Illusions'. *Southeast European and Black Sea Studies* 19(2): 227–42.

———. 2020. 'The Empire Strikes Back: Propagating AKP's Ottoman Empire Narrative on Turkish Television'. *Middle East Critique* 29(2): 177–97.

CHALABY, Jean. 2016. 'Drama without Drama: The Late Rise of Scripted TV Formats'. *Television and New Media* 17(1): 3–20.

ÇİÇEKOĞLU, Feride. 2010. 'Televizyon Dizilerinde Kadının Var Olma Mücadelesi'. *Birikim* (August–September): 48–57.

ÇIFTÇI, Hasan. 2017. 'Televizyon Haberciliğinde Etiksel Bir Sorun Olarak Magazinleşmenin Topluma Etkisi'. *International Journal of Social Science* 58: 475–87.

ÇIFTÇI, Selcen. 2011. 'Uşak'ta Atlı Cirit Sporu ve Cirit Kültürü'. *Milli Folklor* 12(89): 87–99.

ÇİLİNGİR, Sadi. 2009. 'Oyuncu Eğitmeni Anthony Vincent Bova, Temmuz Ayında Yeniden İstanbul'da'. Sadibey.com, 5 June. Available at https://bit.ly/2LmjdtG

ÇINARLI, Gökhan. 2019. Interview by the author, 28 February.

CIVAN, Celil. 2013. 'Yeşilçam'dan Dizilere Mahalle'. *İstanbul Büyükşehir Belediyesi Dergisi* 16: 50–53.

CIVANTOS, Christina. 2006. *Between Argentines and Arabs: Argentine orientalism, Arab immigrants, and the writing of identity*. New York: State University of New York Press.

CIVANTOS, Christina. 2016. 'The Surprisingly Deep Centuries-Old Ties between the Middle East and Latin America'. *Americas Quarterly*, 5 February. Available at https://bit.ly/3fK7Qca

CLARKE, Stewart. 2017. 'Discop Istanbul Will Be Back for 2018'. *Television Business International*, 10 January. Available at https://bit.ly/2ULxfcJ

CLOUGH, Patricia Ticineto, and Jean Halley Affect (eds). 2007. *The Affective Turn: Theorizing the Social*. Durham, NC: Duke University Press.

CNNTURK. 2012. '"JR'ı Kim Vurdu?" Sorusu 80'lerin En Büyük Esrarıydı', 26 November. Available at https://bit.ly/3fHqstH

COE, Neil M. 2000. 'The View from Out West: Embeddedness, Inter-personal Relations and the Development of an Indigenous Film Industry in Vancouver'. *GeoForum* 31(4): 391–407.

COHEN, Ralph. 1986. 'History and Genre'. *New Literary History* 17(2) (Winter): 203–18.

ÇOLAKOĞLU, Murat. 2013. 'Tanıdık Yoksa Vermem'. Campaign Türkiye. Available at https://bit.ly/3B5Yd5C

COOKE, Mervyn. 2008. *A History of Film Music*. Cambridge: Cambridge University Press.

ÇÖPÜR, Mazlum, et al. 2012. 'İstanbul İli Örnekleminde Çocuk ve Ergen Cinsel İstismarlarının Karakteristik Özellikleri'. *Anadolu Psikiyatri Dergisi* 13(1): 46–50.

COŞKUN, Emel. 2014. 'Türkiye'de Göçmen Kadınlar ve Seks Ticareti'. *Çalışma ve Toplum* 42(3): 185–206.

CUMHURİYET. 2016. 'Diriliş Ertuğrul dizisinde ses getirecek iddia', 6 April. Available at https://bit.ly/35QFmKp

DAĞDEVİREN, Yılmaz. 2013. Interview by the author, 22 March and 3 April.

DAĞKIRAN, Lale. 2016. 'Görümce Filminin Setine Konuk Olduk'. *In Style Home* (December): 203–4.

DAĞTAŞ, Erdal. 2006. *Türkiye'de Magazin Basını: Magazin Eklerinin Sektör ve Metin Analizi*. Ankara: Ütopya Yayınevi.

DAILYMOTION. 2012a. 'Cumhuriyet-1. bölüm (TRT)'. Available at https://bit.ly/2y78qAc

DAILYMOTION. 2012b. 'Engin Akyürek in Memory of Meral Okay'. Available at https://bit.ly/34sKDqI

DANCYGER, Ken. 2001. *Global Scriptwriting*. New York: Routledge.

DAVIS, Richard. 2010. *Complete Guide to Film Scoring: The Art and Business of Writing Music for Movies and TV*. Boston, MA: Berklee Press.

DAVULCU, Ebru. 2015. *Meşrutiyet Dönemi Mizah Basınında Osmanlı Modernleşmesi ve Eleştirel Kodlar*. Ankara: Palet Yayınları.

DAVUTOĞLU, Nesteren. 2002. *Ada'da Zaman: Bir Reklamcının Biriktirdikleri '82–92'*. Istanbul: Epsilon.

DEBORD, Jason. 2020. 'The 13th Annual Original Prop Blog "Year in Review" for 2019 (Personal/Professional Update)'. *Original Prop Blog*, 21 January. Available at https://bit.ly/2xc4JJN

DENİZ, Özcan. 2010. 'Dizideki Gibi İmkânsız Bir Aşk Yaşamadım Ben'. *Sabah*, 23 January. Available at https://bit.ly/35Rdeqd

DERE, Cansu. 2013. Interview by the author, 19 March.

DEREN, Kerem. 2014. Interview by the author, 27 May and 18 June.

DERMANCIOĞLU, Esra. 2012. Interview by the author, 3 October.

———. 2015. 'Bir Daha Evlenmem'. Interview by Kezban Aslan Yılmaz. *Posta*, 21 March. Available at https://bit.ly/2YVVWHc

DERRIDA, Jacques. 1980. 'The Law of Genre'. *Critical Inquiry* 7(1): 55–81.

DEVITT, Amy. 1993. 'Generalizing about Genre: New Conceptions of an Old Concept'. *College Composition and Communication* 44(4): 580.

DEVITT, Amy. 2000. 'Integrating Rhetorical and Literary Theories of Genre'. *College English* 62(6): 696–718.

DEVRAN, Yusuf. 2011. *Siyasal İktidar-TRT İlişkisinin Dünü*. Istanbul: Başlık Yayın Grubu.

DİLBER, Mustafa, İsmail Hakkı Eraslan and Mehmet Nafi Artemel (eds). 2012. *Ekonomik ve Toplumsal Etkileri Açısından Türkiye'de Reklamcılık*. Istanbul: Fatih University.

DIMITROVA, Aseniya. 2020. 'Mayor of Cannes Demands Urgent Support for Business after Coronavirus Outbreak'. TheMayor.EU, 5 March. Available at https://bit.ly/3ueB6SP

DINKJIAN, Ara. 2013. 'Ara Dinkjian Quartet Finding Songs'. Krikor Music CD.

DIŞTAŞ, Pelin. 2014. Interview by the author, 31 March.

DİZİLER.COM. 2020. 'Osman Yağmurdereli-Diziografi'. Available at https://bit.ly/3xiO3wR

DİZİSETİ.TV. 2019. 'Bir Zamanlar Çukurova Aladağ Çiftliği Nerede? Bir Zamanlar Çukurova Dizisi Nerede Çekiliyor?' Available at https://bit.ly/2WXi4zU

DOĞU, Ufuk, and Feyzan Erkip. 2000. 'Spatial Factors Affecting Wayfinding and Orientation: A Case Study in a Shopping Mall'. *Environment and Behavior* 32(6): 731–55.

DOLBY-STAHL, Sandra. 1989. *Literary Folkloristics and the Personal Narrative*. Bloomington: Indiana University Press.

DÖNMEZ-COLIN, Gönül. 2013. *Turkish Cinema: Identity, Distance and Belonging*. London: Reaktion Books.

DÖNMEZ, Servet Can. 2019. 'Semt Bizim Ev Kira: 2000 Sonrası Türk Sinemasında Mahalle, Futbol ve Kentsel Dönüşüm'. Gümüşhane Üniversitesi İletişim Fakültesi Elektronik Dergisi 7: 370–97.

DONNELLY, Kevin J. 2005. *The Spectre of Sound: Music in Film and Television*. London: British Film Institute.

DURGUN, Sezgi. 2019. 'Sokağın Hafızasını Tutmak, Hafızanın Sokaklarında Gezmek Örneği'. *Mecmua* 7: 112–16.

DURMAZ, Bahar, Stephen Platt and Tan Yigitcanlar. 2010. 'Creativity, Culture Tourism and Placemaking: Istanbul and London Film Industries'. *International Journal of Culture, Tourism and Hospitality Research* 4(3): 198–213.

DURMAZ, S. Bahar. 2015. 'Analyzing the Quality of Place: Creative Clusters in Soho and Beyoğlu'. *Journal of Urban Design* 20(1): 93–124.

DURMUŞ, Betül. 2012. Interview by the author, 9 May.

DURSUN, Necla, and Aynur Atmaca Can. 2019. 'Sosyal-Çevre Bağlamında Kentte Gündelik Yaşam Estetiği, Sanatçıların Gözünden Kuzguncuk Semti'. *Kent Akademisi* 12(2): 270–87.

DUYAR, Hülya. 2013. Interview by the author, 15 January.

EBOCH, Douglas, and Ken Aguado. 2018. *The Hollywood Pitching Bible*. Sherman Oaks, CA: ScreenMaster Books.

EDEBİYAT VE SANAT AKADEMİSİ. 2015. 'Fatma Nezihe Araz Hayatı ve Eserleri'. *Edebiyat ve Sanat Akademisi*, 27 April. Available at https://bit.ly/2WtR7nb

EDER, Mine, and Özlem Öz. 2015. 'Neoliberalization of Istanbul's Nightlife: Beer or Champagne?' *International Journal of Urban and Regional Research* 39(2): 284–304.

EFENDİOĞLU, Özge. 2016. Interview by the author, 7 October.

EĞİN, Oray. 1999. 'Televole ve Sonrası: Gerçeği Kaybediyoruz!' *Birikim* 117: 104.

EKİNCİ, Ekrem Buğra. 2018. 'Fratricide in Ottoman Law'. *Belleten* 82(295): 1013–46.

EKŞİ SÖZLÜK. 2007. 'Karayılan', 20 November. Available at https://bit.ly/2UQ5QX1

——. 2008. 'Dizi İzleyen İnsanların Zeka Seviyesi', 10 August. Available at https://bit.ly/37xeQ9x

——. 2012. 'İşler Güçler', 2 October. Available at https://bit.ly/2QZmGll

ELİBOL, Muhittin. 2011. 'Dizi Çekmek için Köyde Toprak Yol Bulamadılar'. *Habertürk*, 15 June. Available at https://bit.ly/2Uv3WMB

——. 2016. Interview by the author, 28 October.

EMRE-ÇETİN, Berfin. 2014. 'The "Politicization" of Turkish Television Dramas'. *International Journal of Communication* 8: 2462–83.

——. 2015. *The Paramilitary Hero on Turkish Television: A Case Study on Valley of the Wolves*. Newcastle upon Tyne: Cambridge Scholars Publishing.

——. 2016. 'Pushing the Limits of the Family on Turkish Television: Lost City, an Alternative Voice?' *European Journal of Communication* 31(6): 694–706.

ERAYDA, Naz. 2011. 'Klasik Tiyatro, Çağdaş Gösteri Sanatları ve Sinema Bir Bütünün Parçaları'. Interview by Koray Sevindi and Abdülgafur Şahin. *Hayalperdesi*, 28 October. Available at https://bit.ly/2WXovTA

ERDEM, Umut. 2021. 'Dünyanın televizyon merkezi İstanbul olacak Kaynak'. *Hürriyet*, 14 December. Available at https://bit.ly/3xpd6wq

ERDEMİR, Filiz. 2009. 'Özel Televizyon Yayıncılığına Geçiş Sürecinde TRT'nin Yazılı Basında Sunumu (1990–2007)'. PhD dissertation, Gazi University, Ankara.

ERDEMİR-GÖZE, Filiz. 2011. 'Başlangıçtan Günümüze TRT'nin Reklam Serüveni'. *Gazi Üniversitesi İletişim Fakültesi İletişim Kuram ve Araştırma Dergisi* 32: 205–26.

ERDENİZ, Gülçin. 2011. 'Lust to Go, Obliged to Stay: The Problem of Internal Displacement in Turkey and the Measures for the Return in the eyes of the IDPs Living in Istanbul and Bursa'. PhD dissertation, Istanbul Bilgi University.

ERDOĞAN, Ayten, et al. 2011. 'Türkiye'nin Dört Farklı Bölgesinde Çocuk ve Ergenlere Cinsel Tacizde Bulunan Kişilerin Karakteristik Özellikleri'. *Anadolu Psikiyatri Dergisi* 12: 55–61.

ERDOĞAN, Nezih. 2001. 'Turkish Cinema' in Oliver Leaman (ed.), *Companion Encyclopedia of Middle Eastern and North African Film*. New York: Routledge, pp. 533–73.

———. 2011. 'Bir Seyirci Yapmak: 1896–1928 arası İstanbul'da Sinema ve Modernlik' in Deniz Göktürk, Levent Soysal and İpek Türeli (eds), *Istanbul Nereye? Küresel Kent, Kültür, Avrupa*. Istanbul: Metis, pp. 175–90.

EREN, Hasibe. 2016. Interview by the author, 27 May.

ERGENÇ, Halit. 2011. 'Halit Ergenç Oynadığı Kanuni'yi Anlattı'. Interview by Pelin Çini. *Haber7*, 9 January. Available at https://bit.ly/2WqeldG

———. 2014. Talk given at Mithat Alam Film Merkezi, Istanbul, 27 November.

ERGENEKON, Sema, and Eylem Canpolat. 2015. 'Bir Ölüm Listemiz Var'. Ranini.tv, 1 March. Available at https://bit.ly/2wq2GBs

ERGEZER, Elif. 2019. Interview by the author, 11 February.

ERGİN, Murat, and Yağmur Karakaya. 2017. 'Between Neo-Ottomanism and Ottomania: Navigating State-Led and Popular Cultural Representations of the Past'. *New Perspectives on Turkey* 56: 33–59.

ERGUN, Cengiz. 2017. Mithat Alam Film Merkezi, Türkiye Sineması Görsel Hafıza Projesi Arşivi, 27–28 February.

ERGUN, Köken. 2020. 'How Rituals Maintain Diasporic Communities: Three Contemporary Cases'. PhD dissertation, Free University of Berlin.

ERJEM, Yaşar, and Mustafa Çağlayandereli. 2006. 'Televizyon ve Gençlik: Yerli Dizilerin Gençlerin Model Alma Davranışı Üzerindeki Etkisi'. *C.Ü. Sosyal Bilimler Dergisi* 30(1) (May): 15–30.

ERKİP, Feyzan. 2003. 'The Shopping Mall as an Emergent Public Space in Turkey'. *Environment and Planning* 35(6): 1073–93.

EROĞLU, Nermin. 2012. Interview by the author, 23 May.

EROL-IŞIK, Nuran. 2013. 'Parables as Indicators of Popular Wisdom: The Making of Piety Culture in Turkish Television Dramas'. *European Journal of Cultural Studies* 16(5): 565–81.

EROL-IŞIK, Nuran. 2014. 'TV Drama as a Narrative form: Scenes from a Gendered and a Sacralized Cultural Sphere in Turkish Society' in Valentina Marinescu, Silvia Branea and Bianca Mitu (eds), *Critical Reflections on Audience and Narrativity: New Connections, New Perspectives*. Hannover: Ibidem Verlag, pp. 213–27.

EROL, Ebru Gülbuğ. 2009. 'Asmalı Konak Dizisi ve Filmi Üzerine Anlatı Kuramı Açısından Bir Değerlendirme'. *Erciyes Üniversitesi İletişim Dergisi* 1(1): 100–14.

ERTUĞRUL, Muhsin. 1963. 'Kalkınma Planında Tiyatro'. *Cumhuriyet*, 20 January.

ERTURAN, Ahmet Fatih. 2018. 'Türk dizilerine devlet tanıtımı'. *Yeni Şafak*, 4 November. Available at https://bit.ly/3OsMJxa

ESEN, Nüket. 1990. *Türk Romanında Aile Kurumu*. Istanbul: Boğaziçi Üniversitesi Yayınları.

ESEN, Timuçin. 2019. Talk given at Mithat Alam Film Merkezi, Istanbul, 7 February.

EVCEN, Fahriye. 2011. Interview by the author, 28 December.

EVCEN, Fahriye. 2015. 'Fahriye Evcen Bilinmeyenlerini Anlattı'. *Habertürk*, 28 March. Available at https://bit.ly/3dAWRRs

EVGAR, Demet. 2012. Interview by the author, 28 March.

EVREN, Burçak, and Bircan Usallı Silan. 2012. *Cüneyt Arkın*. Istanbul: Datça Altın Badem Film ve Kültür Festivali Yayınları.

EXPAT.COM. 2019. 'The Work Culture in Istanbul'. Available at https://bit.ly/2XXGN7p

EYÜBOĞLU, Ali. 2008. '"Hatırla Sevgili" Ama Lütfen Doğru Hatırla!'. *Milliyet*, 18 April. Available at https://bit.ly/3awgfhp

FACEBOOK. 2014. '70 ler 80 ler 90 ların TV Dizileri', 22 December. Available at https://bit.ly/2Ccj76G

———. 2017. 'Erol Evgin', 6 July. Available at https://bit.ly/2BjL4cx

FALAY, Barış. 2012. Interview by the author, 25 April.

FALCÓN CASTRO, Víctor. 2018. 'La (Otra) Revolucion Turca'. *El Comercio*, 9 January. Available at https://bit.ly/3aCv7uw

FARMANFARMAIAN, Roxane, Ali Sonay and Murat Akser. 2018. 'The Turkish Media Structure in Judicial and Political'. Context: An Illustration of Values and Status Negotiation'. *Middle East Critique* 27(2): 111–25.

FIDAN, Süleyman. 2018. 'Televizyon Dizilerinde Geleneksel Müzik Belleğinin Kullanımı'. *Uluslararası Sosyal Araştırmalar Dergisi* 11(60): 125–39.

FİLİZTEKİN-TURAN, Şenay. 2018. Interview by the author, 23 November.

———. 2022. Interview by the author, 4 March.

FILM STAGE. 2015. 'The 15 Best Documentaries About Making a Film', 25 February. Available at https://bit.ly/3b5KRXi

FİNANS GÜNDEM. 2019. 'Belediyeden hangi diziye ne kadar para aktarıldı', 18 September. Available at https://bit.ly/3NK8dp4

FISCHER-LICHTE, Erica. 2016. 'Introduction: From Comparative Arts to Interart Studies'. *Paragrana* 25(2): 12–26.

FİŞEK, Emine. 2016. 'Framing Temoignage: Personal Narrative, Theatrical Aid and the Politics of Immigration Activism in France'. *Text and Performance Quarterly* 36(2–3): 77–94.

———. 2018. 'Palimpsests of Violence: Urban Dispossession and Political Theatre in Istanbul'. *Comparative Drama* 52(3–4): 349–71.

FISHELOV, David. 1993. *Metaphors of Genre: The Role of Analogies in Genre Theory*. University Park: Pennsylvania State University Press.

FLICHE, Benoit. 2005. 'The Hemşehrilik and the Village: The Stakes of an Association of Former Villagers in Ankara'. *European Journal of Turkish Studies* 2. Available at https://bit.ly/3A23c6O

Follows, Stephen. 2018. 'How Does the Use of the Terms "Cinematographer" and "Director of Photography" Differ?' *Stephen Follows: Film Data and Education,* 23 April. Available at https://bit.ly/3xICFtU

Fontaine, Gilles. 2017. *TV Fiction Production in the European Union.* Strasbourg: European Audiovisual Observatory.

———, and Marta Jimenez Pumares. 2018. *The Production and Circulation of TV Fiction in the EU28-Television and VOD.* Strasbourg: European Audiovisual Observatory.

Ford, Sam. 2017. 'A Tale of Two Transnational Telenovelas'. *ReVista: Harvard Review of Latin America* 7(1) (Fall). Available at https://bit.ly/3nj9sQi

Formatbiz. 2021. 'Two Words with Can Okan', 12 April. Avilable at https://bit.ly/3HnOM2C

Forrester, Chris. 2019. 'UHD: 4K is Here and Now, But What About 8K?' ibc.org, 10 May. Available at https://bit.ly/2WYonTS

Foster, Susan Leigh (ed.). 1995. *Choreographing History.* Bloomington: Indiana University Press.

Friedman, Ken (ed.). 1998. *The Fluxus Reader.* New York: Wiley.

Frisch, Michael. 1990. *A Shared Authority: Essays on the Craft and Meaning of Oral and Public History.* New York: State University of New York Press.

Ganti, Tejaswini. 2012a. *Producing Bollywood: Inside the Contemporary Hindi Film Industry.* Durham, NC: Duke University Press.

———. 2012b. 'Sentiments of Disdain and Practices of Distinction: Boundary-Work, Subjectivity, and Value in the Hindi Film Industry'. *The Anthropological Quarterly* 85(1): 5–43.

———. 2014. 'The Value of Ethnography'. *Media Industries* 1(1): 16–20.

Gartman, David. 2012. 'Bourdieu and Adorno: Converging Theories of Culture and Inequality'. *Theory and Society* 41(1): 41–72.

Gazetemag. 2019. 'Türk Sinema ve Televizyon Tarihinin Klasikleşmiş Yapımlarının Yaratıcısı Umur Bugay'a saygıyla', 8 August. Available at https://bit.ly/3bwkR74

Gecce. 2012. 'Öykü Karayel'in Yükseliş Öyküsü . . .', 12 November. Available at https://bit.ly/3dyZeEk

Geertz, Clifford. 1983. *Local Knowledge: Further Essays in Interpretive Anthropology.* New York: Basic Books.

Gence, Hakan. 2011. '2 milyon liraya yeni Balat'. *Hürriyet-Kelebek,* 14 August. Available at https://bit.ly/3xHdUOF

Gence, Hakan. 2016. 'Kadir Doğulu: "Neslihan'a ilk görüşte çarpıldım! Çekti ve bitirdi beni"'. *Hürriyet,* 20 August. Available at https://bit.ly/3Kqe3tB

Gence, Hakan. 2019. 'Garson deyip aşağıladılar!' *Hürriyet,* 5 January. Available at https://bit.ly/3ryeXNB

GENETTE, Gérard. 1997. *Palimpsests: Literature in the Second Degree*. Lincoln: University of Nebraska Press.

GEORGE, Nicholas. 2010. *Film Crew: Fundamentals of Professional Film and Video Production*. Las Vegas: Platinum Eagle Publishing.

GEORGEON, François, and Irène Fenoglio (eds). 1996. 'L'humour en Orient'. *Revue du Monde Musulman et de la Méditerranée* 77–78: 89–109.

GERÇEK, Mehmet. 2019. 'Türk Televizyon Dizilerinde Metinlerarasılık/Göstergelerarasılık: Leyla ile Mecnun Dizisi'. MA thesis, Gümüşhane University.

GERÇEK, Merve. 2018. 'Yöneticilerin Babacan (Paternalist) Liderlik Davranışlarının Psikolojik Sözleşme Bağlamındaki Beklentileri Üzerindeki Etkilerine Yönelik Bir Çalışma'. *Eskişehir Osmangazi Üniversitesi İİBF Dergisi* 13(2): 101–18.

GINSBURG, Faye D. 1991. 'Indigenous Media: Faustian Contract or Global Village?' *Cultural Anthropology* 6(1): 92–112.

——, Lila Abu-Lughod and Brian Larkin. 2002. *Media Worlds: Anthropology on New Terrain*. Berkeley: University of California Press.

GİRİTLİOĞLU, Tomris. 2013. Interview by the author, 22 February.

——. 2014. 'Tomris Giritlioğlu: Hâtırla Sevgili'ye Devam Etmeme Kararı Hataydı'. Ranini.tv, 28 October. Available at https://bit.ly/39dxliK

GOFFMAN, Erwing. 1990[1959]. *The Presentation of Self in Everyday Life*. New York: Penguin Books.

GÖK, Cahit. 2012. Interview by the author, 10 May.

GÖKTÜRK-KOBANBAY, Deniz. 2017. 'Sinemada Sanat Yönetmenliği ve Kostüm Tasarımı'. *Timeturk*, 20 November. Available at https://bit.ly/2QXWqHW

GÖKTÜRK, Deniz, Levent Soysal and İpek Türeli. 2010. *Orienting Istanbul: Cultural Capital of Europe?* London: Routledge.

GÖKULU, Gökhan. 2013. 'Representation of Sexual Violence in Turkish Cinema and Television Series'. *Asian Journal of Women's Studies* 19(2): 66–91.

GOMERY, Douglas, and Luke Hockley. 2006. *Television Industries*. London: British Film Institute.

GORBMAN, Claudia. 1987. *Unheard Melodies: Narrative Film Music*. Bloomington: Indiana University Press.

GÖRGÜN-TOPTAŞ, Burcu, and Özlem Yılmaz. 2016. 'İlham Güvenilecek Son Liman!' Interview by Cansu Uras. Ranini.tv, 21 September. Available at https://bit.ly/3bwj6H8

GÖZLÜKAYA-TÜTÜNCÜ, Fatma. 1998a. 'Gündelik Yaşam, Kadınlar ve Pembe Diziler' in *20. Yüzyılın Sonunda Kadınlar ve Gelecek Konferansı, 19–21 November 1997*. Ankara: TODAİE, pp. 425–31.

——. 1998b. 'Television Soap Operas and Women—An Audience Study: Turkish Women's Response to *The Young and the Restless*'. MA thesis, Middle East Technical University, Ankara.

GQ. 2016. 'Yeni Starımız Barış Arduç', 1 April. Available at https://bit.ly/39Sj3dC

GRABOLLE-ÇELİKER, Anna. 2013. *Kurdish Life in Contemporary Turkey: Migration, Gender and Ethnic Identity*. London: I. B. Tauris.

GÜLCAN, Tuvana. 2010. 'Bu Kalp Seni Unutur mu?' *Birikim* (August–September): 64–68.

GÜLEN-OARR, İnci. 2016. Interview by the author, 8 December.

GÜLER, Mine. 2012. Interview by the author, 24 May.

GÜLEREN, Ebru. 2019. Interview by the author, 28 February.

GÜLGEN, Fırat. 2012. 'Ortadoğu'da Kıvanç, Balkanlar'da ise Kenan seviliyor'. *Milliyet*, 19 February. Available at https://bit.ly/2USYXEp

GÜLSOY, Murat. 2012. Interview by the author, 15 June.

GÜLTEKİN, Zeynep. 2006. 'Irak'dan Önce: Kurtlar Vadisi Dizisi'. *İletişim Kuram ve Araştırma Dergisi* 22: 9–36.

GÜLTEKİN-AKÇAY, Zeynep. 2011. 'Türkiye'de Bir Dramedi Türü: Mahalle Dizileri' in Z. Gültekin-Akçay, S. C. Yağcı, S. Büker, F. Erdemir (eds), *Beyaz Camın Yerlileri*. İzmit: Umuttepe Yayınları, pp. 53–84.

GÜNAY-TAN, Zeynep. 2011. '2 Milyon Liraya Yeni Balat'. Interview by Hakan Gence. *Hürriyet Kelebek*, 14 August. Available at https://bit.ly/3dANVfP

———. 2018. 'İstanbullu Gelin Setinde Yönetmen Zeynep Günay-Tan ile Sohbet Ettik'. Interview by Özlem Arıkan Serbez. *Criturk*, 12 June. Available at https://bit.ly/39U7H95

———. 2019. Interview by the author, 6 March.

GÜNDEL, Nergiz. 2003. 'Televizyon Program Türü Olarak Durum Komedileri ve Çocuklar Duymasın Dizisi Üzerine İçerik Analizi'. MA thesis, Selçuk University, Konya.

GÜNDÜZ, Olgun. 2002. 'Türkiye'nin Batılılaşma Serüveninde Özgün Bir Portre: Ahmet Hamdi. Tanpınar'. *Uludağ Üniversitesi Fen Edebiyat Fakültesi Sosyal Bilimler Dergisi* 3(3): 13–28.

GÜNER, Renda. 2012. Interview by the author, 21 March.

———. 2020. Interview by the author, 13 April.

GÜNERBÜYÜK, Çağdaş. 2009. 'Kurtlar Vadisi Dizisinde Politik Söylem'. MA thesis, Marmara University, Istanbul.

GÜNEŞ-AYATA, Ayşe. 1990. 'Gecekondularda Kimlik Sorunu, Dayanışma Örüntüleri ve Hemşehrilik'. *Toplum ve Bilim* 51(52): 89–101.

GÜNSÜR, Mehmet. 2012. Talk given at Mithat Alam Film Merkezi, Istanbul, 3 May.

GÜRBİLEK, Nurdan. 2011. *The New Cultural Climate in Turkey: Living in a Shop Window*. London: Zed Books.

GÜREL, Meltem. 2009. 'Defining and Living Out the Interior: The "Modern" Apartment and the "Urban" Housewife in Turkey During the 1950s and 1960s'. *Gender, Place and Culture* 6: 703–22.

GUTEKUNST, Christina, and John Gillett. 2014. *Voice into Acting: Integrating Voice and the Stanislavski Approach.* London: Bloomsbury Methuen Drama.

GÜVEN, Birol. 2014. Interview by the author, 13 February.

GÜVEN, Erdem. 2011. 'Kuzguncuk as a Village of Mutual Respect and Harmony: Myth or Reality?' *Journal of Modern Jewish Studies* 10(3): 365–82.

HABER GLOBAL. 2020. 'Bihter Ziyagil'in 10. ölüm yıl dönümü sosyal medyada gündem oldu', 24 June. Available at https://bit.ly/3PsXxfe

HABER7. 2011. '"Muhteşem Yüzyıl"a çığ gibi tepki yağıyor', 6 January. Available at https://bit.ly/3xeT4Vq

——. 2020. 'Arka Sokaklar İzleyicisinin Sabırsızlıkla Beklediği Müjdeli Haber! Yeni Bülüm Sürprizi Verildi', 3 April. Available at https://bit.ly/3ekHJbA

HABERLER.COM. 2014. 'Çalıkuşu Dizisi, Rusya'da Türk Edebiyatına İlgiyi Önemli Ölçüde Artırdı', 16 January. Available at https://bit.ly/3deEXVe

——. 2016. 'Sera Tokdemir dizi setinde ölümden döndü', 2 July. Available at https://bit.ly/2VjIA41

——. 2017. 'Söz'den Çok Konuşulacak Sahne . . . ', 27 November. Available at https://bit.ly/2WX6G7c

HABERMAS, Jurgen. 1989. *Structural Transformation of the Public Sphere.* Cambridge, MA: MIT Press.

HABERTÜRK. 2012. 'Gıdı kavgası diziyi bitirdi', 7 April. Available at https://bit.ly/2SRzifq

——. 2015. 'Türkiye, Akıllı Telefonda İnternet Kullanımında Dünya İkincisi', 20 August. Available at https://bit.ly/2WyHgwF

HAFIZOĞULLARI, Zeki, and Ahmet Arif Tarakçıoğlu. 1998. 'Nasıl Bir TRT ve Bir Kamu Tüzel Kişisi Olarak TRT'nin Özerkliği ve Tarafsızlığı Meselesi'. *Ankara Üniversitesi Hukuk Fakültesi Dergisi* 47(1): 1–16.

HALLIWELL, Stephen. 2014. 'Diegesis–Mimesis' in *Handbook of Narratology.* Berlin: de Gruyter, pp. 129–37.

HAMAMCIOĞLU, Alara. 2019. Interview by the author, 28 February.

HARRIS, Charles. 2016. *Jaws in Space: Powerful Pitching for Film and TV Screenwriters.* n.p.: Creative Essentials.

HAUGE, Michael. 2006. *Selling Your Story in 60 Seconds: The Guaranteed Way to Get Your Screenplay or Novel.* n.p.: Michael Wiese Productions.

HAVENS, Timothy J. 2003. 'Exhibiting Global Television: On the Business and Cultural Functions of Global Television Fairs'. *Journal of Broadcasting and Electronic Media* 47(1): 18–35.

HECKER, Pierre, Ivo Furman and Kaya Akyıldız (eds). 2021. *The Politics of Culture in Contemporary Turkey.* Edinburgh: Edinburgh University Press.

HERMONN, Raffi A. 2015. 'Ermeni Tiyatroculardan Güzel Bir Vodvili Türkçe Seyretmeye Var mısınız?' *T24 Bağımsız İnternet Gazetesi*, 19 March. Available at https://-bit.ly/3Kjuecq

HICKMAN, Roger. 2017. *Reel Music: Exploring 100 Years of Film Music*. New York: W. W. Norton.

HIGGINS, Dick. 2001[1966]. 'Intermedia'. *Leonardo Journal of the International Society for the Arts, Sciences and Technology* 34(1): 49–54.

HILL, Andy. 2017. *Scoring the Screen: The Secret Language of Film Music*. Milwaukee: Hal Leonard.

HONTHANER, Eve Light. 2010. *The Complete Film Production Handbook*. Amsterdam: Focal Press.

HORKHEIMER, Max. 1972. *Critical Theory: Selected Essays*. New York: Basic Books.

HOWELL, John. 2018. 'Türkiye'de İş Kültürü'. *Guides Global*, 6 June. Available at https://bit.ly/2ACd8I3

HULLFISH, Steve. 2017. *Art of the Cut*. New York: Routledge.

HÜRRİYET. 1974. 'Kaçak'ı Yakaladık'. *Hürriyet*, 25 June.

———. 2001. 'Sıla Çalıntı Çıktı', 14 September. Available at https://bit.ly/2vO1hUU

———. 2011. 'Muhteşem Yüzyıl dizisine protesto', 30 January. Available at https://bit.ly/3fHncPH

———. 2018. 'Hem Türk İsimleri Hem de Dizilerine Hayranlar! Kıtaları aştı . . . ', 23 September. Available at https://bit.ly/30H117i

———. 2020a. '"Eşkıya Dünyaya Hükümdar Olmaz" Setinde Korona Virüs Önlemi', 30 March. Available at https://bit.ly/3fIvnKJ

———. 2020b. '"Kuşlarla Yolculuk" Dizisi Ramazan Ayında TRT 1'de Ekrana Gelecek', 21 April. Available at https://bit.ly/2NdAYwp

HÜRRİYET DAILY NEWS. 2013. 'Fresh MESH Discusses Entertainment's Future', 18 January. Available at https://bit.ly/39xUNHs

HÜRRİYET-KELEBEK. 2011. 'Kıvanç Tatlıtuğ ve sevgilisi Azra Akın, ünlü organizatör Erkan Özerman'a tazminat davası açıyor: O beni köle gibi kullandı', 20 December. Available at https://bit.ly/2YWcwXp

———. 2016. 'Elçin Sangu'nun 1 milyon Liralık Anlaşması Mahkemelik oldu!', 15 February. Available at https://bit.ly/2SV9e2L

İÇEL, Kayhan. 1985. *Kitle Haberleşme Hukuku*. Istanbul: Istanbul Üniversitesi Yayınları.

İDİL, Neşe. 2020. 'Unions, Performers Urge Suspension of TV Series' Sets amid Coronavirus Outbreak in Turkey'. Duvar.English, 27 March. Available at https://bit.ly/3dkfp86

İKSV. 2020. 'Netflix, İKSV and Cinema and Broadcasting Union Establish New Covid-19 Film and Television Relief Fund for Hardest Hit Workers'. Available at https://bit.ly/3eiKeLN

İLHAN, Attilâ. 1972. *Hangi Batı?* Ankara: Bilgi Yayınevi.

———. 1976. *Hangi Sol.* Ankara: Bilgi Yayınevi.

İLHAN, Erol, and Adalet Görgülü Aydoğdu. 2017. 'Tabloid Journalism and Its Ethics Approach'. *International Journal of Social Sciences and Education Research* 3(5): 1507–21.

İLKKARACAN, Pınar. 1998. 'Exploring the context of women's sexuality in Eastern Turkey'. *Reproductive Health Matters* 6(12): 66–75.

İMİK, Nural. 2006. '2000–2005 Arası Türkiye'de Televizyon Dizilerinde Kullanılan Müziğin Genç İzleyicilere Etkileri'. MA thesis, Fırat University, Elazığ.

İNANOĞLU, Türker. 1984. 'Video ve Sinema Birbirine Düşman Değil'. *Video/Sinema* 1: 68.

———. 2012. Interview by the author, 19 September.

İNCE, Ateş. 2017. 'Ateş İnce: Türk Dizisi Ülkemizin En Değerli ve Başarılı Ürünü, puhutv'nin Misyonu da Bu Ürünü Desteklemek'. Ranini.tv, 7 February. Available at https://bit.ly/3emtove

İNCE, H. Ayça, and Serhan Ada. 2009. '*Zihinsel Değişim? AKP İktidarı ve Kültür Politikası': Türkiye'de Kültür Politikalarına Giriş.* Istanbul: Istanbul Bilgi Üniversitesi Yayınları.

İNCE, Özdemir. 2006. 'Prof. Dr. Nevzat Yalçıntaş'a Mektup'. *Hürriyet*, 24 February. Available at https://bit.ly/2UloPsA

İNCİ, Handan. 2014. *Ayfer Tunç'la Karanlıkta Kelimeler.* Istanbul: Can Yayınları.

İNCİ, Kemal. 2016. *Yeşilçam Anıları.* Istanbul: Pagoda Yayınları.

İNCİ, Sedat. 2020. Interview by the author, 26 May.

INTERNET HABER. 2011a. 'Muhteşem Yüzyıl'a Mehterli Protesto', 5 January. Available at https://bit.ly/2UtQvwr

———. 2011b. 'Muhteşem Hürrem'e Çirkin Saldırı', 16 January. Available at https://bit.ly/2JuBLXK

IŞIKLI, Toygar. 2013a. 'İlham Diye Bir Şey Yok'. *Hürriyet*, 26 March. Available at https://bit.ly/345iaXW

———. 2013b. 'Toygar Işıklı Cine Dergi Röportajı'. *Cine Dergi.* Available at https://bit.ly/2vZX803

İSTANBUL.NET.TR. 2015. 'Morris Metodu ile Eğitim Veren Anthony Vincent Bova, Craft'ta'. Available at https://bit.ly/35WpTbK

JACOBSON, Adam. 2018. 'Turkish Telenovela "Mercy" Hits Hispanic TV'. Multichannel News, 29 March. Available at https://bit.ly/2Ut1lCP

JENKINS, Henry. 2006. *Convergence Culture.* New York: New York University Press.

JENSEN, Klaus Bruhn. 2016. 'Intermediality'. *The International Encyclopedia of Communication Theory and Philosophy.* Available at https://bit.ly/37d1Da9

JORDAN, Jacquie. 2006. *Get on TV! The Insider's Guide to Pitching the Producers and Promoting Yourself!* Chicago: Sourcebooks.

KADIOĞLU, Şebnem. 2010. 'Pembe Dizilerin Kadınlar Üzerindeki Etkisi'. MA thesis, Gazi University, Ankara.

KANAL46. 2010. 'Dizilere 'Yerli Malı' Teşviki Gelecek', 3 January. Available at https://bit.ly/37Mkg0L

KANDIYOTI, Deniz, and Ayşe Saktanber (eds). 2002. *Fragments of Culture: The Everyday Life of Turkey.* London: I. B. Tauris.

KAPLAN, Michael. 2016. 'From Telenovelas to Turkish Dramas: Why Turkey's Soap Operas Are Captivating Latin America'. *International Business Times*, 2 September. Available at https://bit.ly/3dHPhFC

KAPSAL, Hale. 2012. 'Son Dönem Türk Dizilerinde Kadının Toplumsal Kimliğinin Değişimi'. MA thesis, Beykent University, Istanbul.

KAPTAN, Yeşim, and Ece Algan (eds). 2021. *Television in Turkey: Local Production, Transnational Expansion and Political Aspirations.* Cham, Switzerland: Springer International Publishing.

KARA, Aysel Zehra. 2019. 'Türkiye'de Adaptasyon Diziler, Yaratıcı Emek Gücü Olarak Senaristler ve Senaryo Süreçleri'. MA thesis, Hacettepe University, Ankara.

KARACA, Banu. 2012. 'Çağdaş Sanat Üretimi ve Türkiye'de Sansür Politikaları'. *Toplum ve Bilim* 125: 134–51.

KARACA, Doğan. 2013. Interview by the author, 30 October.

KARACAKAYA, Emrah. 2019. Interview by the author, 8 November.

———. 2020. Interview by the author, 18 May.

KARAHAN-USLU, Zeynep. 2002. 'Yazılı ve Görsel Medyada Magazinleşmenin Tarihsel ve Sosyolojik Dinamikleri'. *Gazi İletişim Dergisi* 12: 1–25.

KARAHAN, Mustafa. 2018. Interview by the author, 2 February and 8 February.

KARAKUŞ, Damla. n.d. 'Osman Yağmurdereli Kimdir?' En Son Haber. Available at https://bit.ly/33OZyem

KARATAŞ, Şaban. 1978. *TRT Kavgası.* Istanbul: Emek Matbaacılık.

KARLIDAĞ, Serpil, and Selda Bulut. 2014. 'The Transnational Spread of Turkish Television Soap Operas'. *İstanbul Üniversitesi İletişim Fakültesi Dergisi* 2(47): 75–96.

KARPAT, Kemal H. 1996. 'The Turkish Left'. *Journal of Contemporary History* 1(2): 169–86.

KATIKSIZ, Ahmet. 2013. Interview by the author, 29 October.

KAYA, Ramazan, and Hasan Günal. 2015. 'Tarih Öğretmenlerinin Muhteşem Yüzyıl Dizisi Özelinde Tarih Konulu Film ve Dizilerin Öğretimde Kullanımına Yönelik Görüşleri'. *Türk Tarih Eğitimi Dergisi* 4(1): 1–48.

KAYGALAK, Sevilay. 2009. *Kentin Mültecileri: Neoliberalizm Koşullarında Zorunlu Göç ve Kentleşme*. Ankara: Dipnot Yayınları.

KAZAZ, Mete, and Yasemin Özkent. 2016. 'Televizyon Dizileriyle Eş Zamanlı Olarak Twitter Kullanımı: İletişim Fakültesi Öğrencileri Üzerine Bir Araştırma'. *Selçuk İletişim* 9(2): 205–24.

KENTER, Kadriye. 2017. Interview by the author, 9 March.

KER-LINDSAY, James. 2000. 'Greek–Turkish Rapprochement: The Impact of Disaster Diplomacy?' *Cambridge Review of International Affairs* 14(1): 215–32.

———. 2007. *Crisis and Conciliation: A Year of Rapprochement between Greece and Turkey*. London: I. B. Tauris.

KESİRLİ-UNUR, Ayşegül. 2016. 'Genre, Globalisation and the Nation: The Case of Turkish Police Procedural TV Series'. PhD dissertation, University of Antwerp.

KESKİN, Serkan. 2014. Talk given at Mithat Alam Film Merkezi, Istanbul, 19 November.

KESLASSY, Elsa, and Leo Barraclough. 2022. 'MipTV Gathered More Than 5,000 Guests, Mipcom to Return in Super-Sized Format in October'. *Variety*, 6 April. Available at https://bit.ly/3mLElMW

KEYDER, Çağlar. 1987. *State and Class in Turkey: A Study in Capitalist Development*. London: Verso.

———. 2000. *Istanbul: Küresel ile Yerel Arasında*. Istanbul: Metis Yayınları.

KHAN, Musa, and Yong-jin Won. 2020. 'Transnationalization of TV Serials: A Comparative Study of the Exportation of Korean and Turkish TV Serials'. *European Journal of Social Sciences* 59(2): 193–208.

KIRBAKI, Yorgo. 2005. 'Yabancı Damat Fenomeni'. *Hürriyet*, 13 August. Available at https://bit.ly/3fElFsT

KIRIŞÇI, Murat. 2015. 'Metin Erksan'ın Olay Yaratan TV Filmleri–Bölüm 1'. Öteki Sinema, 2 October. Available at https://bit.ly/3drAqyM

KIVANÇ, Halit. 2002. *Telesafir: 'Bizde TV Böyle Başladı'*. Istanbul: Remzi Kitabevi.

KLICH, Ignacio, and Jeffrey Lesser. 1996. 'Introduction: "Turco" Immigrants in Latin America'. *The Americas* 53(1) (Special Issue: 'Turco' Immigrants in Latin America): 1–14.

KOCABIYIK, Yiğit, and Sibel Erdenk. 2018. 'Güncel Bir Rol Çalışma Yöntemi: Meisner Tekniği'. *Yedi: Sanat, Tasarım ve Bilim Dergisi* 20 (Summer): 1–11.

KOCAKAYA, Ayşe Hanife. 2009. 'Atatürk Dönemi Güzellik Yarışmaları ve Keriman Halis'. PhD dissertation, Dokuz Eylül University, Izmir.

KOCAMANER, Hikmet. 2017. 'Strengthening the Family through Television: Islamic Broadcasting, Secularism, and the Politics of Responsibility in Turkey'. *Anthropological Quarterly* 90(3): 675–714.

KOĞACIOĞLU, Dicle. 2004. 'The Tradition Effect: Framing Honor Crimes in Turkey'. *Differences: A Journal of Feminist Cultural Studies* 15(2): 119–51.

KONDUK, Kandemir. 2012. 'Yasaklar'ı Oynayacağız Tabii Yasaklanmazsa'. Interview by Gülbahar Karakuş. *Hürriyet-Kelebek*, 22 June. Available at https://bit.ly/3auopa9

——. 2014. Interview by the author, 22 April.

KONUR, Tahsin. 1987. 'Cumhuriyet Döneminde Devlet-Tiyatro İlişkisi'. *Ankara Üniversitesi Dil ve Tarih-Coğrafya Fakültesi Dergisi* 31(1–2): 307–59.

KONUŞLU, Fırat. 2010. 'Emek Süreci Analizinden Sınıf Tartışmasına Bir Yol Denemesi: Türkiye Özel Televizyon Dizilerinin Üretim ve Emek Sürecinde Sınıfsal İlişkiler'. *Praksis Dergisi* 32: 222–55.

——. 2016. 'Bir Mücadele Alanı Olarak "Otonomi": Türkiye'de Dizi Üretim Süreçleri Üzerinden Sömürü-Tahakküm İlişkilerini ve Siyasal Özneyi Tartışmak'. *Modus Operandi* 3: 75–110.

KORALTÜRK, Ahmet. 2016. Interview by the author, 8 April.

KOREL, Bergüzar. 2009. 'Şehrazat Değilim Ben'. *Sabah*, 23 August. Available at https://bit.ly/2YRPHUF

KÖROĞLU, Derya. 2019. 'Röportaj Yeni Türkü 40. Yıl'. *Vizyon*, October. Available at https://bit.ly/3zl5nBC

KÖSE, Aynur. 2008. 'Küreselleşme Çağında Bir Aidiyet Zemini ve Örgütlenme Şekli Olarak Hemşehrilik'. *Akademik İncelemeler* 3(1): 221–32.

KÖSEMEN, Begüm. 2015. 'Toplumu Yeniden İnşa Etmenin Kültürel Açılım Aracı Olarak Tüsak'. *Eğitim, Bilim, Toplum* 13: 70–93.

KÖSEOĞLU, Emine, and Deniz Erinsel Önder. 2011. 'İnsan Belleğinin ve Kentin Belirgin Öğelerini Tanımlamak: Ayvalık'taki Öznel ve Nesnel İşaret Öğeleri'. *Arkitekt* 524(78): 40–52.

KÖŞGER, Hüsna. 2018. 'Perran Kutman'ın Efsane Dizisi Meğer O Sanatçı Sayesinde Yazılmış'. JURNAL.İST, 24 May. Available at https://bit.ly/2UcS7dO

KÖSTENDİL, Erkan Kolçak. 2019. Interview by the author, 28 February.

KRAIDY, Marwan M. 2019. 'Boycotting Neo-Ottoman Cool: Geopolitics and Media Industries in the Egypt–Turkey Row over Television Drama'. *Middle East Journal of Culture and Communication* 12(2): 149–65.

——, and Omar Al-Ghazzi. 2013. 'Neo-Ottoman Cool: Turkish Popular Culture in the Arab Public Sphere'. *Popular Communication: The International Journal of Media and Culture* 11(1): 17–29.

KRAJESKI, Jenna. 2012. 'Turkey: Days of Their Lives'. Pulitzer Center, 30 March. Available at https://bit.ly/2UsbmjS

KÜÇÜK, Murat. 2013. 'Aidiyetin Mekânı: Mardin'de Kimlik ve Mekânın Değişimi'. *İdealkent* 4(9): 114–37.

KÜÇÜKURAL, Nihan. 2011. Interview by the author, 12 December.

KÜLTÜR VE TURİZM BAKANLIĞI. 'Dizi Film Desteği'. *Kültür ve Turizm Bakanlığı*. Available at https://bit.ly/3eo01c4

KURT, E. Vona. 2001. 'Televizyon Haberlerinde Magazinleşme'. MA thesis, Gazi University, Ankara.

KÜRÜZ, Murat. 2007. *Son Efsane Gırgır*. Istanbul: Epsilon.

KUŞKAN, Fikret. 2012. Talk given at Mithat Alam Film Merkezi, Istanbul, 15 March.

KUTLUAY, Tolga. 2019. Interview by the author, 23 February and 28 February.

KUYUCU, Michael. 2014. *Müzik Dünyasını Anlamak Müzik Endüstrisinin Sorunları*. Istanbul: Zinde Yayıncılık.

LEPPÄNEN, Sirpa, Samu Kytölä, Henna Jousmäki, Saija Peuronen and Elina Westinen. 2013. 'Entextualization and Resemiotization as Resources for Identification in Social Media' in Philip Seargeant and Caroline Tagg (eds), *The Language of Social Media: Communication and Community on the Internet*. Basingstoke: Palgrave Macmillan, pp. 112–38.

LEVINE, Elana. 2009. 'Doing Soap Opera History: Challenges and Triumphs' in Janet Staiger and Sabine Hake (eds), *Convergence Media History*. London: Routledge, pp. 173–81.

LOVATT, Debbie (ed.). 2001. *Turkey Since 1970: Politics, Economics and Society*. Basingstoke: Palgrave Macmillan.

LU, Ren, Torger Reve, Jing Huang, Ze Jian and Mei Chen. 2018. 'A Literature Review of Cluster Theory: Are Relations among Clusters Important?' *Journal of Economic Surveys* 32: 1201–20.

LUI, Bonnie Rui. 2010. 'New Strength of Competition and Innovation: China's Independent Television Production'. Paper presented at the Conference of the International Communication Association: Matters of Communication, Singapore, 22–26 June. Available at: https://bit.ly/3NitMMd

LUKINBEAL, Chris. 2004. 'The Rise of Regional Film Production Centers in North America 1984–1997'. *GeoJournal* 59(4): 307–21.

LÜKÜSLÜ, Demet. 2018. 'The Political Potential of Popular Culture in Turkey: The Reading of Three TV Series: *Leyla ile Mecnun*, *Ben de Özledim* and *Beş Kardeş*'. TV/Series 13. Available at https://bit.ly/3aShMUo

LUMET, Sidney. 1996. *Making Movies*. New York: Vintage.

LUZI, Evan. n.d. 'Where to Place Your Video Village Monitor'. *The Black and Blue*. Available at https://bit.ly/3a2oYH8

MACNAB, Geoffrey. 2016. 'Midnight Express: The Cult Film that had Disastrous Consequences for the Turkish Tourism Industry'. *Independent*, 16 May. Available at https://bit.ly/30WTJMJ

MAGAZINMAX. 2018. '60 Dakika/Ekrem Catay/Bölüm 1–3', 1 November. Published at https://bit.ly/2Wu790p (currently unavailable; last accessed on 2 February 2020).

MAGGI, Armando. 2009. *The Resurrection of the Body: Pier Paolo Pasolini from Saint Paul to Sade*. Chicago: University of Chicago Press.

MALMBERG, Anders, and Peter Maskell. 2002. 'The Elusive Concept of Localization Economies: Towards a Knowledge-based Theory of Spatial Clustering'. *Environment and Planning A* 34(3): 429–49.

MAMET, David. 1992. *On Directing Film*. New York: Penguin Books.

MANCINI, Michele, and Giuseppe Perrella (eds). 2017. *Pasolini's Bodies and Places*. Zurich: Patrick Frey.

MARCUS, George E. 1995. 'Ethnography in/of the World System: The Emergence of Multi-sited Ethnography'. *Annual Review of Anthropology* 24(1): 95–117.

MARDİN, Şerif. 1991. *'Batıcılık', Türk Modernleşmesi, Makaleler*. Istanbul: İletişim Yayınları.

MARO, Asu. 2013. 'Leyla ile Mecnun Hakkında Her Şey'. *Milliyet*, 25 August. Available at https://bit.ly/3bws6vU

MARSHALL, Alex. 2018. 'Can Netflix Take Turkey's TV Dramas to the World?' *New York Times*, December 27. Available at https://nyti.ms/2CijOvg

MARTIN, Ron, and Peter Sunley. 2006. 'Path Dependence and Regional Economic Evolution'. *Journal of Economic Geography* 6(4): 395–437.

MARTIN, Sylvia J. 2012. 'Of Ghosts and Gangsters: Capitalist Cultural Production and the Hong Kong Film Industry'. *Visual Anthropology Review* 28(1): 32–49.

MATER, Çiğdem. 2002. 'Gazinolar Yeniden'. Bianet Internet Forum. Available at https://bit.ly/2QMknCb

MAYER, Vicki, Miranda J. Banks and John T. Caldwell (eds). 2009. *Production Studies: Cultural Studies of Media Industries*. New York: Routledge.

MCCLOUD, Scott. 1994. *Understanding Comics: The Invisible Art*. New York: William Morrow Paperbacks.

MCKEE, Robert. 1997. *Story: Substance, Structure, Style and the Principles of Screenwriting*. New York: Regan Books.

MCLUHAN, Marshall. 1964. *Understanding Media: The Extensions of Man*. New York: McGraw Hill.

MEDYATAVA. 2012. 'Müjde Ar'ın Dizi Macerası Başlamadan Bitti'. *Medyatava*, 25 September. Available at https://bit.ly/2WkNbVh

———. 2013. 'Popüler dizilerin senaristinden şok karar! Melek Gençoğlu işine neden ara verdi?' *Medyatava*, 20 November.

MEHTA, Monika. 2005. 'Globalizing Bombay Cinema: Reproducing the Indian State and Family'. *Cultural Dynamics* 17: 135–54.

METE, Mehmet. 1999. *Televizyon Yayınlarının Türk Toplumu Üzerindeki Etkileri.* Ankara: AYK, Atatürk Kültür Merkezi Başkanlığı.

METZ, Christian. 1974. *Film Language: A Semiotics of the Cinema.* New York: Oxford University Press.

MIHALAKOPOULOS, Georgios. 2013. 'The Greek Audience "Discovers" the Turkish Soap-Series: Turkey's "Soft Power" and the Psyche of Greeks' in M. Tsianikas, N. Maadad, G. Couvalis and M. Palaktsoglou (eds), *Greek Research in Australia: Proceedings of the Biennial International Conference of Greek Studies, Flinders University, June 2011.* Adelaide: Department of Language Studies, Modern Greek, Flinders University, pp. 179–91.

MILLER, Carolyn R. 1984. 'Genre as Social Action'. *Quarterly Journal of Speech* 70(2): 151–67.

——, and Ashley R. Kelly (eds). 2017. *Emerging Genres in New Media Environments.* Basingstoke: Palgrave Macmillan.

MILLER, James Andrew, and Tom Shales. 2015. *Live From New York: The Complete, Uncensored History of Saturday Night Live as Told by Its Stars, Writers, and Guests.* New York: Back Bay Books.

MILLER, Toby. 2014. 'Turkish Novelas in Chile'. *CTS Online*, 28 November. Available at https://bit.ly/33V3Pgo

MİLLİYET. 2011. 'Hürrem'in dekoltesine Genel Müdür'den eleştiri'. *Milliyet*, 8 July. Available at https://bit.ly/39nroFY

——. 2016. '250 Milyon Dolarlık Dizi İhraç Ettik'. *Milliyet*, 14 January. Available at https://bit.ly/2QRwcab

MILLS, Amy. 2007. 'Gender and Mahalle (Neighborhood) Space in Istanbul'. *Gender, Place and Culture* 14(3): 335–54.

MIPCOM. 2020. 'The World's Entertainment Content Market'. Available at https://-bit.ly/2WZ6l3L

MIPCOM NEWS. 2015. 'Essential Turkey', 20 October. Available at https://bit.ly/2zOniVv

MİZRAHİ, Dario. 1991. 'Diversity and Comedy in Ottoman Istanbul: The Turkish Shadow Performances'. PhD dissertation, Columbia University, New York.

MOORE, Robbie. 2013. 'Soap Opera Diplomacy: Turkish TV in Greece'. *The International*, 27 February, p. 1.

MOORE, Sonia. 1984. *The Stanislavski System.* New York: Penguin Books.

MOORE, Squeaky. 2017. *#100Pitches: Mistakes I've Made So You Don't Have To: The Film and Television Pitching Guide for Content Creators.* n.p.: Moore Squeaky Productions.

MORAN, Albert. 2009. *New Flows in Global TV.* Bristol: Intellect Books.

——, and Justin Malbon. 2006. *Understanding the Global TV Format.* Bristol: Intellect Books.

MORRIS, Eric. n.d. 'The Eric Morris System'. Available at https://bit.ly/35QOnmD

MÜLLER, Timo. 2010. 'Notes toward an Ecological Conception of Bakhtin's "Chrono-tope"'. *Ecozon@: European Journal of Literature, Culture and Environment* 1(1): 98–102.

MURCH, Walter. 2001. *In the Blink of an Eye: A Perspective on Film Editing*. West Hollywood, CA: Silman-James Press.

MUTLU, Dilek Kaya. 2005. 'The *Midnight Express* (1978) Phenomenon and the Image of Turkey'. *Historical Journal of Film, Radio and Television* 25(3): 475–96.

MUTLU, Yeşim. 2009. 'Turkey's Experience of Forced Migration after 1980s and Social Integration: A Comparative Analysis of Diyarbakır and Istanbul'. PhD dissertation, Middle East Technical University, Ankara.

MYNET. 2020. 'Çukur Dizisinden Evden Çekilen Özel Bölüm Sürprizi! Çukur Bu Akşam Var mı?' Mynet, 20 April. Available at https://bit.ly/2YVxRhU

NALÇACI, Nilgün. 2011. Interview by the author, 16 November.

———. 2016. 'Hanım'ın Kimliği Hala Bende Durur'. Interview by Cansu Uras. Ranini.tv, 28 October. Available at https://bit.ly/2WUjOKh

NALÇACI, Nilgün. 2020. Interview by the author, 25 March.

NARİN, Aslı. n.d. 'Sinema ve Edebiyatın Öksüz Çocuğu: Bir Fotokitap Olarak Foto-roman'. Orta Format. Available at https://bit.ly/2yL0h5l

NAS, Tevfik F., and Mehmet Odekon (eds). 1988. *Liberalization and the Turkish Economy*. New York: Greenwood Press.

NORRIS, Sigrid, and Carmen Daniela Maier (eds). 2014. *Interactions, Images and Texts: A Reader in Multimodality*. Berlin: de Gruyter.

NUTKU, Özdemir. 1969. *Darülbedayinin Elli Yılı*. Ankara: A.Ü.-D.T.C.F. Yayınları.

O'NEIL, Mary Lou. 2013. 'Selfish, Vengeful, and Full of Spite: The Representations of Women Who Have Abortions on Turkish Television'. *Feminist Media Studies* 13(5): 810–18.

OBST, Lynda. 1997. *Hello, He Lied, and Other Truths from the Hollywood Trenches*. New York: Broadway Books.

ÖĞET, Cem. 2019. 'Müziğin Filmlerdeki Önemi-2'. *Vizyon*, October. Available at https://bit.ly/3zl5nBC

ÖĞÜT, Adem, and Ayşe Kocabacak. 2008. 'Küreselleşme Sürecinde Türk İş Kültüründe Yaşanan Dönüşümün Boyutları'. *Selçuk University Journal of Studies in Turcology* 23: 145–70.

OĞUZ, Abdullah. 2016. Talk given at Mithat Alam Film Merkezi, Istanbul, 3 March.

OĞUZ, Gül. 2007. 'Töreyi Bitirmek gibi Bir İddiamız Yok'. *Sabah*, Interview by Eylem Bilgiç, 18 February. Available at https://bit.ly/2Jsm4Ra

Oн, Chong-Jin, and Young-gil Chae. 2013. 'Constructing Culturally Proximate Spaces through Social Network Services: The Case of "Hallyu" (Korean Wave) in Turkey'. *Uluslararası İlişkiler/International Relations* 10(38) (Summer): 77–99.

Öncü, Ayşe. 1995. 'Packaging Islam: Cultural Politics on the Landscape of Turkish Commercial Television'. *Public Culture* 8(1): 51–71.

——. 2000. 'The Banal and the Subversive: Politics of Language on Turkish Television'. *European Journal of Cultural Studies* 3(3): 296–318.

——. 2011. 'Representing and Consuming "the East" in Cultural Markets'. *New Perspectives on Turkey* 45 (Fall): 49–73.

Önder, Ümit. 2019. 'Müziğin Filmlerdeki Önemi-2'. *Vizyon*, October. Available at https://bit.ly/3zl5nBC

Önen, S. Mustafa, and Nural İmik Tanyıldızı. 2010. 'The Administrative Supervision of Broadcasting of the Turkish Radio Television Corporation (TRT): Can the British Broadcasting Corporation (BBC) Provide a Model?' *Amme Idaresi Dergisi* 43(3): 125–152.

Öneş, Nilgün. 2017a. 'Nilgün Öneş: "Asi Dizisinin Seçkin Senaryo Yazarı Türk people-news.gr'da"'. *People News*, 18 October. Available at https://bit.ly/2xmzIlM

——. 2017b. 'Nilgün Öneş: Senaryo Yazarı'. *İlham Verenler*, 11 May. Available at https://bit.ly/3dJRXST

Öngen, Betül. 2017. 'Devlet Güdümündeki Medyadan Özel Sermaye Medyasına Geçiş: Turgut Özal Dönemi Medya Sermaye Yapısının Değişimi'. *Akademik Bakış* (59): 26–40.

Öniş, Ziya, and Şuhnaz Yılmaz. 2008. 'Greek-Turkish Rapprochement: Rhetoric or Reality?'. *Political Science Quarterly* 123(1): 123–49.

Orkut, Ercüment. 2019. 'Üyelerimize Sorduk'. *Vizyon*, March. Published at https://bit.ly/3oef3HV

Ortner, Sherry B. 2009. 'Studying Sideways: Ethnographic Access in Hollywood' in Vicki Mayer, Miranda J. Banks, John T. Caldwell (eds), *Production Studies: Cultural Studies of Media Industries*. London: Routledge, pp. 183–97.

——. 2010. 'Access: Reflections on Studying Up in Hollywood'. *Ethnography* 11(2): 211–33.

Öymen, Aslı. 2012. 'Turkish 'TV Series Spring' Continues'. *Hürriyet Daily News*, 17 October. Available at https://bit.ly/93bAN5O5

Öz, Aysun. 2013. 'Sevdaluk Köyü Şenyuva Cennetten Bir Köşe'. *Habertürk*, 15 December. Available at https://bit.ly/2UuSCjG

Öz, Özlem, and Kaya Özkaracalar. 2011. 'What Accounts for the Resilience and Vulnerability of Clusters? The Case of Istanbul's Film Industry'. *European Planning Studies* 19(3): 361–78.

———, and Mine Eder. 2012. 'Rendering Istanbul's Periodic Bazaars Invisible: Reflections on Urban Transformation and Contested Space'. *International Journal of Urban and Regional Research* 36(2): 297–314.

ÖZAKMAN, Turgut. 1978. 'Devlet Tiyatrolarının Sorunları'. *Devlet Tiyatrosu Aylık Sanat Dergisi* 69: 4.

———. 1988. 'Türk Tiyatrosu ve Atatürk'. *Erdem* 5(12): 1045–62.

ÖZALP, Leyla. 2013. *Bir Film Yapmak*. Istanbul: Hil Yayınları.

ÖZALPMAN, Deniz. 2017. 'Transnational Viewers of Turkish Television Drama Series'. *Transnational Marketing Journal (TMJ)* 5(1): 25–43.

ÖZBAY, Ferhunde. 1999. 'Gendered Space: A New Look at Turkish Modernisation'. *Gender and History* 11(3): 555–68.

ÖZBEK, Meral. 1991. *Popüler Kültür ve Orhan Gencebay Arabeski*. Istanbul: İletişim Yayınları.

ÖZCAN, Perihan. 2015. 'Canan Ergüder: Kendimi çok güzel döverim'. *Habertürk*, 12 February. Available at https://bit.ly/37k4T3q

ÖZCAN, Yusuf Ziya, and Abdullah Koçak. 2003. 'Research Note: A Need or a Status Symbol? Use of Cellular Telephones in Turkey'. *European Journal of Communication* 18(2): 241–54.

ÖZÇİVİT, Burak. 2014. Interview by the author, 2 April.

———. 2018. Interview by the author, 21 January.

ÖZDİKİCİ-DUYAL, Ece. 2015. 'Oyunculuk İlke/Kuralları ve Bir Kurum Tiyatrosu Olarak İ.B.B. Şehir Tiyatrolarında Kurum Kültürü'. MA thesis, Kadir Has University, Istanbul.

ÖZELÇİ, Remziye Köse. 2010. 'Toplumsal Belleğin Dramatik Kurgulanması: Hatırla Sevgili TV Dizisi'. PhD dissertation, Marmara University, Istanbul.

ÖZEN, Ayhan. 2014. Interview by the author, 26 May.

ÖZEN, Saadet. 2010. 'Rethinking the Young Turk Revolution: Manaki Brothers Still and Moving Images'. MA thesis, Boğaziçi University, Istanbul.

ÖZEN, Zeynep. 2010. '*Aşk-ı Memnu*: Tüketim Aşkının Yasak Lezzeti'. *Birikim* (August–September): 58–63.

ÖZER, Ayşe. 2012. Interview by the author, 11 April.

ÖZGÖKBEL-BİLİS, Pınar, A. Emre Bilis, and Meerim Sydygalieva. 2018. 'Türkiye-Türk Cumhuriyetleri Kültürel İlişkilerinde Televizyon Dizileri Faktörü: Kırgızistan Örneği'. *MANAS Sosyal Araştırmalar Dergisi* 7(1): 403–25.

ÖZHAN-KOÇAK, Dilek, and Orhan Kemal Koçak. 2014. *Whose City Is That? Culture, Design, Spectacle and Capital in Istanbul*. Newcastle upon Tyne: Cambridge Scholars Publishing.

ÖZIŞIK, Ethem. 2017. 'İyi Bir Senarist, Karakterlerinin Düşmanı Olur'. Ranini.tv, 16 September. Available at https://bit.ly/33GoGUJ

ÖZKAN, Gülden. 2019. 'Bir Halkla İlişkiler Çalışması Olarak Türkiye'de Düzenlenen İlk Güzellik Yarışması'. *Erciyes İletişim Dergisi* 6(1): 587–606.

ÖZKAN, Sarenur. 2019. 'Televizyon Dizi Türü Olarak Absurd Komediler ve Leyla ile Mecnun Dizisi Üzerine İçerik Analizi'. MA thesis, Marmara University, Istanbul.

ÖZKARTAL, Miraç Zeynep. 2011. 'Muhteşem Yüzyıl'ın Senaristi Meral Okay: "Tehtidlerden Korkuyorum!" *Milliyet*, 30 October. Available at https://bit.ly/3KscHi8

ÖZKUBAT, Handan. 2020. Interview by the author, 5 February.

ÖZMEN, Cengiz, Harun Er and Fatma Ünal. 2014. 'Televizyon Dizilerinin Tarih Bilinci Üzerine Etkisi: Muhteşem Yüzyıl Dizisi Örneği'. *Mustafa Kemal Üniversitesi Sosyal Bilimler Enstitüsü Dergisi* 11(25): 409–26.

ÖZMEN, Seçkin, and Y. Yıldızhan. 2004. 'Hikayeyi Yeniden Anlatmak: 'Asmalı Konak'ta İlksel Metinlerin İzleri ve Seriyal Özelliği' in *2nd International Symposium Communication in the Millennium*. Istanbul: Association of Turkish and American Communication Scholars, pp. 291–304.

ÖZÖN, Nijat. 1968. *Karagözden Sinemaya: Türk Sineması ve Sorunları*. Ankara: Kitle Yayınları.

ÖZŞENER, Yiğit. 2012. Interview by the author, 10 May.

ÖZSOY, Aydan. 2004. 'Türkiye'de 1960'lar Dönemi Aile Melodramlarında Kadın ve Erkek İmgesi' in F. Küçükkurt and A. Gürata (eds), *Sinemada Anlatı ve Türler*. Istanbul: Vadi Yayınları.

ÖZSÜMBÜL, Özlem. 2017. Interview by the author, 25 February.

———. 2019. Interview by the author, 1 September.

ÖZTEKİN, Mehmet Ada. 2012. Interview by the author, 2 May.

ÖZTUNCAY, Bahattin (ed.). 2011. *Dynasty and Camera: Portraits from the Ottoman Court, Ömer M. Koç Collection*. İstanbul: AYGAZ.

ÖZTÜRK, Mehmet. 2004. 'Türk Sinemasında Gecekondular'. *European Journal of Turkish Studies* 1. Available at https://bit.ly/2X6cfAv

ÖZTÜRK, Tuğba Aydın. 2014. 'Muhafazakarlık İdeolojisi Çerçevesinde Gelişen Kültür ve Sanat Politikaları'. *Journal of International Social Research* 7(34): 621–27.

ÖZTÜRKMEN, Arzu. 1994. 'The Role of the People's Houses in the Making of National Culture in Turkey'. *New Perspectives on Turkey* 11 (Fall): 159–81.

———. 1998. 'A Short History of *Kadınca* Magazine and Its Feminism' in Zehra Arat (ed.), *Deconstructing Images of 'The Turkish Woman'*. New York: St. Martin's Press, pp. 275–93.

———. 2001. 'Celebrating National Holidays in Turkey: History and Memory'. *New Perspectives on Turkey* 25 (Fall): 47–75.

———. 2002. 'I Dance Folklore' in Deniz Kandiyoti and Ayşe Saktanber (eds), *Fragments of Culture: The Everyday Life of Turkey*. London: I. B. Tauris, pp. 128–46.

——. 2005. 'Turkish Tourism at the Door of Europe: Problems of Image in Historical and Contemporary Perspectives'. *Middle Eastern Studies* 41(4): 605–21.

——. 2006a. 'Domestic Space: Turkey' in *Encyclopaedia of Women and Islamic Cultures*. Leiden: Brill, pp. 527–28.

——. 2006b. 'Female Space: Turkey' in *Encyclopaedia of Women and Islamic Cultures*. Leiden: Brill, pp. 539–40.

——. 2007. 'Folk Dancers and Folk Singers: The Ottoman Empire and Turkey' in *Encyclopedia of Women and Islamic Cultures*. Leiden: Brill, pp. 56–58, 60–61.

——. 2008a. 'Dolmuş' in Pelin Derviş, Bulent Tanju and Ugur Tanyeli (eds), *Becoming Istanbul: An Encyclopedia*. Istanbul: Garanti Gallery, pp. 85–86.

——. 2008b. 'Dress' in Pelin Derviş, Bulent Tanju and Ugur Tanyeli (eds), *Becoming Istanbul: An Encyclopedia*. Istanbul: Garanti Gallery, pp. 84–85.

——. 2009. 'Orality and Performance in Late Medieval Turkish Texts: Epic Tales, Hagiographies and Chronicles'. *Text and Performance Quarterly* 29(4): 327–45.

——. 2011. 'Performance, iconography and narrative in Ottoman Festive Events' in Barbara Sparti, Judy Van Zile, Elsie Ivancich Dunin, Nancy G. Heller, Adrienne L. Kaeppler (eds), *Imaging Dance*. Olms Verlag, pp. 77–86.

——. 2013. 'The Women's Movement under Ottoman and Republican Rule: A Historical Reappraisal'. *Journal of Women's History* 25(4): 256–65.

——. 2014. 'The Park, the Penguin and the Gas: Performance in Progress of Gezi Park'. *TDR: The Drama Review* 58(3) (Fall): 39–68.

——. 2015. 'The Quest for "National Music": A Historical-Ethnographic Survey of New Approaches to Folk Music Research' in Martin Greve (ed.), *Writing the History of Ottoman Music*. Würzburg: Ergon Verlag.

——. 2019. 'Kore Dalgası ve Türk İçerikleri: Televizyon Dizileri Arası Diyaloglar' in Fikret Turan, Filiz Ferhatoğlu, Cezmi Bayram (eds), *Uluslararası İpek Yolu Sempozyumu: Türkiye ile Kore Arasında Uygarlıkların Etkileşimi Bildirileri*. Istanbul: Türk Ocağı Yayınları, pp. 128–39.

——, and Joanna Bornat. 2009. 'Oral History' in Liz Locke, Pauline Greenhill, Theresa A. Vaughan (eds), *Encyclopedia of Women's Folklore and Folklife*. Abingdon: Greenwood Publishing, pp. 433–5.

ÖZYAĞCILAR, Erdal. 2014. Talk given at Mithat Alam Film Merkezi, Istanbul, 13 November.

OZYEGIN, Gul. 2001. *Untidy Gender: Domestic Service in Turkey*. Philadelphia, PA: Temple University Press.

ÖZYILMAZ, Melih. 2018. 'Dünyada da Türkiye'de de En Çok İşleyen Tema İmkansız Aşktır'. Interview by Gizem Yıldız. *Yeni Çağrı* (8 September). Published at https://bit.ly/3ax41oH (currently unavailable; last accessed on 1 February 2019).

PACKARD, Vance. 1957. *The Hidden Persuaders*. New York: Ig Publishing.

PAMUK, Orhan. 2006. *Istanbul: Memories and the City*. New York: Vintage International.

———. 2009. *The Museum of Innocence*. New York: Alfred A. Knopf.

PAPAILIAS, Penelope. 2005. 'TV Across the Aegean: The Greek Love Affair with a Turkish Serial'. *Window to Greek Culture 4*. Available at https://bit.ly/2UIIJyt

PAREDES, Américo. 1958. *'With His Pistol in His Hand': A Border Ballad and Its Hero*. Austin: University of Texas Press.

PARK, Joseph Sung-Yul, and Mary Bucholtz. 2009. 'Introduction. Public transcripts: Entextualization and Linguistic Representation in Institutional Contexts'. *Text and Talk* 29(5): 485–502.

PARLAR, Zafer, and Ali Calkan Menekşe. 2016. 'Türk İş Kültürü Üzerine Beş Tavsiye'. *Skylife*, November. Published at https://bit.ly/39WpWVe (currently unavailable; last accessed on 31 March 2019).

PASCHALIDOU, Nina Maria (director). 2014. *Kismet*. Athens, Greece: Anemon Productions and Forest Troop, DVD.

PEKMAN, Cem, and Selin Tüzün. 2012. 'Turkish Television Dramas: The Economy and Beyond'. *Cinéma and Cie* 12(19): 93–104.

PEKMAN, Yavuz. 2002. 'Tanzimat Dönemi Oyun Yazarlığında Batılılaşma Olgusu'. *Tiyatro Araştırmaları Dergisi* 14: n.p.

———. 2007. 'Türk Tiyatrosunda Bir 'Başrol' Olarak Mahalle'. *İstanbul Üniversitesi Edebiyat Fakültesi Tiyatro Eleştirmenliği ve Dramaturgi Bölüm Dergisi* 10: 28–61.

PERRINO, Sabina, and Michael Lempert. 2007. 'Entextualization and the Ends of Temporality'. *Language and Communication* 37(3): 205–336.

PIÇAK, Murat, and Hamza Kadah. 2017. 'Türkiye'de Sendikalaşmanın Tarihsel Gelişimi' in Selçuk Koç, Sema Yılmaz Genç and Kerem Çolak (eds), *Dünden Bugüne Ekonomi Yazıları*. Istanbul: Küv Yayınları, pp. 198–240.

PINTO, İzzet. 2013. Interview by the author, 8 April.

PIŞKİN, Günseli. 2007. 'Binbir Gece Televizyon Dizisi ve Toplumumuzda Kadın'. *Afyon Kocatepe Üniversitesi Sosyal Bilimler Dergisi* 9(1): 195–215.

PORTELLI, Alessandro. 1991. *The Death of Luigi Trastulli and Other Stories: Form and Meaning in Oral History*. Albany: State University of New York Press.

PORTER, Michael. 1998. *On Competition*. Boston, MA: Harvard Business School Press.

POSTA. 2016. 'Poyraz Karayel'in yönetmeninden zehir zemberek açıklamalar', 13 June. Available at https://bit.ly/39WDHTL

PÖSTEKİ, Nigar. 2007. *Yeşilçam'dan Bir Portre: Ayhan Işık*. Ümraniye: Es Yayınları.

POSTIL, John. 2017. 'The Diachronic Ethnography of Media: From Social Changing to Actual Social Changes'. *Moment, Journal of Cultural Studies* 4(1–2): 19–43, 319–25.

PRESS, Joy. 'The Week the Cameras Stopped: TV in the COVID-19 Era'. *Vanity Fair*, 23 April. Available at https://bit.ly/3fIc98a

PUTRI, Edira. 2018. 'Sinetron: Indonesia's Popular "Telenovellas"'. *Culture Trip*, 19 December. Available at https://bit.ly/3hBmUe6

RADİKAL. 2009. 'Çılgın Türk, Yorgun Savaşçı'yı nasıl yaktı!' 15 October. Available at https://bit.ly/2wpF3Zt

RAVINDRAN, Manori. 2019. 'MIPTV Says "Change Means Change" with New Palais-Centered Strategy'. *TBI*, 23 July. Available at https://bit.ly/2Jr6hls

REDLING, Erik. 2015. 'The Musicalization of Poetry' in Gabriele Rippl (ed.), *Handbook of Intermediality: Literature – Image – Sound – Music*. Berlin: de Gruyter, pp. 494–511.

REDWOOD, Thomas. 2010. *Andrei Tarkovsky's Poetics of Cinema*. Newcastle upon Tyne: Cambridge Scholars Publishing.

REFİĞ, Halit. 2010. *Düşlerden Düşüncelere Söyleşiler*. Istanbul: Kabalcı Yayınevi.

RESMİ GAZETE. 2019. *Resmi Gazete* No. 30671:11, 30 January.

RIBKE, Nahuel. 2011. 'Telenovela Writers under the Military Regime in Brazil: Beyond the Cooption and Resistance dichotomy'. *Media, Culture and Society* 33(5): 659–73.

RODRIGUEZ, Robert. 1996. *Rebel without a Crew; or, How a 23-Year-Old Filmmaker with $7,000 Became a Hollywood Player*. New York: Plume.

ROUSSELIN, Mathieu. 2013. 'Turkish Soap Power: International Perspectives and Domestic Paradoxes'. *Euxeinos: Culture and Governance in the Black Sea Region* 10: 16–22.

ROXBOROUGH, Scott. 2013. 'Sweden's SVT Takes Turkish Drama "20 Minutes"'. *Hollywood Reporter*, 12 May. Available at https://bit.ly/2BmlvHG

RTÜK. 2013. 'Istanbul TV Forum ve Fuarı (İTVF) törenle açıldı'. *Rtük.gov.tr*, 21 June. Available at https://bit.ly/3PFuwwh

SAAT, Beren. 2019. Talk given at Famelog Academy, Istanbul, 17 February.

ŞAHBAZ, R. Pars, and Arzu Kılıçlar. 2009. 'Filmlerin ve Televizyon Dizilerinin Destinasyon İmajina Etkileri'. *İşletme Araştırmaları Dergisi* 1(1): 31–52.

ŞAHİN, Haluk. 2002. 'Tarcan Günenç: Gerçek Bir Televizyoncu'. *Radikal*, 9 February. Available at https://bit.ly/3dcPZdP

——. 2007. 'Köşe Yazısı'. *Radikal*, 26 January. Available at https://bit.ly/2QuOUUY

——, and Asu Aksoy. 1993. 'Global Media and Cultural Identity in Turkey'. *Journal of Communication* 43(2): 31–41.

ŞAHİN, İrfan. 2015. Interview by the author, 11 February.

ŞAHİNLER, Yıldıray. 2017. 'Aslında Bütün Dünya Düzenini İçerde'de Bulabilirsiniz'. Interview by Cansu Uras. Ranini.tv, 1 July. Available at https://bit.ly/2xVxEC9

SAKTANBER, Binnaz. 2010. 'TV Dizileri ve İzleyici "Katılımı": Bloglar Başrolde'. *Birikim* (August–September): 69–76.

SALAMANDRA, Christa. 1998. 'Moustache Hairs Lost: Ramadan Television Serials and the Construction of Identity in Damascus, Syria'. *Visual Anthropology* 10(2–4): 226–46.

——. 2004. *A New Old Damascus: Authenticity and Distinction in Urban Syria*. Bloomington: Indiana University Press.

——. 2008. 'Creative compromise: Syrian television makers between Secularism and Islamism'. *Contemporary Islam* 2: 177–89.

——. 2012. 'The Muhannad Effect: Media Panic, Melodrama, and the Arab Female Gaze'. *Anthropological Quarterly* 85(1): 45–77.

——. 2013a. 'Arab Television Drama Production and the Islamic Public Sphere' in Christiane Gruber and Sune Haugbolle (eds), *Rhetoric of the Image: Visual Culture in Muslim Contexts*. Bloomington: Indiana University Press, pp. 261–74.

——. 2013b. 'Syrian Television Drama: A National Industry in a Pan-Arab Mediascape' in Tourya Guaaybess (ed.), *National Broadcasting Policy in Arab Countries*. Basingstoke: Palgrave Macmillan, pp. 83–95.

——. 2015. 'Introduction: A Legacy of Raised Expectations' in Christa Salamandra and Leif Stenberg (eds), *Syria from Reform to Revolt: Culture, Society and Religion*. Syracuse, NY: Syracuse University Press, pp. 1–15.

——, and Leif Stenberg (eds). 2015. *Syria from Reform to Revolt: Culture, Society and Religion*. Syracuse, NY: Syracuse University Press.

SALLAN-GÜL, Songül, and Yonca Altındal. 2015. 'Medyada Kadın Cinayeti Haberlerindeki Cinsiyetçi İzler: Radikal Gazetesi'. *Akdeniz Üniversitesi İletişim Fakültesi Dergisi* 24: 168–88.

SAMANCILAR, Menderes. 2014. Talk given at Mithat Alam Film Merkezi, Istanbul, 20 February.

SANDIKCI, Özlem. 2015. 'Strolling Through Istanbul's Beyoğlu: In-between Difference and Containment'. *Space and Culture* 18(2): 198–211.

SANDWELL, Ian. 2018. '7 Dark Behind-the-Scenes stories from Your Favourite TV shows'. *Digital Spy*, 20 February. Available at https://bit.ly/3egzEVJ

ŞANLI, Yadigar. 2013. 'Orhan Pamuk'un Romanlarında Doğu-Batı Algısı'. PhD dissertation, Istanbul University.

SARAÇ, Duygu Çeliker. 2019. 'Televizyon Dizilerinin Üretiminde Emek Süreci'. *İletişim Kuram ve Araştırma Dergisi* 48: 419–41.

SARAL, Hilal. 2012. Interview by the author, 29 May.

——. 2015. Interview by foreign journalists, 22 August.

SARFATİ, Moris. Interview by the author, 23 November.

SARIOĞLU, Aydın. 2012. Interview by the author, 1 May.

SATMIŞ, Doğan. 2017. *$urvivor: Yeni Türkiye'nin Rol Modeli Acun Ilıcalı'nın Sıra Dışı Hikâyesi*. Istanbul: Karakarga Yayınları.

SAVCI, Timur. 2014. Interview by the author, 28 May.

——. 2017. Talk given at Famelog Academy, 30 March.

———. 2020. Interview by the author, 26 May.

SAYAN, Pınar. 2010. *New-Nationalist Popular Art in Turkey: The Case of Kurtlar Vadisi.* Saarbrücken: Lambert Academic Publishing.

SAYARI, Sabri. 2010. 'Political Violence and Terrorism in Turkey, 1976–80: A Retrospective Analysis'. *Terrorism and Political Violence* 22(2): 198–215.

SCHECHNER, Richard. 2006. *Performance Studies: An Introduction.* New York: Routledge.

SCHER, Steven Paul. 1992. *Music and Text: Critical Inquiries.* Cambridge: Cambridge University Press.

SCHÜLER, Harald, Yılmaz Tonbul and Tanıl Bora. 1999. *Türkiye'de Sosyal Demokrasi: Particilik, Hemşehrilik, Alevilik.* Istanbul: İletişim.

SCHWEIGHAUSER, Philipp. 2015. 'Literary Acoustics' in Gabriele Rippl (ed.), *Handbook of Intermediality: Literature – Image – Sound – Music.* Berlin: de Gruyter, pp. 475–93.

SCOGNAMILLO, Giovanni. 2001. *Bay Sinema: Türker İnanoğlu.* Istanbul: Doğan Kitap.

———, and Metin Demirhan. 2002. *Erotik Türk Sineması.* Kabalcı Yayınları.

SCOTT, Allen J. 2005. *On Hollywood: The Place, The Industry.* Princeton, NJ: Princeton University Press.

ŞEKER, Mustafa and Fadime Şimşek. 2011. 'Ötekilik Bağlamında "Muhteşem Yüzyıl" Dizisinin Farklı İdeolojideki Gazetelerin Köşe Yazılarına Yansımaları'. *Türkiyat Araştırmaları Dergisi* 29: 483–502.

SEKMEÇ, Ali Can. 2011. *Türk Televizyon Dizileri: 1974–1995.* Antalya: AKSAV Yayınları.

ŞEN, A. Fulya, and Şule Yenigün Altın. 2018. 'Televizyon Dizilerinde Milliyetçi Söylemlerin Yeniden Üretimi: İsimsizler, Savaşçı ve Söz Örneği'. *Ege Üniversitesi İletişim Fakültesi Medya ve İletişim Araştırmaları Dergisi* 3: 113–40.

ŞEN, Can. 2018. 'Televizyon-Edebiyat İlişkisi Bağlamında Ezel Dizisi'. *Littera Turca Journal of Turkish Language and Literature* 4(1): 259–78.

ŞENER, Aydan. 2016. Interview by the author, 29 October.

SEPÚLVEDA, G., Paulina. 2017. 'Nombres de niños inscritos en 2016 reflejan influencia de teleseries turcas'. *La Tercera*, 8 March. Available at https://bit.ly/3DNwGFG

SERBES, Emrah. 2012. Talk given at Mithat Alam Film Merkezi, Istanbul, 28 March.

SERİM, Omer. 2007. *Türk Televizyon Tarihi 1952–2006.* Istanbul: Epsilon.

SERTBULUT, Zeynep. 2022. *Dramas of Turkish Cultural Production On and Off Screen.* PhD dissertation, New York University.

SEVİM, Ö. Yelda. 2000. 'Terör Nedeniyle Elazığ'a Göç Edenlerin Sorunları Üzerine Sosyolojik Bir Araştırma'. PhD dissertation, Fırat University, Elazığ.

SEZGİN, Neslihan. 2006. *Bir popüler kültür örneği olarak Kurtlar Vadisi Dizisinde erkek kimliğinin sunumu.* MA thesis, Maltepe University, Istanbul.

SIMMEL, Georg. 1997. *Simmel on Culture: Selected Writings.* London: Sage Publications.

SİRMAN, Nükhet. 1989. 'Feminism in Turkey: A Short History'. *New Perspectives on Turkey* 1 (Fall): 1–34.

———. 2007. 'Kürtlerle Dans'. *Kültür ve Siyasette Feminist Yaklaşımlar*, 2 February. Available at https://bit.ly/2UHHCiO

———. 2016. 'Yeni Türkiye, Yeni Diziler, Yeni erkeklikler'. *Çatlak Zemin*, 2 November. Available at https://bit.ly/3hpEeTl

ŞİT, Nuran Evren. 2011. 'İyi Gazete Röportajı'. *Nuran Evren Şit Senaryo Yazarı*, 20 February. Available at https://bit.ly/2wEKVOX

SMITH, Peter B., Michael Harris Bond and Çiğdem Kağıtçıbaşı. 2006. *Understanding Social Psychology across Cultures Living and Working in a Changing World*. London: Sage Publications.

SOL. 2013. 'Muhteşem Yüzyıl Yapımcısına Tehdit: "Bir Dizi Yüzünden Gebereceksin"', 13 February. Available at https://bit.ly/3dFlttd

SÖNMEZ, Elif. 2011. Interview by the author, 6 October.

SÖNMEZ, Mustafa. 2010. *Medya, Kültür, Para ve İstanbul İktidarı*. Istanbul: Yordam Kitap.

SÖNMEZ, Şenol. 2016. Interview by the author, 18 May.

SOYDEMİR, Begüm. 2008. 'Gümüş'ün Sırrı Bu İkilide!' *Radikal*, 16 August.

SOYGÜDER, Şebnem. 2003. *Eyvah Paparazzi*. Istanbul: OM Yayınevi.

SÖZCÜ. 2018. 'Türker İnanoğlu Kimdir? Kaç yaşında nereli? İşte Yeşilçam'ın ve Türk Sinemasının usta ismi hakkında merak edilenler . . .', 21 June. Available at https://bit.ly/39qx23T

———. 2020a. 'Arka Sokaklar Yeni Bölüm Çekimlerine Başlıyor! Zafer Ergin Yaş Sınırına Takıldı', 16 April. Available at https://bit.ly/2NfXLI8

———. 2020b. 'Borcumdan üç gün evden çıkmadım', 2 August. Available at https://bit.ly/3x41hNG

SPIRO, Amy. 2019. 'The Turkish Soap Opera That Has Transfixed Israelis'. *Jerusalem Post*, 12 February. Available at https://bit.ly/2V0P1ZV

STEWART, Kathleen. 2005. 'Cultural Poesis: The Generativity of Emergent Things' in Norman Denzin and Yvonna Lincoln (eds), *Handbook of Qualitative Research*. London: Sage Publications, pp. 1027–42.

STIEGLER, Bernard. 2011. 'Suffocate Desire, or How the Cultural Industry Destroys the Individual: Contribution to a Theory of Mass Consumption'. *Parrhesia* 13: 52–61.

STILWELL, Robynn J. 2007. 'The Fantastical Gap between Diegetic and Nondiegetic' in Daniel Goldmark, Lawrence Kramer and Richard Leppert (eds), *Beyond the Soundtrack: Representing Music in Cinema*. Berkeley: University of California Press, pp. 184–202.

STOELTJE, Beverly, and Richard Bauman. 1988. 'The Semiotics of Cultural Performance' in Thomas A. Sebeok and Jean Umiker-Sebeok (eds), *The Semiotic Web*. Berlin: de Gruyter, pp. 585–99.

STOKES, Martin. 1992. *The Arabesk Debate: Music and Musicians in Modern Turkey*. New York: Oxford University Press.

SUNER, Asuman. 2010. *New Turkish Cinema: Belonging, Identity and Memory*. London: I. B. Tauris.

SÜNETÇİOĞLU, Ayşegül. 2012. 'Şahika Tekand ve Stüdyo Oyuncuları (1989–2009)'. PhD dissertation, Dokuz Eylül University, Izmir.

SURURİ, Gülriz. 2003. *Bir An Gelir*. Istanbul: Doğan Kitapçılık.

TACİRLİ, Merve. 2017. 'Bey Mahallesi'nde Gündelik Hayat'. PhD dissertation, Selçuk University, Konya.

TAÇYILDIZ, Asuman. 1995. 'Pembe Dizi Reklam İlişkisi'. MA thesis, Istanbul University.

TALİMCİLER, Ahmet. 2010. 'Bir Meşrulaştırma Aracı Olarak Futbolun Türkiye'de Son 25 Yılı'. Futbol Ekonomi, 25 November. Available at https://bit.ly/2YWaMxl

TANRIÖVER, Hülya Uğur. 2002. 'Türk Televizyon Dizilerinde Aile, Mahalle ve Cemaat Yaşamı'. *İstanbul Dergisi* 40 (January): 93–96.

TANRISEVEN, Ümit. 2017. 'Muhteşem Platolar'. *Türkiye*, 29 January. Available at https://bit.ly/3aBmCAc

TANRIÖVER, Hülya Uğur. 2004. 'Dizi Dizi İnciyiz, Reytinglerde Birinciyiz'. *Pazartesi* 97: 36–37.

———. 2005a. 'Dizi Kullanım Kılavuzu'. *Pazartesi* 102: 18–19.

———. 2005b. 'Diziler Ne Söyler?'. *Pazartesi* 100: 26–27.

———. 2005c. 'Şehnaz'dan Aliye'ye Aynı Tas Aynı Hamam: Dizilerde Değiş(me)yenler'. *Pazartesi* 98: 20–21.

———. 2011. *Türkiye'de Film Endüstrisinin Konumu ve Hedefleri*. Istanbul: Istanbul Ticaret Odası Yayınları.

TANSEL-İLİC, Deniz. 2015. 'Pierre Bourdieu ve televizyon alanı: Türkiye'deki ana akım televizyon haberciliğinde bir saha araştırması'. *Selçuk İletişim* 8(4): 321–40.

TANYELİ, Uğur. 1998. *Üç Kuşak Cumhuriyet*. Tarih Vakfı Yurt Yayınları.

———. 2005. *İstanbul 1900–2000 Konutu ve Modernleşmeyi Metropolden Okumak*. Istanbul: Ofset Yapımevi Yayınları.

TARKOVSKY, Andrei. 1986. *Sculpting in Time: Reflections on the Cinema*. Austin: University of Texas Press.

TATLI, Beşir. Interview by the author, 7 July.

TATLITUĞ, Kıvanç. 2013. 'Kıvanç Tatlıtuğ ile Elle Özel'. *Elle*, 19 May. Available at https://bit.ly/2LhnUFj

———. 2016. 'Yılın Adamı Kıvanç Tatlıtuğ Bilinmeyenleri Anlattı'. Interview by Zeynep Üner. *NTV*, 21 December. Available at https://bit.ly/2yGRIbX

TAYLAN, Ahmet Mümtaz. 2016. Talk given at Mithat Alam Film Merkezi, Istanbul, 27 October.

TAYLAN, Erman. 2015. 'Dijitali Seçen Ulan İstanbul Artık Daha Kısa, Daha Özgür'. Sosyal Medya, 10 February. Available at https://bit.ly/3dfLe1H

TAYLOR, Diana. 2003. *The Archive and the Repertoire: Performing Cultural Memory in the Americas*. Durham, NC: Duke University Press.

TCCİB (T.C. Cumhurbaşkanlığı İletişim Başkanlığı). 2020. 'Kamu Diplomasisi Aracı Olarak Türk Dizileri Çalıştayı düzenlendi'. Available at: https://bit.ly/3oenymi

TCCMBS (T.C. Cumhurbaşkanlığı Mevzuat Bılgı Sıstemı). 2004. 'Sinema Filmlerinin Değerlendirilmesi ve Sınıflandırılmasına ile Desteklenmesi Hakkında Kanun', 14 July. Available at https://bit.ly/2V4zaKB

TCKB (T.C. Kalkınma Bakanlığı). 2018. *On Birinci Kalkınma Planı (2019–2023): Görsel Hizmetler Sektörünün Geliştirilmesi Çalışma Raporu*. Ankara: T.C. Kalkınma Bakanlığı Yayınları. Available at https://bit.ly/3Hqoo8k

TEKELİ, Şirin. 1986. 'Emergence of the Feminist Movement in Turkey' in Drude Dahlerup (ed.), *The New Women's Movement*. London: Sage Publications, pp. 179–99.

TEKİN, Mustafa. 2003. 'Çocuklar Duymasın ya da Bir Sitcomun Çağrıştırdıkları'. *Umran Dergisi* 103: 107–8.

———. 2017. Interview by the author, 18 October.

TEKSOY, Rekin. 2008. *Turkish Cinema*. Istanbul: Oğlak Yayıncılık.

TELEGRAPH. 2018. 'From Poldark to Broadchurch: The Best British TV Filming Locations', 8 June. Available at https://bit.ly/2RcTKGP

TEMEL, Tamer. 2016. 'Türk Modernleşmesinin Taşıyıcı Gücü: Tiyatro'. *idil* 5(26): 1763–76.

TESEV. 2008. *Zorunlu Göç Mağdurlarına Destek, Hizmet ve Yardım Veren Kişi ve Kuruluşlar için Yol Gösterici Kılavuzu*. Istanbul: Tesev Yayınları.

THELEN, Kathleen. 1999. 'Historical Institutionalism in Comparative Politics'. *Annual Review of Political Science* 2(1): 369–404.

THUSSU, Daya Kishan (ed.). 2007. *Media on the Move: Global Flow and Contra-Flow*. New York: Routledge.

TİCARET BAKANLIĞI. 2015. *Döviz Kazandırıcı Hizmet Ticaretinin Desteklenmesi Hakkında Karar*. Available at https://bit.ly/3JrDA4F

TMMOB. 1998. *Bölge İçi Zorunlu Göçten Kaynaklanan Toplumsal Sorunların Diyarbakır Kenti Ölçeğinde Araştırılması*. Ankara: TMMOB.

TODAY'S ZAMAN. 2012. 'Turkish Soap Operas Popular in Greece because of Cultural Similarities', 2 December. Available at https://bit.ly/3OLTSrM

TONNER-CONNOLLY, Brandon, and Alicia van Couvering. 2015a. 'The Seven Arts of Working in Film: A Necessary Guide to On-Set Protocol'. Filmmaker Magazine, 14 April. Available at https://bit.ly/2RvGm0l

——. 2015b. 'What Everyone Does on a Film Set'. Filmmaker Magazine, 24 August. Available at https://bit.ly/2RshW7Y

TOPÇU, Aslıhan Doğan, and Onur Önürmen. 2018. 'Kültür Endüstrisinin Eğlencelik Yüzleri: Fotoroman'dan Caps'e Bir Bakış'. Erciyes İletişim Dergisi 5(4): 263–83.

TOPUZ, Hıfzı (ed.). 1990. Yarının Radyo ve Televizyon Düzeni: Özgür, Özerk ve Çoğulcu bir Alternatif. Istanbul: İletişim Araştırmaları Derneği.

TÖRE, Evrim Özkan. 2010. İstanbul Film Endüstrisi: İstanbul'da Kültür Ekonomisine Yön Veren Dinamikler. Istanbul: Bilgi Üniversitesi Yayınları.

TRACEY, Michael. 1985. 'The Poisoned Chalice: International Television and the Idea of Dominance'. Daedalus 114(4): 17–56.

TREISMAN, Jonathan. 2003. 'Writing Loglines That Sell'. Bi-weekly Ezine, 30 August. Published at https://bit.ly/3ajIi3u (currently unavailable; last accessed on 17 March 2020).

TRT HABER. 2020a. 'Mısır Dizileri Koronavirüs Salgınına Rağmen Setlerde Çekiliyor', 2 May. Available at https://bit.ly/3Jfybx7

——. 2020b. 'Ramazan'da TRT1'de Her Gün: Kuşlarla Yolculuk', 21 April. Available at https://bit.ly/3uTuvw0

TRT. 2017. 'Tarihçe'. Available at https://bit.ly/3dqtgLo

TSA.ORG.TR. 2017. 'Bay E-Tüm Ekip ve Oyuncular'. Available at https://bit.ly/3Ottcwe

TUFAN-TANRIÖVER, Hülya, and Ayşe Eyüboğlu. 2000. Popüler Kültür Ürünlerinde Kadın İstihdamını Etkileyebilecek Öğeler. Ankara: T.C. Başbakanlık Kadının Statüsü ve Sorunları Genel Müdürlüğü Yayınları.

TUĞ, Onur. 2014. 'Dizi ve Sinema Filmlerinde Bir Çok Başarılı İşe İmza Atan Sanat Yönetmeni Onur Tuğ ile Röportajımız'. Interview by Dizisponsorları.com, 22 June. Available at https://bit.ly/2WWskIS

TUĞRUL, Semih. 1975. Türkiye'de Televizyon ve Radyo Olayları. Istanbul: Koza Yayınları.

TUNAYA, Tarık Zafer. 1960. Türkiye'nin Siyasî Hayatında Batılılaşma hareketleri. Istanbul: Yedigün Matbaası.

TUNÇ, Aslı. 2001. 'Gırgır as a Sociological Phenomenon in Turkey: The Transformation of a Humor Magazine'. Humor 14(3): 243–54.

——. 2012. 'Missing Byzantium: Explaining Greeks' Love for Turkish TV Serials'. International Journal of Media and Cultural Politics 8(2–3): 335–41.

——. 2018. 'All Is Flux: A Hybrid Media Approach to Macro-Analysis of the Turkish Media'. Middle East Critique 27(2): 141–59.

TUNÇ, Ayfer. 2001. Bir Maniniz Yoksa Annemler Size Gelecek: 70'li Yıllarda Hayatımız. Istanbul: Yapı Kredi Yayınları.

———. 2010. 'Her Türkün Kullandığı Tek Yerli Malı: Diziler'. *Birikim* (August–September): 38–47. Available at https://bit.ly/3OIlWfN

TUNÇ, Hüseyin. 2012. Interview by the author, 23 May.

TUNCAY, Murat. 2007. 'Modern Türk Tiyatrosu'nun İlk Sıkıntılarına Toplu Bakış'. *Yedi* 1: 20–35.

TUNCAY, Rauf. 1968. 'Türk Tiyatro Tarihi Belgeleri'. *Belgelerle Türk Tarihi Dergisi* 8: 71–75.

TUNCER, Cem. 2019. 'Üyelerimize Sorduk'. *Vizyon*, March. Available at https://bit.ly/3oef3HV

TUNCER, Selda. 2018. *Women and Public Space in Turkey: Gender, Modernity and the Urban Experience*. London: I. B. Tauris.

TURAN, İlter. 1994. *Özelleştirme Uluslararası Sempozyumu*. Istanbul: Koç University.

TURHAN, Mümtaz. 1959. *Garblılaşmanın Neresindeyiz?* Istanbul: Türkiye Yayınevi.

TÜRK, İbrahim. 2001. *Halit Refiğ: Düşlerden Düşüncelere Söyleşiler*. Istanbul: Kabalcı Yayınevi.

TÜRKEŞ, Mustafa. 2001. 'A Patriotic Leftist Development-Strategy Proposal in Turkey in the 1930s: The Case of the Kadro (Cadre) Movement'. *International Journal of Middle East Studies* 33(1): 91–114.

TÜRKİYE GAZETESİ. 2014. 'Enver Ören Ağabey Kendisini Anlatıyor: Ben Enver Abi . . . ' Available at https://bit.ly/3dHitwu

TURKIYETURIZM. 2021. 'Dünyanın televizyon merkezi İstanbul olacak'. Turkiye-Turizm.com, 14 December. Available at https://bit.ly/3xpd6wq

TUROK, Ivan. 2003. 'Cities, Clusters and Creative Industries: The Case of Film and Television in Scotland'. *European Planning Studies* 11: 549–65.

TÜZÜN, Ayşegül. Interview by the author, 10 March 2022.

TÜZÜN, Selin, and Aygün Şen. 2014. 'The Past as a Spectacle: The Magnificent Century' in R. Gülay Öztürk (ed.), *Handbook of Research on the Impact of Culture and Society on the Entertainment Industry*. Hershey, PA: IGI Global, pp. 182–202.

TV AKTÜEL. 2014. 'İşte unutulmaz set kazaları', 8 August. Available at https://bit.ly/2RwQy8T

TV100. 2020. 'Korona Virüse Rağmen Sete Çıkan Dizi Eşkıya Dünyaya Hükümdar Olmaz'dan Kötü Haber', 20 April. Available at https://bit.ly/2BnYNz2

UÇANSU, Hülya. 2012. *Bir Uzun Mesafe Festivalcisinin Anıları: Sinema Günleri'nden İstanbul Film Festivali'ne*. Istanbul: Doğan Kitap.

ÜLKENCİLER, Mustafa Ziya. 2015. 'Sanat Yönetmenliğine Gereken Önem Verilmiyor'. *Milliyet*, 6 June. Available at https://bit.ly/2w17vkr

———. 2019a. Interview by the author, 1 April.

——. 2019b. 'Mustafa Ziya Ülkenciler, yapım tasarımcısı'. *OdaTV*. Available at https://bit.ly/3awhzAS

ULUSUM, Ece. 2016. 'Engin Altan Düzyatan: Teklif gelirse Trump'ı oynarım'. *Haber Türk-Pazar*, 6 November. Available at https://bit.ly/3DT6tp2

ÜNER, Mithat, Evren Güçer, and Aslı Taşçı. 2006. 'Türkiye Turizminde Yükselen Destinasyon Olarak Istanbul Şehrinin İmajı'. *Anatolia: Turizm Araştırmaları Dergisi* 17(2): 189–201.

ÜNLÜ, Derya Gül, and Pınar Aslan. 2016. 'Türk Televizyon Dizilerinde Kadın Rollerine Kadınların Gözünden Bakmak'. *İNİF E-DERGİ* 1(2): 191–206.

ÜNLÜ, Onur. 2012. 'Antalya TV Ödülleri'. Paper presented at Akdeniz University Panel, Antalya, 21 April.

ÜNSALLI, Emre. 2008. 'Sinemanın Yapamadığını 'Hatırla Sevgili Yaptı'. *Vatan*, 18 April. Available at https://bit.ly/2UcY1vy

ÜNÜR, Ece. 2013. 'Türk Televizyon Dizilerinde Toplumsal Kimliklerin Temsili'. *Erciyes İletişim Dergisi* 3(2): 32–42.

URAZ, Abdullah. 1970. *1970 Siyasî Buhranı ve İç Yüzü*. Istanbul: Son Havadis Yayınları.

USALLI-SILAN, Bircan. 2004. *Dört Yapraklı Yonca: Onların Sihri Neydi?* Istanbul: Epsilon Yayınları.

USTA, Murat. 2018. 'Jerzy Grotowski'nin Fiziksel Eylemleri ve Türk Tiyatrosuna Etkisi'. MA thesis, Haliç University, Istanbul.

UYSAL, Makbule. 2015. 'Halk Tiyatrosunun Değişen Bağlamı Medya: Bir Demet Tiyatro Örneği'. MA thesis, Gazi University, Ankara.

——. 2016. 'Seyirci Anlayışı Açısından Geleneksel Türk Tiyatrosu ile Bir Demet Tiyatro Dizisinin Karşılaştırılması'. *Milli Folklor* 28(109): 71–82.

UYSAL, Ülke Evrim. 2013. 'Branding Istanbul: Representations of Religion in Promoting Tourism'. *Place Branding and Public Diplomacy* 9(4): 223–35.

VACHON, Christine, and David Edelstein. 1998. *Shooting to Kill: How an Independent Producer Blasts Through the Barriers to Make Movies that Matter*. New York: William Morrow Paperbacks.

VAN SIJLL, Jennifer. 2005. *Cinematic Storytelling: The 100 Most Powerful Film Conventions Every Filmmaker Must Know*. Studio City, CA: Michael Wiese Productions.

VARIS, Tapio. 1974. 'Global Traffic in Television'. *Journal of Communication* 24(1): 102–09.

——. 1984. 'The International Flow of Television Programs'. *Journal of Communication* 34(1): 143–52.

VAROL, Ziyad. 2016. 'The success story of Turkish TV series in Latin America'. *Daily Sabah*, 2 February. Available at https://bit.ly/2yfB5Dm

VATAN. 2020. 'Arka Sokaklar Yeni Fragmanı!'. *Vatan*, 25 April. Available at https://bit.ly/2NfXO6M

Velİoğlu, Halide. 2011. 'Bosniak Sentiments: The Poetic and Mundane Life of Impossible Longings'. PhD dissertation, University of Texas, Austin.

Vivarelli, Nick. 2016. 'Character-Driven Storylines Abound in Turkish TV Series', *Variety*, 17 October. Available at https://bit.ly/3KtSfxu

Voigts, Eckart. 2015. 'Literature and Television (after TV)' in Gabriele Rippl (ed.), *Handbook of Intermediality: Literature – Image – Sound – Music*. Berlin: de Gruyter, pp. 306–24.

Vos, Eric. 1997. 'The Eternal Network. Mail Art, Intermedia Semiotics, Interarts Studies' in Ulla-Britta Lagerroth, Hans Lund and Erik Hedling (eds), *Interart Poetics: Essays on the Interrelations of the Arts and Media*. Boston: Brill, pp. 325–36.

Vural, Sinem. 2011. 'Bu İşin Matematiği Yok'. *Kelebek*, 2 September. Available at https://bit.ly/33FrX6R

Watson, Ryan. 2018. 'Atresmedia adds Turkish Dramas'. *C21 Media*, 16 April. Available at https://bit.ly/2UO6Lr5

Waugh, Lisa. 2019. 'A Guide to All the Behind-the-Scenes Drama on Your Favorite TV Shows'. *Ranker*, 23 September. Available at https://bit.ly/3a7f1Z7

Williams, Nathan. 2013. 'The Rise of Turkish Soap Power'. BBC News, 28 June. Available at https://bbc.in/2WUwbG5

Williams, Raymond. 1974. *Television: Technology and Cultural Form*. London: Fontana.

Winters, Ben. 2010. 'The Non-Diegetic Fallacy: Film, Music, and Narrative Space'. *Music and Letters* 91(2): 224–44.

Witt, Emily. 2017. *Nollywood: The Making of a Film Empire*. New York: Columbia Global Reports.

Wolf, Werner. 2015. 'Literature and Music: Theory' in Gabriele Rippl (ed.), *Handbook of Intermediality: Literature – Image – Sound – Music*. Berlin/Boston: de Gruyter, pp. 461–74.

Woodard, Kathryn. 2007. 'Music Mediating Politics in Turkey: The Case of Ahmed Adnan Saygun'. *Comparative Studies of South Asia, Africa and the Middle East* 27(3): 552–62.

World Screen. 2014. 'Video Interview: Lovebird Stars Fahriye Evcen and Burak Özçivit', 4 March. Available at https://bit.ly/3bk1Bt9

Yağcı, Sevgi Can (ed.). 2011. *Beyaz Camın Yerlileri*. Istanbul: Umuttepe Yayınları.

Yalçın, Nihal. 2013. Talk given at Mithat Alam Film Merkezi, Istanbul, 21 March.

Yalçınkaya, Can T. 2008. 'Turkish Arabesk Music and the Changing Perceptions of Melancholy in Turkish Society'. *NEO: Journal for Higher Degree Research Students in the Social Sciences and Humanities*: 1–14.

Yanardağoğlu, Eylem. 2022. *The Transformation of the Media System in Turkey: Citizenship, Communication, and Convergence*. London: Palgrave Macmillan.

YANAT-BAĞCI, Yelda. 'Aşk-ı Memnu'da Erkeğin Sunumu'. *Akdeniz Üniversitesi Sosyal Bilimler Enstitüsü Dergisi* 4: 97–108.

YANG ERDEM, Chien. 2017. 'Ottomentality: Neoliberal Governance of Culture and Neo-Ottoman Management of Diversity'. *Turkish Studies* 18(4): 710–28.

YANG, Mayfair Mei Hui. 1994. 'Film Discussion Groups in China: State Discourse or a Plebian Public Sphere?' *Visual Anthropology Review* 10(1): 112–25.

YANIK, Lerna K. 2009. 'Valley of the Wolves-Iraq: Anti-geopolitics Alla Turca'. *Middle East Journal of Culture and Communication* 2(1): 153–70.

YARAR, Betül. 2008. 'Politics of/and Popular Music: An Analysis of the History of Arabesk Music from the 1960s to the 1990s in Turkey'. *Cultural Studies* 22(1): 35–79.

YARAŞ, Ali Can. 2008. 'Ali Can Yaraş: Hayatımın Hiçbir Döneminde Yazıyla Çok İlgim Olmadı'. *Buyrun Buradan Okuyun*, 15 November. Available at https://bit.ly/3cgoKTp

YARAŞLI, G. Y. 2007. 'Destinasyon İmajı ve Trabzon Yöresine Dönük Bir Çalışma'. MA thesis, Başkent University, Ankara.

YARGIÇ, Aytuğ. 2019. 'Müziğin Filmlerdeki Önemi–2'. *Vizyon*, October. Published at https://bit.ly/3aCxspC (currently unavailable; last accessed on 2 February 2020).

YARKIN, Hakan. 2011. 'İşte Sineklidağ Mahallesi'. Interview by Sinem Vural. *Hürriyet Kelebek*, 2 December. Available at https://bit.ly/2R0tiA2

YATES, Jo Ann, and Wanda Orlikowski. 2002. 'Genre Systems: Chronos and Kairos in Communicative Action' in Richard Coe, Lorelei Lingard and Tatiana Teslenko (eds), *The Rhetoric of Ideology and Ideology of Genre*. Cresskill, NJ: Hampton Press, pp. 103–22.

YAZICI, Hilmi. 2016. 'The Art of Opera in Turkey within the Scope of Culture-Art Policies'. *International Journal of Humanities, Arts and Social Sciences* 2(5): 159–64.

YENER, Duygu. 2020. 'Sağlık Bakanlığından Koronavirüse Karşı Yeni Kamu Spotları'. Anadolu Ajansı, 14 April. Available at https://bit.ly/2YSkizZ

YENER, Yasemin. 2012. 'Rape Discourses in Turkey: The Case of Turkish Television Series *Fatmagül'ün Suçu Ne?*' PhD dissertation, Bilkent University, Ankara.

YENGİN, Hülya. 1994. *Ekranın Büyüsü*. Istanbul: Der Yayınları.

YESIL, Bilge. 2015. 'Transnationalization of Turkish Dramas: Exploring the Convergence of Local and Global Market Imperatives'. *Global Media and Communication* 11(1): 43–60.

YEŞİLYURT, Melek. 2016. 'Metin Erksan'ın Deneysel TRT Filmleri'. Film Loverss, 25 July. Available at https://bit.ly/2xkxaom

YILDIZ, Burcu. 2016. 'Turkish "Dizi" (TV Series) Music and the Concept of Professional Dizi Musicianship' in Liz Mellish, Nick Green and Mirjana Zakić (eds), *Music and Dance in Southeastern Europe: New Scopes of Research and Action*. Belgrade: Colorgrafx, pp. 210–16.

YILDIZ, Filiz. 2019. 'Türkiye'de İlk Güzellik Yarışmaları ve Basının Öncü Rolü: Genç Cumhuriyet'in Asri Güzelleri'. *Üsküdar Üniversitesi İletişim Fakültesi Akademik Dergisi Etkileşim* 4: 66–87.

YILMAZ-KARAKOÇ, Nesrin. 2015. 'TAL Tiyatro Araştırma Laboratuarı ve Beklan Algan Vizyonu'. MA thesis, Haliç University, Istanbul.

YILMAZ, Atıf. 1995. *Söylemek Güzeldir*. Istanbul: Afa Yayınları.

YILMAZ, Hakan. 2005. 'Placing Turkey on the Map of Europe' in Hakan Yılmaz (ed.), *Placing Turkey on the Map of Europe*. Istanbul: Boğaziçi University Press.

——, and Medet Yolal. 2008. 'Film Turizmi: Destinasyonların Pazarlanmasında Filmlerin Rolü'. *Anadolu University Journal of Social Sciences* 8(1): 175–92.

YILMAZ, Mehmet, and Güliz Uluç. 2008. '"Hatırla Sevgili" dizisindeki temsili ile bir dönemin anatomisi: 27 Mayıs 1960'. *Selçuk İletişim* 5(2): 136–51.

——. 2009. 'To Be a Relative to "the Other": "Foreign Son-in-law"'. *İletişim* 10: 93–121.

YILMAZ, R. Ayhan. 2001. 'İlanattan İnternete: Türkiye'de Reklamcılık'. *Kurgu Dergisi* 18: 355–67.

YILMAZ, Recep, Ali Çakır and Filiz Resuloğlu. 2019. 'Historical Transformation of the Advertising Narration in Turkey: From Stereotype to Digital Media' in *Brand Culture and Identity: Concepts, Methodologies, Tools, and Applications*. Hershey, PA: IGI Global, pp. 1380–99.

YILMAZ, Servet. 2009. 'Hanımın Çiftliği Adana'da Kuruldu'. *Hürriyet Kelebek*, 4 September. Available at https://bit.ly/2USfCrI

YILMAZ, Ülkü. 2017. Interview by the author, 12 December.

YÖRENÇ, Ece, and Melek Gençoğlu. 2013. Interview by the author, 7 January.

YÖRÜK, Evrim. 2010. 'Televizyon Anlatısı, Tür ve Temsil Açısından Asmalı Konak' in Tezcan Durna (ed.), *Medyadan Söylemler*. Istanbul: Libra Kitap, pp. 313–48.

YÖRÜK, Evrim. 2012. 'Televizyonda Nitelik Sorunu Hakkında Bir Tartışma: Behzat Ç. Örneği'. *Ankara Üniversitesi SBF Dergisi* 67(3): 219–63.

YÖRÜK, Sinan, Mehmet Koçyiğit and Murat Turan. 2015. 'Dizi filmler ve bilgisayar oyunlarının ortaöğretim öğrencilerinin şiddet algısına etkisi nitel bir araştırma'. *Uşak Üniversitesi Sosyal Bilimler Dergisi* 8(4): 127–42.

YOUTUBE. 2011. 'Fatmagül Kerim Türkü Şarkı Sahnesi—Evlerinin Önü Mersin', 28 April. Available at https://bit.ly/2YCyMUo

——. 2012. 'Making of/Behind the Scenes', 26 June. Available at https://bit.ly/2V17lTW

——. 2016. 'Muhteşem Yüzyıl Kösem 28. Bölüm | Kösem'in kara günü!', 26 May. Available at https://bit.ly/3xXF5nd

YÜCEŞAHİN, M. Murat, and E. Murat Özgür. 2006. 'Türkiye'nin Güneydoğusunda Nüfusun Zorunlu Yerinden Oluşu: Süreçler ve Mekânsal Örüntü'. *Coğrafi Bilimler Dergisi* 4(2): 15–35.

YUKARUÇ, Vedii. 2011. '1960'lar ve 1970'lerden Radyo-Televizyon Anıları'. *Tarihten Anekdotlar*, 17 September. Available at https://bit.ly/2Yx2qKX

YÜKSEL, Ayşegül. 2009. 'Türkiye'de 'Yazar Tiyatrosu'. *Tiyatro Araştırmaları Dergisi* 27:' 125–36.

YÜKSEL, N. Aysun. 1999. 'Toplumsal Cinsiyet Olgusu ve Türkiye'deki Toplumsal Cinsiyet Kalıplarının Televizyon Dizilerindeki Yansımaları'. *Kurgu, Anadolu Üniversitesi İletişim Bilimleri Fakültesi Uluslararası Hakemli İletişim Dergisi* 16(16): 67–81.

YÜKSEL, N. Aysun Akıncı. 2013. 'Does Love Forgive Everything? Sexual Assault as an Attack Which Is Normalized in Turkish Television Series'. *Journal of Literature and Studies* 3(8): 469–81.

YÜKSELEN, Cemal, and Emel Gönenç-Güler. 2009. *Antakya Marka Kent: Görüş ve Öneriler*. Ankara: Detay Yayıncılık.

YURDERİ, Mihriye Meral. 2014. 'Romandan Uyarlanan Televizyon Dizilerinde Değişen Değer Temsili'. PhD dissertation, Ege University, İzmir.

YURTSEVER, Nail. 2019. 'Üyelerimize Sorduk'. *Vizyon*, March. Published at https://bit.ly/3oef3HV

ZAMANIAN, Kavon. 2016. '5 Inspirational Behind-the-Scenes Documentaries'. *The Beat*, 13 April. Available at https://bit.ly/2xjEsJi

ZİYALAR, Ahmet. 2017. Interview by the author, 14 November 2017.

———. 2022. Interview by the author, 2 June.

Index

Locators in italics indicate images.

industry. *See* dizi industry; film industry; television industry

Inter Medya, 358, 363–64, 366, 368–69, 372, 387–68

interdiscursivity, 19, 29, 110–12, 119, 119n17, 120–21, 123, 366, 390

intermediality, x, 6, 19, 29, 109–11, 130, 134–36, 135n40, 142, 147–50, 154–57, 340, 390

intertextuality, x, 111, 119n17, 120, 390

Işıklı, Toygar, 10, 149, 155

Kanal D, 5, 64–65, 68, 92, 95, 104–06, 110, 110n4, 177–78, 183, 192n5, 311, 357–58, 357n11–12, 368, 385–86

Karaca, Doğan, 141

Karahan, Mustafa, 66, 81, 103, 174

Karataş, Şaban, 30, 41, 51

Kartallar Yüksek Uçar, 59, 168, 235

Katıksız, Ahmet, 305, 320, 326

Kaynanalar, 57–58, 66, 122, 168

Kiralık Aşk, 124, 161, 176, 198, 199n9, 209n27, 241, 271, 290

Konduk, Kandemir, 101, 170–71, 190, 269

Kösem, 1, 157, 203n13, 260, 286, *350,* 359

Kuruluş, 1–2, 61, 279n30

Leyla ile Mecnun, 124, 183, 183n10

Malmborg, Fredrik af, 109, *351,* 376

media text, 6, 9, 29, 107, 109–12, 119, 122, 129–34, 139–40, 145, 165, 197, 292–93, 311, 319, 340, 374, 390

MIPCOM, 2, 11, 13, 15, 31, 31n40, 149, 230, 313, 341–45, 345n5, 347–48, 350, 353–55, 371–73, 384, 386, 392

MIPTV, 13, 199n9, 229, 313, 341, 341n1, 342–43, 345, 345n5, 347–48, 350, 353–55, 357, 371, 373–74

Muhteşem Yüzyıl, 10, 124, 128, 151n49, 179, *179,* 212, 227, 264, 267, 279–81, 288, 320, 331n30, 332n32, 357, 384–85, 398

Nalçacı, Nilgün, 208, 217, 219, 221

Oğuz, Abdullah, 81, 104, 181

Okan, Can, *346,* 388

Öneş, Nilgün, 136, *137,* 173, 182, 195, 199, 267, 276

oral history, 11, 19, 25, 27n38, 30, 32, 87, 90, 230, 297, 306, 311, 354

Özçivit, Burak, 11, 93, 99n18, 229, 231, 237n17, 242, 271, 318n17, 330n29

Özen, Ayhan, 68n32, 136, 239, 242, 303, 305, 325

Özer, Ayşe, 106, 123, 219, 245

Özşener, Yiğit, 231, 239, 252

Özsümbül, Özlem, 357, 362, 365, 371